BRITONS VIEW AMERICA

RICHARD L. RAPSON

BRITONS
VIEW
AMERICA

Travel Commentary,

1860-1935

University of Washington Press

SEATTLE & LONDON

To Carin

PREFACE

THIS WORK takes up the story of the British traveler begun forty years ago by Jane Mesick in *The English Traveler in America, 1785–1835*[1] and continued twenty years later by Max Berger in *The British Traveller in America, 1836–1860*,[2] but it also departs sharply from the pattern of these two studies. Mesick and Berger devoted their energies to explication of the travelers' views on a wide variety of assorted, sometimes unrelated subjects. They were successful in providing a comprehensive summary of the varieties of views among British visitors to American shores in neat, self-contained monographs that make handy reference guides.

In this book an effort will be made to determine whether the vast body of British travel literature adds up to a coherent commentary, to ascertain whether points of agreement may be extracted from the more prominent and colorful polemics in which the visitors engaged. The peculiar advantage which foreign commentators have over native observers in being struck by that which the native takes for granted will be exploited. Topics which Americans have therefore generally neglected and which the Britons have not will be probed in some detail, while some of those upon which Americans have lavished great attention will be slighted. Differing conceptions of American society between the British visitors and American historians will be examined, and some of the interesting interpretive questions which these differences suggest will be pondered.

I do not assume that because the foreign commentators happened to agree on some subject, that they must consequently have been right. Their accuracy is another question that requires different and more extensive research. Because their books are essentially impressionistic, and because their observations are subject to a variety of limitations that I discuss in the Appendix, I do not want to pretend that my findings, based upon a processing of this kind of indefinite material, are any more definite than in fact they could be. But the observations of the travelers are worth something. They do increase our knowledge of the American past; they add a new dimension to other kinds of data dealing with American social history. Most important, because the stranger sees America freshly, his observations are often original, suggestive, and perceptive in ways which the native's, steeped in his own culture, cannot be. I have tried to take the fullest advantage of the special perspective of the foreigner.

[1] New York: Columbia University Press, 1922.
[2] New York: P. S. King and Staples, 1943.

I have advanced with caution, pointing out the various points at which there does seem to be a consensus among the commentators and which appear to be worthy of our notice. Various other points at which the travelers did not even agree among themselves are frequently of interest, and I have drawn some attention to them. I have tried not to spend undue amounts of time on trivial bits of information or the miscellaneous and often inaccurate reports of passing fads upon which many of the visitors loved to dwell. A rather extensive annotated bibliography at the end of the book undertakes to fill in some of the gaps left by my process of selection.

The travelers asked in years past, in unsystematic fashion, the kinds of questions being raised about contemporary America by sociologists, psychologists, and anthropologists. As the critical approach of the behavioral scientists continues to attract American historians it is certain that foreign travel literature will be taken more seriously than ever before. The clearer we can be about its pitfalls and potentialities, the better our understanding of the American past will be served.

But of major interest to me has been the substance of the British visitors' provocative findings concerning the United States. They crossed the Atlantic in order to see our culture whole. While their bold generalizations were often ill-formed, they were at least attempting to do what the native scholar hesitates to do, namely, to depict the entire sweep of American life and to speculate on the fundamental elements that differentiate the New World from the Old. In making this effort, the tourists, individually and collectively, frequently came up with arresting insights into areas of American culture that are too often taken for granted by our historians. So this book is not simply about British travelers, but it is also a synthesis of their commentary on some of those key, but sometimes neglected subjects: the family, the schools, the women, the churches, the values, attitudes, assumptions, and faiths of Americans. All these topics are contributory to the two omnipresent questions of the commentators: how and why did Americans differ from Englishmen and other national groups? I have, in this book, followed the British down this path of inquiry and have tried to describe where the path ended. Finally, since these travels cover a seventy-five-year period, I have been in a better position than any single visitor to look into the matter of whether, over that period, the British as a group have stuck to pretty much the same picture of this country or whether the America they described after the first fifteen or twenty years of the twentieth century differed essentially from their conception of our nation and people before, let us say, the 1880's.

Several chapters of this book have appeared, in slightly different form, in the following journals: Chapter VI in *American Quarterly*,

XVII (1965), 520–34 (Copyright, 1965, Trustees of the University of Pennsylvania); Chapter IX in *Church History,* XXXV (1966), 3–19; and Chapter II in *History Today,* XVI (1966), 519–27.

Early versions of this manuscript were read by Professors David M. Potter of Stanford and John Higham of the University of Michigan. Late drafts were read by Walter P. Metzger and Robert K. Webb of Columbia, and most drafts were examined by Richard Hofstadter, who supervised the work from beginning to end when it was a dissertation. To those familiar with American scholarship it will be clear that I have received good advice. I have, and I am grateful especially for the uniform insistence of these historians that I confront important and difficult questions of substance rather than seek refuge in the safe harbor of pedantry. This book furnishes one more sign (in this case, a small one) of the incalculable contributions made to the study of American history by David Potter and Richard Hofstadter, whose recent untimely deaths have left so many of us with a terrible sense of intellectual and personal loss.

RICHARD L. RAPSON

March, 1971
Honolulu, Hawaii

CONTENTS

BRITONS VIEW AMERICA

I

The Meeting
of Great Britain
and America

WHEN Mrs. Trollope came to the United States, she found America in arms against Basil Hall's book. She remedied that situation, for after her book appeared in 1832, the caustic Englishman Basil Hall slipped quietly from the memory of Americans. The United States was now in arms against Mrs. Trollope: Hall's work was "actually a mild and flattering treatise compared with her own."[1] The appearance of her book constituted a major event in diplomatic history and played no small part in exacerbating Anglo-American relations. A British visitor who toured in 1833 reported that the controversy it aroused surpassed all others of the time including Jackson's tariff and Bank battles. "At every table d'hote, on board every steamboat, and in all societies, the first question was, 'Have you read Mrs. Trollope?' "[2] So great was the furor that her name became a swear word in the American language to the extent that "not long after the appearance of her volume, the cry of 'A Trollope! A Trollope!' was sufficient to reduce any ill-mannered person in a theatre or other public place to order."[3]

Only one author after Mrs. Trollope, Charles Dickens, managed to generate anything like the general response to his person or his views that she did. When he landed in 1842, no English personality was nearly so well known or well loved as he. *Oliver Twist, Pickwick Papers, Nicholas Nickleby,* and other early works of the thirty-year-old novelist had been as widely read and loved in this country as in England. His arrival was the greatest event of its kind since Lafayette had triumphantly toured

[1] Allan Nevins, *America Through British Eyes,* p. 85 (first published as *American Social History As Recorded by British Travellers*). The books were Basil Hall, *Travels in North America in the Years 1827–28* (3 vols.; Edinburgh, 1829) and Mrs. Frances Trollope, *Domestic Manners of the Americans* (2 vols.; London, 1832).

[2] Lieutenant E. T. Coke, *A Subaltern's Furlough* (London, 1833), quoted in Nevins, *America Through British Eyes,* p. 21.

[3] Nevins, *America Through British Eyes,* p. 83.

the nation in 1824. Dickens received plaudits everywhere, and when he made known his intentions to write a book about the United States, anticipation ran high. After the first copy reached New York, only nineteen hours elapsed before it had been reprinted and placed on sale. Fifty thousand copies were sold within two days, and Philadelphia's original consignment of three thousand copies was sold out in thirty minutes. The shock of pain that went through the nation upon reading the book has become legendary. Said Nevins: "It is a little difficult now to comprehend the mortification that seized the continent upon the publication of Dickens's *American Notes*."[4] Actually Dickens was far less acerbic than either Hall or Mrs. Trollope. He had many kind things to say, but there were at least three reasons for the intense chagrin that Americans suffered: Dickens had been received so lavishly; he had such a large following in the United States; and, probably worst of all, many of his criticisms were accurate.

These years marked the heyday of American sensitivity to foreign criticism. They also gave birth to some of the more pungent denunciations of American society. Supported by the inflammatory work of the Tory periodicals, the times conspired to heighten the impact of British travel books to a point that had never been reached before and has not been reached since.

TRAVEL ACCOUNTS: FROM EVENTS TO MERE BOOKS

After Dickens' historic tour, Americans began to receive the British with greater equanimity than in the past. They awaited future travel works with less anxiety and anticipation, and they greeted the publication of these books with calmer interest. There are a number of reasons for this change. First, Americans were rapidly getting used to the English interloper. The adolescent need for approval from father diminished yearly as the nation matured and grew in strength. These gradual developments steadily made Americans feel less uneasy in the presence of the Briton.

Second, the Tory periodicals inflamed fewer tempers as their importance declined. This happened largely as a result of the internal evolution taking place in Great Britain. The Reform Bill of 1832 signaled England's tentative movement toward a gradual broadening of democracy. *Blackwood's* outcries against democracy and the United States began to take on the desperation of a holding action doomed to failure. Third, as Max Berger noted, "as Britons became more familiar with American ways, there also came about a growing understanding and tolerance. The days of Mrs. Trollope and Basil Hall were past." Berger also

[4] *Ibid.*, p. 90. Charles Dickens, *American Notes for General Circulation.*

thought that the "greater tendency to be fair, and to award both praise and criticism where due" derived from the proportionate diminution of upper class tourists in comparison with those who came from "middle-class backgrounds, and were naturally less hostile to democratic innovations than would be true of the upper classes."[5]

Fourth, there were general developments in both nations serving to bring them into closer harmony, with, in the words of political scientist Raymond English, "political and economic and social realities . . . producing fundamentally similar adjustments behind their superficially contrasted forms of life."[6] Finally, the comparatively low status granted American intellectuals in the nineteenth century prompted them and whatever upper class existed in the United States to reach out for their counterparts across the Atlantic. This constitutes one of the sources of that Anglophilism which by the end of the nineteenth century was to reach such great intensity, and which, to this day, remains a dominant factor in American foreign policy. At first, it was the alienated, unappreciated intellectual who traveled to England either to find his cultural roots or to settle his doubts about his native land. Practically every major American literary figure in the first half of the nineteenth century had to make the inevitable pilgrimage to Great Britain.[7] While the American visitor to England often went not to judge (as did the Englishman in America) but to find himself, many, like Emerson, discovered there precisely what the English found in America: boastfulness, too rapid a life, materialism, and so forth. Curiously enough, other European visitors to England, for example, the Frenchman Hippolyte Taine and the German Wilhelm Dibelius, found these same faults. Either intellectuals will tend to spot these flaws almost anywhere they travel or else industrialism carries with it these vices. I suspect both these explanations contain some truth.

By the end of the century, larger contingents of the American population looked fondly to England for guidance. It is today argued that the spearhead for the Progressive movement came from the "Mugwump" reformers who occupied respected places in certain circles of American life before they were displaced by the new breed of businessmen.[8] The reformers established many ties with English liberals. The businessmen,

[5] Max Berger, *The British Traveller in America, 1836–1860,* pp. 20, 21.

[6] Raymond English, "Britain and the United States: The Myth of Differentiation," *Yale Review,* n.s. XLII (1953), 280–81.

[7] Cushing Strout gives a good account of the changing perception of England among leading American intellectuals throughout our history in *The American Image of the Old World* (New York: Harper and Row, 1963).

[8] See for this view Richard Hofstadter, *The Age of Reform: From Bryan to F.D.R.* (New York: Knopf, 1955) and George E. Mowry, *The California Progressives* (Berkeley: University of California Press, 1951).

too, looked to England for a different kind of support. Everywhere Matthew Arnold went he was entertained not by the poets and artists but by the wealthy businessmen, not always noted for their highly developed aesthetic sensitivity.[9] The best American friend held in common by Arnold and Herbert Spencer was Andrew Carnegie. The comments of critics like these were seized upon with great eagerness by the American business community.

The settlement of the copyright dilemma in 1892 by which literary piracy came to an end aided the growing Anglo-American entente. The literary thefts of British books by American publishers had long justly infuriated British authors, most notably Dickens, and the end to this practice was warmly welcomed in Great Britain. Groups other than writers, respectable old families, and rich entrepreneurs saw Great Britain in a rosier light toward the end of the century. The great middle class reacted with increasing alarm as hordes of new immigrants from Eastern Europe poured into the country in unprecedented numbers from 1880 to 1920. By contrast the English immigrants were elevated. Anglophilism became an integral part of American life with the Anglo-American alliance of World War I, further mitigating the effect of an occasionally hostile assault on the United States from the pen of some Englishman.

The growth of Anglophilism in America predates these more recent developments. In the wake of the Reform Bill of 1832, American sensitivity to British criticism began to relax, with four events felt to be of special significance. Nevins thought the year 1835 of some importance:

> Beginning in 1835, a subtle change in the tone of British commentaries upon the United States can be discerned. That was the year in which Tocqueville published his *Democracy in America,* a work profoundly influential in all Europe. It was especially so in Great Britain, where liberal elements in politics took it up. After Tocqueville visited England and married an Englishwoman, his writings were widely quoted and his best ideas echoed by many journals and reviews.[10]

Berger saw 1848 as a turning point. Diplomatic tension between England and the United States lessened after this time. The revolutions of that year on the Continent, it should be remembered, had pushed America into a secondary position as the symbol of chaos and the spawning ground of revolutionary demons.[11] Few observers have failed to note a further growth of respect granted by England to the United States at the close of the Civil War in 1865. The Union had remained firm, had triumphed, had even prospered during the course of the bloody conflict.

---

[9] Howard Mumford Jones, "Arnold, Aristocracy, and America," *American Historical Review,* XLIX, No. 3 (1944), 393–409.

[10] Nevins, *America Through British Eyes,* p. 89.

[11] Berger, *The British Traveller in America, 1836–1860,* p. 21.

One could still criticize the young nation, but one could no longer consider passing it off with a condescending sneer. In fact Union victory in the Civil War played a leading role in the liberalization of European politics. The Norwegian historian Halvdan Koht noted the manner in which "the Civil War in America influenced and encouraged political progress in Europe, not only by what was conceived as a triumph for democracy, but by sharpening the conflict between the ideas of freedom and servitude." Examples of this influence were to be found in the triple drive in Great Britain for democratic reform, for universal suffrage, with both "mounted together with the movement for friendship with the United States." One immediate outcome of this drive was the reawakened interest in Tocqueville's work on the United States, used to better effect by the friends of democracy than by its opponents. The rest of the Continent responded similarly to Union victory: "Liberals and republicans in France found new support for their ideas. Democrats in Norway learned to direct their energy to the consolidation of their demands into firmly planted institutions."[12]

Another decisive event in the ebbing hostility between England and the United States, one in which Union victory played its part, was the Reform Bill of 1867. "Though there were many forces and factors leading to the long-awaited day in 1867, who," asks the historian George Lillibridge, "will now deny that the role of the American destiny was not a humble one in this decisive triumph of the democratic movement in England in the nineteenth century?"[13]

These dates—1832, 1835, 1848, 1865, 1867, 1892 (the year of the copyright settlement)—all stand for external events which help explain why English travel criticism softened, and even when it did not, why it seemed to cause less and less consternation among Americans as time passed. One must mention also an internal change in the nature of that criticism. Nevins described the period from 1870 to 1922 as the age of analysis in British travel literature. During this period the travels assumed a "superior character" to those of any other period. We have evidence of this in the mere names of the principal authors.

> In all the century-long literature of the subject no descriptive passages show greater vividness and stylistic felicity than those of Kipling; no social and political analysis approaches that of James Bryce in thoroughness or discernment; no sociological generalizations are so forcible as H. G. Wells's.[14]

[12] Halvdan Koht, *The American Spirit in Europe: A Survey of Transatlantic Influences* (Philadelphia: University of Pennsylvania Press, 1949), pp. 147–49.

[13] G. D. Lillibridge, *Beacon of Freedom: The Impact of American Democracy upon Great Britain 1830–1870* (Philadelphia: University of Pennsylvania Press, 1955), p. 122.

[14] Nevins, *America Through British Eyes,* p. 305. The cut-off date of 1922 has no historical significance; Nevins composed his book in that year.

Nevins went on to mention the names of Matthew Arnold, Herbert Spencer, E. A. Freeman, Frederic Harrison, Arnold Bennett, and G. K. Chesterton as proof of the "eminence of the authors." As we know, however, the renown of Dickens added immeasurably to the irritant power of *American Notes*. Even more important than the fame of the authors in lifting "the more recent treatment of the United States to a higher level" was the new character which these books assumed: "a change of character that may be summed up in the statement that for the first time analysis became the dominant note. It completely triumphed over mere narration and description."[15]

Whatever the reasons—external or internal—whenever the turning point, British travel books were not a sore point in Anglo-American relations during the years encompassed by this study. Developments in England, in the United States, on the Continent, changes in the character of the travelogues and in the maturity of the Americans all contributed to the conditions that allowed these works to become vehicles for understanding on both sides of the Atlantic rather than weapons in the hands of irresponsible polemicists.

HERBERT SPENCER'S VISIT: A CASE STUDY

A fuller sense of the ease with which Americans increasingly responded to British criticism can be obtained through a specific example. Perhaps the best (though by no means perfect) analogy to the first visit of Dickens came exactly forty years later. From August 21 to November 11, 1882, Herbert Spencer toured America. Like Dickens, Spencer had received at least as much recognition and adulation in the United States as in England.[16] Like Dickens, Spencer reached New York at an auspicious time. Richard Hofstadter noted that "the peak of Spencer's American popularity was reached in the fall of 1882, when he made a memorable visit to the United States."[17] And like Dickens, Spencer surprised his American audiences with some critical comments which jarred. Although his arrival was anxiously awaited and received good press coverage, no one even got a glimpse of the great man when he disembarked

[15] *Ibid.* Nevins could have added many more illustrious names to the honor roll. Perhaps it should be suggested that there was no guarantee that Oscar Wilde or Aldous Huxley or John Galsworthy would write particularly important books on the United States—as they did not. Many of the most informative works came from lesser luminaries. I also think Nevins overstates the case of the triumph of analysis over narration.

[16] Spencer actually was received more warmly in the United States than in England during his vogue.

[17] Richard Hofstadter, *Social Darwinism in American Thought* (Boston, Mass.: Beacon Press, 1955), p. 48.

from the *Servia* on August 21. The *New York Herald* reported that the arrival "was an event that excited much comment in the city, the more so from the almost instantaneous disappearance of Mr. Spencer, who was carried off bodily by Prof. Youmans before the vessel was fairly at the pier."[18]

Despite Spencer's efforts to travel incognito (perhaps because of them), when the vain philosopher finally relented to publicity, his comments aroused wide interest and received handsome newspaper and magazine coverage. Spencer made two concessions on his tour which permitted Americans to gain first-hand knowledge of the man: he granted an interview for press release and he agreed to appear as guest of honor at a fabulous and now-famous banquet at Delmonico's. The interview was, as Hofstadter appropriately tagged it, a purely "synthetic" affair. Youmans did the questioning; and the questions were Spencer's. "The result," said Spencer, "was that I practically interviewed myself. Two instances excepted, the questions as well as the answers were my own."[19] Nonetheless, the newspapers seized upon the opportunity to print his views on America. Nearly every New York and Chicago paper reprinted the text *in toto*.[20] At the interview, during which he severely chastised American reporters, Spencer belittled all Americans on the following matters: (1) the considerable wealth of the United States had been created neither through superior American ability nor superior American institutions, but rather through the fortuitous circumstance of abundant natural resources; (2) political bosses were depriving Americans of political freedom; (3) the Constitution had not worked; (4) these political failures *could* be explained by traits in the national character (as America's economic success could not); (5) education alone could not be the panacea that Americans assumed it could; (6) Americans tolerated too many inconveniences—inconveniences which though now minor could become important later on; and (7) Americans were remiss for not doing enough

[18] *New York Herald*, August 22, 1882. Professor Edward Livingston Youmans, the founder of *Popular Science,* the nation's leading popularizer of science, and, along with Carnegie, Spencer's closest American friend, had taken years to persuade the philosopher to grant his large American public a look at him. Youmans made all the arrangements for the journey and did his best to spare the ill Spencer overexposure.

[19] Hofstadter, *Social Darwinism in American Thought,* p. 48. Herbert Spencer, *An Autobiography* (2 vols.; New York, 1904), II, 475.

[20] This extensive reporting was not an entirely spontaneous affair, either. Youmans masterminded the whole operation in a manner which would have done Madison Avenue proud. He wrote up the interview himself, set it in type, and distributed it to every major newspaper in Chicago and New York without mentioning a word as to how the interview had been rigged. For a final touch, he delayed the publication a day to October 20 so that the Chicago newspapers could receive his dispatch and print it simultaneously with the New York papers, thus heightening the illusion of spontaneity.

to end these improprieties, and should encourage the government to leg-
islate against shocking travesties such as newspaper sensationalism.[21]

Then as if to make up for the negative, even querulous tone of all these
comments, Spencer concluded his remarks with a pompous tribute. The
future of

> . . . the American nation will be a long time in evolving its ultimate
> form, but that ultimate form will be high. . . . From biological truths it
> is to be inferred that the eventual mixture of the allied varieties of the
> Aryan race forming the population will produce a finer type of man than
> has hitherto existed. . . . Americans may reasonably look forward to a
> time when they will have produced a civilization grander than any the
> world has known.[22]

The tone of the printed American response to this pseudophilosophical
preaching was polite. The journals' first responsibility was to clarify Spencer's meaning. The *New York Times* dismissed the Darwinian flourish at
the end of the interview and thought that the logical conclusion of most
of his remarks was "that this republic is doomed to disaster." The *New
York Tribune,* on the contrary, headlined:

> HIS EXPECTATIONS FAR SURPASSED—RESULTS
> OF FIRST IMPRESSIONS—SUCCESS OF REPUB-
> LICAN INSTITUTIONS—TWO AMERICAN TRAITS
> —A BRILLIANT OUTLOOK.

With Congressional and gubernatorial elections only two weeks away,
his references to bossism were the only items that interested other publications. Erecting Boss Kelly as Spencer's straw man, the *New York Herald* intoned, "Let the people ponder Mr. Spencer's words with this case
of Kelly before them as an illustration." The magazine, *The American,*
excused America by pointing out that Spencer "judges during our house-
cleaning time." *The Critic,* another periodical, rephrased this thought by
naming the pre-election period as a "time of contrition." With comfortable smugness, the *Tribune* assured its readers that "if Mr. Spencer will remain long enough among us he may be able to change his views somewhat in regard to our political affairs."[23]

The Critic admired his insights and hoped to hear more from him.
"Neither Prof. [Matthew] Arnold nor Mr. [Edward A.] Freeman made

[21] Edward Livingston Youmans, *Herbert Spencer on the Americans and the
Americans on Herbert Spencer* (New York, 1883), pp. 19–20. Spencer's laissez-
faire preference was less rigid than is sometimes supposed.

[22] *Ibid.*

[23] *New York Times,* October 21, 1882; *New York Tribune,* October 20, 1882;
New York Herald, October 21, 1882; *The American,* V (1882), 37; *The Critic,*
II (1882), 298.

any distinct impression on us," commented that journal. "But now we have among us a philosophical observer whose training in the art of judging social and political forces is beyond that of any man of our time." *The American,* on the other hand, felt that "Mr. Spencer's criticisms are not very profound." The *New York Times,* while referring to him repeatedly as "highly respected" or "truly distinguished," while also comparing him favorably with Freeman, nonetheless gently discredited the philosopher's logic by highlighting the basic contradictions between his criticisms and his philosophical works. Even his glowing prognostication was subject to sophisticated disparagement, with *The Nation* referring to his prophecy as "the old-fashioned—we might also say Fourth-of-July—view."[24] From even this brief sampling, it is clear that the American press had no intention of undergoing another Dickens trauma, no matter what Mr. Spencer had to say. They were interested in his comments, but they did not take them personally (or, in some cases, seriously). Spencer himself appreciated this show of maturity.[25]

At the banquet in his honor at Delmonico's, before a gathering of 168 of the most distinguished Americans, Spencer rose to the occasion by telling his guests that they and their fellow-Americans worked too hard! The irony that this came from a tired and sick old man did not go unnoticed by the *New York World*'s editorial writer who wryly observed: "Spencer may have mistaken his own incapability to enjoy us for our incapability to enjoy ourselves." Other newspaper reaction to his talk continued in the same unruffled vein as before. The *New York Tribune* charitably commented that "the philosopher has not discovered a new truth, but he puts an old one plainly." The *New York World* added: "If his remarks were a trifle arid, they were without doubt instructive." The *Philadelphia Press,* somewhat unnecessarily, accused Spencer of keeping himself "far from the strife of the market-place and the clatter of chaffing men."[26]

At any rate, when Spencer sailed for home on the *Germanic* on November 11, 1882, the United States of America experienced no difficulty in recovering from the highly regarded philosopher's steady stream of complaints. The maturing nation resumed its business as though Spencer had never existed; the days of a national blow-up such as that which accompanied the visit of a Dickens or a Trollope or a Marryat had receded into the past.

[24] *The Critic,* II (1882), 298; *The American,* V (1882), 37; *New York Times,* October 21, 1882; *The Nation,* XXXV (1882), 348.

[25] Youmans, *Herbert Spencer,* p. 29.

[26] *New York World,* November 10, 1882; *New York Tribune,* November 10, 1882; *Philadelphia Press,* November 11, 1882. Hofstadter, viewing the banquet in historical perspective, also found Spencer's talk "somewhat disappointing" (*Social Darwinism,* p. 48).

ARNOLD AND KIPLING

The two strongest American reactions to British visitors were occasioned by the lecture tour of Matthew Arnold (1883–84) and the first publication of Rudyard Kipling's *American Notes* (1891).[27] Both cases, too, are analogous to the Dickens trip, and for both one can draw conclusions similar to those made for Spencer's. When Arnold came "he was so well known that, as one informant assured him, the very conductors and brakemen of the railway lines had read his books."[28] Yet he crossed the Atlantic with aristocratic, preconceived, and insufferably snobbish notions about the United States. While England's upper, middle, and lower classes were disposed of as Barbarians, Philistines, and Populace, respectively, a description not always favorably received in Great Britain, his famous characterization of America as "just ourselves, with the Barbarians quite left out, and the Populace nearly"[29] was not well designed to win him friends in the Land of the Philistines either.

Arnold looked haughty: " 'He has harsh features, supercilious manners, parts his hair down the middle, wears a single eyeglass and ill-fitting clothes.' "[30] He did not know how to lecture, a fault forever immortalized by Major Burton Pond's remembrance of his first lecture. The talk was attended by General and Mrs. Grant and an overflow crowd.

> We had just heard the last few sentences of Mr. [Chauncey M.] Depew's introduction when Matthew Arnold stepped forward, opened out his manuscript, laid it out on the desk, and his lips began to move. After a few minutes General Grant said to Mrs. Grant, "Well, wife, we have paid to see the British lion; we cannot hear him roar, so we had better go home." They left the hall. A few minutes later there was a stream of people leaving the place. All those standing went away early. Later on, the others who could not endure the silence moved away as quietly as they could.[31]

Unfortunately, even the few who could hear him were not very pleased by the substance of his talk. Andrew Carnegie's mother answered Ar-

---

[27] Americans have always reacted more vigorously to foreign criticism than foreign praise. The works of Tocqueville and Bryce have made more lasting impacts, but the immediate reactions to their works lacked the intensity granted the more negative critics. Perhaps masochism should be added to the list of major American traits.

[28] Nevins, *America Through British Eyes*, p. 359.

[29] Matthew Arnold, *Civilization in the United States: First and Last Impressions of America*, pp. 79–80.

[30] Nevins, *America Through British Eyes*, p. 359, quoting an unnamed Chicago newspaper.

[31] Quoted in Jones, "Arnold, Aristocracy, and America," p. 397.

nold's expectant query as he returned to the hotel after the disastrous lecture—"Well, what have you all to say? Tell me! Will I do as a lecturer?" She chided him with the perfect reply: "Too meeneesterial, Mr. Arnold, too meeneesterial." As if to insult further the American people Arnold went around the country hobnobbing exclusively with rich Americans and members of society (he never called them Barbarians to their faces), dropping cruel remarks about the vulgar Philistines. To top it off, his main and avowed purpose in exposing the vulgarity of American life was to make sufficient money from his lectures to retire![32]

Thus one had all the ingredients for an American reaction to make that caused by Dickens seem quite mild. This seemed especially likely in light of the ammunition that he furnished conservative groups in the country in their fight against reform, ammunition that they used repeatedly. Arnold was indeed the subject of extensive criticism. But the tone of it differed altogether from the stunned and defensive hurt caused by Dickens. Arnold was laughed at, abused, satirized, mocked, reduced to insignificance. Walt Whitman said of the illustrious critic: "It is a great comfort for me to think that the Lord finds a place for them all: and if the Lord can afford to do so, so can we—and not stand off being critical. We must have the bedbug, the rat, the flea: they all have their places."[33] So Americans attended Arnold's ill-delivered lectures in good numbers without suffering serious psychic wounds in the process. "The common hearer seems to be impressed by the fact," said Charles Eliot Norton, "that it is the matter not the manner of his speech that is of primary consequence."[34] Perhaps if they had been able to hear him there might have occurred louder repercussions. As it was, Arnold completed the lyceum circuit with, as the *New York Tribune* put it, "$6000 of the Philistines' money in his pockets."[35] Instead of leaving Americans with lasting moral lessons and injured egos, he provided them with an ever-amusing stereotype.

The case of Rudyard Kipling was much the same. When his first version of *American Notes* appeared as a book in 1891, its bruising satire caused unnecessary alarm in some publishing quarters, so that the book was almost completely suppressed.[36] Kipling had crossed the continent from west to east as a brash young author of twenty-five and had used

[32] *Ibid.,* pp. 397, 402.

[33] *Ibid.,* pp. 403, 409. The *New York World,* in the context of Arnold's money-making lecture ambitions, followed mention of his own words about American vulgarity with "it is doubtful if sweetness will melt in his mouth." This kind of refusal to take him seriously greeted Arnold far more often than thoughtful attempts to answer his not insubstantial claims. *Ibid.,* p. 402.

[34] Quoted in Nevins, *America Through British Eyes,* p. 359.

[35] Quoted in Jones, "Arnold, Aristocracy, and America," p. 402.

[36] After the 1892 copyright agreement, no American publisher took the necessary steps to circulate the English edition or print an American one.

his agile pen to crush the spirits of native San Franciscans and, with even more devastating effect, Chicagoans. His portraits of these two cities (from which excerpts will later be quoted) remain classics in the literature of debunking, even though his over-all verdict of the United States was mixed with generous dashes of praise.

When his American impressions reappeared in 1899, Kipling was one of the most individual and powerful figures in the literary world of the day. He had created a new movement in poetry and fiction. How did Americans react to this now-eminent author's constant chiding? Had Americans truly matured in this regard? The evidence seems to bear out Allan Nevins' verdict that the book's "disagreeable passages were not more taken to heart by Americans than they should have been."[37]

THE BRITISH BACKGROUND

No full-scale or highly sophisticated treatment of Victorian Britain can be attempted in this study, but a few remarks touching upon the background from which the travelers emerged and which inevitably conditioned their approach to the New World are necessary. In so far as Americans have any conception of Great Britain in the nineteenth century, three views seem to compete for favor. First, Victorian Britain was aristocratic. Second, Victorian Britain, especially after the Reform Bill of 1832, was increasingly democratic. Third, Victorianism is a term synonomous with smug self-satisfaction, with moral prudery and hypocrisy, with a fatuous optimism that rested at a dead center between aristocracy and democracy.

Although Americans, in their preference for simple conclusions, do not often like to admit of apparent contradiction, an adequate picture of the society that sent over the visitors would have to embrace at least all of these conclusions. It would also compel separate discussion of developments in Scotland and those in England. The "myth" that unequivocally emphasizes democracy as the characteristic expression of Scotland in the nineteenth century, earlier and more pervasively than it could be applied to England, has, according to L. J. Saunders, a strong foundation in fact. The growth in early nineteenth-century Scotland, for instance, of public education as "an instrument of social justice" contributed strongly to the enhancement of opportunities for more of her citizens regardless of their social backgrounds.[38] This may help explain why, among all the travelers, the Scots were generally more favorably disposed to American institu-

[37] Nevins, *America Through British Eyes,* p. 323.
[38] Laurance James Saunders, *Scottish Democracy, 1815–1840: The Social and Intellectual Background* (Edinburgh: Oliver and Boyd, 1950), pp. 1, 3.

tional experiments than were the English.[39] Scotland and the United States had made roughly similar egalitarian commitments and, as the English historian Edward A. Freeman has noted, Scotland can be regarded as having been more foreign than America to many Englishmen of the nineteenth century.[40]

When our attention turns specifically to England during the reign of Queen Victoria (1837–1901) the first thing that strikes the American (as, two generations apart, it struck Ralph Waldo Emerson and Henry James) is the hierarchical class structure. To talk glibly about this era as the noon of the "middle class," as has been done so often and not always with great precision, may be to miss the continuing hold on power of the upper classes. G. Kitson Clark has noted that a wanderer from the 1750's lost in the 1850's would find much that was strange, puzzling, and frightening in the new age, "the machines, the factories and their masters, the busy crowds, the newspapers, the subjects which all men earnestly debated." The marks of the Industrial Revolution were permanent and had altered forever the rural landscape of the eighteenth century. "But when he reached those who might be considered to be at the head of society," Kitson Clark continued, "he might feel himself to be reasonably at home. Many of them would be the grandchildren of men he had known, nor would many of their thoughts and habits be altogether strange to him."[41]

Let the stranger wander even into the England of the middle 1880's, after the burst of reform signaled by the 1867 Reform Bill and by the Liberal majority voted into office in the following year, and caste would still be seen to reign. There had been, it is true, a broadening of the definition of "gentleman"; the proper education, membership in the expanding professional classes, and even new money made from the new industries could open the doors to the upper class where they were once closed. But the importance of such membership and respectability did continue to exist, and it had in some ways grown stronger by adapting to changing conditions; members of the upper classes still wielded the power in late Victorian England.[42] Even though there were large numbers of Liberals and Conservatives, Nonconformists and Anglicans among the visitors to the United States, a large proportion of all of them were drawn from these upper classes and much of their perspective was determined by that fact.

[39] Of the twenty travelers who were most enthusiastic about the United States, nine were Scotsmen. This is about double the proportion that one should statistically expect from the whole sample used in this study.

[40] Edward Freeman, *Some Impressions of the United States* (New York, 1883), p. 10.

[41] G. Kitson Clark, *The Making of Victorian England* (London: Methuen, 1962), p. 206.

[42] *Ibid.*, pp. 273–74.

At the same time one can view this era in England as a time of reform and democratic ferment. The legislation enacted by Parliament after the Reform Bill of 1832 makes an impressive list, some of the leading examples of which are: the Poor Law Reform Act of 1834; the Municipal Corporations Act of 1835; the repeal of the Corn Laws in 1846; the Factory Act of 1847; the Public Health Act of 1848; the Reform Act and Factory acts of 1867; the disestablishment of the Irish Church in 1869; Forster's great Education Act in the following year, along with the Ballot Act and the opening of the civil service to competitive examination; the abolition of religious tests at the universities in 1871; the Public Health Act of 1875; and so on. It was also the period of the Chartist agitation, the novels of Dickens, the formulas of Jeremy Bentham, and the philosophy of John Stuart Mill.

The contrast between the reformist impulse and the maintenance of aristocratic dominance suggests a polarity and tension in nineteenth-century England. No understanding of this period can be complete without a sense of this conflict and polarization. Yet Victorianism also implies a smug complacency, an imperturbability, an unquestioning acceptance of the unmatched excellence of English life, an unruffled faith in a benign future. The great century of peace after Waterloo contributed to this sense of well-being. So did the unexampled prosperity of the epoch that reached its peak in the mid-Victorian decades of the fifties and sixties, and that appeared to be eternal—eternal, that is, until the depression of 1873 struck and further severe blows to the traditionally important sectors of English agriculture (beginning with the depressed prices on corn) followed after 1874. In addition to prosperity and peace, the sanguine faith in progress was reinforced by visible signs of improvement right on the streets of London and other cities; slowly the bestiality, deprivation, and drunkenness for which the British lower classes were notorious abated as "society learnt more of its duty to protect those who were at the mercy of economic and social forces which were too strong for them."[43] Even so, travelers to England as late as the 1860's, most memorably Hippolyte Taine, were disgusted by the wretched degradation of the lower classes who could find comfort only in drink.[44]

Although democracy and aristocracy coexisted with moderate com-

[43] *Ibid.*, p. 278.
[44] Hippolyte Taine, *Notes on England*, trans. W. F. Rae (New York: 1872): "On the stairs leading to the Thames they swarm, more pale-faced, more deformed, more repulsive than the scum of Paris; without question, the climate is worse, and the gin more deadly. Near them, leaning against greasy walls, or inert on the steps, are men in astounding rags; it is impossible to imagine before seeing them how many layers of dirt an overcoat or a pair of trousers could hold. . . . For a creature so wasted and jaded there is but one refuge—drunkenness. 'Not drink!' said a desperate character at an inquest. 'It were better then to die at once' " (p. 34).

placency, different elements dominated at different times. While British historians warn their readers not to exaggerate the literal importance of the reform bills that extended the suffrage in 1832, 1867, and 1884 they also feel that the bills are at least of great symbolic import and that they can usefully serve as demarcations of various stages of nineteenth-century English culture. The period beginning in 1832, five years prior to Victoria's accession to the throne but commonly called "early Victorian," is generally viewed as a period of humanitarian agitation and political turbulence, an outburst of energy after the post-Napoleonic years of retrenchment.

The mid-Victorian era, dated by W. L. Burn from about 1852 to 1867, characterized by some as a lull or a pause, or a consolidation, has been brilliantly described by Burn as "the age of equipoise," that moment in English history when the nation, whatever its faults, "neither was nor was regarded as being decayed or decadent." Not only were notions of *laissez-faire* and public responsibility becoming reconciled, but here was "a generation in which the old and the new, the elements of growth, survival and decay, achieved a balance which most contemporaries regarded as satisfactory."[45] Norman Gash describes the period from 1830 to 1850, when Peel dominated the political stage, as "the age of violence." By 1850 when Palmerston had replaced Peel, "the major problems of the age had been met and solved." Palmerston dominated in a more peaceful era; Peel had lived in a more turbulent and politically fertile era with "profounder issues to confront."[46]

Equipoise was upset by the Reform Bill of 1867 and even more by the surprising majority won by the Liberals in the parliamentary elections in 1868. A long series of reforms were enacted during the next two decades, by Disraeli's Conservative ministry as well as during the years of Gladstone's Liberal ascendancy. Yet the continuity between Gladstone's purposes in the seventies and eighties and those of earlier Victorians like Peel, Cobden, and Bright should not be overlooked; nor should it be forgotten that this later epoch sustained and invigorated the old hierarchical society that had seemed on the verge of decay in the 1840's.[47]

The breakdown of traditional conservatism did not occur until the middle of the 1880's when the union of cottage and throne had to yield before the realities of an industrial order in which no one could any longer reasonably expect the newly rich to perform traditional obligations gracefully. The influence of Joseph Chamberlain, the rise of the new

[45] W. L. Burn, *The Age of Equipoise: A Study of the Mid-Victorian Generation* (New York: Norton, 1964), pp. 16–17.
[46] Norman Gash, *Politics in the Age of Peel: A Study in the Technique of Parliamentary Representation, 1830–1850* (London: Longmans, 1953), p. xxi.
[47] H. J. Hanham, *Elections and Party Management: Politics in the Time of Disraeli and Gladstone* (London: Longmans, 1959), p. xiv.

Labor Party at the end of the nineteenth century, and the emergence of the efficient administrative mentality in government announced a new day in English politics.[48]

Perhaps it can be said of all cultures when viewed from a distance that they are changing rapidly from what they once were, and that they are holding on to old familiar landmarks in order to maintain sanity, that they are always liberal and conservative at one and the same time. The difference between nineteenth-century England and other cultures, as seems implicit in the writings of many British historians, revolves around the heightened self-consciousness of the Victorian Englishman in the face of the conflict. More than others he appeared to know that he lived in an age of great change. He also prized the traditions that through the centuries had made his country unique. Perhaps it was out of this consciousness that many an Englishman felt compelled to proclaim with such rhapsodic exaggeration his satisfaction with his world, his country, and his future.

This sharpened awareness on the part of the articulate Englishman doubtlessly contributed to his desire to see the United States. It would be an error to assume that he came to this country primarily to use the American example as a means of scoring political points back home. The intellectual Englishman was also genuinely curious about developments in the New World; he wanted to learn; he wanted to understand America so that he could better come to grips with movement in England. For this reason the observers were surprisingly serious in their choice of subjects upon which to write. They directed their attention not only to the capricious and sensational, but also to the essential structure of American society. They delved at length into the institutions which supported American culture (and most other cultures), and to which Englishmen at home were giving a great deal of thought: educational organization, religious arrangements, and the family. These are the three institutions that are chiefly charged with transmitting values to the young. In England religion and family furnished major links with the past, and an educational system standing separate from these two had not truly come into existence despite increasing clamors for its development. Because they were citizens of a nation keenly aware of rapid change within her borders and just as keenly valuing tradition, one can begin to comprehend why the English commentators were so attentive to American practices in these fundamental areas of life.

Amidst all the confusion of the Industrial Revolution, the Victorian family mythically became the residue of all virtue and the source of much stability. Although O. R. McGregor has every right to demonstrate the

---

[48] K. B. Smellie, *A Hundred Years of English Government* (London: Macmillan, 1937), p. 184.

gap between ideal and reality in this most sacrosanct of English institutions,[49] it is still necessary to realize the extent to which the family was idealized. Here the father was sovereign, the child learned to be moral and to appreciate the best in the British past, and here was the place for the fragile, tender mother. The family was represented as the refuge of goodness in an unstable, often predatory world. When the travelers noted that the American family was structured in a different way, they wrote endlessly about it, and more severely than they did upon most other subjects. G. M. Young, in his evocative portrayal of Victorian England, was disturbed at statements that "the Victorians did this and the Victorians believed that, as if they had all lived within the sound of the town-crier's bell." Imputations of such monolithic behavior and thought are incorrect. Young continued:

> What creed, what doctrine, what institution was there among them which was not at some time or other debated or assailed? I can think of two only: Representative Institutions and the Family. I am speaking of sincere debate and earnest assault, of doubts widely felt, and grounded on the belief that there is a better way: and for the ordering of public and private life that age could imagine none better.[50]

The subject upon which Englishmen debated each other with perhaps more intensity than any other was religion. At the center of a most earnest controversy lay the claims of the Established Church. Anglicans were at war with Dissenters. The Anglicans also fought each other, most notable among the debates being that inspired by the Oxford Movement led by Newman and Pusey. Nonconformists were divided between each branch of Protestantism. Evangelicalism, Sabbatarianism, Tractarianism, the problem of the Irish Church, and the relation between religion and education were great issues of the day in England.

Debate of this sort can be misleading. It attested not to the breakdown of religion, but to its strength in Victorian England.[51] This has even been called a time for the revival of religion after the assaults of the Enlightenment; bitter polemicism should be taken as an indication that Englishmen took religion very seriously. The existence of a handful of rationalists, agnostics, and atheists in the 1850's did not amount to much of a threat to the dominance of the religious sensibility. Not until the 1870's and after were the challenges to faith posed by Darwinism, pseudo-Darwinism, and the higher criticism very important. Religion "pervaded all society, challenged men and women of every level of society or education

[49] O. R. McGregor, *Divorce in England: A Centenary Study* (London: Heinemann, 1957), pp. 61–63.

[50] G. M. Young, *Victorian England: Portrait of an Age* (London: Oxford University Press, 1936), p. 150.

[51] W. L. Burn, *Age of Equipoise*, pp. 275–78.

and became fused with objectives of most political parties and the hopes of every class."[52] When Englishmen observed American religious institutions they were primarily interested in how the separation between church and state worked in practice, and then whether it contributed to genuine faith or whether it opened the gates to secularism. The preconceptions of the visitors and their particular religious affiliations prejudiced their views and made detached observation on this topic more difficult than on any other.

As long as a child learns about the world chiefly from his father and from his church he tends to receive a conservative education. The family and religion, despite theological and organizational controversies concerning the latter, were forces making for stability in a changing order. To entrust the training of the young to those who stood outside the home and the church was deemed too risky by the large and influential group of people who felt alarmed by the strange new world that industrialism had introduced. Consequently a coherent educational system made little headway in nineteenth-century England. Politicians could never disentangle educational questions from religious ones, and this proved a thorn in the side of many Englishmen who desperately felt the need for public education for all classes. At times the dilemma seemed to have no solution. Efforts at a voluntary educational system had not succeeded. In the two universities the church was paramount and all schools of a public character were essentially church institutions.[53] Not until Balfour's Education Act of 1902 could England be said to have a reasonably comprehensive educational system. Even that act and Forster's important Education Act of 1870 still constituted halting and difficult compromises with the church, not solutions.

In the United States compulsory public schooling had been a reality in most sections of the nation outside the South since the end of the 1830's. This system stood as a model that appealed to most of the visitors—men and women of education themselves. Here education had been successfully separated from religion, and from state control; and Americans of the lower classes impressed the visitors as being infinitely more respectable (an important concept to the Victorian), because of their schooling, than their English counterparts. The English travelers were not consistently enthusiastic about the American separation of church and state, but they were envious that such a separation did make educational advances possible in the New World, advances that most Englishmen valued but could not equal.

The English observers, then, could not help examining the parallel

[52] Clark, *The Making of Victorian England*, p. 147.
[53] John William Adamson, *English Education, 1789–1902* (Cambridge: At the University Press, 1930), p. vii.

American institutions with English questions in mind. Because the visitors were highly sensitive to the tensions and pulls in England concerning the issues of the church, the schools, the family, and the class structure, their views were often biased, but their sensitivity also gave their analyses a heightened perspicuity. The American historian should be grateful that the British were exercised over subjects that Americans already had, for the most part, settled and then ignored, for the visitors were peculiarly equipped to throw considerable light upon those subjects.

When, in the twentieth century, these questions became fairly well resolved in England, and the institutions of the two nations tended to converge,[54] the travelers turned their attention to issues of diplomacy, war and peace, prosperity and economic administration, and politics. They became, that is, amateur political scientists and economists instead of cultural anthropologists. In so doing they asked more specific questions than they had before. They thus lost some of that grand perspective that contributed to their most useful insights upon the New World.[55] If the Victorians had been as calm and unified about their world as is often claimed, their comments upon America surely would have been less relevant and far less penetrating than they commonly were.

GREAT BRITAIN AND THE UNITED STATES

In looking back on nineteenth-century Britain from the context of the end of the Victorian era, the eminent English historian George Macaulay Trevelyan made this assessment: "Though all was not well in 1897, yet, in those sixty years past, millions had come out of the house of bondage and misery into which the unregulated advent of the Industrial Revolution had plunged its victims." In an earlier statement, Trevelyan tried to sum up some of the greater movements of the nineteenth century in his country:

> Change was never more rapid, nor the advance of the equalitarian spirit more observable. It was due, not to political propaganda, but to environment and conditions of life. A profound transmutation was in process towards a more mechanical and a more democratic world, the world of the great city instead of the country village, a world expressing itself through science and journalism and less through religion, poetry and literature.[56]

[54] See again English, "Britain and the United States: The Myth of Differentiation," pp. 280–81.

[55] In the Appendix I explain why I find the greatest value of the travelers to inhere in their role of amateur anthropologists rather than in their self-proclaimed roles as experts or *luminati* of one sort or another.

[56] George Macaulay Trevelyan, *British History in the Nineteenth Century and After (1782–1919)* (London: Longmans, Green and Co., 1938), pp. 405, 424.

In appraising the impact of the American experiment upon the course of nineteenth-century British society, it would be tempting to infer simply that the impact helped push Great Britain on to the road of democratization.[57] Such an inference, however, rests on a number of precarious assumptions: that "democratization" adequately describes the course of nineteenth-century British history; that the same characterization fits nineteenth-century America; that there is a causal line running from the latter to the former. More modest, but perhaps more reliable statements, can be made as one attempts to examine the immediate British response to the travel books themselves. Throughout the nineteenth century the British press tended to react in a more partisan manner to these travel works than did the American press, even with the decline of the Tory journals. In commenting upon Herbert Spencer's American journey, for example, the English *Saturday Review* could only muster praise for his remarks about the United States when Spencer had been critical; likewise the *Spectator* met his praise for the future of the United States with ridicule.[58]

One interesting measure of British reaction can be found in George Harmon Knoles, *The Jazz Age Revisited: British Criticism of American Civilization During the 1920's*. In this book, Knoles deals with a wide range of British opinion, encompassing a wider area than simply the travel reports. For each book listed in his annotated bibliography, Knoles notes all the major British periodicals that reviewed that book, with an indication of the reviewer's evaluation.[59] Forty-four of the authors included in his list belong to the cast of characters in this study. Only four of their American travel accounts were *not* reviewed at all by any of the publications studied by Knoles. The forty works that were reviewed received an average of four reviews apiece.[60] The evaluation tended to vary more with the individual reviewer than with the particular magazine; that is, no journal had a consistent policy of panning or extolling works that praised or reprimanded American civilization. The verdict on the books seemed to reside with the reviewer rather than the editor. These findings

[57] This is basically the thesis of George Lillibridge's book, aptly titled *Beacon of Freedom: The Impact of American Democracy upon Great Britain 1830–1870*. I am not persuaded that the story of Anglo-American relations could be that simple and neat.

[58] *Saturday Review*, LIV (1882), 557; *Spectator*, LV (1882), 1, 405.

[59] The publications to which Knoles referred, in order of decreasing regularity, were: *The Times Literary Supplement, The Saturday Review, The Spectator, The New Statesman, The Nation and Athenaeum, The Dublin Review, The Contemporary Review, The English Review, The Quarterly Review, The London Mercury*, and *The Graphic*.

[60] When one realizes that Knoles laid stress on the first five journals listed in note 59, and that the vast majority of reviews were drawn from those five publications, one must conclude that these books were well reviewed on the whole. As books, they were taken seriously.

suggest a couple of simple conclusions. First, these books continued to evoke considerable interest; British curiosity concerning the United States has not flagged in modern times. But, second, these books less and less became threats or weapons in English domestic politics and diplomacy; more and more they came to be regarded as books, to be judged by the standard canons of literary criticism.

One good reason for this development could be found in the course of *American* history, beginning a generation after the Civil War, which made it very difficult for British travelers to use their reports for simple propaganda purposes as they had during the Jacksonian period. During the early years of the nineteenth century the United States was more egalitarian in nearly every way than England. The British liberal could use the example of the American experiment to demand reform; the conservative could use American failures to damn the liberals. But by the end of the nineteenth century it was no longer self-evident, with the growth of trusts, political corruption, the rise of nativism, and a host of other subjects to be dealt with later in this study, that the United States was to the "left" of Great Britain. Britain, by 1890, had taken several halting but large steps in the direction of social and political reform, while it was unclear whether the United States of 1890 was more egalitarian in fact or in belief than the United States of 1835. The American woman may have been freer than the Englishwoman, but was the American laborer? American public education may have been more advanced than British, but could the same be said about American municipal government?

These developments also complicate any explication of the use made of the travelogues by Americans. The general public no longer cringed at rebukes and swelled at the smallest tokens of British esteem, making it most difficult to speak any longer of a public response to these works. The picture of the United States drawn by the commentators in these works grew more complex and hence the use made of it becomes harder to trace. Still we can presume that American opinion-makers did make some use of the travel books to further their own designs and that they were in some degree influenced by what the British travelers wrote. For example: the wealthy classes quoted Matthew Arnold constantly; the Progressive intellectuals appealed to the authority of H. G. Wells; the newspapers turned Herbert Spencer against Boss Kelly; the city planners invoked British descriptions of American urban chaos. Along these lines, several important questions suggest themselves. To what extent did American parents respond to British disgust with our permissive child-rearing habits? How did the universal British approval of American public education effect their own school reforms? Is there any relation between the British loss of interest in the Negro after the Civil War and the

Negro's desertion by the northern elite? Did the British travelers' infatuation with modern American woman speed the process of emancipation in England? Did British condemnation of the Fenians reach the American Irish? Did their abomination of Mormon bigamy touch that community? I do not know the answers to these questions, but they would appear to be legitimate ones in any further study of Anglo-American history. The simple relations of the 1830's very quickly had given way to conditions in which comparisons between Great Britain and the United States grew very complicated.

In the next chapter we shall follow the travelers around as they toured the United States (Chapter Two) and then examine their efforts to describe the American character (Chapter Three). As a substitute for character analysis an attempt will be made to isolate those British statements which bear directly on American values, beliefs, on the unquestioned (and sometimes unarticulated) articles of faith—which bear on, that is, the American "mythology" (Chapter Four). To follow this up we shall pursue in the ensuing chapters the British inquiry into the basic institutions of American culture: the schools (Chapter Five); the family (Chapter Six); the status assigned to women (Chapter Seven); the state (Chapter Eight); and the churches (Chapter Nine). In a harmonious culture, these institutions should at least refract the deep-seated credos of the people and, by their success of failure in history, modify, alter, or reenforce those faiths. An investigation of these institutions should be important in revealing the interaction of idea and practice in the American past. In effect, for reasons outlined in the third chapter, I shall be deserting character analysis for cultural analysis in these pivotal chapters; that is, I shall be using the travelers to analyze creeds and norms as embodied in institutions.[61] Since creeds can change, the final two chapters will be devoted to an examination of continuity and change in America over the seventy-five years spanned by this study, concluding with some attempts to generalize about America on the basis of these travel reports. The Appendix contains a composite portrait of the British visitors and confronts the major methodological problems involved in the use of these materials by historians.

[61] These are the institutions to which professional anthropologists pay the greatest attention. Except for long tales of sightseeing, the Britons on the whole devoted their most extensive literary efforts to these same topics.

II   The American
                      Landscape

B EFORE 1850 a voyage from Liverpool to New York was a hazardous
and wearying experience. Only those with high motivation, unusual courage, ample time, substantial income, or a specific mission dared risk the
passage. The ordinary tourist rarely satisfied these conditions, and did not
invade America in significant numbers until transportation had improved.[1] In 1835 a transatlantic crossing could last as long as ninety
days; in 1856, the *Persia* traversed the three thousand miles of ocean in
one tenth that time.[2] As early as 1847 the Collins Line was established,
specializing in rapid service; those who were less in a rush and more accustomed to luxury usually chose the Inman Line.[3] Within American
borders at this time the steamboat, stagecoach, and sleigh were yielding
to the excellent railroads. The triumph of the railroads was virtually
sealed in 1869 when the Union Pacific met the Central Pacific at Promon-
tory, Utah, rendering transcontinental travel a commonplace and hence
altering for all time the itineraries of future visitors.[4]

These transportation innovations virtually eliminated what had been

[1] Berger, *The British Traveller in America, 1836–1860*, p. 15.
[2] F. C. Bowen, *A Century of Atlantic Travel, 1830–1930* (New York: Little,
Brown and Co., 1930), pp. 15–95, cited also in Berger, *The British Traveller in
America, 1836–1860*, p. 18. The crossings around 1835 usually took about a
month.
[3] Berger, *The British Traveller in America, 1836–1860*, p. 17.
[4] No one liked the stagecoaches. See Alexander Mackay, *The Western World*,
II, 34, to share in his misery and be disabused of any romantic notions concerning these vehicles. Some of this misery could be accounted for by the abomi-
nable roads in the United States one hundred years ago (David Macrae, *The
Americans at Home*, p. 417). Macrae shared his comrades' high regard for
steamboats. They are, said Greville Chester, "very justly the pride of the
country. They are as good as possible" (*Transatlantic Sketches in the West
Indies, South America, Canada, and the United States*, p. 355). The railroads,
though, received the greatest degree of approbation. Macrae has an excellent
description of their features, including the one that struck the Britons most
forcibly and was such a visible manifestation of American equality—the lack
of separation of classes on the trains (*The Americans at Home*, pp. 455–60).

the major obstacle (except for money) blocking the potential tourist market. By 1870 American shores swarmed with Britons who came to hunt, to fish, or, most commonly, simply to see sights. Individuals still came on special journalistic, agricultural, diplomatic, labor, and government missions, and many eminent personalities readily accepted lucrative offers to lecture, first on the lyceum circuit, and later to women's clubs and the like. But tourism replaced all these as the leading motivation for the British to venture into the wilds of the New World.

The tourist covers more ground in less time than any other animal species. After the Civil War, most of this breed ambled over at least a thousand miles of American countryside and passed through at least a half dozen major cities. Few lingered more than four months, contributing no doubt to the superficiality that marked too many of the travel accounts. After the completion of the Union Pacific, half a dozen cities and a thousand miles amounted to a modest circuit. A veritable Grand Tour emerged for the English in America—as inevitable as a Cook's Tour in Europe today. By the 1870's, the visitor usually traversed a minimum of six thousand miles from coast to coast and back, before scurrying home to get his impressions into print and recover some of his expenses.

THE GRAND TOUR: FIRST IMPRESSIONS

Although few of the tourists had as long a voyage as Edward Sullivan in 1850, who "had a very tedious one of forty-two days,"[5] most were relieved of considerable boredom when the pilot boarded ship near New York. Lady Emmeline Stuart-Wortley, also in 1850, anticipated later sailing experiences when she marveled at the speedy shrinkage of the globe. "In my transatlantic travels," she happily noted, "I do not feel so far away from home as I thought I should; the Cunard steamers are so regular and rapid in their passage, they are now generally here to the day they are expected. What a fast age we live in!"[6]

The Statue of Liberty did not greet arrivals until 1886, but, barring fog and rain, the entrance into New York harbor began the tour with a dramatic flourish. Mrs. Clara Bromley enthusiastically told of how "the first view of New York surpasses in splendour any town in the world I have seen, and of those the number is not small. . . . Sea and river, mountain and garden, houses, ships, trees, all seem to vie with each other in adding to the charm of this matchless scene." Early in the nineteenth

---

[5] Edward R. Sullivan, *Rambles and Scrambles in North and South America*, p. 10. It took Alfred Pairpont only twenty days to reach Britain from New York in 1854 (*Uncle Sam and His Country*, p. 327).

[6] Emmeline Stuart-Wortley, *Travels in the United States*, p. 15.

century the tall edifices of New York City were already overwhelming the new arrivals. "My attention on landing," remarked Alfred Pairpont in 1854, "was first of all attracted by the great height of the buildings, which rise from seven to nine and even ten stories above the street."[7]

After passing through a customs inspection that rarely turned out to be as harrowing an encounter as the visitor anticipated, a cab—first horse-drawn and later motor-powered—whisked the innocent newcomer away for an intolerably high price. This gave him a foretaste of the exorbitant fees that would confront him in large cities and came as a surprise to many who, in ante-bellum days, could expect to travel economically in the United States.[8] In 1874, J. W. Boddam-Whetham echoed a common plaint that

> . . . travelling is much cheaper in Europe than in the United States, and that the cost of living at American watering-places and at all favourite resorts is so enormous that a whole family can enjoy some months of European travel for the same sum that a short sojourn at any of these fashionable places would entail. . . .[9]

The cab deposited its passenger at one of New York's great, palace-like hotels. The early irritation at the size of the cab fare mounted quickly when the driver aggressively stuck out his hand for a tip and kept it there until satisfied. Irritation, though, quickly changed to awe when the arriving tourist beheld the magnificent sight before his eyes. Not only the grandeur of the hotel, but the efficiency, caused visitors like William Fraser Rae to utter high praise. "They materially differ," he said, "from what he has seen either at home or on the Continent of Europe. For convenience of arrangement the first-class American hotel is unrivalled. Everything the visitor may require is within his reach."[10]

Two items did perturb the Englishmen in connection with these institutions. Newlyweds and entire families lived in the hotels, which hardly provided the healthiest atmosphere either for familial warmth or for the raising of young and impressionable children.[11] By the 1880's this habit had all but disappeared and few worries were afterwards voiced. Second, many authors drew their American impressions from the characters who inhabited the hotels; not often did the travelers find this sampling reassuring. Happily, as time went on, more Britons recognized that the mob that circulated in the lobby of the Astor or the sitting room of a

[7] Clara F. Bromley, *A Woman's Wanderings in the Western World,* p. 42; Pairpont, *Uncle Sam and His Country,* p. 25.

[8] Berger, *The British Traveller in America, 1836–1860,* p. 15.

[9] John Whetham Boddam-Whetham, *Western Wanderings: A Record of Travel in the Evening Land,* p. 362.

[10] William Fraser Rae, *Westward by Rail: The New Route to the East,* p. 375.

[11] William and W. F. Robertson, *Our American Tour,* p. 9.

boardinghouse, or the hordes who raced for tables in the huge, noisy, chaotic dining rooms of these establishments, were not a representative cross-section of people inhabiting the United States. William Ferguson made this point simply:

> In the hotels and public places, one meets with men who impress you with the idea that they and their fellow-countrymen are a frivolous, reckless, worldly set of rash speculators, money-worshippers and money-getters, while contact with the other class, in their Christian homes, supplies the corrective to the former misleading aberrations.[12]

NEW YORK AND THE EAST COAST

New York City assumed a place of special significance for the guest, quite apart from its size and commercial activity. Everyone visited it and nearly everyone began his tour there. All wondered how representative of the nation it was. The literary critic Ford Madox Ford, in 1927, coined a phrase when he entitled a book *New York Is Not America.* He claimed, as did his illustrious predecessor James Bryce, that the Midwest typified the United States more than New York City did.[13] The other side of the issue was argued sixty-five years earlier by Anthony Trollope:

> New York appears to me infinitely more American than Boston, Chicago, or Washington. It has no peculiar attribute of its own, as have those three cities. . . . That it [New York] is pre-eminently America is its glory or disgrace,—as men of different ways of thinking may decide upon it. Free institutions, general education, and the ascendancy of dollars are the words written on every pavingstone along Fifth Avenue, down Broadway, and up Wall Street.[14]

Whatever differing symbolic significance each author may have attached to life in Manhattan, they all did see the same life. Rush, scramble, frantic pace, movement, noise, excitement—these they all discovered in New York, and this push and raw vitality, they thought, were the city's unique attributes. The Marquis of Lorne, entering New York in 1866 after a peaceful stay in Cuba, could hardly maintain his equilibrium when confronted with the immediate contrast: "Instead of the lazy, half-alive movements we had been accustomed to for a month or two, there was a frantic haste and hurry, a general movement and bustle, that told of an eager life and dollar-scramble refreshing to witness." If money-seeking actually did characterize the United States, then one would have

---

[12] William Ferguson, *America By River and Rail,* p. v. Also he wished that the bellboys and porters might be a bit more respectful (p. 1).

[13] Ford Madox Ford, *New York Is Not America,* pp. 233–34.

[14] Anthony Trollope, *North America,* I, 290–91.

to put New York at the hub of that pursuit, as did Lorne and Theresa Longworth. "Teresina" (as she called herself) claimed that "in the matter of dollars it reigns supreme—and nothing more is needed to make it the worshipped of all worshippers, the sun and centre of American life." Some saw no end to the hustle and were convinced that New Yorkers had simply caught a mad, infectious disease. Charles Dilke recalled a joke that was going the rounds even in 1866: "Every New Yorker has come a good half-hour late into the world, and is trying all his life to make it up."[15]

Some of the visitors were infuriated by the metropolis's disgraceful paving and by the absence of a distinguished boulevard; some were appalled by its mixed population. Others were enraptured by Central Park or taken with the city's night life. But all reacted strongly to a city with a clearly delineated personality. The final verdict, as still it is, was mixed. The commentators either loved or hated Gotham; none failed to react. George Steevens never saw "a city more hideous or more splendid." Perhaps his conclusion came closest to echoing the general sentiments of the observers: "Uncouth, formless, piebald, chaotic, it yet stamps itself upon you as the most magnificent embodiment of titanic energy and force."[16]

The Eastern seaboard from Boston to Washington, D.C., has always furnished America's chief tourist attractions; and this now-megalopolitan region, though challenged by California in the twentieth century, maintained this position for the period to 1935. From New York, the newcomer chose to head either for the Capital or for the Hub of the Universe. Boston usually won out, by dint of its favorable reputation, and it generally provided a pleasant second stop for the tourists.

The Englishmen liked Boston because they found it very English: clean, orderly, refined, and (most important) intellectual.[17] Boston-

---

[15] John Argyll, *A Trip to the Tropics and Home Through America By the Marquis of Lorne*, p. 171; Maria Theresa Longworth [Therese Yelverton], *Teresina in America*, I, 4; Charles Wentworth Dilke, *Greater Britain: A Record of Travel in English-Speaking Countries during 1866 and 1867*, p. 33.

[16] George Warrington Steevens, *The Land of the Dollar*, p. 10. "Fling together Tyre and Sidon, the New Jerusalem, Sodom and Gomorrah, a little of heaven, and more of hell, and you have a faint picture of this mighty Babylon of the New World" (Macrae, *The Americans at Home*, p. 75).

[17] See, for example, Robert Ackrill, *A Scamper from Yorkshire to the United States, with a Glance at Canada*, p. 148; William Archer, *America Today: Observations and Reflections*, p. 91; Argyll, *Trip to the Tropics*, p. 206; Emily Katherine Bates, *A Year in the Great Republic*, I, 249; Charles Beadle, *A Trip to the United States in 1887*, p. 181; Isabella Lucy (Bird) Bishop, *The Englishwoman in America*, p. 321; Alexander Craib, *America and the Americans*, p. 230; Samuel Phillips Day, *Life and Society in America*, I, 208; Archibald W. Finlayson, *A Trip to America*, p. 35; A. Mackay, *The Western World*, I, 28; Pairpont, *Uncle Sam and His Country*, p. 39; Archibald Porteous, *A Scamper through Some Cities of America*, p. 100; Annie S. Smith [Annie

Cambridge stood for culture and taste. Alexander Mackay saw these qualities on the very faces of typical Bostonians: "The countenances of those we pass bespeak a very general diffusion of intelligence, an intellectuality of expression being, as I afterwards discovered, more common to the Bostonians than to the inhabitants of any other city in the Union."[18]

The Marquis of Lorne had a wonderful time in Boston. "One feels the town to be the abode of all that are first in literature, culture, and civilization in America."[19] Longfellow did much to create this warmth; he seemed to grant an audience to every Britisher who came to town. As time went on, however, the love affair between the English and Boston cooled a bit. The Hub of the Universe became the Hub of Italy and the Hub of Ireland, and this, especially the Irish influence, robbed the city of much of its charm as far as many Britons were concerned. Even Boston's fine old, lingering culture came under attack as effete and archaic.[20] H. G. Wells, who may not have had the proper temperament ever to have felt himself emotionally attuned to Boston, nonetheless most brilliantly depicted the tired, over-refined, over-reverential quality of Boston culture at the beginning of this century:

> . . . there broods over the real Boston an immense effect of finality. One feels in Boston, as one feels in no other part of the States, that the intellectual movement has ceased. Boston is now producing no literature except a little criticism. The publishers have long since left her, save for one firm (which busies itself chiefly with beautiful reprints of the minor classics). Contemporary Boston art is imitative art, its writers are correct and imitative writers, the central figure of its literary world is that charming old lady of eighty-eight, Mrs. Julia Ward Howe. . . . Boston commits the scholastic error and tries to remember too much, to treasure too much, and has refined and studied and collected herself into a state of hopeless intellectual and aesthetic repletion in consequence.[21]

The novelist W. L. George, who, in 1921, celebrated modernity wherever he saw it, did the same for Boston. Even though "Boston still stands for good taste and for the appreciation of learning," he preferred

> . . . the spectacle of Boston, with its swarming tenements, its crowds of yelling children, its resounding trolley cars. . . . All this is really sane

Burnett-Smith], *As Others See Her*, p. 102; Stuart-Wortley, *Travels in the United States*, p. 68; Sullivan, *Rambles and Scrambles*, p. 68; Oscar Wilde, *The Writings of Oscar Wilde*, III, 246.

[18] A. Mackay, *The Western World*, I, 28.

[19] Argyll (Lorne), *Trip to the Tropics*, p. 206.

[20] The English feminist Emily Faithfull feared that the aristocracy of letters was dying out. Between her first visit in 1872 and her second a decade later, "many a valued presence [had turned] into a 'majestic memory'" (*Three Visits to America*, pp. 97–98).

[21] H. G. Wells, *The Future in America: A Search After Realities*, pp. 316–17, 320.

and splendid and full of promise for a luminous future. I weep no tears over Old Boston that lies in its own dust, nor smile, for instance, at the Boston Mushroom Society.[22]

Even though most Britons, especially Englishmen, felt more comfortable with the old Boston, it is not an overstatement to say that over the entire span of American history Boston has been heaped with more British praise than any other American town.[23] Even in the modern era, it maintains its position (if Cambridge is included) as one of the favorite cities of the English visitors.

Washington reversed Boston's path; it began as the most jeered at of cities and became widely esteemed as it aged. In its early stages, "The City of Magnificent Distances" was no more than a plan: wide, empty avenues with buildings on neither side, dustbowls before the rains, and swamps after them. Charles Dickens composed the classic description of early Washington (1842) when he outlined his blueprint for constructing a replica on the site of a slummy suburb of London:

> Burn the [present suburb] down; build it up again in wood and plaster; widen it a little, throw in part of St. John's Wood . . . plough up all the roads . . . erect three handsome buildings in stone and marble, anywhere, but the more entirely out of everybody's way the better; call one the Post Office, one the Patent Office, one the Treasury; make it scorching hot in the morning and freezing cold in the afternoon, with an occasional tornado of wind and dust; leave a brickfield without the bricks in all the central places where a street may naturally be expected; and that's Washington.[24]

But as the plans took shape and the avenues were lined with stately buildings, the Capital's reputation underwent a rapid transformation. By 1877, Rae could say:

> Among the changes wrought during a few years in the United States none has been more striking than that which concerns the exterior aspect of the city of Washington. Whoever reads what was written about it by the travellers whose remarks I have quoted, and looks on the city as it now exists, will have great difficulty in believing that the place before his eyes, and that about which he has read, are the same.[25]

Two years later, Sir George Campbell described Washington as "the pleasantest and best of American cities," and Karl Marx's son-in-law, E. B. Aveling, in 1887 called it "incomparably the most beautiful city

[22] Walter Lionel George, *Hail Columbia! Random Impressions of a Conservative English Radical,* p. 31.

[23] Clare Sheridan, a year after George, still insisted that Boston was very English (*My American Diary,* p. 357).

[24] Charles Dickens, *American Notes for General Circulation,* p. 300.

[25] William Fraser Rae, *Columbia and Canada,* p. 149.

I saw in America." After that date, Washington overshadowed all other cities located between it and New York, and indeed W. E. Adams compared it favorably with Paris, London, Copenhagen, Berlin, Brussels, and Edinburgh.[26]

Philadelphia, although widely visited, did not inspire the strong emotions of Manhattan; rarely disliked, it scarcely ever aroused more than the tepid compliment of being "clean." Baltimore, which previously had achieved fame as the city of beautiful women, eventually turned into the last obstacle to be passed before gaining admittance to its marbled neighbor to the south. Other spots along the eastern seaboard that attracted visitors included Atlantic City, about which the journalist A. Maurice Low composed a chapter entitled "The Middle-Class Playground." The autumnal beauty of the Hudson area around West Point deeply touched Lady Duffus Hardy. Niagara Falls had been the great natural tourist attraction in the early part of the nineteenth century. Most of the travelers groped for the words to depict its beauty and, like Lady Emmeline Stuart-Wortley, they eventually surrendered to its magnificence. "If one saw the sun for the first time," she breathlessly asked, "could one describe it?" But sixty years later, in 1906, H. G. Wells bitterly noted how its splendor had been "long since destroyed beyond recovery by the hotels, the factories, the power-houses, the bridges and tramways and hoardings that arose about it." Giving expression to one of the tragedies of a growing America, Wells imagined that the Falls "must have been a fine thing to happen upon suddenly after a day of solitary travel . . . but it's no great wonder to reach it by trolley-car, through a street hack-infested and full of adventurous refreshment-places and souvenir shops and the touting guides."[27]

DOWN SOUTH, OUT WEST, AND HOME

The cities south of the Mason-Dixon line suffered the greatest relative loss of tourist traffic in the nation after the Civil War. A good many Englishmen before the war found their spiritual home away from home in Dixie, that mythical dreamy land removed from the scramble and

[26] Sir George Campbell, *White and Black: The Outcome of a Visit to the United States*, p. 33; Edward Bibbins Aveling, *An American Journey*, p. 60; William Edward Adams, *Our American Cousins: Being Personal Impressions of the People and Institutions of the United States*, p. 33.

[27] Longworth, *Teresina in America*, II, 131; A. Maurice Low, *America at Home*, pp. 172–83; Mary (McDowell) Hardy, *Through Cities and Prairie Lands: Sketches of an American Tour*, pp. 70–71; Stuart-Wortley, *Travels in the United States*, p. 5; Wells, *The Future in America*, p. 52.

sordidness of life in the American North and West.[28] After 1865, except
for those with a special interest in the war or Reconstruction or in racial
problems, the average tourist bypassed this section of the nation;[29] and
the majority of those who did venture there were not happy with what
they saw. James Stirling, a Scots jurist, anticipated this trend of thought
when in 1857 he sighed with relief as he returned to the North after a
stay down South: "Thank Heaven! I am once more in the North. Behind me is despotism and desolation; around me is freedom and prosperous industry. One breathes more freely. The little step from South to
North is a stride from barbarism to civilization; a leap from the sixteenth
to the nineteenth century."[30] Each traveler to Dixie at some time found
occasion to contrast it with the buzzing North.[31] Many post-bellum observers predicted that the development of a new, industrial South might
eventually blur the contrast, but this never fully materialized during the
period 1860–1935; stark, dramatic differences told the story of the two
sections.

The slower pace and softer outlines of southern life continued, of
course, to attract some visitors. The majority, however, viewed the
slower pace as lethargy; western energy became more romantic than
southern sluggishness. Samuel Smith, for example, noted in 1896: "In
the South, partly from climate, partly as a relic of slavery, there is much
less energy and progress than in the other sections of the Union." Forty
years later, Morgan Phillips Price said the same thing, except that by
his time it was just as appropriate to compare the South to the West as

[28] Amelia M. Murray loved the ease of the South (*Letters from the United States, Cuba, and Canada*, p. 183). An English cleric who resided in the South for twenty-one years beginning in 1841 stressed the great natural abundance of the land which would, he confidently asserted, manifest itself during the Civil War, culminating in a mighty Confederate triumph (T. D. Ozanne, *The South as It Is*, pp. 35–36). Just as many Britons, especially Scotsmen, however, found the region dirty, desultory, and depraved. Even the mild Alexander Mackay remarked with disgust upon the "spiritless and even dilapidated as-pect" of the South (*The Western World*, I, 250). It would not do to exaggerate the myth of British-Southern *gemütlichkeit*. Before the Civil War there was a definite correspondence between one's attitude toward the South and one's at-titude toward slavery.
[29] This statement would seem to be belied by *Travels in the New South*, ed. Thomas D. Clark (2 vols.; Norman: University of Oklahoma Press, 1962), with its overwhelming accumulation of travelers to the post-bellum South. The great majority of these, however, were Americans; and my statement is a relative one, referring to the proportion of British observers who ventured into the South after 1865 as compared with the proportion before the Civil War.
[30] James Stirling, *Letters from the Slave States*, p. 353.
[31] Mackay said the North-South transition "is as great as is the change from the activity of Lancashire, to the languor and inertness of Bavaria (*The Western World*, I, 250). Macrae has the fullest set of comparisons (*The Americans at Home*, pp. 270–76).

to the North. The eighty years between Price and Stirling seem as one when Price tells of how "we were coming into another America, whose customs and traditions were different from those of the Americas we had seen. . . . How different from the great prairies out West, where the limitless prospect and exhilarating air seem to make everyone energetic!"[32]

New Orleans did not suffer the tourist slack of her southern sisters, but New Orleans has never been a typical southern city.[33] Instead of going to Mobile, Charleston, and Richmond, the tourists headed toward Pittsburgh, Cincinnati, St. Louis, Detroit, and especially toward Chicago to discover "the real America." These cities did not evoke great enthusiasm, but they seemed somehow to be authentically American. "The West," suggested James Bryce, "may be called the most distinctively American part of America, because the points in which it differs from the East are the points in which America as a whole differs from Europe." He later amplified these remarks by naming as some of these points of difference "unrestfulness, the passion for speculation, the feverish eagerness for quick and showy results."[34]

One special manifestation of these western attributes was the astonishing way in which midwestern cities mushroomed from nothing. W. E. Adams could scarcely catch his breath at the American's total disregard for time and difficulty. "Cities," he wrote, "rise up in that country almost in a night-time. It has taken Newcastle something like 800 years to attain the dignity of a city." No city illustrated this phenomenon more completely than did Chicago. The sequence outlined by Henry Hussey Vivian in 1878 bordered on the miraculous, for in 1830 it had but 12 houses and 100 inhabitants; in 1871 it burned to the ground; in 1878 it

[32] Samuel Smith, *America Revisited,* p. 21; Morgan Phillips Price, *America After Sixty Years: The Travel Diaries of Two Generations of Englishmen,* p. 193.

[33] The fortunate geographical location of New Orleans would, thought Mackay, make it one of the world's great commercial entrepôts of the future (*The Western World,* II, 90). A good many visited the Miami area, but not to gain insight into the spirit of the Confederacy; see Low, *America at Home,* pp. 159–71.

[34] James Bryce, *The American Commonwealth,* III, 86, 647. Low conceived of the United States as two separate nations—East and West, sobered adult and confident youth (*America at Home,* p. 60). W. L. George said that "the civilization that the Middle West creates within the next fifty years will be the American civilization" (*Hail Columbia!* p. 72). Ford Madox Ford was not pleased by the prospect of a nation dominated by midwestern types: "As far as I can see, the design of the denizens of the land round, say, Chesterton, Ind., and of hundred-per-centers in general is to create an American—an AMERICAN— who shall have all the characteristics of the Scandinavian–North–German– Lutheran farmer. There will be about him nothing of any culture that has come down the ages. He will have no trace of French or English wisdoms" (*New York Is Not America,* pp. 263–64).

approached a population of 500,000. Just as the Middle West represented the United States, so Chicago stood for the Middle West. Chicago was synonymous with movement; the winds blowing off Lake Michigan seemed themselves to stir motion and create energy. When Boddam-Whetham observed how "everything must keep moving in Chicago" he did not grossly overstate the case, for dozens of tourists remarked how even houses were transferred intact from one place to another.[35] The city's amazing recovery from the Great Fire excited the admiration of the visitors; such indomitable spirit represented the best in the youthful vigor of the New World. Sir Rose Lambart Price tried to capture this quality, writing soon after the fire:

> Of all the extraordinary towns in the United States, Chicago may certainly be looked upon as being the most so. Twice almost entirely destroyed by fire within an unprecedentedly short space of time, it has on each occasion risen like a Phoenix from its ashes, invariably improved by the fiery ordeal. If it continues burning and improving at the same rate, there is no telling to what pitch of magnificence it may not ultimately arrive.[36]

The haste and drive of this prototypical town naturally had its less fortunate side, somewhat apparent even in Price's good-willed sarcasm. Not all agreed with the Irish wit, Shane Leslie, who thought Chicago a very handsome place: "Chicago has the finest walk of any city in the world: along Michigan Avenue between the lake and the skyscrapers: with the wind blowing fresh and keen as on Brighton front minus only the salt."[37] Many Englishmen demurred strongly, finding Chicago's beauties to be, at best, patchy and accidental. These commentators, rather than being invigorated by the Windy City, were repelled by the utter lack of planning, order, dignity, taste, and purpose. If Chicago symbolized anything for H. G. Wells, it was vulgarity, crassness, and chaos. For all of Wells's distaste for Boston, at least it had what Chicago lacked as a city: a plan.[38] Chicago, like New York, aroused both high regard and

[35] Adams, *Our American Cousins,* p. 35; Henry Hussey Vivian, *Notes of a Tour in America,* p. 86; Boddam-Whetham, *Western Wanderings,* p. 33.

[36] Sir Rose Lambart Price, *The Two Americas: An Account of Sport and Travel with Notes on Men and Manners in North and South America,* pp. 335–36.

[37] Shane Leslie, *American Wonderland: Memories of Four Tours in the United States of America (1911–1935),* pp. 182–83.

[38] Wells, *The Future in America,* pp. 78–81; even though Daniel H. Burnham had designed a plan for Chicago. Walter Gore Marshall defended the solidity of the architecture and atmosphere of Chicago in a minority dissent (*Through America,* p. 87). The Chicago World's Fair of 1893 attracted visitors from all over the world, but curiously elicited few books of travel. One exception (of small merit) was Robert Anderson Naylor, *Across the Atlantic.* The same can be said for the 1904 Exposition at St. Louis, which assembled many of

great contempt. No one gave vent to this latter sentiment with more gusto than Kipling upon leaving Chicago. "Having seen it, I urgently desire never to see it again. It is inhabited by savages. Its water is the water of the Hugli, and its air is dirt. . . . After those swine and bullocks at Chicago I felt that complete change of air would be good."[39]

While the twenty-five-year-old Kipling headed east, for most tourists the clean air could be found west of Chicago. They, along with the migrant native population, swarmed in vast numbers to the western two thirds of the nation after 1870. No Grand Tour could any longer exclude that portion of the continent. Daniel Pidgeon's description of the route traversed by the typical traveler merits extended quotation for, while it does not come from the pen of one of England's eminent literary figures, it does accurately recreate the tempo and spirit, as well as the westward thrust which increasingly marked the visitors' itineraries.

> The average American tourist of to-day spends, usually, a few weeks in cosmopolitan New York, pays flying visits to the Falls of Niagara, the political capital, and the greater cities of the Union, but thinks his trip only beginning when, turning his back on the Atlantic slope, he joins the ranks of the great army of civilization which is always on the march to the Far West.
>
> His chief halts are made, probably, at Chicago, St. Louis, the City of the Saints, the mining-camps of the Rocky Mountains, and the cattle-ranches of their western flanks; on the peaks and passes, or by the blue lakes of the Sierra Nevada; in the cities of her silver kings, or among the wheat-fields of Central California and the orchards and vineyards of the Pacific slope. At length, he reaches the city where the old and the new worlds meet, and, through the portals of the Golden Gate, sees the sun set beneath the misty western horizon. Then he turns, to recross, in a single flight of seven days' duration, three thousand miles of mountain, desert, river, prairie, cultivation and forest. During all that time he passes rude camps, remote homesteads, farming villages, mushroom towns and settled cities, the homes of miners, ranchmen, pig and grain growers, lumberers, husbandmen and citizens.
>
> Finally, he steps on board ship to return, in the full belief that he has seen America.[40]

Pidgeon composed these lines in 1884, just fifteen years after the official opening of the transcontinental railway. The exotic unknown of the virgin

the world's greatest minds; see George Haines, IV, and R. H. Jackson, "A Neglected Landmark in the History of Ideas," *Mississippi Valley Historical Review*, XXXIV (1947), 201–20. One tourist account is William Winget, *A Tour in America and a Visit to the St. Louis Exposition*. As a city, second only to Chicago, St. Louis received the most attention among midwestern towns. In 1868 William A. Bell argued that St. Louis was easily the best place for the Federal Capital (*New Tracks in North America*, I, 10). In the same year Foster Barham Zincke explained why it was a finer, more substantial, more urbane city than Chicago (*Last Winter in the United States*, p. 165).

[39] Kipling, *American Notes*, pp. 215, 234.
[40] Daniel Pidgeon, *Old-World Questions and New-World Answers*, pp. 1–2.

West beckoned all travelers who sought adventure and, perhaps more realistically, those who sought a reading market back home. Few could resist this double temptation, so the cultured Britons rode staunchly into the primitive territory.[41]

Denver, except for its breathtaking situation, reminded the explorers of Chicago and other towns which, like Topsy, just grew. The barrister, William Ballantine, observed that Kansas City and Denver had "both sprung up to their present dimensions [in 1884] with that rapidity which seems characteristic of all American undertakings."[42] By this time Mormonism, the obsession of the earlier tattlers, had become more of a commonplace,[43] and Salt Lake City became a pause before the final push into "paradise": California.[44]

California supplied the authors with an opportunity for belletristic release, a chance to turn loose their poetic impulses upon scenes of natural beauty for which the precommercialized Niagara Falls had earlier been the inspiration. Listen, for example, to Sir Charles Dilke:

> The names of The Golden State and El Dorado are doubly applicable to California; her light and landscape, as well as her soil, are golden. Here on the Pacific side, Nature wears a robe of deep rich yellow: even the distant hills, no longer purple, are wrapped in golden haze. No more cliffs and canyons—all is rounded, soft, and warm. The Sierra, which faces eastward, with four thousand feet of wall-like rock, on the west descends gently in vine-clad slopes into the California vales, and trends away in spurs toward the sea . . . [etc.][45]

Even more than the Pacific slope and Yosemite, San Francisco was the climax of the long westward trek.[46] Some visitors were put off by a

[41] The romantic, primitive quality of the virgin West is well evoked in the writings of W. F. Butler, especially *The Great Lone Land: A Narrative of Travel and Adventure in the North-West of America,* and of Paul Fountain, e.g., *The Great Deserts and Forests of North America.* Somewhat more prosaically, R. L. Price wrote of the West as the future seat of the nation's power and population (*The Two Americas,* p. 345).

[42] William Ballantine, *The Old World and the New,* p. 171. Denver's magnificence greatly moved W. G. Marshall (*Through America,* p. 401).

[43] The unfair treatment given the Mormons by American journalists and British visitors appalled Phillip Stewart Robinson who, in his own words, "lived *among* the Mormons and with them . . . as no Gentile has ever done before me." This probably truthful claim gave him authority to "assure my readers that every day of my residence increased my regret at the misrepresentation these people have suffered" (*Sinners and Saints: A Tour Across the States, and Round Them: with Three Months among the Mormons,* pp. 247–48).

[44] For the best description of Yellowstone, read Windham Thomas Wyndham-Quin, *The Great Divide: Travels in the Upper Yellowstone in the Summer of 1874;* for the Rockies, William A. Baillie-Grohman, *Camps in the Rockies.*

[45] Dilke, *Greater Britain,* pp. 179–80.

[46] Yosemite enthralled William Henry Barneby in 1883 (*Life and Labour in the Far, Far West,* p. 50). The eminent Darwinist, Alfred Russel Wallace,

certain rowdy quality rampant by the Golden Gate in the two or three decades after 1849; but very rapidly San Francisco replaced Boston as the American city most generally admired. Edward Money declared in 1886 with some enthusiasm: "I have travelled much and seen many cities and towns in different parts of the world, but I have seen nothing to equal San Francisco." Fifty years later A. G. MacDonell, after complaining about all the "semi-literate pests" who spew out fanciful adjectives in exaggerated encomiums to San Francisco, when he saw the city had to conclude, somewhat to his dismay, that all they could "say in praise of its harbour can only be understatement. It is the most beautiful thing that I have seen in my life."[47]

By the second decade of the twentieth century, an area a little over four hundred miles to the south began to mushroom into prominence with incredible speed: Los Angeles became a major tourist attraction. Practically to a man, however, the travelers mercilessly derided this strange world. Los Angeles provided license for a different kind of literary release than that furnished by the Sierras and the Bay Area. A defense of this growing region came from Sir Charles Igglesden at the end of the 1920's:

> From what I could glean, San Francisco is sore at the rapid growth of Los Angeles, founded as a tiny place only a few years ago and now so large that it promises to be the biggest city of the West before many decades have passed. . . . The city itself already boasts of fine streets, many superb buildings, especially hotels, and charming boulevards or avenues. Then there is the scenery all around—the Pacific coast-line . . . The Beverly Hills . . . are a dreamland. . . . Flowers run riot in their sun-kissed beds. One of the most beautiful places I have ever seen is Pasadena. . . .[48]

A half dozen years later, however, MacDonnell spoke for the majority of Britons, though in rather brutal fashion, by saying: "I pottered about the streets in goggling amazement that any place could be so ugly and at the same time contain so many ugly people."[49]

---

was disappointed with Lake Tahoe in 1886, even before it became an outpost of Reno culture (*My Life: A Record of Events and Opinions*, II, 174).

[47] Edward Money, *The Truth about America*, p. 94; A. G. MacDonell, *A Visit to America*, p. 198. The opium dens fascinated scores of travelers like George Augustus Sala, *America Revisited: From the Bay of New York to the Gulf of Mexico, and from Lake Michigan to the Pacific*, II, 266–73. I am fond of Philip Guedalla's image of San Francisco in *Conquistador: American Fantasia*, in his chapter "The Tilted City": "I was always half afraid that San Francisco would slip off her hills into the water. If she did, I should certainly run to pick her up; and I feel quite sure that she would lie charmingly in one's arms for just an instant before saying 'Thank you' " (p. 266).

[48] Sir Charles Igglesden, *A Mere Englishman in America*, pp. 92–93.

[49] MacDonnell, *America Revisited*, p. 220.

The critic and novelist J. B. Priestley compared the two California adversaries:

> Only at night does it [Los Angeles] lose its air of being determinedly third-rate. It has always seemed to me symbolical of an America I do not like, just as its rival, San Francisco, a real city with a sparkle and a charm of its own, has always seemed to me symbolical of an America I love, the large, hearty, devil-may-care, romantic America. Los Angeles has always appeared to me to be a city of boosters and boomers. . . .[50]

Lest the San Franciscans feel too smug at this flattery (a vice that some observers detected), they needed only to recall Kipling's description of their city: "ragged, unthrifty sand hills, to-day pegged down by houses." Or one might be reminded of his verdict on San Franciscans: "perfectly insane," "barbarians."[51]

More gracious champions came to the defense of other cities: H. H. Vivian spoke for Cincinnati, Robert Ackrill for Cleveland, J. F. Muirhead for Colorado Springs—a western retreat for easterners and the English—W. E. Adams for Milwaukee, E. A. Freeman for Albany.[52]

After his days in San Francisco, the traveler, thoroughly exhausted by now, entrained and rapidly recrossed the continent to New York. A day or two after arrival there he embarked for home. His basically big-city expedition of more than six thousand miles invariably filled him with a heightened sense of the overwhelming size of the United States, which Ackrill, the Yorkshire editor, tried to convey by asking his readers whether they could imagine the experience of riding in one train within one sovereign nation for "a journey as long as that of a steamer from Liverpool to New York."[53] The astonishing magnitude of the nation left most of these highly vocal visitors awed and speechless, and undoubtedly was one reason for the upsurge of respect that came to characterize most British writing about the United States in the last quarter of the nineteenth century.

Nonetheless, few found in the United States a tourist paradise: simply too big, too expensive, and too often monotonous. Bryce could find little difference between one American city and another.[54] Muirhead, a decade

---

[50] J. B. Priestley, *Midnight on the Desert*, pp. 172–73.

[51] Kipling, *American Notes*, pp. 118–19, 22, 24. It must be conceded, in all fairness, that he did derive some delight from San Francisco's lunacy. The visitors to Los Angeles often enjoyed themselves too, even if they could not admit it in print.

[52] Vivian, *Notes of a Tour in America*, p. 189; Ackrill, *A Scamper from Yorkshire*, p. 101; James Fullarton Muirhead, *America, the Land of Contrasts: A Briton's View of His American Kin*, pp. 212–13; Adams, *Our American Cousins*, p. 27; Freeman, *Some Impressions of the United States*, p. 245.

[53] Ackrill, *A Scamper from Yorkshire*, p. 57.

[54] Bryce said: "In all [of the cities] the same shops, arranged on the same

later, took exception to this point: "I should simply ask what single
country possessed cities more widely divergent than New York and New
Orleans, Philadelphia and San Francisco, Chicago and San Antonio,
Washington and Pittsburg?"[55]

The tourists frequently differed as to what was beautiful and what was
hideous. All the visitors, though, came upon sights of extraordinary
beauty and incredible ugliness; they all encountered the most cosmopoli-
tan metropolises and the most provincial hamlets;[56] they enjoyed superb
tourist accommodations and survived the most primitive hotels and
meals; they beheld places they adored and spots they despised. The British travelers ventured only two generalizations concerning the physical
aspects of the nation as a whole: the United States was huge, and, as
James Fullarton Muirhead, editor of Baedeker's guide to the United
States, put it in the title of another of his books, it was pre-eminently
"the land of contrasts."

---

plan, the same Chinese laundries, with Li Kow visible through the window,
the same ice-cream stores, the same large hotels with seedy men hovering
about in the dreary entrance hall . . ." (*The American Commonwealth*, III,
621–23). See also Joseph Hatton, *To-day in America: Studies for the Old World
and New*, p. 54.

[55] James Fullarton Muirhead, *America, the Land of Contrasts*, p. 190. James
M. Phillippo in 1857 drew a series of sharp delineations between the peoples
of the various sections which "render a general description [of the nation as a
whole] difficult, if not impossible. The New-Englanders are industrious, frugal,
pious, patient, and inperturbable. In the Middle States, Pennsylvania excepted,
where the people are of a staid and sober aspect, they are, in addition to these
qualities, eminently energetic. In the Southern States, where slavery exists, they
are generous, indolent, haughty, and reckless. In the Western States, frank,
hospitable, industrious, and lovers of adventure; but at the same time, possessed
of many deteriorating qualities" (*The United States and Cuba*, p. 97). Half a
century later, J. Nelson Fraser contended: "Differences of tone may be noticed
between East and West, between North and South. But these are all trivial,
compared with the strong community of sentiment and manners which, as a
whole, unites the country" (*America, Old and New: Impressions of Six Months
in the States*, p. 367). For this later period, Fraser's view more than Phillippo's
represented the consensus of the visitors. Such attempts to define a national or
regional character will be analyzed in the next chapter.

[56] "The average small American town is crude, vulgar, and ugly. *Main
Street* was, in the main, an accurate picture of the desolation of a thousand
Middle-Western towns, with their dirty streets, their dilapidated Fords, their
glaring drug stores, soda fountains, placards, iron-roofed villas, clothing stores
displaying 'ox-blood Oxfords with bull-dog ties,' lunch-counters with wet oil-
cloth and thick handleless cups, Christian Science libraries, pool rooms, yellow-
brick school buildings, gasoline pumps, etc., etc., etc." (Beverley Nichols,
The Star Spangled Manner, pp. 270–71). He conceded that " 'Main Street' in
England" was also a nightmare. "Let us admit both those facts, and lament
the common depravity of them" (*Ibid.*, p. 271). As early as 1882, T. S. Hudson
remarked on the way advertising marred the landscape (*A Scamper through
America*, pp. 43–44).

III

The American Character

WHEN the Reverend David Macrae arrived in the New World in 1867, he recorded his first impressions for posterity:

> The moment I set foot in the United States I felt that I had got amongst a new people. It is very remarkable that a country still in its infancy should have already produced so distinct a type of man. There are great differences between the people of the North and the people of the South, between the people down East and the people out West; and yet a common nationality has its mark upon them all. An American is everywhere recognized. You know him by his speech; you know him by a certain ease and grandeur of manner, which is inspired by the greatness of his country and his personal share in its government; you know him by his features—the long sharp face, the eagle eye, and the pointed chin.[1]

The attempt to define that "common nationality" and to single out the identifying marks of the American has spurred on countless numbers of writers on the American scene, foreign and native, from before Crevecoeur down to the latest scholarly publication. Americans do seem to be different from other national groups, and British commentators have striven manfully to uncover the areas in which Americans stray from British norms. For the most part they have had to rely on the immediate evidence of their senses and, in consequence, they have amassed a very long list of misleading idiosyncracies which purport to define the American character.

[1] Macrae, *The Americans at Home*, p. 33. I do not assume that the travelers thought of us as a melting pot. Tocqueville and Harriet Martineau, for example, and many other tourists approached America in terms of cultural pluralism, while others insisted that Americans tried to imitate English norms.

41

MANNERS AND CUSTOMS

The English language had a different sound when spoken in the New World. Sir Philip Burne-Jones, son of the famous painter, never quite reconciled himself to the American "audacity to refer to an *English accent! . . .* For an American to speak of an English *accent* is like a singer who habitually sings flat commenting on someone else who is singing in tune! It's absurd. An American may speak English with an American accent, but surely an Englishman speaks English." Not all Britons were as perfectly British about American English as Burne-Jones was. Alexander Francis smiled at this predictable sort of response. "Americans, with characteristic good-humor," he pointed out, "express their sense of this weakness of ours in the story of one of us who, on his return to England, reported of the speech of Americans that they say 'Where am I at?' when we should say 'Where is my 'at?' The rebuke is not undeserved."[2]

Americans also looked different from the British, according to such visitors as David Macrae. "Strangers on their arrival in America," James Burn graciously observed, "cannot fail to be disagreeably impressed by the almost skeleton forms and sallow complexions of the male population." The difficulty in evaluating such observations is that American physical characteristics were apparently susceptible to rapid alteration. Only forty-five years after Burn's comments the Yankee physiognomy, as described by British travelers, had undergone a total revolution. James Nelson Fraser in 1910 gazed and saw that "the Uncle Sam face is rarely to be seen now, unless it be in the old-fashioned Southern States. The classic example of this type is the face of Abraham Lincoln; the face which has superseded it is that of MacKinley [*sic*]; full, massive, and oftentimes blue-eyed."[3] Harold Spender, in 1920, also noted this metamorphosis:

> Since my last visit, there has asserted itself a remarkable change in the American man. The older type of American—"Uncle Sam"—as depicted in all our British cartoons, is a long, lanky, thin man with a goatee beard. The American man of today is clean-shaven, of medium height and possessed of a resolute chubby face which gives him the appearance of a formidable cherub.[4]

Two years later Sir Arthur Conan Doyle made this same point in contrasting the new "American business man of the best type—clean-shaven,

[2] Sir Philip Burne-Jones, *Dollars and Democracy*, pp. 177–78 (author's italics unless otherwise stated); Alexander Francis, *Americans: An Impression*, pp. 4–5.
    [3] [James Dawson Burn,] *Three Years among the Working Classes in the United States during the War*, p. 3; Fraser, *America, Old and New*, p. 369.
    [4] Harold Spender, *A Briton in America*, p. 260.

steady-eyed, alert, and smiling" with the older generation, which was "hirsute, angular, full of whimsical character, and humorous exaggeration, as different as posible from their quiet, efficient successors."[5] Doyle offered no clues in explanation of this mysterious transformation, nor did any of the authors.

One thing was certain: Americans did eat differently from average mortals; they switched forks to the right hand and they ate with astonishing rapidity. "We found out," said J. F. Campbell, "why British tourists talk so much about Yankee haste in dining. Arriving at a country station, it was somehow communicated to us that we stopped ten minutes to feed." Americans even satisfied their thirst oddly. "All day long," Foster Barham Zincke noted, "throughout the winter as well the other seasons of the year, people are drinking water with ice floating in it."[6] Liquid refreshment of a more potent sort also interested the tourists, especially those who came in the nineteenth century when drunkenness among the lower classes in England constituted one of that nation's most formidable social problems.[7] "The main difference between the drinking habits in America and our own country," wrote the Reverend Mr. Macrae, "is this—the Americans drink more at bars and less at home." The British thought the American lower classes had a much better record for moderation in drinking than their counterparts in England, who so often stumbled through the streets in a drunken stupor. During prohibition, Edith Somerville seemed to feel cheated that "at our first dinner party, we did not find ourselves rising from the table and leaving our fellow guests under it."[8]

Moving outdoors, Macrae discovered that he liked the American weather; he found it vivifying. It quickened "all the pulses of life," accounting for, in part, the ambition and energy of the American, the speed of his life.[9] There was a general healthiness about life in the United States reflected in outdoor living, climate, and food. "I never saw a table," said Alfred Pairpont, "even in the house of the very poorest, where there was not an abundance of excellent food for every meal." In touching upon the "plenty" of American life, Pairpont connected it with conditions that allowed for a rough material equality whose consequences reached everywhere: "With regard to dress, too, they far surpass us; for

[5] Sir Arthur Conan Doyle, *Our American Adventure,* p. 17.

[6] John Francis Campbell, *A Short American Tramp in the Fall of 1864,* p. 267; Zincke, *Last Winter in the United States,* p. 66.

[7] Visitors to Victorian England often testified to the prevalence of this vice. See Taine, *Notes on England,* p. 5.

[8] Macrae, *The Americans at Home,* p. 530; Edith Somerville, *The States Through Irish Eyes,* p. 88.

[9] Macrae, *The Americans at Home,* p. 35. Alexander Mackay wrote a wonderful description of American thunderstorms and their stimulating effect during summertime (*The Western World,* I, 245).

no matter how subordinate the position, all dress well; nor could a stranger always tell by the clothes, the difference between a merchant and an artizan—between a lady and her female servant or 'help.' "[10]

Americans had droll customs. They called their servants "help"; yet for a supposedly democratic nation they loved to endow each other with pretentious titles like "colonel" and "judge." The men mechanically gave up their train and carriage seats to women and the women just as automatically took the seats without a word of thanks to the gentlemen. Pairpont was astonished that Americans weighed themselves on scales. Alexander Mackay commented with repugnance on the perpetuation of dueling in the South, though he admitted that the North despised it. With equal repugnance, almost a century later, William Teeling wrote a chapter about "Morticians' Parlours or Funeral Homes" whose practices "made me pray I never die there [in America]."[11] Another American habit was that the males actually chewed tobacco. This idiosyncracy recalls the most renowned Americanism, spitting, to which the British somehow could never accustom themselves. Nearly every travel book before the Civil War contains at least one tale of spitting. Macrae recounted these two:

> A Southern poet [was] reading me some of his verses, with a large plug of tobacco in his mouth; and every now and then, when his mouth became too full, stopping in the middle of some beautiful line to squirt another mouthful of tobacco-juice toward the grate. In Courts of Justice you sometimes see the officer give a squirt, and call up the next witness; the witness takes up the Bible, and gives a squirt before kissing it; and the Mayor squirting in the spittoon at his feet before proceeding to put the man upon his oath.[12]

Edward Sullivan said he "would much rather be shut up with a madman than with a genuine expectorator." However, this venerable example of free enterprise soon vanished from the sight of the horrified onlookers. Macrae himself, writing five years after Appomattox, noted with an audible sigh the demise of expectoration. "Happily," he said, "it is disappearing in New England, and from amongst the classes of highest refinement all over the States. . . . The increasing refinement of the country . . . is setting its face against this disgusting practice."[13] Aversion to spitting did spread throughout all classes in the nation, and

[10] Pairpont, *Uncle Sam and His Country*, p. 336.

[11] Alfred Pairpont, *Rambles in America: Past and Present*, p. 166; A. Mackay, *The Wesern World*, I, 143; William Teeling, *American Stew*, p. 305. References to Southern dueling were very rare after the Civil War.

[12] Macrae, *The Americans at Home*, p. 401.

[13] Sullivan, *Rambles and Scrambles*, p. 193; Macrae, *The Americans at Home*, pp. 400, 402.

before the end of the 1880's mention of it disappeared altogether from the pages of the travelogues.

Nearly all the travelers felt that American newspapers should bear a major burden of responsibility for the sometimes crude manners of the Americans. Newspapers in the United States devoted themselves to scandal and sensation on a scale not yet fully matched in Victorian England. "The American paper," said the friendly Muirhead, "represents a distinctly lower level of life than the English one; it would often seem as if the one catered for the least intelligent class of its readers, while the other assumed a standard higher than most of its readers could reach." Matthew Arnold, who was less favorably disposed to American civilization than Muirhead, thought the newspapers had a pre-eminently baneful effect on American manners. "I should say that if one were searching for the best means to efface and kill in a whole nation the discipline of respect, the feeling for what is elevated, one could not do better than take the American newspapers."[14] Only an occasional voice was raised in vindication of the press. A. Maurice Low spoke one of the more authoritative defenses when he stated:

Despite all its faults, the American newspaper Press has been a great civilising and educational instrument, and has tended to elevate rather than lower the moral tone. In an essay written by the late Charles Dudley Warner several years ago he remarked that the American newspaper voiced the moral sentiment of its particular community, and no matter how objectionable the character of the paper might be it was always a trifle better than the people upon whose patronage it relied for support.[15]

American gadgetry and ingenuity brought more consistent praise; these attributes captured the fancy of the Britons as a spate of remarkable inventions came into wide use in the United States in the last quarter of the nineteenth century. Admiration for the rocking chair gave way before more impressive accoutrements to living which rapidly found their way into average American homes.

But let us enter the house [bade Harold Spender in 1920], and then we have revealed to us the new and extraordinary facilities of living which America is discovering—the marble bathrooms, the shaded verandahs, and the cool basement rooms, built for the summer heats: the ingenious devices of cookery and cleaning which make them so independent of domestic aid: the spacious rooms, the simple and restful decorations, the general air of ease and comfort.[16]

[14] Muirhead, *America, the Land of Contrasts,* p. 143; Arnold, *Civilization in the United States,* p. 177.
[15] Low, *America at Home,* p. 217.
[16] Harold Spender, *A Briton in America,* p. 270.

Visitors gaped over electric lights, typewriters, telephones, and Pullman sleepers[17] no less than they have marveled more recently over movies, automobiles, and radios during those intervals in which the United States was in advance of Great Britain.

As much as the inventions themselves, the commentators, even Tories like Sullivan, admired the practicality of the Americans, which led them to "make every use of the progressive improvements of the age, adapting in the most astonishingly short time all modern inventions to the everyday concerns of life." Saunders, twenty-five years after Sullivan, in 1877, ignored American originality and emphasized the practicality by which "the people in the States have a habit of adopting English inventions and bringing them into use, before we can tell whether we like them or not." His examples of "English inventions" were watches and telephones![18]

TRAITS OF BEHAVIOR CONFUSED WITH TRAITS OF CHARACTER

So long as the commentators recognized these various quirks, achievements, and customs for what they were, they served as little windows through which one could get a glimpse into the daily life of the American. These items add to the color and detail which a finished portrait of the nation would require; they serve, also, as useful data for the social historian.

On the basis of these specific observations, however, too many writers thought they could read the character of the nation. Americans eat fast; Americans eat fast because Americans are always in a hurry; Americans are always in a hurry because they want to make money and more money; *ergo,* the United States is a money-mad society. Other absurdities abound in the travel accounts. The existence of crime, of corrupt politicians, of cutthroat businessmen translates into total social depravity; expectoration equals lack of culture; or large attendance at a church service proves the piety of the people.

The most persistent crime committed by the writers in the name of analysis has been to personify the nation on the basis of one or a few personal interviews with "typical" Americans. It has been out of this logical error, more than any other, that the commentators have constructed erroneous portraits of the "American character": "The love of

[17] W. F. Rae loved the Pullmans (*Westward by Rail,* p. 377), but the Robertsons could not adjust to the "startling commingling" of men and women in the cars (William and W. F. Robertson, *Our American Tour,* p. 90).

[18] Sullivan, *Rambles and Scrambles,* p. 190; William Saunders, *Through the Light Continent,* p. 380.

gain, the spirit of practical achievement, curiosity, a rather supercilious exclusiveness and contempt for the foreigner."[19] It has been because of this tendency, more than any other, that travel literature as a whole has been disparaged by some historians. Americans are, according to Robert Ferguson on the basis of a small number of individual encounters, "one of the most reserved and taciturn of peoples." "The Americans, I imagine," affirmed James Stirling in an equally impossible statement, "are the most serious people in the world." William Saunders called Americans "the quietest and most orderly people upon the face of the earth."[20] In reverse, the same error of overgeneralization was committed by others. George Steevens made his visit at a time in which solemnity and taciturnity were not in style: during a presidential election campaign. Steevens, in fact, had been assigned to cover that noisiest of campaigns in 1896 between Bryan and McKinley. Little surprise then that he found that "the demonstrative nature of the race [the national, not the electoral race], once discovered . . . soon appeared a master-key which would unlock most of the puzzles in the American."[21]

Another ubiquitous trait attributed to the American by the English has been his extreme sensitivity to criticism and his consequent need to be praised. The inevitable question put by Americans to J. J. Aubertin in 1886 went, "Now that you have been there, what would you say was your opinion of the effects of republican institutions upon the morals, intellect, and genius of a young and aspiring nation?" Only three years before, Russell had expressed pleasure at the "one great change [which] has come over Americans since I was last here [in 1862]. . . . Except by a professional interviewer, not one of the party was asked, 'What do you think, sir, of our country?'" The boastfulness (or insecurity) that expressed itself through questions like these made a declining impression on the Britons in the generation after the Civil War.[22] Mrs. Desmond Humphreys in 1910 claimed that "the essence of bravado is still latent in the American citizen, but it is tempered now with a citizen's dignity,

[19] John Graham Brooks, *As Others See Us,* p. 45, quoting the French traveler, Edmond de Nevers.
[20] Robert Ferguson, *America during and after the War,* p. 7; Stirling, *Letters from the Slave States,* p. 369; Saunders, *Through the Light Continent,* p. 13.
[21] Steevens, *Land of the Dollar,* p. 310. A trait frequently connected with demonstrativeness was what the English called the "recklessness in dealing with human life." Once this was accepted as part of the American character, it was then possible to explain the considerable amount of crime in the United States that many observers professed to see. A good example of this logic can be found in William Howard Russell, *Hesperothen: Notes from the West,* II, 167; also, Elijah Brown [Alan Raleigh], *The Real America,* p. 271.
[22] J. J. Aubertin, *A Fight with Distances,* p. 5; W. H. Russell, *Hesperothen,* II, 185. Sir John Leng spoke of the maturing Americans who had no need to boast (*America in 1876: Pencillings during a Tour in the Centennial Year,* p. 331); see also Hatton, *To-day in America,* p. 2.

and a citizen's pride." Rudyard Kipling probably got closest to the point when he indicated quite simply that Americans "believe in their land and its future, and its honor, and its glory, and they are not ashamed to say so," a passionate conviction "to which I take off my hat and for which I love them." By the 1930's L. P. Jacks was contending that, rather than flourishing on flattery, "as a people the Americans are the most self-critical on the face of the earth."[23] Then again, perhaps this was the very reason they needed flattery.

These statements highlight the analytic errors that the travelers were prone to commit. They often assumed that every bit of behavior was characterologically significant; they preferred psychological explanations to sociological ones even when the latter would have made more sense. Further, they used a single disposition to describe the whole of a person's character, preferring to deal with types, as some novelists do, than with the frequencies of specific traits. Laying aside for the moment the question of whether their samples were adequate, Alexander Mackay admonished his colleagues, well in advance of those visitors above quoted, with specific reference to the question of the reserve of Americans:

> An American can be reserved as anybody else, when he comes in contact with one whom he does not understand, or who will not understand him—and this is the reason why so many travellers in America, who forget to leave their European notions of exclusiveness at home, and traverse the republic wrapped in the cloak of European formalism, find the Americans so cold in their demeanour, and erroneously regard their particular behaviour to themselves as the result of a general moodiness and reserve.[24]

One can list indefinitely the number of traits placed in the national composite by the tourists: friendliness, suspiciousness, inventiveness, moral purity, moral laxity, love of quantity rather than quality, humorlessness, humor, individualism, conformity, reckless violence, benevolence.[25] Freud has shown us that character can be understood in terms

---

[23] Eliza Humphreys [Rita], *America—Through English Eyes*, p. 236; Kipling, *American Notes*, p. 237; Lawrence Pearsall Jacks, *My American Friends*, p. 53. See also Alexander Francis, *Americans: An Impression*, pp. 9, 13. Jacks, a prominent Unitarian, may have seen America through the eyes of American Unitarians—generally a critical lot. But as early as 1917 the sensitivity seemed rapidly to be switching to the British side. Hector MacQuarrie was alarmed because the British acted condescendingly to Americans. "We don't mean to run them down really, but we assume a superior air that must be perfectly awful. . . . One would like the Americans to know us at our best, because we are not really unpleasant people" (*Over Here: Impressions of America by a British Officer*, pp. 182–83).

[24] A. Mackay, *The Western World*, I, 126.

[25] Other sample traits: courtesy (Stuart-Wortley, *Travels in the United States*, p. 11), a quality which surprised her; preference for the flashy effect rather than

of polarities, but these contradictory terms assuredly cry out for greater analytic precision.

DIFFERENCES BETWEEN TRAITS OF BEHAVIOR AND TRAITS OF CHARACTER

In one of the best discussions of the idea of national character, David Potter observed:

> Long experience has repeatedly shown that a traveler visiting the United States and meeting, let us say, a property-owning, Methodist electrician, age twenty-five, is likely to explain all the traits of the individual, whether deriving from his occupation, his religion, his economic status, or even his youth and his sex, as attributes of his Americanism. This is to be expected.

Not to be expected, however, is that the historian would succumb to the same gambit and make the same mistake as the misguided visitor. As Potter continued: "But when the historian or the social analyst draws upon the traveler's report, a discrimination between the various factors becomes his responsibility. By and large, the responsibility has not been met, and many historians writing on national character have not refined very much beyond the traveler." The portrayal of the American as an unmannered, idealistic, hurrying, egalitarian, sallow-looking, anti-intellectual, ice-water–drinking, materialistic expectorator unacceptably jumbles together too many different levels of abstraction.

> Very often a catalogue of traits ranges from the profound to the trivial. Thus we may be told in the same breath that Americans are optimistic (a trait of temperament), that they attach great value to productive activity (a trait of character), that they are fond of jazz music (a cultural trait), and that they are remarkably prone to join organized groups (a behavioral trait which may provide overt evidence of some underlying trait of character).[26]

In recent years there has grown up a vast literature on the uses of the construct of national character.[27] Although the approaches have

---

the substantial and long-lasting achievement (Yelverton, *Teresina in America,* I, 12); hospitality (Mrs. J. B. G. Jebb, *A Strange Career: Life and Adventures of John Gladwyn Jebb,* p. 147); etc. *ad infinitum.*

[26] David M. Potter, *People of Plenty* (Chicago, Ill.: University of Chicago Press, 1954), pp. 12, 18–19; the entire first chapter, "The Historians and National Character" is relevant to this discussion.

[27] Among the more interesting discussions in addition to Potter's are: Walter P. Metzger, "Generalizations about National Character," pp. 77–102, and Thomas C. Cochran, "The Historian's Use of Social Role," pp. 103–10 in Louis

varied, they have generally pointed to two conclusions. First it has been felt almost universally that the clumsy analysis of national character typically found in the accounts of travelers and often directly appropriated by the scholar is totally indefensible. The indiscriminate mixture of categories illustrated by Potter, the "heavy freight of contrary and unclear meanings, accumulated through the years" by "national character"[28] has led not only to faulty logic in which a character trait accounts for a mode of behavior which, in turn, accounts for that character trait, but it has led to the entire abandonment in some circles of any attempt to use the idea of national character at all.

This abandonment has not been accepted, however, by most of the recent writers on national character. "It would be premature," said Walter Metzger, "to conclude that the term is beyond redemption."[29] These researchers have felt that national character is not only a redeemable tool of research but may be a highly useful model by which the social scientist can come to understand the workings of a given culture. What is needed, above all, is rigor and consistency of definition. Different writers have looked to different seminal thinkers—Max Weber, Freud, Marx—as guides to clearer uses of "national character." But all of the writers have agreed upon the need for precision, for discrimination, for exacting logic when any analyst assembles "traits" in the effort to erect a character portrait of a particular nation.

While this general subject is complicated, of decisive importance, and methodologically enticing, Potter suggested one particular distinction among traits that is of special value for this study. "There is a vast difference," he explained, "between mere traits of behavior, such as writing from left to right or eating with a fork, which a given people may have

---

Gottschalk, ed., *Generalization in the Writing of History* (Chicago, Ill.: University of Chicago Press, 1963); Alex Inkeles and Daniel J. Levinson, "National Character: The Study of Modal Personality and Sociocultural Systems," in Gardner Lindzey, ed., *Handbook of Social Psychology* (2 vols.; Reading, Mass.: Addison-Wesley, 1954), II, 977–1020; Lindzey's book contains a good collection of essays dealing with general problems of culture and personality. Another useful collection is Eleanor E. Maccoby, Theodore M. Newcomb, Eugene L. Hartley, eds., *Readings in Social Psychology* (3rd ed.; New York: Holt, 1947), especially Theodore R. Sarbin and Daniel S. Jones, "An Experimental Analysis of Role Behavior," pp. 465–72. Other important works are A. Kardiner, *The Individual and His Society* (New York: Columbia University Press, 1939); Clyde Kluckhohn, "The Study of Culture," in D. Lerner and Harold Lasswell, eds., *The Policy Sciences* (Stanford, Calif.: Stanford University Press, 1951), pp. 86–101; and K. Lewin, "Some Social Psychological Differences between the United States and Germany," in Gertrude Lewin, ed., *Resolving Social Conflicts: Selected Papers on Group Dynamics, 1935–46* (New York: Harper, 1948), pp. 3–33. Other items from this vast literature which I have found of value will be referred to throughout this book.

[28] Metzger, "Generalizations about National Character," p. 84.
[29] *Ibid.*

in common, and traits of character, in which a deeply intrenched system of value is involved."[30] The British visitors, acting in their broad-ranging capacity as amateur anthropologists, have been quite amateur in their general failure to make this distinction, and yet it is absolutely incumbent upon any analyst who uses their travel accounts to try to do so.

The difficulties and potentialities of turning the travelers loose on national character, as so often has been done, may best be grasped by being specific. One of the very best discussions of the American character was conducted by Muirhead in a chapter called "International Misapprehensions and National Differences." In it he made a series of perceptive comparisons between the English and the Americans. Among the differences, Muirhead mentioned that:

1. The American mind is discursive, open, wide in its interests, alive to suggestion, pliant, emotional, imaginative; the English mind is concentrated, substantial, indifferent to the merely relative, matter-of-fact, stiff, and inflexible.
2. The American is, on the whole, more genially disposed to all and sundry. . . .
The American tends to consider each stranger he meets—at any rate within his own social sphere—as a good fellow until he proves himself the contrary; with the Englishman the presumption is rather the other way.
3. In domestic and social morality the Americans are ahead of us, in commercial morality rather behind than before, and in political morality distinctly behind.

According to Muirhead, Americans are kinder to women, children, and animals, but not to competing businessmen or political constituencies.[31]

In these three areas of mental disposition, personality, and morality, the author has tried to avoid "making the mistake that nine out of ten of . . . [my] countrymen constantly make in swooping down on a single *outré* instance as *characteristic* of American life."[32] Yet one must still ponder seriously whether these generalizations describe traits of character "in which a deeply intrenched system of value is involved" or whether they are merely generalizations of traits of behavior based upon, in Muirhead's case, wider experience and maturer judgment than is usually the case with the British traveler. They look like statements about the national character; value systems are certainly implicit in them; but they form a dangerous brew randomly mixing the behavioral and the characterological. It would be safer and wiser to separate these ingredients.

The frequent attention given to the American's capacity for humor

[30] Potter, *People of Plenty,* p. 11.
[31] Muirhead, *America, the Land of Contrasts,* pp. 90, 92, 99.
[32] *Ibid.,* p. 105.

further illustrates the close connection between behavior and character. Muirhead could not help "noticing how humour penetrates and gives savour to the *whole* of American life. There is almost no business too important to be smoothed over with a jest." Earlier in his book, Muirhead mentioned that "the sense of enjoyment is more obvious and more evenly distributed [than in Great Britain]; there is a general willingness to be amused, a general absence of the *blasé*." Lord Bryce found, a decade earlier, this "remarkable faculty for enjoyment, a power of drawing more happiness from obvious pleasures, simple and innocent pleasures, than one often finds in overburdened Europe." In 1921 Harold Spender said: "The American man is not a cynic. That is where he chiefly differs from the European. The American is really anxious to enjoy and appreciate." In the same year G. K. Chesterton arrived at this same point somewhat obliquely when he mentioned that the American "is not only proud of his energy, he is proud of his excitement."[33]

Laughter is a form of behavior. Lack of cynicism suggests a deeper commitment to some scheme of values. Chesterton began to take his readers to that latter world when he explained how American adults "are like children."[34] Children have the power of "drawing more happiness from obvious pleasures, simple and innocent pleasures," to switch the context of Bryce's words. Muirhead, as just noted, spoke of the American kindness to children, of the adult's own genial disposition, of his mind "alive to suggestion, pliant," of his willingness to assume the best about each stranger he meets until given reason otherwise. Connections of this sort furnish hope that one can filter out "the deeply intrenched system of value" hidden in the confused semianthropological generalizations of even the most perceptive British visitor. This constitutes the major effort of the following pages, but it will be carried out along different lines than those pursued by character analysts.

INSTITUTIONS, VALUES, AND CHANGE

The phrase "American character," despite its potential value as a model and despite its frequent usage by the foreign observers (who are then used as delineators of the national character by scholars), will not often appear in the remainder of this study. The travelers' overt comments on this topic are too murky to meet the rigorous standards of clarity justly demanded by contemporary scholars. Yet the rough discrimination made

[33] *Ibid.*, pp. 138, 35; Bryce, *The American Commonwealth*, III, 614; H. Spender, *A Briton in America*, p. 263; G. K. Chesterton, *What I Saw in America*, p. 263.
[34] Chesterton, *What I Saw in America*, p. 268.

by Potter between traits of behavior and traits of character that reveal value commitments is a discrimination that will be held to insofar as it is possible to do so without violating the spirit of the travel accounts. I am interested in using travel literature to shed light on American *values*. Values are sometimes revealed in character analyses, but, as the following chapters will show, they come out more directly and clearly when the British commentators write of American "philosophy" or when they describe American institutions.

Values, however, can change; and the historian, whose unique dimension is time, must concern himself with change as much as he does with continuity. It is the contention of this study that the British travelers writing about America presented a picture of a society which held to a certain group of values from as early as 1830 until around 1900. At the same time, the travel accounts reveal that these old beliefs were being fundamentally re-examined, threatened, and even altered in part from about 1885 to the First World War, and that the initial shock of challenge came between 1885 and 1900. Those "old beliefs" are defined in Chapter Four and placed in time from 1860 to the beginning of this century. A reading of travel material before 1860 suggests, in fact, that these earlier values were continuous from about 1830. This implies that the traditional watershed in American history, the Civil War, the event which presumably made a rural land urban, an agricultural country industrial, and a weak nation united, had, by British testimony, surprisingly little effect on American values.[35] The travelers, to be sure, noted these significant political and economic changes (although they were already writing in the 1850's about the rapid urbanization and industrialization taking place in the North and West). They certainly did call attention to the emergence of a powerful, united nation with whom English diplomats would have to reckon seriously. But rather than telling of a fundamental break in the American structure of values, they seemed to tell a tale of consummation. It is interesting to note that when the British wrote of the United States and her values, they meant the northern and western states. Both before and after the Civil War, the travelers usually considered the South as a separate land, and they referred to the South specifically by name.

[35] The early date of 1860 in the title of this book is inherited from the closing date of Berger's study, just as Berger inherited his opening date of 1836 from Miss Mesick's work. It does not imply any preconceived acceptance of the standard date of 1860 (the dividing point in every two-volume textbook of American history) as the great turning point in American development. In order to ascertain whether the Civil War ushered in a new era in American belief according to the foreign commentators, I read widely in the travel literature before 1860. Some of the more important books of travel written between 1845 and 1860 are included in the Bibliography.

The tenor of the British version of the American spirit ("American" always being above the Mason-Dixon line) began to change rapidly around the years 1885–1900. The discussion of American beliefs and attitudes in Chapter Ten is dated from 1885–1935. The overlap between Chapter Four (1860–1900) and Chapter Ten of the years 1885–1900 is shorthand for the self-evident fact that ideas change slowly. In fact, the transition period might better be dated from 1885 (or earlier) to 1920. No new, recognizably modern system of values to replace the old appears consistently in the travel accounts until after World War I. This war did more to alter British impressions of the quality of American life than did the Civil War. The closing date in this study, 1935, takes us far enough ahead to enable us to determine whether the new tone of British generalization in the 1920's carried over into a decade undergoing such different experiences, or whether the new values elevated during the 1920's were merely an exception to the general pattern of American history. The evidence of the accounts of travel actually underlines the philosophical continuity between the 1920's and 1930's and it suggests that the transformation of American life following Versailles and ushered in during the Jazz Age was fundamental enough to survive the crisis of profound economic depression.

The problem of change is also important in the chapters that deal with education, religion, government, children, and women. While in most cases the years at the end of the nineteenth century seemed to be years of quickened activity and re-evaluation, there is no attempt here to impose a uniform periodization on subjects that have their own internal history. Thus new developments connected with the churches, with politics, and with the feminist movement around the turn of the century are not, for the sake of uniformity, automatically ascribed also to child-rearing patterns, which appear to follow a more continuous course in the accounts of British observers.

Recent American scholarship is brought into the discussion in the final chapter to examine critically the problem of change and continuity in American values. It is hoped that by concentrating on the interaction between values and institutions which emerges from these books of travel spanning seventy-five years, and by checking the conclusions against some of the more authoritative studies of American scholars, some light may be thrown on just what makes the American "everywhere recognized," without the necessity of closely following the travelers down their own windy trail of "the American character," which too often before has led to nowhere.

IV
Land of Youth, 1860–1900

THE APPEARANCE of de Tocqueville's renowned study of American democracy was the event of 1834," said the historian J. B. Bury in his excellent intellectual history, *The Idea of Progress*. Tocqueville was convinced, continued Bury,

> . . . that he had discovered on the other side of the Atlantic the answer to the question whither the world is tending. In American society he found that equality of condition is the generating fact on which every other fact depends. He concluded that equality is the goal of humanity, providentially designed.

The British historian then quoted the French writer to underline the way in which Tocqueville had married the idea of progress to actual American conditions of equality:

> The gradual development of equality of conditions [said the Frenchman], has the principal characteristics of a providential fact. It is universal, it is permanent, it eludes human power; all events and all men serve this development. . . . If the men of our time were brought to see that the gradual and progressive development of equality is at once the past and the future of their history, this single discovery would give that development the sacred character of the will of the sovran master.[1]

There is no necessary or logical connection between equality and progress, as Bury took pains to point out. The idea of progress simply means "that civilisation has moved, is moving, and will move in a desirable direction."[2] Equality represents only one of many possible directions. Those Victorian aristocrats who, at the *fin de siècle,* never ques-

---

[1] J. B. Bury, *The Idea of Progress: An Inquiry into Its Origin and Growth,* with an Introduction by Charles A. Beard (New York; Macmillan, 1932), pp. 314–16. The first editions of Tocqueville's work (in French and in English) actually appeared in 1835.

[2] *Ibid.,* p. 2.

tioned the idea of progress, did not dream of Marx's classless society of the future as humanity's ultimate destination. Nor does belief in equality automatically include faith in progress. The egalitarian utopia, as will be discussed later in this chapter, having reached perfection, has no need for the idea of progress. Equality is an ideal which envisions a final destination. Progress is an idea centering on a process, one that generates a temperamental vitality and optimism.

Upon observing the American scene during Jackson's first administration, Tocqueville was struck by the way in which Americans believed in *both* the egalitarian ideal and the idea of progress, and he was impressed by the Americans' success in translating these values into tangible institutional realities. While the British travelers were not as deterministic, abstract, or prophetic as Tocqueville, nevertheless, from at least as early as his American travels until more than a generation after the end of the Civil War, they shared his conviction that the beliefs in equality and in progress were the central faiths of America.

THE BELIEF IN THE EGALITARIAN PRINCIPLE

Max Berger concluded, in generalizing upon the British books of travel written during the twenty-five years previous to the outbreak of the Civil War: "Most prominent of the many impressions of America that Britons took back with them was the aggressive egalitarianism of the people."[3] The British visitors did not always understand what they meant by equality, nor did they always use the concept consistently. They spoke of equality in four distinct though not wholly unrelated categories. First was historical equality, or the absence in America of feudal inheritances, with their time-laden baggage of military, noble, clerical, and peasant classes. Second, the authors often talked of actual material equality, even classlessness. This was a source of some confusion. In the third place, they referred to equality of opportunity, to the fact that every American citizen, no matter what his origins, was regarded as a human being and deserved the chance, by merit, to improve his station in life.

Their final use of equality was indirect and very widespread; they described its manifestations in American life. Sometimes these applications were quite prosaic, and fell under the rubric of "manners and customs" outlined in the preceding chapter. Hotel porters were arrogant, railway carriages were usually one-class, strangers greeted each other with familiarity, servants were called "help," and the British did not in general receive the deference to which they were accustomed. Sometimes, on other occasions, the commentators used generic terms—freedom, mate-

[3] Berger, *The British Traveller in America, 1836–1860*, p. 54.

rialism, democracy, individualism, competition, liberty—to call up general features of American life, but which, in their descriptions, could have been more fruitfully understood as logical consequences of their other definitions of equality. This thought will be developed in this chapter. Then again, they saw equality in operation in various American institutions. The next five chapters deal with this phenomenon.

The Britons were not rigorous, precise, or consistent in their use of the concept of equality. But they were clear enough to make unmistakable their belief that it was somehow the organizing principle of American life for most of the nineteenth century. Let us examine their words on the subject.

Historic Equality

After his travels in 1846–47, Alexander Mackay, one of the most astute of the British commentators, decided that the historic roots of European and American society reached down in different soils:

> . . . that society, in the two hemispheres, rests upon very different bases. In the old world, where the feudal relations are still permitted so largely to influence the arrangement of the social system, society presents an agglomeration of distinct parts, each having its determinate relation to the rest, and the members of each having the range of their sympathies confined to their own particular sphere.

European society, he said, is organized in layers which "only partially fuse into each other." There is no common feeling pervading European society. The "distinctiveness of class," accompanied by "an inequality of position" produces a "constraint and formalism which renders one class, by turns, arrogant and awkward, and the other supercilious and condescending." Social graces are cultivated, refinements of life displayed. "In its general aspect, therefore, the internal intercourse of European society is less marked by kindness than by formality, less regulated by sympathy than by rule." The contrast with the United States, he argued, is vivid:

> Very different from this are both the basis and the manifestation of society in America. There social inequality has never been a recognised principle, moulding the social fabric into arbitrary forms, and tyrannically influencing each person's position in the general scheme. Society in America started from the point to which society in Europe is only yet tending. The equality of man is, to this moment, its cornerstone. . . . American society, therefore, exhibits itself as an indivisible whole, its general characteristics being such as mark each of the different classes into which European society is divided. That which develops itself with us as the sympathy of class, becomes in America the general sentiment of

society. There is no man there whose position every other man does not understand; each has in himself the key to the feelings of his neighbour, and he measures his sympathies by his own. The absence of arbitrary inequalities banishes restraint from their mutual intercourse, whilst their mutual appreciation of each other's sentiments imparts a kindness and cordiality to that intercourse, which in Europe are only to be found, and not always there, within the circle of class.[4]

Mackay was much more favorably disposed to the United States than was Matthew Arnold forty years later. But Arnold, too, was aware of the absence of historic classes in America. "Not only have they not the distinction between noble and bourgeois, between aristocracy and middle class; they have not even the distinction between bourgeois and peasant or artisan, between middle and lower class. They have nothing to create it and compel their recognition of it." Arnold was sure that Americans "deserve no praise for not having invented" class distinctions. They were historically lucky:

The United States constituted themselves, not amid the circumstances of a feudal age, but in a modern age; not under the conditions of an epoch favorable to subordination, but under those of an epoch of expansion. Their institutions did but comply with the form and pressure of the circumstances and conditions then present.

History favored the Americans, but even so, Arnold grudgingly commended their "strong good sense . . . to have forborne from all attempt to invent class distinctions at the outset, and to have escaped or resisted any fancy for inventing them since." So deeply imbedded in the American past was the opposition to feudal, "fixed-status," ascribed class distinctions that Arnold demurred from Lord Macaulay's famous prediction that American cities would soon fill up and the nation develop the same embarrassing class divisions as England.[5]

The debt owed to these views by present-day American historians is great, for after flirting with theories of divine determinism, environmental determinism, and economic determinism, many leading contemporary scholars have reverted basically to many of Tocqueville's insights —insights that many British travelers after him developed with a greater acuity and feeling for the facts. Thus we read today that Americans, that is, *white* Americans, were "born free"; being so born, the body politic was spared the fury of social revolution, which leaves in its wake hatred, division, and extremism. Inheriting no rigid classes and blessed with natural economic abundance, the new nation advanced on all fronts without the albatross of revolutionary philosophies. American thought

[4] Mackay, *The Western World*, I, 125–26.
[5] Arnold, *Civilization in the United States*, pp. 121–23.

converged around a consensus at the core of which was the egalitarian faith, which elevated the common man and common tastes, and glorified practical, pragmatic approaches to life, typified by the rising entrepreneur. Aristocratic exclusiveness and, unfortunately, intellectual excellence were sacrificed at the altar of a society in which most men searched for wealth in the quite realistic hope of attaining it.[6] This general interpretation is not confuted by a reading of British travel accounts—at least during the twenty-five years on either side of the Civil War. Some of the visitors made certain implications about American equality, however, which are alien to this historical definition of the concept.

Material Equality

The movement toward equality, carried to its logical extreme, ends in a communistic classlessness in which all citizens possess the same wealth. This never has been an American ideal; yet some commentators came close to confusing a condition of widespread opportunity with classlessness. This confusion stemmed naturally enough from one particular circumstance: the observers hardly ever came across beggars in the United States, whereas at home the terrible gap between the rich and the woebegone poor was a most visible part of life. This elementary fact meant much to the visitors—more than it did to natives, who tended to take it for granted. Sir S. Morton Peto, the great liberal railroad builder, shows how easy it is to derive notions of complete material equality from his observation that few beggars roamed in the streets of America:

> On their return from the United States, travellers are not unfrequently asked what feature struck them most forcibly in their journey through the country. Looking to the territory, I should certainly answer to such a question, its wide expanse and its abundant resources; but looking to the people, I should say, the *absence of pauperism*. Nothing is more striking to a European than the universal respectability of appearance in all classes in America. You see no rags, you meet no beggars. In London the painful scenes, whether of real or of fictitious woe, that are encountered at every turning are in the highest degree distressing.

Absence of pauperism seemed to imply a second negative discovery: absence of a wealthy aristocracy. This led Peto to place undue emphasis on material equality: "The equal distribution of wealth in the United

[6] The most notable examples of this view in recent American historical writing can be found in Louis Hartz, *The Liberal Tradition in America: An Interpretation of American Political Thought since the Revolution* (New York: Harcourt, Brace, 1955); Daniel J. Boorstin, *The Americans: The Colonial Experience* (New York: Random House, 1958); Richard Hofstadter, *The American Political Tradition and the Men Who Made It* (New York: Knopf, 1948); and Potter's *People of Plenty.*

States is, certainly, a very marked feature of the nation. Whilst there may be said to be no poor, the number is also comparatively few of those whom we should class as very rich."[7] Peto never quite ascribed complete classlessness to the United States. But he, and other travelers, came close, and such misunderstandings perhaps help account for a great deal of the obscurity in the discussions of equality by many British authors.

The tendency toward an equitable distribution of wealth was, of course, a component of the American style of equality, for as the missionary Phillippo demonstrates, if large sections of a population live in poverty, if there is great economic inequality in fact, it will be very difficult to achieve substantial social and political equality. He wrote of America:

> Property is not accumulated in a few hands, and political power confined to certain privileged orders; nor do the middle and higher ranks enjoy, in the fruits of wealth, exuberance, and luxury, while larger sections of the population are either entirely destitute of the means of subsistence, or earn them by unrequited toil and degradation. And the opposite ingredients in her social and political state are not only the source of the social welfare of America, but the basis on which her political institutions rest.[8]

Equality of Opportunity

America was spared the burden of degraded masses living an impoverished, subhuman existence not only because she had skipped the historic stage of feudalism, but because her natural resources were abundant and rich. For more than two and a half centuries after settlement the demand for labor exceeded the supply. The chance to become wealthy was a real one. Most of the British commentators knew that equality meant to the American that no matter what his origins, *every man had the opportunity to rise.*

There were classes, as a good many Britons realized. In fact, as Mackay pointed out, "in America there is a broad and distinct line drawn between the two conditions of master and servant." The difference from Europe stems from the fact that "both parties look to the time when that relation will be dissolved, by the servant becoming himself a master."[9]

[7] Sir S. Morton Peto, *Resources and Prospects of America,* pp. 386, 388. It is almost impossible for the upper-class Englishman to get used to American equality, remarked T. L. Nichols: "Accustomed to the differences of caste, position, and rank in England, they are shocked with American equality and freedom. They miss the refinement and insolence—it is not quite the word—of the upper classes, and the servility and—brutality, shall I say?—of the lower" (*Forty Years of American Life, 1821–1861*), p. 9.
[8] Phillippo, *The United States and Cuba,* p. 94.
[9] A. Mackay, *The Western World,* I, 142.

One's present status was temporary; one could change it through initiative and ability.

> Perhaps in no other quarter of the world [wrote Alfred Pairpont in 1854], "is the fact so observable, as in America, that men have risen from the masses, to that of wealthy attainment; and ye who condemn our transatlantic cousins, as too fast with the go-a-head mania, will here see, that many of them find sufficient time to create ideas, to trade advantageously, and to build up large fortunes from very humble beginnings.[10]

The reasons for the fluidity of American classes were clear to F. B. Zincke, "for in America there are employment, food, and position for everybody, and no old and firmly established antagonistic institutions to be fought against and overthrown in opening the course for the new order of things." As W. H. Russell expressed it, "It would seem as if Nature had been engaged for myriads of ages to provide for their happiness and grandeur—all climes and all products are theirs—the bounteous plain, the ore-filled mountain, the treasures of the deep, the heaven-made ways by lake and river. . . ."[11]

Joseph Hatton told of the following, rather revealing conversation:

> "Why do we get along so well in this great establishment, and how is it every man and boy about the place looks so earnest and so hopeful?" asked the chief of a remarkable New York institution, repeating my question. "Because every boy and man in the place knows that he has a clear prospect of advancement. If the lad who sweeps the office comes to me to-morrow morning and says, 'Sir, I think I have discovered a plan whereby you can save an hour or a dollar in a particular operation,' I should listen to him with respect and attention. In your country, I am told, he would very likely be kicked out of the place for his impertinence." He had struck the true cause of much of the hopelessness of the prevailing toil among the English masses.[12]

The consequences of these conditions went far beyond the economic; they went to the core of human existence, as Anthony Trollope pointed out in the concluding sentences to his three volumes on America:

> Men and women do not beg in the States;—they do not offend you with tattered rags; they do not complain to heaven of starvation; they do not crouch to the ground for half-pence. If poor, they are not abject in their poverty. They read and write. They walk like human beings made in God's form. They know that they are men and women, owing it to themselves and to the world that they should earn their bread by their labour, but feeling that when earned it is their own. If this be so,—if it

[10] Pairpont, *Uncle Sam and His Country*, p. 152.

[11] Zincke, *Last Winter in the United States*, p. 201; W. H. Russell, *Hesperothen*, II, 152.

[12] Hatton, *To-day in America*, p. 8.

be acknowledged that it is so,—should not such knowledge in itself be sufficient testimony of the success of the country and of her institutions?[13]

Many Englishmen naturally failed to share Trollope's generosity. After all, when "the fact is," as Robert Ferguson asserted, "that while in England it is the upper ten thousand that are most cared for, in America it is the lower million,"[14] then no one should be surprised that many English travelers—most of whom belonged to the upper ten thousand—were appalled by this state of affairs.

The Britons may have exaggerated the actual degree of opportunity in America because there was so little chance to rise, relatively speaking, for the British lower classes. Since the gap between the classes in England surpassed that of most bourgeois nations, they may have magnified the extent to which Americans received equal treatment before the law and the extent to which Americans truly regarded their fellow white citizens as human beings. As long as opportunities for advancement appeared wide open in America, however, there was no good reason to deny the plausibility of the British claims of American opportunity. Toward the end of the nineteenth century, seeing the pressure of new immigration, amid the bitterness of labor-management hostilities, commentators began to wonder out loud in increasing numbers whether Lord Macaulay's prediction might be coming to pass, whether Americans had even begun to abandon their egalitarian ideals. James Muirhead, however, as late as 1898, aware of these growing problems, still managed to conclude, after a lengthy discussion filled with qualifications and fears, that "in spite of anything in the foregoing that may seem incompatible, the fact remains that the distinguishing feature of American society, as contrasted with the societies of Europe, is the greater approach to equality it has made."[15]

Democracy, Materialism, and Individualism as Manifestations of the Belief in Equality

If an American were to guess how Englishmen would respond on a word-association test to the phrase "the United States," it is not unlikely that three words would occur to him before "equality": "democracy," "materialism," and "individualism." The commentators did, in fact, employ "democracy" and "materialism" (though not "individualism") with some frequency. But they applied these terms to the American scene with special meanings which do not fit the usual stereotype, and which, upon examination, add more body to our developing definition of "equality."

[13] A. Trollope, *North America*, III, 291.
[14] R. Ferguson, *America during and after the War*, p. 24.
[15] Muirhead, *America, the Land of Contrasts*, p. 28.

Democracy. When the authors wrote of democracy, they rarely applied it to the American system of government. They not only were unimpressed by American politics, but they did not even feel that the government was particularly democratic. Berger said that American democratic government and politics were criticized by the ante-bellum British visitor more than any other aspect of American life except slavery.[16] This British verdict did not change after the Civil War. How might this strong derogation of American democracy be explained? Did not Tocqueville, after all, entitle his tome to the world on the promise of the American experiment *Democracy in America?*

The explanation appears as soon as the question is asked. Tocqueville's version of democracy was not primarily political; it referred to the entire social and economic condition of the American people as sketched in the preceding section; it referred to a way of life more than to a structure of government. He even understood political democracy in America to be an egalitarian rather than a libertarian phenomenon.

This distinction meant even more to the British than the French commentators. True political democracy in Britain did not rest on the assumption of man's equality and the political axiom that all men should have a voice in government. British political democracy, rather, harked back to John Locke and, later, John Stuart Mill. It anchored itself on the very different assumption (if one may oversimplify) that the best ideas could triumph in society only if men's minds were unfettered; its political axiom was that official interference with men's free thought must be stripped to the barest minimum. American political democracy, according to the British, concerned itself with *all* men, with rule by the *demos.* To the English, this bore little resemblance to authentic political democracy in which rational exchanges between free men would *select* the *best* ideas, in which maximum dissent must be tolerated.

Tocqueville's use of "democracy" in its broadest cultural sense as a synonym for "equality" paralleled British usage in describing the American scene. The Britons endowed "democracy" with two lesser meanings also. The first of these did refer to democratic government, that is, the manner in which the three branches of the federal government and the state and local authorities managed their business. This sense of political democracy meant, for them, corruption, and an evil sort of tomfoolery manifest wherever the tourists peered; and they peered most often into Congress in session, into City Hall in any large city, into election campaigns, and into Washington "cocktail" parties.

Bryce distinguished quite sharply between the broad and narrow meanings of democracy. At the end of his definitive volumes on Ameri-

[16] Berger, *The British Traveller in America, 1836–1860,* p. 106.

can government, he described the general condition of American life by the word "uniformity." This bore a meaning very close to Tocqueville's use of "equality." Bryce then suggested that the governmental functionings he had so painstakingly detailed must not be equated with this larger and more significant condition of life. He said:

> Those who have observed the uniformity I have been attempting to describe have commonly set it down, as Europeans do most American phenomena, to what they call Democracy. Democratic government has in reality not much to do with it, except in so far as such a government helps to induce that deference of individuals to the mass which strengthens a dominant type, whether of ideas, of institutions, or of manners. More must be ascribed to the equality of material conditions, still more general than in Europe. . . .[17]

The final meaning of democracy dealt with a particular political practice which was, according to the British, America's most characteristic political commitment: universal suffrage. The more perspicacious of the travelers found other political commitments of greater significance than mass suffrage: for example, the federal principle, or the loyalty to party, or the balance of power, or the written constitution itself. The majority of the visitors, however, were simplistic on this point, and argued continually that the great difference between the political systems of the two nations centered on the issue of suffrage. Consequently, it was around universal suffrage that political debate raged most hotly among the British commentators, perhaps because this issue lay at the center of British political debate during these years. "The American and the Englishman are both Republicans," insisted Anthony Trollope:

> The governments of the States and of England are probably the two purest republican governments in the world. . . . And yet no men can be much further asunder in politics than the Englishman and the American. The American of the present day puts a ballot-box into the hands of every citizen and takes his stand upon that and that only.[18]

This statement having been made, it required no elaborate logic to demonstrate the connection between the ballot in every hand and the idea of equality.[19] With its assumption that one man's vote is as good as anoth-

---

[17] Bryce, *The American Commonwealth,* III, 629–30.
[18] A. Trollope, *North America,* I, 311–12.
[19] One result of granting suffrage to all males was, as Alexander Francis noted in 1909, to insulate the nation from class-wedded ideologies such as Marxian Socialism. In America, he wrote, "all enjoyed equally all the dignity that is given by a vote in a democratic community; and this prevented the growth, not of classes, but of a well-defined system of classes and of a servile class; and this policy, persistently pursued to the present day in relation to immigrants, has maintained this measure of social equality. This, in turn, has proved

er's, universal suffrage can be characterized as the political manifestation of equality, as Peto characterized it one hundred years ago:

> Where every man has his proportionate share of the good things of this world, all feel entitled to claim a fair share in the administration of the affairs of the nation. . . . Equality and brotherhood they regard, not in theory only (as the idea of mammon worship would imply), but in truth and in reality, as of the essence of the Constitution under which they live and of their social well-being and existence.
> It is from this point of view that the suffrage comes to be regarded in America not only as a right common to all, but as a primary necessity.[20]

The British libertarian democrat, rather than taking his stand on the ballot-box "and that only," would no doubt display more interest in the conditions, freedom, and quality of political debate.

Materialism. "And *how* they talk of money! In snatches of conversation caught in the streets, the restaurants, and the cars, the continual cry is always 'dollars—dollars—dollars!' You hear it on all sides perpetually, and money does truly rule here, as politics in England seem to be an end in itself, instead of a means to an end."[21] Surprising though it may seem, Burne-Jones' predictable cry that money is king never mounted to a crescendo among the nineteenth-century travelers. To make money certainly did count as a major Yankee ambition. But most of the writers during this period noted, with surprising perspicacity, that riches themselves, or even the things money could buy, were not held in the highest esteem. "As to worship of the 'Almighty Dollar,' " commented the philosopher and critic Frederic Harrison at the same time as Burne-Jones, "I neither saw it nor heard of it; hardly as much as we do at home."[22] Well before the era of conspicuous display chronicled by Thorstein Veblen and before sociological discussions of "status-seeking" and "other-directedness," Edward Dicey announced with some insight:

> Money-making is the chief object of the nation; but they value the possession of the "almighty dollar" rather as a proof of success in life than as an end of existence. The mere ownership of wealth is less valued there than with us. The man who has made his money is infinitely more re-

---

a bulwark against Socialism" (*Americans: An Impression,* pp. 223–24). The effects of equality pushed the American Communist into a very solitary corner of American life even in 1935–36, during the depths of the Depression (Priestley, *Midnight on the Desert,* pp. 38–39). The tendency in American politics toward a large consensus of the population sometimes inhibited the exercise of dissent and resulted in the phenomenon Tocqueville called the "tyranny of the majority." This important topic and its evident relationship to the leveling tendencies in American society will be further explored in Chapter Eight.

[20] Peto, *Resources and Prospects of America,* pp. 389–90.
[21] Burne-Jones, *Two Sides of the Atlantic,* p. 74.
[22] Frederic Harrison, *Memories and Thoughts: Men-Books-Cities-Art,* p. 200.

spected than the man who has inherited it. Millionaires are rare in the second generation; and the bare fact of wealth gives a man fewer advantages in the North than in any Old World country.[23]

Wealth has "no power in America," said Mackay, "to alter the essential characteristic of society—that universal equality which is based on universal independence." "I think whatever may be said of the worship of the almighty dollar in America," added Matthew Arnold four decades later, "it is indubitable that rich men are regarded there with less envy and hatred than rich men are in Europe." The reason for this, thought Arnold, was "because their condition is less fixed, because government and legislation do not take them more seriously than other people, make grandees of them, aid them to found families and endure."[24]

Wealth in itself held no magic; it was, as Dicey said, "a proof of success in life," or as George Thomas Smart put it, "the sign of an inward power."[25] The philanthropical tendencies of the wealthy have been recalled by many commentators for many years, as another token of the cohesion between all groups in American society.[26] In America, where opportunities were open to all, wealth became the yardstick of one's ability, of one's manhood. Englishmen were neither surprised nor disgusted by the pursuit of riches because the pursuit seemed so natural and sensible in a land where success actually could be attained through effort and talent. The British saw that work in the United States was honored, even exalted, since that work (in which the men seemed to immerse themselves so single-mindedly) simply had to be done in order to scale the economic heights. "Labour as a profession is more dignified in America than in the old country, . . . entirely owing to the unlimited demand there is in the country for industry," concluded the author of *The Working Classes in the United States*.[27]

If history and abundance blessed Americans with the opportunity to rise, it also forced upon them the consequent necessity to work hard, to compete, and to achieve. There was no choice. "The essentially commercial spirit of the people . . . is nowhere else so universally, or so unreservedly displayed," Mackay remarked. "There is no class affecting to scorn the avocations of trade—no one compromises his position by being a trader. With every stimulus to exertion, idleness is not, in America, deemed an honourable pursuit." The growing community had needs, new

[23] Edward Dicey, *Six Months in the Federal States*, I, 304.
[24] A. Mackay, *The Western World*, I, 127; Arnold, *Civilization in the United States*, p. 123.
[25] George Thomas Smart, *The Temper of the American People*, p. 6.
[26] For example, A. Trollope, *North America*, I, 295, and, almost seventy years later in 1929, Igglesden, *A Mere Englishman in America*, p. 180.
[27] [Burn,] *The Working Classes in the United States*, p. 19.

commercial innovations were always in demand, and so "business never, for any length of time, assumes in America that overdone aspect, which is too familiar to it in older and less-favoured communities. Besides, it is the rapid road to wealth; and wealth gives great, if not the greatest consideration in America." The learned professions were not "one whit more honourable," and did not lead quickly to wealth.[28]

Anyone planning to emigrate to the United States to take advantage of the abundant conditions and egalitarian dispositions of the New World should not look for a short-cut to riches, nineteenth-century Englishmen warned their countrymen. A successful industrialist, Sir John Leng, indicated that "every workman is in a sense his own master, but the probability is that if he starts business for himself, however hard he worked for another, he will work still harder on his own account. Hard work," he continued, "is the rule in America, and no man need go there and expect to prosper unless he is ready to do his very utmost, and certainly to do much more than even hard-working men do here." The atmosphere was so ripe for the aspiring entrepreneur, that some Americans found themselves swept into realms of wealth and work beyond those which they desired to enter. Leng noticed this: "From the greatness of the country and the wonderful development of its requirements and resources, many can scarcely help themselves. They find their businesses grow at a rate beyond all their calculations and arrangements. They try to cope with it as it grows, but are always underhanded."[29]

The familiar diatribes against "crass American materialism" and the slothfulness of its people became common only in the 1920's when writers such as C. H. Bretherton wrote that America's vigor "is being applied exclusively to material and not at all to spiritual and intellectual things. It is becoming a gigantic Babbitt warren, minus the useful habit of proliferation. Everyone waxes fat and skips in the bright moonshine."[30]

Even before 1920 critics were disturbed at the apparently low level of intellectual and artistic attainment, but they understood that Americans were too busy for those things. George Smart noted perceptively:

[28] A. Mackay, *The Western World*, I, 71–72. The desire to make money in a land where new vocations were constantly coming into being and where labor was scarce led to the development of the jack-of-all-trades type of worker very common in America, said David Macrae (*The Americans at Home*, p. 37). Here is an instance where a commonly noted behavioral trait—versatility—can be joined to environmental conditions in the New World, which in turn color the values of the people.

[29] Leng, *America in 1876*, pp. 318–19. Recall Spencer's address at Delmonico's six years later.

[30] C. H. Bretherton, *Midas, or, The United States and the Future*, p. 87. Walter Metzger suggests that we might be able to account for this change by making a distinction between the older materialism of thrift and the materialism of expenditure, the latter being the target of British critics of the 1920's.

The American works longer, to a later age; he has hardly yet begun to feel the monotony of labor or business. In a measure this is why he is indifferent to the arts, for he does not yet feel the need of their solace. The conquest of his continent is a fine art to him. He thinks he has little time to give to meditate on aesthetics. He spares a little for politics, but not enough to get at first principles, or to carry but remedial measures to a completion. He is essentially uncritical because he is laboring so intensely. And he makes labor *per se* an obscuring idolatry. His joy of living is a joy in working that exceeds the patient laboriousness of Europe; and the *élan* that Europe keeps for military and social life he keeps for work alone.[31]

Before the 1920's, American materialism, placed in the context of a healthy scramble for wealth open to all, was more often associated with the phrase "electric energy" than with "money-madness." The opening of a continent made Americans proud, not ashamed, of this enterprise. They indeed cast these activities in essentially moral terms. Given the natural abundance and the egalitarian preferences of Americans, the hurry to become rich and the whole achievement ethos was, as Alexander Mackay once again so easily saw, the most natural thing in the world, for "America is a country in which fortunes have yet to be made. Wealth gives great distinction, and wealth is, more or less, within the grasp of all. Hence the universal scramble. All cannot be made wealthy, but all have a chance of securing a prize. This stimulates to the race, and hence the eagerness of the competition." What prevented Englishmen from joining the race was not their superior refinement, but the fact that in England "the lottery is long since over, and with few exceptions the great prizes are already drawn."[32]

Individualism. Frederick Jackson Turner notwithstanding, the visiting authors did not think of the American citizenry as individualists, even though Americans frequently claimed the distinction for themselves. Among men of their station in life, the British definition of "individualism" meant individuality—the right to be different as a human being, to think one's own thoughts. The British thought Americans were a "uniform" people. Hence, while Americans might think the following anecdote an illustration of Yankee individualism, the story-teller, A. M. Low, found it an obvious example of the egalitarian phenomenon. He told of a United States Senator returning home and finding a workman standing at his door. " 'Well, my man,' said the senator good-naturedly, 'what can I do for you?' 'I'm not your man; I'm nobody's man except my wife's,' the fellow answered, with some asperity. 'I've come to paint the house.' "[33]

[31] Smart, *Temper of the American People*, p. 81.
[32] A. Mackay, *The Western World*, II, 296.
[33] Low, *America at Home*, p. 79.

The exercise of true individualism, for the traveling Briton, demanded more than the peevish insistence on being given equal treatment, more even than material equality. It required an acceptance of differences among people. But, complained Edward Dicey:

> In a moral as opposed to a material point of view, the most striking feature about American Society is its uniformity. Everybody, as a rule, holds the same opinions about everything, and expresses his views, more or less, in the same language. These views are often correct, almost invariably intelligent and creditable to the holders. But still . . . you cannot help wishing, at times, for a little more of originality.[34]

Rather than American individualism, the commentators more often spoke of liberty and freedom, by which they meant that the state, the powerful, the wealthy, must not infringe upon the opportunity of any citizen to rise in the world. Neither through law nor even through superciliousness must an American be denied the "liberty" to prove his mettle. If one's position is not inherited it must be earned; if it is to be earned, one must be left "free" by society to earn it; if one reaches the top, he has achieved it by his own "individual" efforts. Individualism in America thus refers to the achievement ethos arising out of the competitive process. The competitive process is, in turn, the inevitable economic manifestation of equality of opportunity.

The American sociologist Robin Williams has recently shown the interrelatedness of these various elements of individualism, achievement, competition, freedom, and materialism—all within the framework of an equality that refers to opportunity (not to classlessness):

> By "American" ideals, *position should be based upon personal qualities and achievements.* . . . It is held that our society is and *should be* one in which the individual is free to move into those positions in the society that he has earned by ability, skill, effort, and moral worth. He is supposed to rise or fall according to his own merits; his position is determined by what he is and does or can do *as an individual.*

All this, he thought, "becomes an internally consistent scheme that satisfactorily explains and justifies the entire system. It runs as follows:

> 1. This is a society of equality of opportunity and free competitive placement. ("Anyone who has it in him can get ahead.")
> 2. Hence, success is solely a matter of individual merit.
> 3. Hence, those who are at the top deserve to be there, and those at the bottom are there because of lack of talent or effort; it is "their own fault."

[34] Dicey, *Six Months in the Federal States,* I, 305–6.

4. Thus the placement of individuals could not be otherwise without violating individual achievement.[35]

Williams, a modern commentator, thus confirms the estimate of Tocqueville and the British travelers that American individualism, novelty, and self-reliance were concentrated on the economic sphere rather than in the area of opinions and ideas. The Britons did not go beyond the Frenchman's explanation that the compartmentalization of individualism in America was a further manifestation of the equality of conditions; equality in the United States simultaneously stimulated economic innovation and stifled intellectual independence.

THE BELIEF IN A GLORIOUS FUTURE

In 1888, toward the close of the period under discussion, and perhaps in a way symbolic of the end of the egalitarian era, a book appeared which portrayed a classless utopia that would undo the miseries and injustices of the contemporary world by the year 2000. Edward Bellamy's *Looking Backward* postulated the perfection of a socialist society in which true equality had been achieved, stating, of course, that it had not been achieved in his own society. Bellamy's utopia was not the same as the American society outlined by the travelers from Tocqueville's time to Bellamy's. Not only was Bellamy's classless ideal alien to the American egalitarian aspiration, but joined inextricably to equality in every travel account was a description of the American's passionate faith in progress, an absolute conviction that America's future would reach heights of glory never matched in the history of civilization. Whereas the future of the United States had no final classless goal and the American vision was dynamic, Bellamy's dream society was perfect, static, and bland.

The belief in equality that pervaded life in the New World was carried along by the temperamental product of a belief in progress—an extraordinary optimism, a boundless enthusiasm that gave to American equality an altogether different spirit from Bellamy's, one consonant with the American stress on opportunity rather than sameness. The best way to evoke that optimism to which the affirmations of progress and equality naturally led—"that Titanic energy that grasps at the impossible,"[36] that sense of destiny that the travelers saw bring equality to life—is to let the Britons describe these impressions in their own words.

Charles Richard Weld (1855): Americans are, he wrote at the end of his book, "a mighty people triumphing in the splendour of immeasurable

[35] Robin Williams, *American Society: A Sociological Interpretation* (New York: Knopf, 1951), p. 91. Williams makes an enlightened effort to define American equality, pp. 78–135.
[36] Stirling, *Letters from the Slave States*, p. 361.

habitation, and haughty with hope of endless progress and irresistible power."[37]

James M. Phillippo (1857): "They have literally a 'faith to remove mountains,' they hesitate at nothing,—they regard nothing as impossible. It does not appear that they ever ask the question, Is such a thing easy or difficult of accomplishment? but, Can it be done?—meaning that if it is possible to be effected by human effort and ingenuity, it *shall* be accomplished. They seem to act as though difficulties were made to be surmounted; while, like all other men of energy and enterprise, they find that both body and mind are improved by the toil that fatigues them."[38]

Henry Latham (1867): "Hope may spring eternal in the human breast in Europe, but the yield, the number of gallons per minute at which it springs in every breast in America, cannot be realised without living in the atmosphere, surrounded by the people. To an American nothing appears impossible, nothing chimerical. Every man is going to make a fortune before he dies."[39]

James Bryce (1888): "The hopefulness of her people communicates itself to one who moves among them, and makes him perceive that the graver faults of politics may be far less dangerous there than they would be in Europe. A hundred times in writing this book have I been disheartened by the facts I was stating: a hundred times has the recollection of the abounding strength and vitality of the nation chased away these tremors."[40]

James Muirhead (1892): Americans possess "a sense of illimitable expansion and possibility; an almost childlike confidence in human ability and fearlessness of both the present and the future . . . above all, an inextinguishable hopefulness and courage."[41]

Sir Alfred Maurice Low (1905): "The future is the keynote of Uncle Sam's daily song. . . . The American believes in himself. That alone carries him far. The American believes in his destiny. That gives him confidence to face the future. The future for him is always one of promise. . . ."[42]

[37] Charles Richard Weld, *A Vacation Tour in the United States and Canada,* p. 394. Many books ended on just this note.

[38] Phillippo, *The United States and Cuba,* p. 324.

[39] Henry Latham, *Black and White,* p. viii. Herbert Spencer grumbled that Americans are *too* future-oriented: "The American, eagerly pursuing a future good, almost ignores what good the passing day offers him; and when the future good is gained, he neglects that while striving for some still remoter good" (*Essays: Scientific, Political, and Speculative,* III, 482).

[40] Bryce, *The American Commonwealth,* I, 14. He warned later that a growing material inequality seriously threatened America's future (III, 526, 528). The fate of the American faith in progress and equality in the twentieth century will be examined in the final two chapters of this book.

[41] Muirhead, *America, the Land of Contrasts,* p. 274.

[42] Low, *America at Home,* pp. vii, 219.

THE METAPHOR OF YOUTH

If constant repetition among the traveling Britons furnishes any reliable standard, then the belief in equality sustained by the faith in the future were, together, the guiding myths of nineteenth-century America. These two creeds, borne out by actual developments in American history, and their many ideological, temperamental, and physical offshoots—democracy, materialism, optimism, energy—constituted the ingredients for the all-embracing metaphor that so many travelers seemed to find appropriate for depicting the United States: America, Land of Youth. The picture of a youthful people summed up all these qualities in one image. Note for example the similarity of literary expression and sociological observation in the remarks of the following four authors, each of whom wrote on the basis of visits between 1878 and 1883.

Sir William Howard Russell called the United States "a lusty youth, promising a manhood of irresistible vigour and strength in time to come if the body politic fulfils its early hope." Professor Edward A. Freeman, the noted historian, commented upon the importance of a nation thinking itself young, even if, as he tried to demonstrate, it was not truly youthful: "In a young country everything is affected by the fact of youth. . . . Everything seems to be young together, while in an old country some things are old and some young. This air of newness in the United States is often, as I hope presently to show, only an air; but the air of seeming newness practically affects everything." Joseph Hatton compared the United States to England as he would a boy to a man: "Youth will be better pleased with the New World than with the Old, since youth dwells upon the future, age upon the past. America looks forward. England looks back. The boy strains his eyes toward coming days; the man turns to those which have fled." And the novelist, Moreton Frewen apologetically made a request: "I want them [the Americans] without resenting it to let me regard them as children—not yet half through the schools—children who play with all the fire-crackers of a vast continent; who are strangely irresponsible in their ways. Orators, yes! Artists, yes! Philosophers, yes! but amazingly *young;* so young the world will not as yet take them seriously."[43]

The British tourists practically to a man, both before and after the Civil War, found youthfulness a suitable expression for the land that had inherited the venerable tradition of England. It became less suitable in the twentieth century, but as late as 1906 Frederic Harrison

[43] Russell, *Hesperothen*, I, vi; Freeman, *Some Impressions of the United States*, pp. 2–3; Hatton, *To-day in America*, pp. 2–3; Moreton Frewen, *Melton Mowbray and Other Memories*, p. 197.

enthusiastically invoked the vision of a nation that "offers a new life, a fresh start, a world detached, on a virgin soil unencumbered with our antique civilisation and its burdens."[44]

Equality, optimism, and youth did not always stimulate admiration. Critics could confront these attributes with scorn as well, for youth suggested a certain rawness and crudity, qualities that came out when the observers turned their attention specifically to American children; it suggested a lack of sophistication, a lack of dignity, taste, and culture; it suggested bad manners and insufficient respect for superiors. A nation without the proper regard for the past, without a sense of tradition may be reckless; a nation unappreciative of beauty may be ugly; a nation apathetic about higher intellect may be dumb and dull. America lacked "what we in Europe regard as the Corinthian capital of society, . . . the literary element," wrote Zincke. Fifty years later in 1906 Charles Whibley took note of the irony that while the United States encouraged independence in the economic realm, it "has not invented a new method of expression, that the country which questions all things accepts its literature in simple faith."[45]

What the Britons said for literature, they said for all matters intellectual. Americans are not materialists in the ordinary sense of the word, stated George Steevens; they are intellectual materialists. "Materialistic in the sense of being avaricious, I do not think they are: they make money, as I have said, because they must make something, and there is nothing else to make. But materialistic, in the sense that they must have all their ideas put in material form, they unquestionably are." In one of his most carefully chosen words, Matthew Arnold finally decided that the United States was "uninteresting."[46] Youth can have energy, hope, and humor; it rarely has wisdom. That takes time, and in a land where children were like adults and adults like children —perhaps the most extreme form which equality took in America— age and maturity were, according to many Britons, regarded as liabilities.

THE INTEGRATED SOCIETY

British understanding of the twin American faiths in equality and progress, and of the youthful, uncynical, optimistic, idealistic spirit that

[44] Harrison, *Memories and Thoughts*, p. 173.

[45] Zincke, *Last Winter in the United States*, p. 175; Charles Whibley, *American Sketches*, p. 250. The Britons generally failed to appreciate the freshness and novelty in the mode of expression of the best of American literature.

[46] Steevens, *Land of the Dollar*, pp. 311–12; Arnold, *Civilization in the United States*, pp. 170–72.

they elicited, did not come to rest with these various generalized expressions. The visitors wrote extensively of American institutions; they found these creeds and this buoyant temperament embedded and embodied in tangible institutions: in the schools, in the government, in the family, in the churches. These form the subjects of the next five chapters. Nothing impressed the travelers more about nineteenth-century America than the symmetrical blending of belief, natural resources, animating spirit, actuality, and invented institutions into a harmonious whole. The fundamental institutions created by Americans expressed almost perfectly their youth, their confidence in the future, and their affirmation of equality; and the success of these institutions no doubt contributed to strengthening the credibility of those faiths and their hold on the minds of Americans.

That is why Americans asked foreign visitors what they thought of republican institutions. "Intimately connected with the pride of country which generally distinguishes the Americans," said Mackay, "is the feeling which they cherish towards their institutions." The European attachment to one's country was different. The Swiss might identify with his soil, the Scottish mountaineer with the rugged features of his own land.

> But the American exhibits little or none of the local attachments which distinguish the European. His feelings are more centered upon his institutions than his mere country. He looks upon himself more in the light of a republican than in that of a native of a particular territory. His affections have more to do with the social and political system with which he is connected, than with the soil which he inhabits.[47]

"Until I went to the United States," wrote Matthew Arnold, "I had never seen a people with institutions which seemed expressly and thoroughly suited to it." He pursued the organic coherence of American society when he pointed out that "in France, though the institutions may be republican, the ideas and morals are not republican. In America not only are the institutions republican, but the ideas and morals are prevailingly republican also."[48]

America, said James Bryce

> . . . is made all of a piece; its institutions are the product of its economic and social condition and the expression of its character. The new wine

[47] A. Mackay, *The Western World*, II, 288.

[48] Arnold, *Civilization in the United States*, pp. 115, 125. I have made a tandem of Mackay and Arnold throughout this chapter for several reasons. Their writings are separated by forty years and fall on both sides of the Civil War. Their feelings about the American experiment were quite different from each other. Yet their generalizations were almost identical. I chose them also because they were both rather perceptive observers.

has been poured into new bottles: or to adopt a metaphor more appropriate to the country, the vehicle has been built with a lightness, strength, and elasticity which fit it for roads it has to traverse.[49]

[49] Bryce, *The American Commonwealth,* III, 354. At the beginning of his work, Bryce mentioned that American institutions are supposed to be "of a new type. They form, or are supposed to form, a symmetrical whole, capable of being studied and judged all together more profitably than the less perfectly harmonized institutions of older countries" (*ibid.,* I, 1).

V   The Schools

I T WOULD BE IMPOSSIBLE to exaggerate the importance that the travelers attached to the system of free public education developed by the Americans. The ante-bellum visitors, according to Berger, found it to be "the foundation upon which the entire superstructure of American institutions rested." Not only was education deemed important, but no matter what their other views, "most British visitors thought very highly of American education. . . . Even observers sharply critical of democratic institutions agreed that the common school was 'one of the glories of America.' "[1] Seen in the context of England's tortured efforts to disentangle religious issues from educational matters, it is not difficult to comprehend the Englishman's envious approbation of American schools.

These two themes of praise and prominence were played from early in the nineteenth century to well into the 1880's and frequently beyond. Said the geologist Charles Lyell in 1846 of the public school system: "It is the most original thing that America has yet produced." In 1857, James Phillippo commented that "education has ever been a subject of deep interest and importance in America; and there is no country in the world where it has to so great a degree reached the masses. . . . Almost every village has its school-house as well as its place of worship." Anthony Trollope, five years later, reflected the continuing approval accorded the grammar schools when he remarked simply that "it is almost impossible to mention them with too high a praise." In 1869, a year before the passage of Forster's Education Act in England, W. A. Harris and Alex Rivington decided that "the public school system of the United States is the foundation of their political edifice, and is the real cause, as well, of the general intelligence, as of the industry and

---

[1] Max Berger, *The British Traveller in America, 1836–1860,* pp. 147, 161. He attributed the enclosed quotation to Mrs. I. L. Bishop, H. A. Murray, and T. C. Grattan.

commercial prosperity of its people, and of its political safety as a nation."[2]

EDUCATION AND EQUALITY

The common schools had four cardinal properties: they were public, compulsory, free, and secular. All children attended them; all children *had* to attend them; no student paid tuition since state funds, through taxes paid with a minimum of public complaint, met the expenses; and, of greatest moment to the Englishman, being public in a land where church and state were separated, the schools were nondenominational.[3] These features could be expressed differently. Lawrence Cremin, in one of the best of the few modern studies of the common school, emphasizes the four properties that illustrated the close connection between education and the community in the America of 1850. They were:

1. A common school was a school ideally common to all, available without cost to the young of the whole community.
2. A common school was a school providing students of diverse backgrounds with a minimum common educational experience, involving the intellectual and moral training necessary to the responsible and intelligent exercise of citizenship. It was carefully to avoid in the process those areas which in terms of conscience would prove so emotionally and intellectually divisive as to destroy the school's paramount commitment to universality.
3. A common school was a school totally supported by the common effort of the whole community as embodied in public funds.
4. A common school was a school completely controlled by the whole community (usually through its representatives) rather than by sectarian political, economic, or religious groups.[4]

These principles have often been tabbed as "democratic," but such an equation may not be as natural as first it seems. A good democratic society could have made different educational choices. For example, an educational system need not be undemocratic which: (1) divides itself along religious lines; (2) makes attendance voluntary rather than com-

[2] Sir Charles Lyell, *A Second Visit to the United States of North America,* I, 205; Phillippo, *The United States and Cuba,* p. 199; A. Trollope, *North America,* I, 317; [W. A. Harris and Alex Rivington], *Reminiscences of America in 1869,* p. 131 (since Harris wrote the section on education, the best portions of the book, citations hereafter will refer only to Harris).
[3] Issues that relate to the separation of church and state will be detailed in the chapter on religion.
[4] Lawrence A. Cremin, *The American Common School: An Historic Conception* (New York: Bureau of Publications, Teachers College, Columbia University, 1951), p. 219.

pulsory; or (3) is financed privately or through selective taxation, based upon ability to pay, and collected from parents whose children actually attend school. Such a system, in fact, being voluntary and discriminating by individual needs, might easily be said to be more democratic in the libertarian sense than that which actually developed. American schools, however, never divided students along any lines: religious or sexual or intellectual or economic or social. All children came together in the same classroom; all children came; all received basically the same grammar school and high school training; all of society bore the responsibility for all the children.[5]

The key word for the authors was "all." An education without distinctions could only belong to a society that disowned predetermined distinctions, that is, to an egalitarian society. Education was the instrument par excellence of equality; the schoolroom was its home. "The coachman who drives you," wrote Anthony Trollope, "the man who mends your window, the boy who brings home your purchases, the girl who stitches your wife's dress,—they all carry with them sure signs of education, and show it in every word they utter." "Here the sons and daughters of the rich meet together," intoned the wealthy John Leng. "Here the same classes are open to all, and the only distinctions recognized are those which attend superior diligence and mental endowments."[6]

The tourists liked not only the educational ideal, but many of the techniques and practices that followed in its wake. Zincke vigorously applauded the effort to teach the essentials. Reading and writing skills in American schools, he asserted, rightly preceded lessons in taste and accumulations of useless information. Latham thought the extension of equality even to girls would likely have far-reaching and positive consequences in the future. He also liked the institution of free school (and public) libraries.[7]

David Macrae and John Tod remarked with delighted wonder at the relative absence of corporal punishment. Perhaps the women teachers

[5] This excludes, naturally, those who chose to attend private or parochial schools and had the money or conviction to do so. A. Mackay noted the paradox that America had reversed the traditional European pattern, for here education was compulsory and religion voluntary, rather than vice versa: "They have left religion to fortify itself exclusively in the heart of man, whilst they have treated secular education as a matter which essentially concerned the State" (*The Western World,* II, 253). As noted before, though frequently ignored by the British, "all" really meant all *Caucasians.*

[6] A. Trollope, *North America,* II, 78–79; Leng, *America in 1876,* p. 274.

[7] Zincke, *Last Winter in the United States,* pp. 312–13; Latham, *Black and White,* pp. 244, 250. For sharp indictments of coeducation, in theory and practice, see Humphreys, *America—Through English Eyes,* p. 91, and Woodruff, *Plato's American Republic,* p. 81. They were minority opinions.

(who outnumbered the men) were not physically able to hand it out.[8] More likely, since the lack of corporal punishment in the home as well as in the school was widely remarked, this benevolence reflected the American sentimentality toward children. Still, many of the visitors were much impressed by the women teachers and they were sure that the ladies needed no recourse to the cruder ways of caning simply because of the talent they exercised in the classroom. They taught with charm, strength, ingenuity, and intelligence; they taught their charges to think rather than to amass facts. Phillippo wrote that the teachers, male and female, were more interested in inculcating the desire for self-knowledge in their students than in training them to memorize. The teachers achieved this, said Lucy Soulsby, through the "great use of discussion classes." And the teachers were so good because they listened to and learned from their students. This is why the instructors were so young in spirit as well as in years, suggested James Hannay.[9] The emphasis on discussion over recitation should not occasion great surprise. A lecture betokens a kind of autocracy; a seminar more closely approximates the ideals of egalitarian democracy. Perhaps this contributes in part to "the careful study" that Americans "devote to the science of education."[10]

One author accounted for the teachers' sturdy good sense by pointing out their egalitarian backgrounds, which so equipped them for egalitarian schools, coming as they did primarily from farmer and tradesman stock.[11] That the Britons thought of the pre-Dewey elementary school as highly progressive would be, surprising though it may seem, a quite correct inference to draw. The goal of the school system had been achieved, proclaimed Harris in 1869: "Every traveller in the United States is struck with the general intelligence of the people."[12] No finer inducement to emigrate to the New World could he think of when he concluded that

[8] Macrae, *The Americans at Home,* p. 603; John Tod [John Strathesk], *Bits About America,* p. 149. Tod said corporal punishment would be regarded as an assault on "a free-born citizen."

[9] Phillippo, *The United States and Cuba,* p. 340; L. H. M. Soulsby, *The America I Saw in 1916–1918,* pp. 75, 80; James Owen Hannay [George A. Birmingham], *From Dublin to Chicago: Some Notes on a Tour in America,* p. 296.

[10] Archer, *America Today,* p. 67.

[11] Zincke, *Last Winter in the United States,* p. 306. Zincke also commented upon the high social position of the teachers, as did many others, including Hugh Seymour Tremenheere, who displayed an unintended bias toward these people when he spoke of their "very high social position, considering the nature of their employment" (*Notes on Public Subjects Made During a Tour in the United States and in Canada,* p. 58). Despite the high esteem in which they were held by all, they were underpaid (Pidgeon, *Old-World Questions and New-World Answers,* p. 87, and Faithfull, *Three Visits to America,* p. 75).

[12] [Harris], *Reminiscences of America in 1869,* p. 128.

"the great privilege of a working man in America is the fact that a good and gratuitous education is offered to his children."[13]

A good many Englishmen naturally objected to the common schools on the same grounds that they rejected the idea of equality. Common schools were common and encouraged commonness rather than excellence. Schools without distinctions would inevitably be without distinction.[14] Richard De Bary anticipated contemporary criticisms of progressive teaching when he admonished Americans about their laxness: "School is not taken to be a place for tasks, but rather for easinesses." Thomas Hughes, the reforming author of *Tom Brown's Schooldays,* feared that public schools were too easily falling prey to the society that financed them, and were inculcating the cheaper public values. "Were I living there I should certainly try the public schools first for my boys," he charitably admitted. "But they say that the teaching there is too forcing in the earlier stages and afterwards not liberal enough in the direction of *'the humanities,'* so that the boys get trained more into competitive money-making machines than into thinking cultivated men."[15] Annette Meakin later cynically remarked, in this vein, that Americans "prize education because they think it will help them to rise, and everyone wants to rise over here."[16]

Fewer conservatives and critics, however, objected to the egalitarian schools than objected to other, broader manifestations of the principle, simply because they respected learning and could at least hope that common schools, if anything could, might elevate the common man. Furthermore, they could not boast about England's educational system. The vast majority of nineteenth-century visitors agreed with Miss Bird, who remarked in 1856 that American schools were "worthy of the highest praise."[17]

EDUCATION AND THE FUTURE

It did not escape British attention that the American population footed the bill for the educational enterprise. Few of the authors could conceal

[13] *Ibid.,* p. 318. This important factor may have carried more weight with prospective Jewish emigrants from Russia or Poland, for example, than, say, with Sicilians.

[14] For this general view, see especially Boddam-Whetham, *Western Wanderings,* p. 176; [Burn,] *The Working Classes in the United States,* pp. 159–64; Harrison, *Memories and Thoughts,* pp. 182–85.

[15] Richard De Bary, *The Land of Promise: An Account of the Material and Spiritual Unity of America,* p. 131; Thomas Hughes, *Vacation Rambles,* p. 174. Although his book was published later, Hughes visited the United States several times between 1870 and 1887.

[16] Annette M. B. Meakin, *What America Is Doing: Letters from the New World,* p. 289.

[17] Isabella (Bird) Bishop, *The Englishwoman in America,* p. 434.

their mild surprise at this national willingness to contribute private money to the public domain in the land of free enterprise.[18] What moved the Americans to make this costly kind of investment was not simply a reaffirmation of the revolutionary Enlightenment Gospel that all individuals can benefit from an education. The society willingly paid the bill not just to uphold a noble hope for each individual, but because it expected to profit more by this investment than by any other. The society was investing in its own future as a society.[19]

What must be stressed in discussing American public education, as pointed out by Cremin, was the total involvement of the community. Its commitment went beyond approval of the philosophical maxims of a Condorcet; it went so deep that only a few Americans wondered, with Trollope, whether their public education "is not advanced further than may be necessary." Americans, in Mackay's opinion, could not ask that question because they regarded education "in its true light, not merely as something which should not be neglected, but as an indispensable coadjutor in the work of consolidating and promoting their scheme." Since that scheme was the future glory of the United States of America as a republic, there could never be enough education. It was the chief instrument of the progress in which they so fervently believed. As Mackay continued, "The stability of the republic is intimately identified with the enlightenment of the public mind—in other words, with the great cause of public education; it is to the promotion of education that it will in future chiefly owe its success."[20]

The purposes of education and the nation were held to be inseparable. J. Nelson Fraser insisted that

> . . . it must be recognised by all who have studied America that there is a breadth about her views of education not yet attained in England. Education is felt to be a function of society; society needs to study itself from an educational point of view, to take stock continually of its needs, and to measure its progress.[21]

"The object of education in America," said Daniel Pidgeon in connecting it with national aspirations, "is not so much the production of the learned

---

[18] Zincke properly noted that wide property distribution made this taxation more feasible in America than England (*Last Winter in the United States*, p. 305).

[19] Archer, *America Today*, pp. 51–52; Arnold Bennett, *Your United States*, p. 156; Fraser, *America, Old and New*, p. 302; Low, *America at Home*, p. 116; Lyell, *A Second Visit*, I, 193; Pairpont, *Uncle Sam and His Country*, p. 334; Phillippo, *The United States and Cuba*, p. 199; Smart, *Temper of the American People*, pp. 222–23; Soulsby, *The America I Saw*, pp. 79–80.

[20] A. Trollope, *North America*, II, 177; A. Mackay, *The Western World*, II, 230, 291.

[21] Fraser, *America, Old and New*, p. 302.

man, or even the good man, as of the good citizen." Thus, he continued, now quoting Fraser, the school itself

> . . . is a microcosm of American life. There reigns in it the same free-dom and equality; the same rapidity of movement and same desire to progress, easily catching at every new idea, ever on the watch for im-provements; the same appeals to ambition; the same subordination of the individual to the mass; the same prominence given to utilitarian over pur-suits of a refining aim; the same excessive strain on the mental and physi-cal powers; the same feverishness and absence of repose.[22]

Leng felt compelled to rhapsodize upon the societal effects of the school system. He composed a hymn to "the Common School" whose lyrics paid homage to "the grand fuser of heterogeneous races in America —the centre round which all its institutions revolve—the security for its permanent peacefulness, welfare, and progress." Most of the nineteenth-century commentators associated such mystic adoration with the typical American's attitude toward his schools. They insisted that Americans worshipped the public schools as the panacea for all social ills, as the tangible assurance of an uncommonly enlightened populace, as the guar-antor of a soaring future. "I suppose," said Fraser, "that in no country is the spirit of Progress so closely associated with that of Education. No country believes so much in this or owes so much to it. . . . America believes in education."[23]

Americans believed in education because they believed in the future; they believed in the future because they had their schools. The Britons well understood that if Equality and the Beautiful Future were the God and Heaven of the American religion, then Americans regarded the little red schoolhouse as the Church, as the means to Salvation. As George Smart said: "The fundamental feeling of the American is that education is indispensable. This is not only for the salvation of the state, but for the salvation of his own soul."[24] Or as Miss Meakin put it:

> If the practical American people has one superstition it is—education. In America, especially as you travel westward, the most stately and impres-sive edifices that meet your eyes are schools, colleges, and libraries. These

[22] Pidgeon, *Old-World Questions and New-World Answers*, p. 90. This is a very important point, for it indicates that the communal hopes for education figured more prominently than the individual. See also on this distinction A. Mackay, *The Western World*, II, 237, and [Harris], *Reminiscences of America in 1869*, p. 128. Travelers always spoke of the "general intelligence" of the peo-ple, of "an informed populace," of "general readers." They hardly ever spoke of "excellence." See Freeman, *Some Impressions of the United States*, p. 184, for the best discussion of America's general readers, large in number, not deserving, he contended, of the derision to which they were often subjected.

[23] Leng, *America in 1876*, p. 274; Fraser, *America, Old and New*, p. 364.

[24] Smart, *Temper of the American People*, p. 222.

are tokens of the national faith in education, just as the cathedrals and monasteries of the middle ages were monuments of religious faith. . . . They give, and give in blind faith.[25]

The religious metaphor for the schools is not altogether accidental. Whereas in most societies of the past the church had been the chief transmitter of values to the young, its place had been pre-empted in the United States by the schools. Whereas the state in most societies of the past had allied with the church to maintain order and its own stability, the state in the United States relied chiefly on the schools to make good citizens. Whereas religion was usually compulsory and education voluntary, the United States had completely reversed the Continental pattern.

Nor was the church the only institution whose authority was pre-empted by the schools. The place of the family in the United States became ambiguous as more and more authority for the teaching of children passed from the home to the schoolhouse. The centrality of the schools as the chief transmitter of values to the young reveals something about both the nature of the values and the place of the young in the New World. The church and the family have traditionally been conservative teachers. The church taught the eternal, unchanging truths. The family reinforced these and trained the children to repeat the tasks that had always been carried on by the father and mother.

The schools in the United States trained children for new tasks. As a few of the more sensitive commentators recognized, the children, upon coming home from school, knew more about many things, were more up-to-date, more *American* than their parents. And their training as citizens was general, equipping them to deal with new, unimagined possibilities in the future rather than teaching them to see what their parents saw. The transmission of values in the United States was directed toward the future instead of the past. In placing the schools at the center of American institutions, Americans were further betraying their overwhelming respect in theory and practice for the chief carriers of the future: the children. And the child knew it. As Arnold Bennett expressed it after visiting an experimental school:

I knew the secret of the fine, proud bearing of young America. A child is not a fool; a child is almost always uncannily shrewd. And when it sees a splendid palace provided for it, when it sees money being showered upon hygienic devices for its comfort, even upon trifles for its distraction, when it sees itself the center of a magnificent pageant, ritual, devotion, almost worship, it naturally lifts its chin, puts its shoulders back, steps out with a spring, and glances down confidently upon the whole world. Who wouldn't?[26]

[25] Meakin, *What America Is Doing,* p. 289.
[26] Bennett, *Your United States,* p. 153.

The strange paradox that education was the source of so much faith in a land noted for its anti-intellectualism may be better understood by seeing that faith more as an expression of the belief in children, equal opportunity for all, and the future than as an affirmation of the power of thought.

MOUNTING DOUBTS ABOUT EDUCATION

Blind faith in an institution that promised salvation could maintain its hold only as long as salvation seemed at hand. Only as long as progress in the United States remained visible and the millennium seemed imminent could the "myth" maintain its magic. Toward the end of the nineteenth century, however, that millennium seemed further away than ever. Old problems, instead of vanishing, persisted, and new ones emerged: problems of labor-management strife, of political corruption, of rising racial tension, of mushrooming slums daily enlarged by hordes of new and strange immigrants, of crime, of depressions, of moral decay and skulduggery, of a symbolically closed frontier, of new ideologies.

In such a real world, it was only a matter of time before the mass of Americans would begin to raise questions about their educational panacea. Given the identification of the common schools with social progress, the intuition that something was amiss in the land could be easily translated into the query: what's wrong with the schools? In the 1880's Britons reported hearing this kind of question more and more persistently. Writing in 1881, the renowned journalist William Howard Russell could not fail to notice the powerful hold that the common schools still exerted upon the souls of Americans. He said: " 'Philosophers,' in all the doubts and fears which the condition of the Republic inspires at times, cling with confidence to the palladium which is, they think, to be found in the system of free schools of the States." But by this time, more than a few Americans began to wonder whether the reality would ever rise to the ideal, for as Russell said, "if Americans are to be trusted as authorities, the result of the largest and most liberal system of education ever devised is not as happy in practice as it ought to be according to theory." Russell then quoted American authorities in order to specify the "serious doubts [which] are intruding themselves respecting the success of the common schools." Attendance, he said, was low. Interest had declined. The quality of instruction had dipped "ridiculously" below the level of public schools in Bedford, Manchester, and London. Teachers endlessly roamed from school to school in search of the decent salaries that were nowhere to be found. The majority of students could not read, write, spell, or add. They recited rather than understood. And to top it off, the breakdown of the system displayed itself in the alarming fact that "crime and pauperism are increasing far more rapidly than population." Russell's remarks are irresponsible and foolish, but they serve as prelude to the more judicious criticisms to which the schools were subjected, with increasing regularity, on both sides of the Atlantic, from the 1880's on. Herbert Spencer, for instance, in the same year as Russell, went right to the heart of the educational problem by asking whether human nature can be altered by *any* external process. He solemnly warned Americans that morality, purity, and responsibility cannot be taught the average man. "The common citizen, educate him as you like, will habitually occupy himself with his personal affairs, and hold it not worth his while to fight against each abuse as soon as it appears. Not lack of information, but lack of certain moral sentiment is the root of the evil."[27] Undoubtedly this was an *a priori* judgment rather than one based on observation, fitting in so neatly as it did with his own philosophical presuppositions. But was Helvetius really more empirical in deciding that good learning can make the good man?

Two years after Spencer's remarks, Matthew Arnold made much of James Russell Lowell's aphorism of Americans as "the most common-schooled and the least cultivated people in the world." George Smart, a responsible observer, ruefully wrote in 1912 of the growing emphasis on technical education and claimed that "the results of American education in former days seem to many observers finer than those of today." Continuing his comparison with bygone days, Smart added that "America, today, is insecure about its education as it was not a decade ago. Education is now more often seen to be no automatic good. . . . There are those who affirm that America is far behind other nations." It was in 1935 that H. G. Wells coined his famous phrase that "human destiny is a race between ordered thought made effective by education on the one side, and catastrophe on the other," and that in America "catastrophe seems to be leading."[28]

Although the tides of opinion were in the process of turning, the school system still found its ardent defenders in the early 1900's. "In America," affirmed the liberal journalist W. T. Stead, "everybody, from the richest to the poorest, considers that education is a boon, a necessity of life, and the more education they get the better it is for the whole country." Stead had no doubt that the results justified the faith. William Archer explicitly tried to refute the "most common-schooled, least cultivated" charge. Ar-

[27] W. H. Russell, *Hesperothen*, II, 152–54; Spencer, *Essays*, III, 476. One of the chief factors inducing doubts about the schools was their presumed failure to reach the new immigrants. With a very few exceptions, the travelers missed this.

[28] M. Arnold, *Civilization in the United States*, p. 91; Smart, *Temper of the American People*, p. 221; H. G. Wells, *The New America, The New World*, p. 45.

nold Bennett was convinced that America was still "intensely interested in education." "The zeal for education, and the amount of money now being spent upon it, is probably greater than in any other country in the world," Miss Meakin claimed in 1911. S. P. B. Mais, in 1933, "was struck by the genuine desire for knowledge," the "exemplary" conduct of the students, and the fact that they "obviously liked their work. Their reading was done for pleasure." And the Unitarian schoolmaster, L. P. Jacks, also in 1933, argued that American education had been unjustly maligned for fifty years.[29]

While one cannot determine here which side was right, the realization can be underlined that compared to the period before the 1880's the common school system for the fifty years before 1933 was in fact often abused. Its friends were on the defensive. Although it is hard to measure, one would still have to conclude that the American school system continued to elicit more good words than bad; but the reverential tone appeared rarely. This change of tone may reflect advances in English education after Forster's Act in 1870 and Balfour's Act in 1904 as much as it reflects an actual decline in the quality of American schooling.

Whatever the reasons, a mighty bulwark of America's faith in the future was losing its infallibility; faith lingered, but faith with reservations cannot move mountains. Ethel Tweedie summarized in a dozen words the substance of the British and American criticism that was going around in the early years of the twentieth century: "This education produces high mediocrity, but apparently retards the inspiration of genius." This charge, echoed by many Americans as well, matches precisely, of course, those that the earlier Britons made concerning the effects of equality in general. Americans came to listen in large numbers when Frederic Harrison reminded them that "literature of a high order is the product of a long tradition and of a definite social environment. Millions of readers do not make it. . . . Literature, politics, manners and habits, all bear the same impress of the dominant idea of American society—the sense of *equality*."[30] Harrison's remarks followed his characterization of the educational system as admirable, but, if intellectual pre-eminence "of a high order" was at all deemed desirable, self-defeating. By the twentieth century Americans, too, were restlessly scanning the educational scene, searching for different results, and looking beyond the sixth grade. The observant Briton watched the Americans shift their gaze; and he,

    [29] William T. Stead, *The Americanization of the World, or The Trend of the Twentieth Century*, p. 387; Archer, *America Today*, pp. 51–52; Bennett, *Your United States*, pp. 153, 156; Meakin, *What America Is Doing*, p. 293; S. P. B. Mais, *A Modern Columbus*, p. 51; Jacks, *My American Friends*, pp. 7–8.
    [30] Ethel Brilliana Tweedie [Mrs. Alec-Tweedie], *America As I Saw It*, p. 134; Harrison, *Memories and Thoughts*, p. 185.

similarly, turned his head in this new direction to ascertain the object of their attention.

FROM GRAMMAR SCHOOL TO COLLEGE

When it appeared evident that the common schools could not eradicate evil single-handedly, and when, for a variety of reasons, American colleges were transformed into universities, British interest began to turn in the direction of higher education. Whereas before the 1880's American education evoked the image of rich and poor, boy and girl learning together in one classroom under the aegis of a committed and hopeful society, the spirit of later education resided on the college campus. The travelers in the twentieth century looked at the universities, while the lower levels were eclipsed in their works.[31] In the nineteenth century, the typical British comparison of American universities and public schools with their British counterparts could be found in statements like this:

> The primary and secondary schools in the United States seem to me, on the whole, better adapted to the general requirements of youth in America than are the similar schools in Scotland, and more particularly in England. But with one or two exceptions, like Harvard and Yale, the Universities are far inferior to ours.[32]

Seven years later, in 1883, while struck by "the amazing number of universities and colleges," Edward Freeman, in company with many others, deplored their "tendency to mediocrity."[33] Even by 1914, Americans, according to Hannay, were still unwilling to boast about their universities:

> The ordinary American citizen is proud of every single thing in his country except his universities. He is always a little apologetic about them. He compares his country with England and is convinced that America is superior in every respect, except the matter of universities. When he speaks of the English universities he shows a certain sense of reverence and makes mention of his own much in the spirit of Touchstone who introduced Audrey as "a poor thing, but my own."[34]

[31] This rule has many exceptions. Colleges were discussed with great avidity by such nineteenth-century visitors as: Dilke, *Greater Britain,* p. 69; Freeman, *Some Impressions of the United States,* pp. 180–82; Leng, *America in 1876,* p. 285; and A. Trollope, *North America,* II, 38. The primary schools received enthusiastic attention from such twentieth-century commentators as: Harrison, *Memories and Thoughts,* pp. 182–85; Samuel Reynolds Hole, *A Little Tour in America,* p. 125; Low, *America at Home,* p. 116; Soulsby, *The America I Saw,* pp. 75–80; and others.

[32] Leng, *America in 1876,* p. 285.

[33] Freeman, *Some Impressions of the United States,* pp. 180, 182.

[34] Hannay, *From Dublin to Chicago,* pp. 297–98.

Such insecurity is perfectly understandable. American education had been directed toward raising the level of the common people; Old World universities for seven centuries had nurtured genius and scholarly excellence, whose requirements tended to be unfamiliar to egalitarian America. Yet not long after Birmingham's comments the proudest emblem an American parent could wear, the badge of his success in life as a parent, was the insignium of his child's college or university.[35]

One cannot account for this switch simply by tracing the commentators' explanations of the workings of the colleges; they rarely agreed upon what higher education was attempting or whether it was succeeding. Did the universities, for example, carry on the egalitarian ethos of the nation? Yes, said Bryce: "It is the glory of the American universities, as of those of Scotland and Germany, to be freely accessible to all classes of people."[36] No, said H. G. Wells: "The American universities are closely connected in their development with the appearance and growing class-consciousness of this aristocracy of wealth."[37] On this question much naturally depended upon whether one was talking about the rapidly multiplying state universities, in which case Bryce made sense, or whether one stayed in the East amidst the ivy, making Wells seem more realistic. Charles Dilke compared the University of Michigan with Harvard and Yale in just these terms in 1866. What kind of course of study did the colleges stress? Liberal, scholarly, and creative, but tending toward dilettantism, answered William Archer. Narrow, technical, and mean, accused Douglas Woodruff and G. Lowes Dickinson. Research- and science-oriented, agreed Ramsay Muir, but rather than being narrow, this activity was vital, fresh, and was, more than any other factor, responsible for American prosperity.[38]

Schoolmaster Jacks, most judiciously, thought they were all right in some cases and wrong in others. The colleges approached learning in a variety of ways, and they were always experimenting:

> While some of the great universities have committed the fatal error of including in their curricula "everything that anybody wants to know," thereby losing the character proper to a university . . . there are others, mostly smaller, where the traditions of sound learning are faithfully upheld and the elements of a universal culture held together. . . . In the

[35] See, for example, Jacks, *My American Friends*, p. 160.

[36] Bryce, *The American Commonwealth*, III, 438.

[37] H. G. Wells, *Social Forces in England and America*, p. 363. The college population, though growing, was still being drawn from a narrow band of society when Wells wrote this. Also the fraternity system was becoming established, even in the supposedly more democratic state universities.

[38] Dilke, *Greater Britain*, p. 69; Archer, *America Today*, p. 62; G. Lowes Dickinson, *Appearances: Notes of Travel, East and West*, p. 194; Woodruff, *Plato's American Republic*, p. 90; Ramsay Muir, *America the Golden*, p. 31.

multitude of American colleges both extremes are to be met with: superficiality at one end, thoroughness at the other.[39]

Why did students go to college? To make more money in the future,
asserted Woodruff. Because they were thirsty for knowledge, insisted Sisley Huddleston. What could one say as to the total educational impact of
the colleges? George Steevens decided that "superficial" was the best he
could say. Hannay demurred: "I take it that the American universities,
both those for men and women, are the greatest things in America today."[40] Thus one can learn little about the workings of American higher
education from these outsiders. These questions demanded more first-
hand knowledge than the typical casual visitor possessed; general impressions were not enough.

What the travelers failed to perceive may be of as much interest as that
which did strike them directly. There were a number of educational matters which aroused great debate among professional educators at the turn
of the century but which the Englishmen passed over. Among these were
the government of the universities, problems of academic freedom and
faculty tenure, the quality of the doctoral programs, and the extent of
business domination of the governing boards. We have here further evidence of the failure of the foreign observer to get down to hard, occasionally technical, but frequently meaty questions. This may also be a sign
that these were not burning problems in Great Britain at the beginning of
this century when more basic pre-university issues were still unresolved
in England.

These recent writers did agree, though, that they should be visiting the
colleges rather than the grade schools, simply because Americans displayed far more interest in their colleges than in the lower schools. The
travelers noted, to cite one revealing example, that Americans who had
attended college always identified themselves with their college instead
of their high school or preparatory school. Hannay was genuinely puz-
zled when he wrote that "of American men whom I met most frequently,
I know about several of them whether they are Yale men, Princeton men
or Harvard men. I do not know about any single one of them what school
they belonged to. I never asked any questions on the subject." They all
affirmed that the universities, whatever the learning process they pursued,
commanded fierce loyalty, great attention, and vast publicity. Authors,
journalists, musical comedy lyricists were fascinated by some sort of

[39] Jacks, *My American Friends,* p. 171. He did insist, though, that the level
of academic attainment was below England's. Furthermore, "I have never met
an American educator who would dispute it" (*ibid.*, p. 165).
[40] Woodruff, *Plato's American Republic,* p. 81; Sisley Huddleston, *What's
Right with America,* p. 113; Steevens, *Land of the Dollar,* p. 309; Hannay,
From Dublin to Chicago, p. 297.

atmosphere which the campuses evoked. In 1926, J. St. Loe Strachey, editor of *The Spectator,* hailed "the greatest thing in modern America . . . the splendid and growing manifestation of the University spirit."[41] Strachey never really defined whether he meant intellectual spirit or that exhibited at football games, but he felt it nonetheless.

There are several good explanations for the coming of age of American universities in modern times. First, we know that higher education did not emerge as a truly creative force in American education until after the Civil War. According to Richard Hofstadter and Walter Metzger the college rather than the university had been the dominant model in higher education before 1860, and "founded by evangelical fervor, the denominational college allied Christian piety and humanistic study against the skeptical rationalism of the Enlightenment." Its role had been the essentially conservative one of endowing "a haphazard [frontier] society with religious truths and values."[42] But after the Civil War the university, not the college, became the model institution. In the ante-bellum period the growth of the emergent universities was held in check by the very existence of the powerfully entrenched denominational colleges. After 1865 the universities reshaped to some extent all but a few of the backward colleges. This change approached the proportions of a major educational revolution, for now research joined teaching as a major function of the university. Religion lost many prerogatives as science and the experimental method began to usurp the traditional authority of theology.[43]

Nothing could be more natural for a society that had invested so much money and emotion in primary and secondary education than to enlarge the sphere to include the universities. "Therefore," as Strachey aptly expressed it, "though not neglecting, yet not stressing, primary education, except as a necessity like food, drink, and clothing, America has fixed her firm gaze upon knowledge and truth in their higher aspects." The success as much as the inadequacies of the common schools may have inspired the critical scrutiny that they received toward the end of the nineteenth century, resulting in the national desire for *more* education. The republic's new concern with higher education may simply have been part of the effort to supply, as Bryce put it, "exactly those things which European critics have hitherto found lacking in America": scholarship, refinement, love of learning.[44]

[41] Hannay, *From Dublin to Chicago,* p. 283; John St. Loe Strachey, *American Soundings: Being Castings of the Lead in the Shore-Waters of America, Social, Literary, and Philosophical,* p. 93.
[42] Richard Hofstadter and Walter P. Metzger, *The Development of Academic Freedom in the United States* (New York: Columbia University Press, 1955), pp. 277–78.
[43] *Ibid.,* p. xii.
[44] Strachey, *American Soundings,* p. 94; Bryce, *The American Commonwealth,* III, 464.

This endeavor confronted egalitarian America with the awful dilemma of balancing quantity and quality, a dilemma that has produced an
unresolved educational ambiguity in modern times. It is not easy to impart "knowledge and truth in their higher aspects" to the multitudes.
Thus, as the visitors have indicated, the best and most prestigious universities have been private, highly selective, and extremely expensive; not
public, accessible to all, or free. To say "I am a Princeton (or Harvard
or Yale) man" does not carry egalitarian overtones, nor does it signify
the nation's commitment to education any more than the existence of Oxford and Cambridge did for England. Yet even a century ago, it must be
admitted, ordinary Americans had more opportunities to receive a college
education than their counterparts anywhere else in the world, though
much of the work in the colleges was of gymnasial grade. And today
Americans are wrestling seriously but not altogether successfully with the
problem of making mass college education a valuable intellectual experience for the student and not simply a vocational necessity. The effort to
furnish free public college education to vast numbers inevitably posed the
problem of quality. The twentieth-century Britons have not been satisfied with the results for generally the same reasons outlined by Mary
Agnes Hamilton in 1932:

> . . . there is little help or light coming from the Universities, rich
> and large as they are, and objects, as they are, of so much national pride.
> Open to every child, no matter where born or how conditioned finan-
> cially, is an education extending from the primary through the secondary
> school, on to the University. This looks like being an Open Sesame for
> the nation to genuine civilisation, and as constituting an advantage over
> us in Great Britain rich in unmeasured possibility. But the more one sees
> of the actual teaching given, whether in school or university, the cooler
> grows one's envy. Here, at bottom, the object pursued is the familiar one
> of putting boys and girls, young men and women, in a position to "make
> good"—the terms of this making being the standard terms of business.
> At the colleges, the system of "assembling credits," by which the courses
> and the studies of the average student is governed, is calculated to under-
> mine any respect for disinterested work or thinking, and is absolutely
> hostile to the putting of awkward questions about "What is it all for?"[45]

Despite the fact that the national government was soon to draw much
help and light from the universities under the collective name of the
"Brain Trust," Miss Hamilton would still have had some justification in
bringing the private universities explicitly within the range of her indictment, because many of them were doing the same thing as the public universities. The issue of private versus public higher education, however, is
only one of the many confronting educators today. Should the university

[45] Mary Agnes Hamilton, *In America Today,* pp. 147–48.

reflect the values of the community or forge new ones? Can one afford the luxury of asking "What is it all for?" when the individual is herded together with 25,000 other students in educational "factories"? Should the universities be turning out generally educated humanists or highly trained specialists?

The egalitarian common schools of the nineteenth century had simpler questions and easier answers. Their job was to turn all the children into good citizens who would lead the republic into the better world of tomorrow. The twentieth-century universities and the society to which they belong, unclear as to their goals and unsure how to balance egalitarian aspirations with quality education, are still groping for productive solutions to their dilemmas but, with a few exceptions, they have done no more than prolong the difficulties by adding graduate school training to the requisites for a good job.

Clearly the new quandaries facing American education in the twentieth century, as traced by the travelers, belong in the context of larger problems that have confronted American society as a whole as it has "progressed." Whether the progression from the egalitarian and idealistic nineteenth-century common school to the large, research-centered, complex, and perhaps educationally uncertain universities of the twentieth century faithfully mirrors changes in the values of American society is a question that can only be dealt with after other institutions have been examined. Perhaps the new complexities of the age demanded a specialization that never before had been required. Perhaps America was simply growing up, emerging from an eager, sanguine youth to a maturity that could not afford to rely on panaceas. Whatever the explanation, change there was, and perhaps the next few chapters will help unravel more of its meaning.

VI

Children and Parents

THE BRITISH TRAVELERS thought that the American public school system was, on the whole, quite admirable. With near unanimity, during the entire period covered by this study, they found the children detestable. This adds up to a paradox, for if free public education was so excellent, if it was the source of potential salvation for the republic, surely some decent effect upon the schools' young charges should have been faintly discernible. Yet the visitors were not at all charmed by the youngsters, and had very few kind words to say in their behalf.

Fortunately, "the unendurable child does not necessarily become an intolerable man."[1] Still, in a nation characterized by its "youth," implying more often than not the positive qualities inherent in that term, one would with reason expect some association between the metaphor and the actual young people of the country.

PRECOCITY

There was no question as to what quality in the children most nettled the Englishmen. As David Macrae said in 1867: "American children are undoubtedly precocious." In the same year, Greville Chester repeated this theme, which appeared with more monotonous regularity than did any other in these books. "Many of the children in this country," he said, "appear to be painfully precocious—small stuck-up caricatures of men and women, with but little of the fresh ingenuousness and playfulness of childhood."[2]

Again in that same year of 1867, the Robertsons embellished this developing portrait:

[1] Muirhead, *America, the Land of Contrasts*, p. 70.
[2] Macrae, *The Americans at Home*, p. 45; Chester, *Transatlantic Sketches*, pp. 230–31.

Their infant lips utter smart sayings, and baby oaths are too often encouraged . . . even by their own parents, whose counsel and restraint
they quickly learn wholly to despise. It is not uncommon to see children
of ten calling for liquor at the bar, or puffing a cigar in the streets. In the
cars we met a youth of respectable and gentlemanly exterior who thought
no shame to say that he learned to smoke at eight, got first "tight" at
twelve, and by fourteen had run the whole course of debauchery.[3]

Every year American youth was again berated for its precocity. "Precocity" politely expressed the British feeling that American children were
impertinent, disrespectful, arrogant brats. But "precocious" meant more
than that; it implied that American children were not children at all.
Three British mothers made this point. Theresa Longworth exclaimed
that

. . . in the course of my travels I never discovered that there were any
American *children*. Diminutive men and women in process of growing
into big ones, I have met with; but the child in the full sense attached to
that word in England—a child with rosy cheeks and bright joyous laugh,
its docile obedience and simplicity, its healthful play and its disciplined
work, is a being almost unknown in America.[4]

Daniel Boorstin in the introduction to a new edition of *A Lady's Life
in the Rocky Mountains* wrote of how Isabella Bird "saw a society where,
in a sense, everyone was young, yet where the most painful sight was 'the
extinction of childhood. I have never seen [she said] any children, only
debased imitations of men and women.' " And Lady Emmeline Stuart-
Wortley, before the Civil War, commented: "Little America is unhappily,
generally, only grown-up America, seen through a telescope turned the
wrong way. The one point, perhaps, in which I must concur with other
writers on the United States, is there being no real child-like children
here."[5]
One favorite example frequently recalled by the tourists was the
"train-boy," who vended any and all kinds of articles to susceptible travelers. Not only was he an incipient capitalist, but he lacked any qualities
that the ordinary Englishman would associate with childhood.

The train is hardly started before the boy comes through selling newspapers. He is generally a sharp lad, who has clearly before his mind two
facts. The first is, that if you have forgotten to buy a newspaper before
starting, you will, by-and-by, begin to miss one very much, and be willing

---

[3] William and W. F. Robertson, *Our American Tour*, pp. 9–10.
[4] Longworth, *Teresina in America*, I, 263. She also found them to be "inso-
lent, unruly, and rude" (*ibid.*, p. 269). Oscar Wilde thought that little girls were
more charming in their precocity than little boys (*Writings*, III, 251).
[5] Isabella (Bird) Bishop, *A Lady's Life in the Rocky Mountains*, p. xxii;
Stuart-Wortley, *Travels in the United States*, p. 67.

to pay a little extra rather than want it. The second is that, as the train is now fairly off, he (the boy) enjoys a monopoly, there being no longer any outside competition, and therefore that he can charge just as much as he thinks your paperless condition will tempt you to pay: which he does.[6]

These specimens were not always unpleasant people. On the contrary, Robert Louis Stevenson recounts the story of one who helped make it possible for him to survive the long cross-country journey on an emigrant train after a previous boy had made his trip hellish. Eyre Crowe tells how he and his traveling companion, William Makepeace Thackeray, came across a youngster reading a newspaper, "already devouring the toughest leaders, and mastering the news of the world whilst whiffing his cigar, and not without making shies at a huge expectorator close at hand."[7] The picture of the cigar-smoking cherub flashed recurrently in these accounts.

PUSILLANIMOUS PARENTS

The visitors did not have to search far for an explanation—at least a superficial explanation—for this disconcerting childhood behavior. Although a few of them remarked at the leniency of the common schools and regretted the lack of corporal punishment handed out there, many more felt that the only doses of discipline ever received by the child were administered, even if in small quantities, in the schoolrooms. It was unquestionably in the home that the child was indulged, and indulgence gave him his swagger. Parents either could not or else chose not to discipline their offspring. To be sure, the school system was not blameless. Many, like Fraser, regarded the school "as an extension of the family," which by its very effectiveness made matters more difficult for mother and father.

> . . . it must be allowed that schools are robbing parents of the power to control their families. The school has drawn to itself so much of the love and veneration of the young that in their homes missing its spell they grow unruly. Parents are not experts in the management of children, nor have they the moral weight of an institution to back them up, hence they fail to keep up the smooth ascendancy of the school.[8]

P. A. Vaile blamed the American mother: "She is refusing to perform her part of the contract. First she 'went back' on raising her children, now she does not want to have any children at all." Mrs. Humphreys raged at "the conspicuous absence of maternal instinct as a feature of American

[6] Macrae, *The Americans at Home*, pp. 456–57.

[7] Robert Louis Stevenson, *Across the Plains, With Other Memories and Essays*, pp. 37–39; Eyre Crowe, *With Thackeray in America*, p. 21.

[8] Fraser, *America, Old and New*, pp. 280, 282.

marriages." Many others accused fathers, but usually with greater sympathy. After all, the father simply worked too hard all day to have much time, interest, or energy to devote to his little ones. "The husband has his occupations, friends, and amusements."[9]

No matter which parent had to bear the burden of guilt, many an Englishman simply felt that home life in the United States just was not homelike; it lacked atmosphere, comfort, love, play, and warmth. It never became the cozy, friendly hearth that imparted to a family a sense of kinship, identity, or oneness. Long after young couples had forsaken the custom of dwelling in boarding houses or hotels and exposing their tiny ones to the dregs of society—a custom deplored by every Englishman—W. L. George, along with most others, still refused to admit that Americans had any idea what constituted a "real" home:

> The hard child suggests the hard home, which is characteristic of America. I visited many houses in the United States, and, except among the definitely rich, I found them rather uncomfortable. They felt bare, untenanted; they were too neat, too new . . . one missed the comfortable accumulation of broken screens, old fire irons, and seven-year-old volumes of the *Illustrated London News,* which make up the dusty, frowsy feeling of home. The American house is not a place where one lives, but a place where one merely sleeps, eats, sits, works.[10]

George may have been a bit unfair to expect to find "seven-year-old volumes of the *Illustrated London News*" lying about, but he had a right to notice the lack of age; it takes years for a family to implant its brand on a structure of brick and mortar. Perhaps, as many visitors rightly pointed out, Americans were too much on the go, too mobile for them ever to fulfill George's requirements for home-ness.[11] This nonetheless did not excuse the parents from their failure to bring up their children appropriately. Joseph Hatton, in 1881, begged mothers and fathers to take their responsibilities seriously and to realize, as any sensible person must, that their over-indulgence of the child was "excessive and injurious."[12]

Little Fritz, a pretty little American boy who sat as the subject for one of Philip Burne-Jones' paintings, told his grandmother, in the artist's presence, "I'll kick your head!" After being chided and asked to apologize there was "dead silence on the part of Fritz." Finally, after some more pleading, Fritz relented and uttered "a few perfunctory and

[9] P. A. Vaile, *Y., America's Peril,* p. 111; Humphreys, *America—Through English Eyes,* pp. 161, 165.

[10] George, *Hail Columbia!* p. 199.

[11] Said George Steevens: "You cannot call a people who will never be happy ten years in the same place . . . home-loving in the English sense" (*Land of the Dollar,* p. 313).

[12] Hatton, *To-day in America,* p. 7.

scarcely audible sounds, which were generously construed by the family as expressive of contrition and penitence; and Fritz started again with a clear record, for a brief period. His mother had absolutely no influence on him whatever, and she admitted as much."[13] Other American parents also admitted as much; they were fully aware of their inability to control their little ones, but they did not know what to do about it. L. P. Jacks, in 1933, let an American mother declare her utter helplessness and frustration in a way that was rather revealing and even poignant:

> We mothers are rapidly losing all influence over our children, and I don't know how we can recover it. We have little or no control over them, whether boys or girls. The schools and colleges take them out of our hands. They give them everything for nothing, and that is what the children expect when they come home. Their standards and their ideals are formed in the school atmosphere, and more by their companions than by their teachers. They become more and more intractable to home influence and there is nothing for it but to let them go their own way.[14]

But the majority of the Britons accepted neither the influence of the schools nor the social fact of mobility as sufficient explanation for the precocious child; they would have had little justification for disliking the child with the fervor they did and for deploring the parents' follies so strongly if these impersonal forces explained the situation adequately. They felt, rather, that causes ran deeper, in more insidious channels. Not only did the parents spoil their children, but they *wanted* to spoil them. Not only did the mothers and fathers put up with more than they should have, but they were actually proud of their babies. The Britons deplored with special intensity the parents' complete lack of guilt about their own efforts or over the way their children were turning out. The travelers came not to the conclusion that American parents were unable to discipline their sons and daughters, but that they deliberately chose to "let them go their own way." This either infuriated the by-now bewildered visitor, or else made him desperate to figure out how this insanity could possibly reign. William Howard Russell could not accept the excuse that the schools pre-empted parental power since "there is nothing in the American [school] system to prevent the teaching of religious and moral duties by parents at home; but it would seem as if very little of that kind of instruction was given by the busy fathers and anxious mothers of the Republic."[15]

Horace Vachell, like many others, told a child story that turned into a mother story. It seems that one day the author was in the parlor of a

---

[13] Burne-Jones, *Dollars and Democracy*, p. 36.

[14] Jacks, *My American Friends*, p. 149. Notice the young mother's stress on the influence which the peer-group culture held over her children.

[15] W. H. Russell, *Hesperothen*, II, 156.

ship filled with ailing people, including the author's own mother who was suffering from a bad headache. Into this sickly assemblage trooped our hero—a small American boy who decided to soothe the aches of all by playing on the bagpipes. "The wildest pibroch ever played in Highland glen was sweet melody compared to the strains produced by this urchin." He naturally continued to play, louder than ever, despite the glances hurled at him from all around the parlor; he stopped only when he tired. Then, instead of permitting peace, "he flung down the pipes, walked to the piano, opened it, sat down, and began to hammer the keys with his feet." At this turn of events, our long-suffering author had had enough: " 'You play very nicely with your feet,' I ventured to say, as I lifted him from the stool, 'but some of these ladies are suffering with headache, and your music distresses them. Run away, like a good boy, and don't come back again.' " But Vachell's story did not end here: "The mother was furious. Had I been Herod the Great, red-handed after the slaughter of the Innocents, she could not have looked more indignant or reproachful. I was interfering with the sacred rights of the American child to do what he pleased, where he pleased, and when he pleased." Vachell's first conclusion inevitably was that American children were monsters, utterly lacking in "sense of duty, reverence, humility, obedience." His second conclusion was, however, more interesting and more important, namely that parents actually "encourage the egoism latent in all children, till each becomes an autocrat."[16] Once this discovery had been accepted, it occurred to the more curious of the Britons to raise the appropriate question: how could American parents be proud of these diminutive devils?

THE EQUALITY OF CHILDREN

Sir Edwin Arnold presented a question of this sort, in more general form, to one whom he regarded as an expert on the American character: Walt Whitman. " 'But have you reverence enough among your people?' I asked. 'Do the American children respect and obey their parents sufficiently, and are the common people grateful enough to the best men, their statesmen, leaders, teachers, poets, and "betters" generally?' " To this fundamental inquiry, Whitman responded: " 'Allons, comrade!, your old world had been soaked and saturated in reverentiality. We are laying here in America the basements and foundation rooms of a new era. And

[16] Horace Annesly Vachell, *Life and Sport on the Pacific Slope*, pp. 79–80. One should bear in mind at all times the difficulty the travelers had of meeting representative American families since, as W. L. George candidly admitted, "truly representative families generally keep themselves rather to themselves" (*Hail Columbia!* p. viii).

we are doing it, on the whole, pretty well and substantially. By-and-by, when that job is through, *we will look after the steeples and pinnacles.' "*[17]

Whitman and Arnold included childhood precocity within the larger framework of a new people refusing to revere their "superiors." Such reverence constitutes one of the necessary ingredients of an aristocratically oriented society. Lack of that reverence suggests an egalitarian society, and these two distinguished men of letters were implying that the precocious child was symptomatic not merely of weak, stupid, willful parents, but rather of the pervasiveness in American society of the principle of equality. Captain Marryat, as early as 1839, related a well-known example illustrating this point:

> Imagine a child of three years old in England behaving thus:—
> "Johnny, my dear, come here," says his mamma.
> "I won't," cries Johnny.
> "You must, my love, you are all wet, and you'll catch cold."
> "I won't," replies Johnny.
> "Come, my sweet, and I've something for you."
> "I won't."
> "Oh! Mr. ———, do, pray make Johnny come in."
> "Come in, Johnny," says the father.
> "I won't."
> "I tell you, come in directly, sir—do you hear?"
> "I won't," replies the urchin, taking to his heels.
> "A sturdy republican, sir," says his father to me, smiling at the boy's resolute disobedience.[18]

In 1845 Francis Wyse generalized upon incidents like these, placing them in a broad social context. "There is seldom any very great restraint," he noted, "imposed upon the youth of America whose precocious intellect, brought forth and exercised at an early, and somewhat premature age, and otherwise encouraged under the republican institutions of the country, has generally made them impatient of parental authority."[19]

Parental authority did not sensibly differ from any other exercise of power: royal, military, governmental, or private. Americans had established their independence in rebellion against authority; they had rejected all artificially imposed forms of superiority; and they had proclaimed the equality of man. Surely these principles should extend to the family. Indeed, Jacks talked aptly of the way in which children had applied (with considerable parental approval) the Declaration of Inde-

[17] Sir Edwin Arnold, *Seas and Lands,* p. 79.
[18] Quoted in Lawrence A. Cremin, *The American Common School: An Historic Conception* (New York: Bureau of Publications, Teachers College, Columbia University, 1951), p. 217.
[19] Francis Wyse, *America: Its Realities and Resources,* I, 294–95.

pendence to themselves. And Muirhead, who composed one of the most informative chapters on this topic, formulated the grand generalization thus: "The theory of the equality of man is rampant in the nursery." He referred to the infants as "young republicans," "democratic sucklings," "budding citizens of a free republic." Here then was another application of the theory of equality—one which even the friendly Muirhead could not get himself to smile upon. It "hardly tends," he patiently tried to explain, "to make the American child an attractive object to the stranger from without. On the contrary, it is very apt to make said stranger long strenuously to spank these budding citizens of a free republic, and to send them to bed *instanter*."[20]

One must sympathize with the British travelers as they suffered through each encounter with these young specimens of the New World. But their dislike of American children is as beside the point as is their love of the schools. Both child rearing at home and the nationwide system of compulsory, public education were faithful to the ubiquitous thrust of equality, and the paradox that began this chapter turns out to be no paradox at all. The commentators liked what they saw in the classrooms because some authority was being exercised. It was being exercised by teachers who wielded it in the interests of learning and morality. When the travelers confronted the child outside the context of the school and inside the context of home and family they were appalled by what they believed to be the universal and inexcusable betrayal of authority by the parents.

This reversal in the roles of authority between teacher and parent disoriented the visitors to such an extent that many of them never realized that, just a few chapters before their excoriation of the American child, they had been blessing his development in the schoolrooms. Although the traveler frequently sensed that the "success" of the teachers and the indulgent "failures" of the parents were related to each other, and that both stemmed from the same peculiar, general assumptions in which American society was rooted, not one of them ever managed to pose squarely the problem of how and whether dual authority *could* be exerted on the child, of just how parent and teacher *should* combine their efforts in child rearing, given the public school system and the widespread assumption that the child was an equal partner in the family team.

The origins of the dilemma may be traced back to colonial days, where under the pressure of new conditions the familiar family pattern brought over from the Old World suffered major transformations affecting both child-rearing practices and the role of education. The traditional family was the wide kinship group with the source of power vested

[20] Jacks, *My American Friends*, pp. 150–51; Muirhead, *America, the Land of Contrasts*, pp. 63–65.

in the father and extending outward to include not only wife and children, but cousins, other relatives, and servants as well. The father was the chief educator, transferring the traditions of his culture and even vocational training to his sons. But authority and traditionalism were, as revealed in an excellent study by Bernard Bailyn, inadequate for conditions in the New World, where problems were new, land abundant, labor scarce, and old solutions to old problems irrelevant. In these circumstances . . .

> . . . the young—less bound by prescriptive memories, more adaptable, more vigorous—stood often at advantage. Learning faster, they came to see the world more familiarly, to concede more readily to unexpected necessities, to sense more accurately the phasing of a new life. They and not their parents became the effective guides to a new world, and they thereby gained a strange, anomalous authority difficult to accommodate within the ancient structure of family life.[21]

One of the effects on the child reported by Bailyn concerned the passage of the child into society after "the once elaborate interpenetration of family and community dissolved." A result was that "the individual acquired an insulation of consciousness," a "heightened . . . sense of separateness" from society, and particularly from the state, which no longer could "command his automatic involvement." Perhaps this is what the British meant by precocity.

THE FAMILY TEAM

The commentators who believed that parents must exercise authority over children were not pleased by what they saw in American families. In order to muster any kind words it was necessary to revise traditional conceptions of the family and accept a measure of equality in the home, accept the notion that the various family members could be close friends. Dicey was one who was able to take this step. He concluded one of his volumes in 1863 in praise of "the great charm which surrounds all family relations in the North. Compared with Europe, domestic scandals are unknown; and between parents and their grown-up children, there exists a degree of familiarity and intimacy which one seldom witnesses in this country."[22]

There were other companions within the family besides the parents and grown-up children. Growing boys and their fathers were companions, wrote Zincke in 1868. "In America the father never loses sight of

[21] Bernard Bailyn, *Education in the Forming of American Society* (Chapel Hill: University of North Carolina Press, 1960), pp. 22–23.
[22] Dicey, *Six Months in the Federal States,* I, 310.

his child, who thus grows up as his companion, and is soon treated as a companion, and as in some sort an equal." Zincke went on to relate a pleasant incident he observed on a train between a fourteen-year-old boy and his father:

> They had long been talking on a footing of equality. . . . At last, to while away the time, they began to sing together. First they accompanied each other. Then they took alternate lines; at last alternate words. In this of course they tripped frequently, each laughing at the other for his mistakes. There was no attempt at keeping up the dignity of a parent, as might have been considered necessary and proper with us. There was no reserve. They were in a certain sense already on an equal footing of persons of the same age.[23]

Mothers and daughters were companions, Low maintained:

> Daughters are much with their mothers, and they become their companions younger than they do in Europe. At an age when the French girl, for instance, is still demurely attending her convent, or the English girl is in the hands of her governess, her more emancipated sister across the Atlantic is calling with her mother on her friends, or assisting her in the drawing-room on her reception days.[24]

Sons and daughters received equal treatment, claimed William Saunders. Whereas "in an English family, as a rule, the greatest consideration is shown to the boys," in America, if anything, "the wishes of the girls would be first listened to, and their education provided for." The boy, after all, "is as eager to start life on his own account as is a greyhound to rush after the hare. . . . In the matter of early independence both sexes are equal."[25]

Husbands and wives were also companions. While the wife "will not consent to being submerged by her children, she gives much of her time to them, and is still able to find time to be with her husband. The average American husband makes a confidante and a companion of his wife."[26]

The patriarchies and matriarchies of the past had been replaced by a family team composed of equals. The British perceived this family revolution as being directly parallel to the fundamental cultural difference between the New World which blurred distinctions and the Old which honored and preserved them. As Muirhead put it:

[23] Zincke, *Last Winter in the United States,* pp. 70–71.
[24] Low, *America at Home,* p. 74.
[25] Saunders, *Through the Light Continent,* pp. 399–400. Also enlightening on these leveling tendencies in the home are Fraser, *America, Old and New,* p. 246, and Harold Spender, *A Briton in America,* pp. 253–54.
[26] Low, *America at Home,* p. 82.

The reason—or at any rate one reason—of the normal attitude of the American parent towards his child is not far to seek. It is almost undoubtedly one of the direct consequences of the circumambient spirit of democracy. The American is so accustomed to recognise the essential equality of others that he sometimes carries a good thing to excess. . . . The present type of the American child may be described as one of the experiments of democracy.[27]

THE LEADERS OF TOMORROW

Americans enthroned their children not merely out of obedience to some social ethos that compelled them to do in the home something consonant with what the nation proclaimed to the world as its faith. Americans, as Zincke's story of the singing father and son so nicely shows, were often quite fond of their children, and rather than being harried and intimidated, they were frequently joyful parents. In fact, the Americans, according to the British, believed in their young ones in much the same way that they believed in their future. Let the youths' natural spirit triumph and they would not only participate in a grand future, but they would be the chief forgers of that future; the child was the future. Children could be heard as well as seen because they represented hope in "the land of youth." "Nowhere," said Muirhead, "is the child so constantly in evidence; nowhere are his wishes so carefully consulted; nowhere is he allowed to make his mark so strongly on society in general." Richard De Bary chimed in that "America is wholly convinced . . . that the young child can take it all in. The child is given kingship and becomes the king."[28]

Those few Englishmen who thought well of American children praised precisely the same qualities that the detractors abominated. The novelist Arnold Bennett, for example, came across one "captivating creature whose society I enjoyed at frequent intervals throughout my stay in America. . . . [She] was a mirror in which I saw the whole American race of children—their independence, their self-confidence, their adorable charm, and their neat sauciness." The reformer George Holyoake liked "the American habit of training their children to independence" more than he did England's "unwise domestic paternalism, which encourages a costly dependence." John Tod did not employ the term "precocious" in a depreciating manner when he decided that "the girls

---

[27] Muirhead, *America, the Land of Contrasts,* pp. 70–71.

[28] *Ibid.,* p. 63; De Bary, *Land of Promise,* p. 128. "Young America does not sit at the master's feet and worship; it has definite opinions, which it deems as much deserving of hearing as other people's, and it gives them forth with the bold confidence born of youthful inexperience and immaturity" (Faithfull, *Three Visits to America,* p. 89).

and boys of America are very frank, even precocious."[29] And Sir Philip
Gibbs expanded upon this theme:

> The children of America have the qualities of their nation, simplicity,
> common sense, and self-reliance. They are not so bashful as English boys
> and girls, and they are free from the little constraints of nursery etiquette
> which make so many English children afraid to open their mouths. They
> are also free entirely from that juvenile snobbishness which is still culti-
> vated in English society, where boys and girls of well-to-do parents are
> taught to look down with contempt upon children of the poorer classes.[30]

Even Vachell, who told the story of the boy with the bagpipes, had to
confess to the "originality, independence, pluck, and perspicuity" of the
children.[31]

It can be noticed that the adjectives used to depict the child are similar, whether used in delight or disgust: saucy, self-reliant, original,
plucky, arrogant, wild, spontaneous, immodest, independent, demanding, irreverent. It can also be observed that they bear resemblance to
adjectives that some Englishmen thought applicable to the young nation
as a whole. Some visitors, it must be noted, found the terms suitable for
characterizing American adults as well.

PARENTHOOD AND THE CULT OF YOUTH

The blurring of lines between young and old in the New World furnished
an invitation to some British writers to caricature both American parents
and American children. But to Margaret Mead this leveling tendency
forms an explicable part of a peculiarly national approach to child-
rearing which she has called "third-generation American." The American child, contends this anthropologist, is expected to traverse a course
very different from his father's, and "with this orientation towards a different future for the child comes also the expectation that the child will
pass beyond his parents and leave their standards behind him." Thus "it
comes about that American parents lack the sure hand on the rudder
which parents in other societies display." Or, approaching the matter
from a different perspective than that used by either the historian Bailyn
or Miss Mead, Erik Erikson supports their findings when he writes that
"the psychoanalysis of the children of immigrants clearly reveals to

[29] Bennett, *Your United States,* pp. 147–48; George Jacob Holyoake, *Among
the Americans and a Stranger in America,* p. 183; Tod, *Bits About America,* p.
149.
[30] Philip Gibbs, *People of Destiny,* p. 88.
[31] Vachell, *On the Pacific Slope,* p. 83.

what extent they, as the first real Americans in their family, become their parents' cultural parents."[32]

The most repeated consensus at which the travelers arrived concerning the "American character" was that that character resembled, at heart, the character of a child. If there were no childlike children, if there were only miniature adults in "the land of youth," then the reverse was equally true—there were few adultlike adults; there were only adults trying to be young. It was as though Americans of all ages felt compelled to play the part of a youth between fifteen and twenty-five years of age. "There are no old in America at all," said George Steevens in 1900. By this he meant two things. First, that adult virtues are uncultivated in the New World; the American "retains all his life a want of discipline, an incapacity for ordered and corporate effort." Steevens' second meaning centered on the fate of those who were actually aged. "They are shouldered unmercifully out of existence," he claimed. "I found in New York a correspondence on the open question whether the old have any right to respect. Many of the public thought, quite seriously, they had no right even to existence."[33] In exalting childhood and early youth to the consummative positions in life, it follows that maturity and old age should become anticlimactic.

Thirty years after his 1869 visit to America, the Reverend Mr. Macrae returned and noted that the "independence and precocious intellect of the American children" had not diminished; but he was "less struck with these features this time." The reason that he was less struck was precisely the same reason that made Harold Spender think better of the American children in 1920, twenty years after *his* first visit. "Our English child in the interval," said Spender, substituting his native land for Macrae's Scotland, "has become a little more American."[34] By the early years of the twentieth century, America's startling departure in raising children and in inflating the status of the youngsters in the family hierarchy was, like various other American innovations, becoming more general in the Old World also.

[32] Margaret Mead, *And Keep Your Powder Dry: An Anthropologist Looks at America* (New York: William Morrow, 1965), pp. 45, 41, 43; Erik Erikson, *Childhood and Society* (2nd ed.; New York: Norton, 1963), p. 294.

[33] Steevens, *Land of the Dollar,* p. 314.

[34] David Macrae, *America Revisited and Men I Have Met,* p. 24; Spender, *A Briton in America,* p. 271.

VII   Women

THE BRITISH TALE of women in the United States should, one would
guess, have a simple plot. Dominated for centuries by the male sex, it was
in the New World that the women, along with their children, were supposedly granted equality by the end of the nineteenth century, or at least
by 1920. The moral of the story would be that inequality cannot survive
in America. In a rough sort of way this scenario bears some resemblance
to that which the British visitors wrote; and yet, the story is a great deal
more complicated. In the nineteenth century, the foreign observers took
relatively small notice of American women, and that notice centered
not on their equality with men, but on their very special position in the
culture. When in the twentieth century the females came to dominate
these books of travel in a most ambiguous condition of equality, they
were so popular with the Britons that they practically made the visitors
forget their stepped-up criticism of most other aspects of American life.

IN THE NINETEENTH CENTURY

American women did not go unnoticed between 1845 and 1900; but
their attraction for the commentators inhered not in any particularly remarkable attributes of the women, in their independence or prominence,
but rather in the exaggerated chivalry accorded them by the men. Pay-
ing homage to no one or no thing, it was as though American men had
saved up all their reverence to shower it upon their women. Phillippo remarked: "The gallantry of the old world may at least borrow something
from the chivalrous homage which all American gentlemen pay to the
fair sex. It is said that Americans sometimes go so far as to say that a
man who contradicts a woman is not a gentleman. This gallantry, perhaps, is one of the principle [sic] elements in their rapidly growing civili-

zation."[1] All visitors marveled at the absolute freedom from molestation
allowed women on the streets and while traveling; only in the United
States could a female traverse a continent unescorted without fears for
her safety. If she chose, she could be left in privacy; if she preferred
company, she could expect no less than royal treatment.[2] Men even fore-
bore to indulge in their favorite pastime—spitting and chewing—in the
presence of the gentler sex. Alexander Mackay was sure the women
couldn't fully appreciate the medieval sublimity of this most painful of
all sacrifices. "Little do the ladies know," he sympathetically revealed,
"the agony to which their admirers sometimes subject themselves by this
gallant self-denial. 'Oh! for a chew'; whispered on one occasion under
these circumstances, into my ear, a young man in tones indicative of the
deepest distress. I advised him, if he were in pain, to step into the next
room and take one; but he shook his head despondingly, saying that 'they
(the ladies) would smell it on my breath.' " In other words, as Panmure
Gordon put it, "the reverence that is paid to women in America, is outstanding."[3]

Many explanations were put forward for this exceptional behavior,
most common of which was that it rested on the scarcity of females in
the American population. "So long as women are in a minority," declared
James Burn at the end of the Civil War, "it is only natural that men
should pet and flatter them."[4] The scarcity of females had actually ended
by the Revolution. But the high male-female ratio in colonial days, and
later on the frontier, undoubtedly contributed to an attitude that persisted long after the original reason for it had vanished.

Mentioned nearly as frequently was the desire of the men to soften
some of the rough edges of the new, expanding society by raising upon a
pedestal man's symbol of civilization, beauty, and grace. Perhaps it was
a case of overcompensation for the American's total unwillingness to
revere anything else in the land; the chivalry in this one case may even
have made it psychologically easier for Americans to tear down distinctions in all other cases. It may also have concealed the fact that the
female was not granted equality, that she was denied basic liberties per-
taining to work, property, and marriage.

The Britons rarely suggested as an hypothesis for male chivalry,
however, that the American woman deserved it by dint of her own special charm, warmth, and gratitude. On the contrary, many Englishmen

[1] Phillippo, *The United States and Cuba,* p. 99.
[2] Longworth, *Teresina in America,* p. 306.
[3] A. Mackay, *The Western World,* I, 101; H. Panmure Gordon, *The Land of the Almighty Dollar,* p. 68.
[4] [Burn,] *The Working Classes in the United States,* p. 86.

found her spoiled, arrogant, plain, and completely oblivious to the heroic favors bestowed upon her. The women, thought the tourists, took this worship for granted, and indeed came to expect and demand special treatment. Anthony Trollope expressed the indignation of many of his fellow countrymen when he charged that the American women

> . . . have acquired a sufficient perception of the privilege which chivalry gives them, but no perception of that return which chivalry demands from them. Women of the class to which I allude are always talking of their rights; but seem to have a most indifferent idea of their duties. They have no scruple at demanding from men everything that a man can be called on to relinquish in a woman's behalf, but they do so without any of that grace which turns the demand made into a favour conferred.[5]

The Englishmen were invariably galled whenever they kindly turned over their carriage seats to a member of the fair sex only to be greeted by—nothing, no thanks, no appreciation, no recognition at all of this display of graciousness.

The young girls in the land of youth received the lion's share of British attention. "There is no feature common to all departments of American society," said Mackay, "which will so soon impress itself upon the stranger as the prominent position occupied in it by the young ladies. . . . The mother is invariably eclipsed by her daughters." The shocking precocity of American girls, coupled with the premature retirement into the social background of the older set (otherwise known as married women, forced from the scene at the antique ages of eighteen and nineteen by their marriage) brought into the open the latent indignant Victorianism of visitors like Mrs. Longworth, who cried: "At about thirteen a girl begins to exercise her vocation as a young lady, to devote herself to dress, to look out for flirtations, to promenade with gentlemen, and to read novels."[6]

W. A. Harris made the same general point more precisely, simply by describing the situation: "Young ladies 'come out' at the age of seventeen, and marry earlier than in European countries; and when married they retire very much from general society." That expert on the female sex and other matters, Viscount Bryce, summed up the situation by pointing out, "In no country are women, and especially young women, so much made of. The world is at their feet. Society seems organized for the purpose of providing enjoyment for them." W. L. George, himself an admirer of the older woman rather than "the bread-and-butter miss,"

[5] A. Trollope, *North America,* I, 304. The deference paid them, said Burn, has been "claimed by the darlings themselves as a prescriptive right" (*The Working Classes in the United States,* pp. 86–87).

[6] A. Mackay, *The Western World,* I, 134; Longworth, *Teresina in America,* I, 321.

wrote of this distressing but familiar situation: "Everything goes to the girl—money for college, for training, social consideration; she is encouraged to waywardness, as if the men took a delight in her freshness, her mischievousness, and enjoyed her youthful petulance."[7]

If one can accept the evidence of the eyes, then the travelers supplied an excellent reason for the disproportionate notice paid the unwed girl-woman of the nineteenth century as compared to the older married woman. By common consent the young girls were said to be the only pretty females in the United States. Early bloom was immediately followed by the fabled fading of good looks at a premature stage of life. All beauty was said to have vanished by age twenty-five. After portraying the frail beauty that characterized the American woman at her best, Phillippo launched into a weighty discourse upon the matter:

> . . . it is remarkable that owing, as it supposed, to some peculiarity of climate, in concert with other causes, their beauty is not durable.
> In England, a woman is in the prime of her attractions at thirty-five, and she frequently remains almost stationary till fifty, or else declines gradually and gracefully like a beautiful day melting into a lovely evening. In America, twenty-five is the farewell line of beauty in woman. At this age, and sometimes earlier, the bloom of an American belle is gone; and the more substantial materials of beauty almost as quickly follow. At thirty, the whole fabric is on the decline. At the same time, the development of females is more rapid than in Europe. Girls are women at fifteen or sixteen, which may account in some degree for their premature decay.[8]

As Burn suavely expressed it: "American women are all 'scrags' before the term of middle life." Miss Bird thought the female at thirty "looks passee, wrinkled, old."[9] This indictment was very commonly made and undoubtedly reflects (rather than the results of a strange climate) the society's attitude toward the older woman: it never seemed important for her to dress well and "fix herself up." The emphasis on youth in the United States that encouraged early marriage contributed to this premature decay. Because the woman was giving birth and nursing her children in her teens and early twenties, her ability to preserve her beauty was more sorely tested than had she given birth five or ten years later.

These comments should not leave the impression that the American women repelled British travelers. On the contrary, many of the Britons found an ebullience and an intellectuality among American women which went a long way in easing the visitors' resentment against the more primitive aspects of life in the United States. Henry Latham, with

[7] [Harris,] *Reminiscences of America in 1869,* p. 60; Bryce, *The American Commonwealth,* III, 515; George, *Hail Columbia!* p. 131.
[8] Phillippo, *The United States and Cuba,* p. 108.
[9] [Burn,] *The Working Classes in the United States,* p. 10; Isabella (Bird) Bishop, *The Englishwoman in America,* p. 362.

a secret sort of thrill, professed himself "astonished at their touching without reserve upon all manner of topics which English ladies would ignore." And Macrae thought that they spoke not only widely, but well, because their common school training "has furnished them with a great deal of general information, and has quickened their desire for more. An American girl will talk with you about anything."[10] This quality had some amusing drawbacks, as W. L. George illustrated in this mythical but highly possible conversation at a typically American "cocktail" party:

> YOUNG LADY: "Mr. George, I'm just crazy to know what you think of Miss May Sinclair."
> MR. GEORGE: "Well. . . ."
> YOUNG LADY: "Don't you think her books are full of cosmic universality? Oh, do tell me what you think."
> MR. GEORGE: "You mean. . . ."
> YOUNG LADY: "What I like about Miss Sinclair is just that—her sense of the universal cosmos. Now in my home town in Oregon they want to know just what you think."
> MR. GEORGE: "From the. . . ."
> YOUNG LADY: "If you think she co-ordinates the analyses of the psyche of the characters, then what I want to know is how she correlates the theory of the moron with that of the urning. . . ."
> MR. GEORCE: "I. . . ."
> YOUNG LADY *discusses Bergson and the Matriarchate.*
> MR. GEORGE: "You. . . ."
> YOUNG LADY *discusses Sinn Fein and the decay of taste.*
> MR. GEORGE: "If. . . ."
> YOUNG LADY *discusses Mr. Carl Sandburg, Longfellow, psychoanalysis, Mrs. Fiske, prohibition, spooks, Alexander Hamilton, the negro question, the Barrymores, the exchange problem, and Yellowstone park.*
> MR. GEORGE: "When. . . ."
> YOUNG LADY (*rapturously*): "I'm so glad to have met you. You've no idea, Mr. George, how they hang upon your slightest word way out in Oregon. I do love to hear you talk."
> *She continues.* MR. GEORGE *is later discovered concealed in the refrigerator.*[11]

This little vignette, written in 1921, has a very modern and condescending ring to it. But commentators as early as Alexander Mackay in 1849 (and long before) generalized on the features of the comparatively independent and fearless young woman. Mackay said:

A young girl in America is in every way a freer agent than her European sister; the whole course of her education is one habitual lesson of self-reliance—the world is not kept a sealed book to her until she is tolerably advanced in years . . . she soon acquires a strength of character, to

[10] Latham, *Black and White*, p. 251; Macrae, *The Americans at Home*, p. 42.
[11] George, *Hail Columbia!* pp. 135–36.

which the young woman of Europe is a stranger, and acts for herself whilst the latter is yet in leading-strings.[12]

Exactly thirty years later Sir George Campbell agreed that "the American girls are certainly more independent than our girls are." By European standards, then, or at least by English standards, the nineteenth-century American woman was no wallflower. She had begun to assert herself, and the New World's egalitarian conditions undoubtedly inspired and aided her in that assertion. Bryce, for example, attributed to equal educational opportunities, regardless of sex, the observation that "among American women an average of literary taste and influence [prevails] higher than that of women in any European country."[13]

The position of women of the nineteenth century fell far short of real equality, however. By the last quarter of the century women had not achieved economic equality. It took the inventions of the telephone and the typewriter to open the gates of the labor market to them. The British visitors in the nineteenth century did not think it worth their while to assess the economic significance of the unleashed female simply because they did not think she had been unleashed. She was granted suffrage only in 1920. The fact that the feminist movement failed to gather much momentum until late in the nineteenth century does not deny the long and legitimate set of unredressed grievances under which women still suffered. Despite their conversational independence, most women were apathetic about politics and were given very little real power. Latham doubted in 1867 "if the women do interfere much in politics. Politics are man's work in war time. I should like to have the evidence of some experienced diplomatists on this point, whether women have not much more influence over politics in France than in America."[14]

Muirhead, though no "diplomatist," wrote a good analysis of American women. He continually stressed that their signal importance in American life had nothing to do with political involvement or the wielding of official power. As an example he cited state and local elections in Connecticut where "of 175,000 women of voting age . . . the numbers who used their vote in the last three years [probably 1896–98] were 3,806, 3,241, and 1,906. . . . The sphere of the American woman's influence and the reason of her importance lie behind politics and publicity." More important, she was not treated by the men as an equal; the males made her a goddess. They treated her with respect, bordering on idolatry, but they would not let her compete with them on equal terms. It was just this reverse discrimination which maddened the feminists as they

[12] A. Mackay, *The Western World*, I, 137–38.
[13] Campbell, *White and Black*, p. 29; Bryce, *The American Commonwealth*, III, 521.
[14] Latham, *Black and White*, p. 252.

sallied forth to do battle. As H. G. Wells said: "They do not want to be owned and cherished, and they do not want to be revered."[15]

For the bulk of the nineteenth century, then, the British report on American women was equivocal. Compared to the European women, the Americans were freer, granted greater equality, more self-reliant. Most of the British, however, were not particularly struck by woman's place, especially when one compares their statements during the nineteenth century with their reactions in the twentieth. In general, they still tended to place the American woman in the medieval mode—recipients of gallantry, chivalry, even reverence. Conditions had improved somewhat from those described by the American historian Harvey Wish for the years just before the reform movements of the 1830's. He wrote how "Harriet Martineau, Alexis de Tocqueville, and other European visitors condemned the life of upper-middle-class American wives as intellectually dull, restricted to formal duties at home, and pampered after the fashion of pet animals." Even though their daughters were freer from chaperonage than European girls, they and *their* daughters were still strongly influenced by the Victorian stereotype of feminine delicacy. One should be a "lady," fragile, subject to fashionable faints. One should not exercise after marriage. Better to play languidly with one's ringlets or idly move one's delicate fingers over the piano keys.[16] Most of the British commentators after this period wrote of somewhat more energetic American women, in the upper-middle classes as well as in all the other groups in society. But they did not fall over themselves in admiration of the vigorous American woman achieving equality until the twentieth century.[17]

THE TWENTIETH-CENTURY AMERICAN WOMAN

The political females of the late nineteenth century did not want the pedestal of inequality, flattering though it was; they wanted economic and political rights, and the right to be judged, not simply as women,

[15] Muirhead, *America, the Land of Contrasts,* p. 47; Wells, *Social Forces in England and America,* p. 371.

[16] Harvey Wish, *Society and Thought in Early America* (2 vols.; New York: McKay, 1950), I, 417.

[17] It is very difficult to periodize these general changes with much exactitude. In reading these works of travel, one can easily discern that the American woman of 1920 or even 1910 was portrayed as a very different creature from the women of 1860 or 1870. The transition in these many books is not sudden, and not always consistent. One event or even a series of events does not alter an entire sex. The best I can do is use the shorthand comparing the nineteenth-century with the twentieth-century American female, without denying that the English observers have *always* felt that American women had achieved a greater degree of freedom and equality than had their own women.

but as Americans. If British judgment can be taken seriously, the results of their efforts in the twentieth century have constituted an international revolution of unparalleled force. Nothing that the United States has ever done, the British tone seems to suggest, surpasses in magnitude the exertions and achievements of American woman. While American historians continue to describe their nation's history and character in exclusively masculine terms, the British visitors to the United States in the twentieth century thought that in their required chapter on the fair sex lay the key to a true understanding of the new nation.

In this twentieth-century republic noted for the masculine virtues of wealth and power, the travelers alleged, paradoxically, that women set the tone and dominated the life of the nation. Commentators from Bryce to Brogan made the point that American women exceeded in influence not only European women, but American men as well. Bryce, for example, opened his chapter on "The Position of Women" with this general proposition: "It has been well said that the position which women hold in a country is, if not a complete test, yet one of the best tests of the progress it has made in civilization." He concluded that the growing influence of women in the United States not only testified to that progress, but was an overarching cause of it as well. "No country," he said, "seems to owe more to its women than America does, nor to owe to them so much of what is best in social institutions and in the beliefs that govern conduct."[18]

"The European visitor to the United States *has* to write about American women," wrote the expert Muirhead, "because they bulk so largely in his view, because they seem essentially so prominent a feature of American life, because their *relative* importance and interest impress him as greater than those of women in the lands of the Old World, because they seem to him to embody in so eminent a measure that intangible quality of Americanism."[19] What did Muirhead mean when he talked of women as symbolic of "that intangible quality of Americanism?" Low defined it by turning toward pictorial embodiments:

> The American cartoonist who depicts his country, especially when it is a representation of America triumphant, or America pathetic, or America in all the dignity of the strength, always draws a woman—a woman young and graceful and beautiful, who faces the world with the serenity of confidence that comes from the knowledge that she rules. It is appropriate that Columbia is a woman. In the United States woman dominates. . . . In all that goes to make America unlike any other country,

[18] Bryce, *The American Commonwealth,* III, 504, 524.
[19] Muirhead, *America, the Land of Contrasts,* p. 46. He further declared (p. 48) that "the average American woman is distinctly more different from her average English sister than is the case with their respective brothers."

nothing so marks the contrast as the difference between the American girl and the European girl.[20]

Life in America, declared Hannay, is "gynocentric. It is arranged with a view to the convenience and delight of women." Stead was obliged to decide that "among the influences which are Americanizing the world, the American girl is one of the most conspicuous, and the most charming." "When all's said and done," sighed Burne-Jones, "America is the land for women—they are the queens of the situation all round."[21]

Women rose in prominence when the egalitarian conditions of the land, belatedly applied as they were in the case of the ladies, eventually penetrated into the kitchens and parlors, the offices and the boudoirs. The early educational opportunities had not only expanded their intellectual horizons, but had sent forth women with the ability to articulate the plight of their sex. More important, the prevailing spirit of the land made the goals of their crusade clear; women insisted upon equal treatment and equal opportunities. They demanded quite logically that they had the right, without loss of their previously gained prerogatives, to assert their natural humanity at least as much as did their children. Low put the feminist drive solidly in the context of the national spirit:

> The American girl is the product of her environment, she is what she is because America is America. Admitting that a woman is always physically the inferior of man, he [the American male] sees no reason why women are to be regarded as mentally or morally his inferiors; why they are to be treated as dependents and not as equals; why the "sphere" of woman travels in a different orbit to his own.[22]

The egalitarian spirit did finally open up job opportunities, and the new jobs, in turn, further enlarged that spirit. Bryce claimed that in the last quarter of the nineteenth century "it is easier for women to find a career, to obtain remunerative work of an intellectual as of a commercial or mechanical kind, than in any part of Europe." Miss Faithfull reported that since Harriet Martineau's visit in 1836, the number of occupations open to women had increased from seven to the point where, in Massachusetts alone in 1882, "there are nearly three hundred different branches of industry by which women can earn from one hundred to three thousand dollars a year." In fact, she added with genuine surprise, "the ten years even which elapsed between my first tour in 1872 and my second in 1882, had brought about marked changes." During that eventful decade, Miss Faithfull singled out the development of telephone

[20] Low, *America at Home,* p. 70. It might be worth mentioning that Britannia is also a woman.

[21] Hannay, *From Dublin to Chicago,* p. 214; Stead, *The Americanization of the World,* p. 318; Burne-Jones, *Dollars and Democracy,* p. 75.

[22] Low, *America at Home,* pp. 70, 71.

and typewriter as giving an extra fillip to the woman's case for equality. "Both these marvellous inventions are giving hundreds of girls throughout the States remunerative work."[23]

Another national innovation noted by the travelers, this one with some alarm, may also have contributed to the growing emancipation of the females—the relative ease with which a divorce could be obtained. Travelers were complaining of the runaway divorce rate of the United States as early as the 1830's.[24] But the great acceleration seems to have occurred later. During the years 1867–1906 the divorce rate grew from 27 to 86 per 100,000 population. This was a period of rapid urbanization and the time when feminists such as Susan B. Anthony and Elizabeth Cady Stanton achieved some success in liberalizing divorce laws. Before 1867 divorce meant social ostracism; there were fewer than ten thousand divorces granted in the land. In 1907 over 72,000 marriages were ended by divorce in the United States. This total surpassed the number of divorces in all of the other nations of the Christian world combined.[25] Although usually deplored by the Britons, relatively permissive divorce laws aided the woman who was not allowed to indulge in the remedies open to the husband of an intolerable marriage; the psychological effect of this potential remedy, even when not used, may have armed the American woman with a threatening weapon of liberation.

Another symptom/cause of inestimable psychic consequence may have been what the travelers surprisingly tended to feel were frank and natural relations between the sexes. Rather than stressing the "Puritan strains" in American culture, the visitors preferred to underline the effects of boys and girls attending school with each other from the earliest ages. The artificial formality and the mystery of the sexual relationships were both relatively absent from American life when compared to relations between the sexes in Europe. Muirhead explained that since "the American girl is thrown into such free and ample relations with the American boy from her earliest youth," then boys and girls "are not thought of as opposite sexes; it is 'just all the young people together.' The result is a spirit of good comradeship. There is little atmosphere of the unknown or mysterious about the opposite sex." The result of this natural interaction, according to Muirhead, was that "one certainly meets more husbands and wives of mature age who seem thoroughly to enjoy each other's society." This would superficially seem to contradict the observation of frequent divorce. But if a society deems "love

[23] Bryce, *The American Commonwealth,* III, 506; Faithfull, *Three Visits to America,* p. 275.

[24] Berger, *The British Traveller in America, 1836–1860,* p. 83.

[25] Wish, *Society and Thought,* II, 132.

matches" of value, wherein true intimacy is not only a worthy, but an attainable goal for both husband and wife, then failure to achieve it would incline the partners to seek for relief and try again with someone else—especially if it is felt that the wife has as much claim on marital satisfaction as the husband. David Potter has mentioned that "even our divorce rate is an ironic tribute to the fact that the interests of the individual, and perhaps in a majority of cases the individual woman, are placed ahead of the protection of a social institution—namely the family."[26]

Margaret Mead has called the American marriage ideal "one of the most conspicuous examples of our insistence on hitching our wagon to a star. It is one of the most difficult marriage forms that the human race has ever attempted." In fact the hope to choose freely the person with whom you can share your entire being rather than having your mate chosen for you with different, more limited, traditional purposes in mind has led to surprisingly few casualities "considering the complexities of the task."[27]

It is true that on the point of the healthy relations between the sexes, one could find healthy debate. W. L. George conducted an interesting examination of the "suppressions" in American sexual life, but on balance the British tendency was to support claims like those of Frederic Harrison to the effect that the relations between men and women in the United States had developed "in normal ways."[28]

George did share the majority sentiment on one related point. In a complete reversal from authorities only two generations earlier, the modern commentators, with practically one voice, affirmed that American women not only did not lose their beauty after their mid-twenties, but reached heights of beauty that the youngsters never approached. Although, as George sized up the physical attractions of the American female he decided that "where the European woman suggests, the American woman proclaims," he nonetheless agreed with the general verdict that the twentieth-century American woman devoted great time, energy, and money to her physical appearance well past the age of twenty-five, perhaps as the best guarantee of her freedom. She aged gracefully, the

[26] Muirhead, *America, the Land of Contrasts*, pp. 32–35; David M. Potter, "American Women and the American Character," *Stetson University Bulletin*, LXII, No. 1 (1962), 21.

[27] Maragaret Mead, *Male and Female: A Study of the Sexes in a Changing World* (New York: Morrow, 1949), p. 342.

[28] George, *Hail Columbia!* p. 151; Harrison, *Memories and Thoughts*, p. 201. Aldous Huxley analyzed the mixture of American Puritanism and American sexual laxity (*Jesting Pilate: The Diary of a Journey*, pp. 286–87). See Bryce, *The American Commonwealth*, III, 513–14, for a good discussion of America's "easy," "natural" social life, and for his defense of American girls, who he claims were not "fast."

British connoisseurs decided. She "has the art of growing old with comely dignity" was the way the drama producer William Archer phrased it. Instead of the frail beauty that fades all too soon, Macrae, in contrasting the women of 1898 with those of 1868, found that the ladies he met on his second excursion were "stronger and better developed, and their beauty . . . of a healthier type." "Married women and older women generally hold a far more important place in American Society than they held a generation ago," wrote J. St. Loe Strachey in 1926.[29]

L. P. Jacks and Harry Greenwall, writing during New Deal days, both credited this change less to America's appreciation of older age than to the effectiveness of cosmetics at covering up the lines. "As to the women," Jacks found that "most of their faces are so extensively over-laid with colouring matter and otherwise sophisticated that it is hard to say what lies beneath. As reconstructed by the beauty shops their appearance inclines to be predatory—an effect much favoured in those artistic establishments." Writing of stenographers in New York, Greenwall indicated that "paint and powder and scent gives them all a certain resemblance." Equality had its price. According to some of the men the woman of America knew of her power, her charm, and did not hesitate to use it—on the helpless males. Oscar Wilde called her "the most fascinating despot in the world"—a world in which, according to George Steevens, the men "toil and slave, in which they kill themselves at forty, that their women may live in luxury and become socially and intellectually superior to themselves." Horace Vachell, out West, described the typical woman who "does what she likes rather than what she ought," this "in startling contrast to other women." In short, as Muirhead expressed this new state of affairs, "the American woman has never learned to play second fiddle."[30]

BRITISH REACTIONS TO THE NEW WOMAN

In view of their negative reaction to the assertiveness of American children, the British visitors might have been expected to trace the ascendancy of the new woman with dismay. Although some shrieks of catastrophe and accusations of shrewishness were heard, they were very few. The British men were effusive in their praise of the American woman and exulted in her "triumph." American women, they proclaimed, are su-

[29] George, *Hail Columbia!* p. 118; Archer, *America Today*, p. 54; Macrae, *America Revisited*, p. 22; Strachey, *American Soundings*, p. 86.

[30] Jacks, *My American Friends*, pp. 42–43; Harry J. Greenwall, *American Scene*, p. 9; Wilde and Steevens quoted in Faithfull, *Three Visits to America*, p. 316; Vachell, *On the Pacific Slope*, p. 51; Muirhead, *America, the Land of Contrasts*, p. 48.

perior to American men in every way. Better, they surpass all females ever created in God's universe. Rudyard Kipling compared them to English and French maidens and announced that "the girls of America are above and beyond them all. They are clever; they can talk. Yea, it is said that they think. Certainly they have an appearance of so doing. They are original, and look you between the brows with unabashed eyes as a sister might look at her brother."[31]

Matthew Arnold, who was not given to enthusiasm or to delight with the "civilization" of the United States, found an exception, and almost mustered a smile when he thought on the ladies. He conceded that

> . . . there is a charm in American women—a charm which you find in almost all of them, wherever you go. It is the charm of a natural manner, a manner not self-conscious, artificial, and constrained. It may not be a beautiful manner always, but it is almost always a natural manner, a free and happy manner; and this gives pleasure. Here we have, undoubtedly, a note of civilization, and an evidence, at the same time, of the good effect of equality upon social life and manners.[32]

Muirhead differed in personality from the brash, young Kipling as much as he did from the erudite old Arnold. Yet he couched his compliments in precisely the same terms as they did, and as did many others. He noted how "what chiefly strikes the stranger in the American woman is her candour, her frankness, her hail-fellow-well-metedness, her apparent absence of consciousness of self or of sex, her spontaneity, her vivacity, her fearlessness." Perhaps Frank Dilnot dramatized the British man–American woman encounter most memorably when he exposed the way in which he and his colleagues weakened when an American girl sauntered by. "It must be very hard," he murmured, "for a bachelor from the other side, whatever prejudices and affections he brings across, to keep from trying to marry an American girl." C. V. R. Thompson, a British Prince Charming who actually did marry an American girl, was in an interesting position to evaluate the relations between American husbands and their spouses. His comments closely paralleled those of his compatriots: "I adored the American woman. But the men—!" He need not have gone on, but Thompson felt he should explain this expostulation. "It would be difficult indeed," he pointed out, "for a nation to produce a breed of men able to maintain the supposed superiority of his sex among such women, and so in my eyes the American suffered by contrast. Most of them bored me. They were bores because they were naturally bores or because they worked so hard to prove they were not bores."[33]

[31] Kipling, *American Notes*, p. 55.
[32] M. Arnold, *Civilization in the United States*, p. 168.
[33] Muirhead, *America, the Land of Contrasts*, p. 50; Frank Dilnot, *The New America*, p. 37; C. V. R. Thompson, *I Lost My English Accent*, pp. 65, 67.

The American male simply could not keep up with his vivacious, intelligent wife. "It is certain," remarked the unkind Woodruff, "that in America the women are more alive than the men." Muirhead insisted that the wife is "conspicuously superior to her husband in looks, manners, and general intelligence. This has been denied by champions of the American man; but the observation of the writer, whatever it may be worth, would deny the denial." It probably took a woman to put it most abruptly. Mrs. Tweedie, in comparing the two sexes, simply said that the women "have all the innings."[34]

But it took a British male with sufficient gall to come up with the inexorable conclusion. If the American maidens outshone their male counterparts and even surpassed English women; and if British men were superior to the Yankee males (as few British travelers would deny), it followed that American women should wed British men. James Hannay, who usually wrote tongue-in-cheek, was deadly serious when he set forth this formula, which many twentieth-century male British visitors seemed to believe: "The truth appears to be that American women, apart from any question of their dowries, are attractive both to English and American men. English men, on the other hand, are attractive both to English and American women." Tactfully, Hannay did not bother to spin out the rest of his logic. Because of her superior endowments, it was only right that the American woman dominate the husband-wife relationship, and this the British said she certainly did. There is evidence of this domestic domination over a century ago, such as Mackay's comment that "in America, the ladies exercise an undisputed sway over the domestic hearth." But there the reason was different from those advanced by later travelers. It was because the rest of life was closed to the women that their domain was clearly defined as being the home, and only the home. "Home is their sphere, and to them all the arrangements of the home are exclusively left. . . . Wives in America know their place."[35]

Even so, Burn wrote in 1865, in the homes of the married "it is a common thing for the man to do a considerable part of the slip-slop work. In the morning he lights the stove fire, empties the slops, makes ready his own breakfast, and if his work lies at a distance he packs up his midday meal, and leaving his wife in bed, he packs himself off to his work." C. R. Enock, in a one-paragraph survey of the history of womankind brought the epic to an end in the American home: "Woman, in the United States, seems to be in the midst of a reaction in the history of her

[34] Woodruff, *Plato's American Republic*, p. 14; Muirhead, *America, the Land of Contrasts*, p. 49; Tweedie, *America As I Saw It*, p. 60.
[35] Hannay, *From Dublin to Chicago*, p. 232; A. Mackay, *The Western World*, I, 129.

sex. Woman has been veiled and shut up in harems and zenanas for nearly the whole of known time, but now, in America, the reaction has come, and the pendulum has swung almost to the other extreme; and she occupies first place in the American home." "In America," said Bryce, "the husband's duty and desire is to gratify the wife and render to her those services which the English tyrant exacts from his consort." "Next in power after madame in an American household," wrote Hector Mac-Quarrie, "is the offspring in the house." "There should be a little more equality of the sexes in America," the British husband of an American girl wryly joked. "I mean the men should have a little more to say."[36] "America," declared Emily Faithfull, "is a paradise for married women."[37]

This extravagant celebration of American women, when compared to comments by the British on other subjects, seems wildly overdone. Few contemporary social scientists or laymen would fully credit the British suggestions that women were fully emancipated, that they were so remarkably brilliant, or that they were so completely dominant in American life. There are several reasons for discounting British enthusiasm and for being wary of fully accepting their observations. In the first place, the standard of comparison to which the visitors referred in writing of American women was, naturally, the women of Great Britain. The authors' treatment of the former may have been as much a comment on the limitations of women in British society as upon the full emancipation of women in American society. It must be remembered that the Victorian idealization of the helpless, homebound female lasted longer and with more intensity in England than in the United States. One should read "emancipation and equality" as "emancipation and equality *relative to conditions in England.*" Second, the type of woman with whom the Englishman came into contact in the New World was undoubtedly not so representative of the total population as the men he encountered. The tourist could pick up a conversation with almost any male in the hotel lobby, on the railway carriage, or on the street; he could not do so as easily with the women without getting arrested. The evidence seems clear that much British evaluation of American woman was derived from his *tête-à-têtes* with the most charming, the best edu-

[36] [Burn,] *The Working Classes in the United States,* p. 77; C. Reginald Enock, *Farthest West: Life and Travel in the United States,* p. 154; Bryce, *The American Commonwealth,* III, 516; MacQuarrie, *Over Here,* p. 43; Thompson, *I Lost My English Accent,* p. 119.

[37] Faithfull, *Three Visits to America,* p. 322. One of the costs of growing equality for the woman was that she now had to fight for her carriage seat, and could no longer travel unescorted across the nation and expect the queenly treatment that marked the old chivalric days (*ibid.,* p. 319).

cated, and the wealthiest of them in their drawing rooms and dining rooms as invited guests to the most glittering affairs. Finally, one must remember that a lovely woman can warm the heart of the most demanding social critic. Many of the "analyses" that dotted these books resembled love poetry, composed under a spell of infatuation. It was love not only because of that infatuation, but because the observers *wanted* women to set the tone in the United States. Few of them had ever felt comfortable in the rough and tumble world of business, of frontier expansion, of social equality; they understood and they liked the world inhabited by women—the world of the parlor, the good conversation, the mellow glass of wine. The ladies they most often encountered cultivated these graces; they made the Englishman feel at home. They made him feel that "civilization" had finally come to the United States, that the raw, youthful land was maturing. The Englishman, charmed by the American woman, was bound to believe that the United States, under her influence, was becoming more like Great Britain every day, and this made it possible for him to return to British shores not displeased by the United States despite the many criticisms he had showered upon other aspects of American civilization.

Feminine graces touched the rest of society, affected the children, and even reached the men. As Bryce explained:

> If women have on the whole gained, it is clear that the nation gains through them. As mothers they mould the character of their children; while the function of forming the habits of society and determining its moral tone rest greatly in their hands. But there is reason to think that the influence of the American system tells directly for good upon men as well as upon the whole community. Men gain in being brought to treat women as equals rather than as graceful playthings or useful drudges. The respect for women which every man either feels or is obliged by public sentiment to profess, has a wholesome effect on his conduct and character. . . .[38]

Some of the commentators had harsh things to say about the women. Not a few of them declared that the sex had never produced more ambitious charlatans than those in America. Others were indignant at the manner in which the females employed their wiles in order to have their unsuspecting spouses satisfy their every whim; moreover these whims, they felt, were hideously excessive. W. L. George contended that the consequences of this process went beyond arrogance, shrewishness, hardness, aggressiveness—the characteristics of the so-called masculine female. He worried that the American woman, by her very success, al-

---

[38] Bryce, *The American Commonwealth*, III, 523–24.

ready "may have lost part of her capacity for giving." The woman who cannot love, George regretted to say, is an unfortunate creature. William Woodley insisted that "they are as cold as the ice water they drink. She can live without being loved or loving."[39]

George also cautioned that the women have succeeded only superficially; they had achieved illusory supremacy, but not real equality. In their behalf George advised them to fight and not to be deluded by flattery, for "it would be foolish to believe that woman's battle has been completely won in the United States. She still has a great deal to do to achieve equality; she had better realize this, and struggle for it, than be led away by sentimental eulogies of her achievements, and more or less dishonest proclamations of her supremacy."[40]

The new woman was greatly admired by the British; she was charming, intelligent, and attractive. But, giving expression to a typical male duality on this subject, the authors were not convinced either that she was a very good wife or that she was very happy in her equality. In both these respects equality seemed to have led to consequences more mixed than with other social groups, in no small part because women were more fundamentally different from men than, say, were the rich and poor children whom society united the classrooms. J. B. Priestley, in 1936, believed that his colleagues who assumed that American women were happy were mistaken. If one saw behind superficial appearances one would perceive the tremendous pressures placed on her as she strove for equal treatment in a culture which deposited real power with the men. He asked the women:

> Why be so aggressively feminine day and night? Why not relax, let up? A few wrinkles, a washed pale cheek, a mouth without lipstick, comfortable old clothes—in short, an appearance "like nothing on earth"—how welcome a sight that would be, especially over the orange juice in the early morning, at least to one traveling Englishman, perhaps homesick for his native frumpiness. . . . The vitality, courage, and enterprise of American women are famous, needing no words from me. But how they must have to draw on these qualities! It is a bad business being a woman in most places, but in the United States it must be hell. No relaxation. No letting up for a second. Never relieved from the frontline trenches. Never dropping out of the race till Death rings the bell. . . . [The ordinary American woman] is an unusually competitive being. She has only been freed from most of the drudgery of the European woman in order to lead a still more strenuous life. She has to compete all the time.[41]

[39] George, *Hail Columbia!* p. 150; William Woodley, *The Impressions of an Englishman in America*, p. 43.
[40] George, *Hail Columbia!* p. 128.
[41] Priestley, *Midnight on the Desert*, pp. 56–58.

THE DOUBLE STANDARD FOR AMERICAN WOMEN

The dilemmas that lie at the base of Priestley's compassionate remarks have become quite familiar to modern authorities on the American woman. How reminiscent they are of Herbert Spencer's observations on the overworked, overcompetitive male made in 1882. They also recall the thought that the behavior of the precocious child may also have been a symptom of this same overcompetition—all of which may have been brought on in part by the absence of status assigned the members of the egalitarian society. This in turn gave birth to the intense need to establish, with extraordinary zeal, one's "place." The egalitarian ideal has compelled the males to let females compete with them on nearly equal terms in many phases of life. But the males distrust the woman who does too well—and, curiously enough, so do the women. The egalitarian ideal has not quite penetrated either the British or American traditions (or the actuality) of sexual differentiation and the many social roles that go along with that differentiation. As David Potter writes: "Sexual fulfillment seems to depend upon one set of psychological attitudes—attitudes of submissiveness and passivity—while the fulfillment of equality seems to depend upon an opposite set—attitudes of competitiveness and self-assertion."[42]

Because the equality sought by women differed from that of other groups seeking emancipation, we may have an insight into the fact that, despite the pessimistic tone of much of the analytic literature on the American woman, the British travelers as a group could so loudly sing her praises. They praised not her achievements, but her personality. For them emancipation was less of an external social movement than the freeing of minds and souls long imprisoned. Perhaps in this internal emancipation we have the beginning of an explanation for Potter's positive judgment of the job being done by the American woman in the face of seemingly insurmountable odds. "In short," he states, "she is constantly holding in balance her general opportunities as a person and her distinctive needs as a woman, and when we consider how badly these two go together in principle can we not say that she is maintaining the operative equilibrium between them with a remarkable degree of skill and success?"[43]

[42] Potter, "American Women," p. 15.
[43] Potter, "American Women," 22.

THE SCHOOLROOM AND THE DRAWING-ROOM

From these remarks it should be evident that the British commentators depicted the movement for female equality quite differently than they did other apparently parallel reforms such as the common school movement. The movements belonged to different centuries; their motivating spirits were dissimilar. A comparison of the two images to which the travelers frequently returned to epitomize nineteenth- and twentieth-century America—the child in the classroom and the new woman, respectively—yields interesting results. The school child stood for future promise, for the transformation and growth of human personality regardless of class background. He stood for hope, for social progress, for youth. The school system itself embodied a great social dream: the forging of an entire republic of enlightened, intelligent, respectable, useful citizens—citizens who would rule. In this image were united the twin faiths that the travelers placed at the heart of nineteenth-century American belief—progress and equality.

The woman, on the other hand, was freed for her own sake more than for society's. The British did not see her running too many corporations, settling too many new lands, leading too many diplomatic missions. She did not enter the professions, don clerical robes, teach at the universities, or run for political office in great numbers. The new woman had new opportunities, but her chief responsibility was still to the home, which she ran like a wizard. She could receive a thorough education, but she was expected to use it to be an interesting person and a good mother rather than a successful tax lawyer. She could drink whiskey, take a more active part in sexual relations, and tell off-color jokes, but her men wanted her to be a considerate, attractive, feminine, and affectionate wife.

As Potter remarked, "Women have never renounced the roles of wife and mother," preferring "to reconcile a new condition with an old one." They did not want to obliterate the old one which brought such reverence. Their movement was less an affirmation of the nation's faith in progress than an expression of the women's desire for personal fulfillment. The rise of women in America struck the Britons as a major revolution, but one with very conservative, very practical, short-run (as opposed to millennial) goals in mind, and one that has produced highly ambiguous results. Low wrote:

> No one who really knows America well would contend that the American woman competes with her husband for supremacy or endeavours to become his rival. She is quite content to acknowledge him as the head of the house and to respect him accordingly. . . . She interests herself

in his affairs, whether they be the affairs of the countinghouse or the forum, but she seldom advises him. And her peculiarly dependent and subordinate position is in no way better illustrated than in her abstention from any active interests in politics. One would naturally suppose that in America of all countries women would play an active part in politics and wield great influence, but the "political woman" is quite unknown. . . . For the American has no love for the strong-minded masculine woman. He likes her to be healthy and to golf or fish if he goes in for those forms of recreation; but he wants her always to be a woman, to have the peculiarly feminine touch; to wear a dash of his favourite colour at her throat or waist, even if she is sitting in a boat all day drawing fish out of the water and no one sees her except himself.[44]

Low underemphasized the egalitarian aspirations of the women just as some critics passed over the purely feminine side of the precarious balance which American women sought and still seek to maintain. But he expressed nicely the idea that the rise of the American women meant, for most of the travelers, in a way which later chapters will elaborate upon, that the United States had actually begun to disavow the extreme, unqualified, egalitarian idealism which many Britons could respect, but with which few of them could feel comfortable.[45]

The elevation of the woman in the New World meant that America, through its women, was achieving in some measure that grace, restraint, beauty, and culture that so many Englishmen valued highly in judging civilizations. The Old World traveler had never intimately participated in the nineteenth-century American dream. But now the United States, in the first thirty-five years of the twentieth century, was becoming for him, despite its many grievous, masculine faults, a land he could enjoy, a land in which, for the first time really, he could almost begin to feel at home.

[44] Low, *America at Home,* pp. 82–83.

[45] In the same vein I suspect that most British male travelers to America after 1965 have been as uncomfortable as are most American men with the definitely egalitarian thrust of the current movement for the liberation of women. But that "new" thrust would seem simply to be a delayed attempt to fulfill the promises made and often extended to American white males and their children during the nineteenth century.

VIII   The State

THE BRITISH VISITORS may have regarded the manner in which the Americans conducted their government as comic, colorful, confusing, disgraceful, or fascinating; but they did not regard it as especially significant. American politics, to them, resembled some rough-house but harmless game played for thrills, but not for serious stakes. American "democracy" may have been fraught with meaning; American government had little to do with it, however. Bryce's distinction between the two, though made more consciously by him than by others, still cropped up in similar form in the works of most of the travelers, seen usually as the difference between theory and practice.[1]

Max Berger's composite portrait of the comportment of the House of Representatives as witnessed by the ante-bellum commentators sets the proper tone for the general British view of American government in action.

> Upon entering the House gallery, the visitor's first impression was that he had inadvertently stepped into a madhouse. Precariously treading away through the maze of spittoons and expectorations, a variety of odors and noises assailed him as he took a seat. . . . The scene that greeted his eye was both comic and disillusioning. Below him sat the Representatives of the Sovereign People. Some slept; others whittled; a few, chairs tilted backward and feet on desks, stared intently at the ceiling. On one side, a number were busily engaged in throwing spitballs. Elsewhere, groups of men were holding informal meetings. Above it all, could be heard reports like pistol shots, made by slapping the desk with a paper to attract the attention of a page-boy. Despite everything, however, the speaker droned futilely on, as oblivious to his surroundings as his fellow-members appeared to be of him. Regardless of whatever else he was doing, every male in the place busily chewed his tobacco plug, and spat vast streams of saliva in every direction.[2]

[1] *The American Commonwealth*, III, 629, 630.
[2] Berger, *The British Traveller in America, 1836–1860*, p. 92.

The Senate conducted itself with a bit more dignity, and conditions in the House improved with time; but the over-all view of American political life as a carnival never entirely vanished. Englishmen wrote extensively not only about Congressional decorum, but about the machinations of the parties, the noise of the nominating conventions, the low level of political debate, the scandals of the bosses, and especially the madness of the election campaigns—always with a mixture of delight and derision. "Politics in America?" asked one American citizen, as Kipling tells it. "There aren't any. The whole question of the day is spoils. That's all. We fight our souls out over tram-contracts, gas-contracts, road-contracts, and any darned thing that will turn a dishonest dollar, and we call that politics. . . . If I had money enough, I could buy the Senate of the United States, the Eagle, and the Star-Spangled Banner complete."[3]

Occasionally the Briton rose to indignation at the tawdry, demeaning behavior of the politicians. Occasionally he saw something to commend in this informal attitude toward politics. Countless visitors, for example, either alone or in a large group, were able to obtain an interview with the President of the United States himself, and the easy access to the highest office in the land invariably impressed the commentators. Laughter, however, sarcastic or friendly, most commonly greeted American politics because few felt, except in times of crisis, that it made much difference who won the debates, the nominations, or the elections. The hoopla, accusations, tantrums, violence, and sound and fury of political debate truly signified little; on the important matters that occasionally arose, the two parties were said to have thought (if the word could be used) alike. Henry Nevinson was nostalgic about it in his valedictory to America: "Good-bye to politicians contending for aims more practical than principles! Good-bye to Republicans and Democrats, distinguishable only by mutual hatred!" "The essence of the American party conflict," Harold Laski contended, "has been an absence of any real distinction between the rival claimants for power."[4]

If few outside observers considered themselves taken in by all the noise, it might be remarked that some, like Matthew Arnold, insisted that the Americans were no more hoodwinked than the English. They, too, knew it was all a boy's game and simply liked to play along. Arnold disparaged all the charges of corruption and scandal that Americans hurled at each other by pointing out that "the practice so common in America, of calling a politician 'a thief' does not mean so very much." Others disposed of the tumult by indicating that the best men shunned

[3] Kipling, *American Notes,* pp. 16–17.
[4] Henry W. Nevinson, *Farewell to America,* p. 11; Harold J. Laski, *Democracy in Crisis,* p. 44.

politics in the United States; the true test of one's competence could be found in the business or scientific or professional world, but certainly not the world of politics where incompetence was so pervasive. "The great men of the United States," said J. A. Spender, "are the big businessmen, not the politicians. . . . Far too little of the brains and character of the country is going into its public affairs."[5]

It was clear in the 1880's that the "best men" shunned the contamination of politics. "Political life in America is at a low ebb," declared Miss Faithfull in 1884, "owing to the disinclination of the best section of society to have anything to do with it. 'You can't touch politics here and remain uncorrupted' has been frequently said to me by those who are content to stand passively by, while a crowd of wire-pullers and professional politicians fight for place and spoil." At the same time, Edward Freeman noted that "the divorce between politics and the higher culture, strikes one very strongly. . . . The questions which come more immediately before him, the politics of the State or the city, may well have a side which is repulsive to the cultivated man; and the result may be that federal politics themselves fall too largely into the hands of a class of professional 'politicians.' "[6]

Although this was the heyday of the machine politician, criticism of their ilk continued fairly steadily in succeeding years. The men who staked out political careers were, according to Douglas Woodruff, "the less successful and able of the community." C. H. Bretherton believed that if the contemporaries of Jefferson, Madison, and Washington had had all the conveniences of modern life, "they too would have left the comparatively tedious business of politics to the professional politicians, the men who play the game of politics for what there is in it."[7]

Bryce was one of a small contingent who managed to understand the American practice of government and to see it in some sort of perspective. First he assembled a list in a chapter entitled "The Supposed Faults of Democracy," including the following:

> Weakness in emergencies, incapacity to act with promptitude and decision.
>
> Fickleness and instability, frequent changes of opinion, consequent changes in the conduct of affairs and in executive officials.
>
> Insubordination, internal dissensions, disregard of authority, a frequent resort to violence, bringing on an anarchy which ends in military tyranny.

[5] M. Arnold, *Civilization in the United States,* p. 119; John Alfred Spender, *Through English Eyes,* pp. 312–13.

[6] Faithfull, *Three Visits to America,* p. 9; Freeman, *Impressions of the United States,* p. 202.

[7] Woodruff, *Plato's American Republic,* p. 22; Bretherton, *Midas,* p. 36.

A desire to level down, and intolerance of greatness.

Tyranny of the majority over the minority.

A love of novelty: a passion for changing customs and destroying old institutions.

Ignorance and folly, producing a liability to be deceived and misled; consequent growth of demagogues playing on the passions and selfishness of the masses.[8]

Bryce decided "that the defects commonly attributed to democratic government are not specifically characteristic of the United States." Instead, in his next chapter, modestly called "The True Faults of American Democracy," Bryce stressed four factors that he found more relevant to the peculiar case of the United States. "Firstly, a certain commonness of mind and tone, a want of dignity and elevation in and about the conduct of public affairs, an insensibility to the nobler aspects and finer responsibilities of national life." Second, withdrawal from the political arena of the best people. Third, a lack of administrative knowledge, experience, and professional judgment. And, "fourthly, laxity in the management of public business."[9]

Bryce came equipped with the necessary knowledge, and experience, and skill to undertake the kind of study that the typical Briton, in his three-month race across the continent and back, could not even contemplate doing.[10] The average tourist could do two things: tell colorful political anecdotes or pontificate in the most abstract terms. These abstractions should not be dismissed, for they sketch the very broad political outlines that the expert may miss in his fuller knowledge. Why, for example, did the visitors laugh at the presidential nominating conventions and elections? Why did they think politics in the United States a sordid and funny game? How did they think it got that way? What made American democracy different from English democracy? Did they take anything about it seriously? What did they mean by American "democracy?"

---

[8] Bryce, *The American Commonwealth*, III, 305.

[9] *Ibid.*, pp. 323, 326–27.

[10] *The American Commonwealth* is, of course, the classic study of American political institutions—either by an outsider or a native. Bryce not only dealt fully with national government, but he pioneered in the study of local and state governments. The only other British travel work that adds appreciably to our knowledge of these lower levels of government can be found in Gaillard Lapsley, ed., *The America of Today* (Cambridge: Cambridge University Press, 1919). This book of essays contains one by Eustace Percey, a former Secretary at the British embassy in Washington, called "State and Municipal Government." Percey contended that the state governments would be more likely to spawn reform than any other arm of the American government.

IN THEORY: GOVERNMENT BY THE PEOPLE

To all these questions the answer was the same: universal suffrage. With an odd myopia, the British centered their attention on this innovation as the cornerstone of the American political system, as that which separated the "democracies" of England and the United States. Bryce discerned that a broad, positive principle lay behind universal suffrage, put simply, that the government of the United States was no less than "the direct government of the multitude." "The American Republic," said Alexander Mackay earlier, "differs essentially from all that have preceded it [in being] a Democratic Republic, in the broadest sense of the term. If it is not a monarchy, neither is it an oligarchy. It is the people in reality that rule."[11]

Here again the point might be made that democracy could mean a government *for* the people by an enlightened leadership—this meaning approximating the democracy with which the Victorian Englishman operated. The idea of rule actually *by* the people was fairly new in history, as attested to by Ortega y Gasset in *The Revolt of the Masses*. Nor was Ortega alone with British Tories in his discomfort with the ascendancy of "mass man." Two thousand years before, Aristotle defined democracy as "the rule of the Many for the good of the poor," a rule which does not serve "the interest of the community at large," a form of government which he characterized as a perversion of the more beneficial and oligarchical form of polity.

For many Englishmen, rule by the people meant quite simply rule *not by the best people,* nor even by the most qualified or experienced people. Since anyone could run for office, and since theoretically everyone elected anyone, standards of dignity would necessarily suffer and the lack of elevation in American political discourse was thus easily accounted for. "No one but a mule in stupid obstinate perversity . . . can help noticing," sputtered Sir Rose Lambart Price with no little asperity, "that men of the highest social and hereditary rank are conspicuous by their absence from the legislative councils of their country." The bogey was universal suffrage and it was around this device that friends or foes of American government rallied. Either it represented the essence of democracy in its most exalted guise, or it was, above all, the cause of the corruption, ignorance, decay, and sickness rampant in American society. Price expressed this latter point of view quite typically, when after his exposé of the scandals, bosses, and rings degrading American life, and

[11] Bryce, *The American Commonwealth,* III, 326; A. Mackay, *The Western World,* II, 291,

just before his outcry at the absence of dukes and barons from the United States Senate, he concluded: "Universal suffrage, unaccompanied by either an educational or property qualification, is the fundamental root of all these evils; and to universal suffrage all the existing ills, in all existing republics, distinctly can be traced."[12]

No one underestimated the consequences of universal suffrage; it was the symbol of American political ideas and practices. Its connections with the principle of equality are direct. The travelers tended to take the political exclusion of the Negro for granted. In fact, it is incredible to realize the extent to which the visitors, except in isolated instances, managed to ignore the plight of the American Negro. They were disturbed, however, at the low rate of actual voting among eligible whites. Their primary explanation for this apathy was that politics simply did not matter very much in American life. John Macgregor, in 1859, manufactured a conversation between "B" (the Briton) and "A" (the American) which managed to bring together many of the arguments against universal suffrage, arguments that happened to be just as usable against equality. "B" wanted his countrymen to adopt the universal ballot, but "A" had been burned by experience.

> B. I think the Ballot and universal suffrage would give us upright legislators, who would not waste our money.
> A. Just the reverse. Our men try to please the most voters; most voters pay the least taxes individually, so the more the members spend, the more money flows *to* the poorest and *from* the more industrious! . . .
> B. But we must get really good men into Parliament, and they will not do thus badly. They will represent the wishes of the community.
> A. I hope ours *don't*. If they do, the wishes of the community must be mighty bad! Why, our general run of members are the laughing-stock of all sober-minded people. You know the old story, I dare say. 'Tis far too true to be forgotten because it is old:—
> "Poor Johnson! You know what became of Johnson. Ah! poor fellow, he went down hill sadly, till, from bad to worse, he got at last so low he was elected a member of Congress."
> Our elections are abjured by the good men; and they are managed by a set of regular paid partisans, who make it their daily business. The proved corruption and bribery in every department of the state exceeds what you can even imagine. . . .
> B. All these objections are American frailties incident to a new people, which we in England might overcome?
> A. Yes; but the ballot tolerates them all: nay, it produces them; and it steadily sanctions every one. Did you ever hear of a man being elected by ballot and universal suffrage, to protest against these flagrant wrongs?

[12] Price, *The Two Americas,* pp. 344–45. The city "bosses," especially the Irish ones, received very harsh treatment at the hands of the travelers. One of the few analysts who attempted to explain their function was Harold Laski, *The American Democracy,* pp. 59–60, 158–60.

B. We could soon get them elected, if we paid our members as you do.

A. Men who can't make money enough to live on by their own business, ought not to be paid, as members, to manage the business of the public.[13]

The bonds between universal suffrage and the American faith in the future are less direct, but also fairly conspicuous. The success of universal suffrage, as Mackay previously indicated, was "intimately identified with the enlightenment of the public mind—in other words with the great cause of popular education; it is to the promotion of education that it will in future chiefly owe its success."[14] Hence, according to the Britons, Americans never assumed that their political life had reached a state of perfection. But it would do so year by year as the effects of universal schooling, whose chief function was to create good *citizens,* reached the minds of the universal voters. Americans looked beyond contemporary political imperfections into a future in which the enlightenment fashioned by education would eradicate the evils by making all-powerful public opinion an informed opinion.[15] When Sir Charles Lyell, for example, presented to Americans his objections on the way they ran their governments, he was told by Americans that "every political system has its inherent vices and defects, that the evil will soon be mitigated by the removal of ignorance and the improved education of the many."[16] Thus were equality and universal suffrage, education and the future wrapped up together in the same American-made satchel.

THE POWERLESS GOVERNMENT

The Britons made two criticisms of American government which overshadowed all others; but they were not obvious ones. One might have expected the seasoned Englishman to recoil at the passage of political power into the hands of the unruly mob. Instead of recoiling, he admon-

[13] John Macgregor, *Our Brothers and Cousins: A Summer Tour in Canada and the States,* pp. 145–48.

[14] A. Mackay, *The Western World,* II, 291.

[15] Bryce made the political dominion of public opinion the central theme of his monumental volumes. Public opinion, he said, "stands above the parties, being cooler and larger minded than they are; it awes party leaders and holds in check party organizations. No one openly ventures to resist it. It determines the direction and character of national policy. It is the product of a greater number of minds than in any other country, and it is more indisputably sovereign. It is the central point of the whole American polity. To describe it, that is, to sketch the leading political ideas and habits and tendencies of the American people, and show how they express themselves in action, is the most difficult and also the most vital part of my task" (*The American Commonwealth,* I, 8).

[16] Lyell, *A Second Visit,* I, 101.

ished. He chided Americans for: (1) erecting a weak and ineffective government; and (2) supporting a government less democratic than that of Great Britain. The government, especially from the Grant era on, was generally regarded as the only American institution whose practices were *not* to the "left" of the comparable British institutions.

It was argued by some that the American government thrived on studiously avoiding the major problems of the nineteenth century. The one it did confront—slavery—did not add sheen to the government's already tarnished reputation. Early twentieth-century commentators reported a greater effort by Americans to have their political leaders face up to critical issues and to stop pretending that democracy meant the absence of governmental power. By the end of the 1920's, however, not much had changed. Harold Laski characterized the American state as a non-state, and certainly not the source of America's strength. "Until quite recently," he said, "the state, in its European substance, has hardly been necessary in American life: with the result that popular interest has never been deeply concentrated upon its processes." Writing during the early depression days of 1931, Laski greatly lamented this condition. "Now, when a state is necessary, the American people lacks that sense of its urgency which can galvanize it into rapid and effective action. It has been so long tutored to believe that individual initiative is alone healthy that it has no appreciation of the plane which must be reached in order to make individual initiative significant." He went on to note with a wry warning in his words that "only once before—in the Civil War—have its political institutions been tested in a crisis." Then he specified some of the reasons for the ineffectuality of American government:

> The defects of the American political scheme are, to the outsider, little less than startling. The Congressional system seems based upon principles so checked and balanced against one another that they paralyse the power to act. The states are historical entities; but industrial development has largely deprived them of effective reality as governmental units. City government, for nearly a century, has been a dismal failure; cities like Chicago, Philadelphia, New York, resemble, in their internal governance, rather the British municipal position before 1835 than the possibilities of modern administrative technique. The public business, save in periodic movements for reform, has been no one's business in an orderly and coherent way.

Looking at affairs in 1931 he concluded: "There is in America a wider disillusionment with democracy, a greater scepticism about popular institutions, than at any period in its history."[17]

[17] Laski, *Democracy in Crisis,* pp. 45–47.

This notion of the weakness, of the abdication of responsibility in American politics, is found in British travel literature long before 1931.[18] Charles Mackay in 1858 blamed universal suffrage for the timidity of the Presidents, the hopeless diffusion of power, and the refusal of politicians to exert power positively. "Universal suffrage," he was quite sure, "is not only the substratum on which the whole political edifice rests, but the supreme arbiter in all cases." "Universal suffrage," he afterward contended, "extending not only to the choice of the chief magistrate, but to the whole course of his policy, and to the whole personnel of his appointments, leads inevitably—as in America—to a weak government."[19]

Different commentators at different times were convinced that America would begin to activate its government. Peto, writing just as the Civil War ended, was sure that with the issue of slavery removed, the nation "will henceforward be consolidated." The result of the conflict "relieves the nation of its one great difficulty. Apart from bloodshed, it was worth any sacrifice to America, to be rid of slavery. Whilst that system existed, it was impossible that the nation could have a settled, firm, or united administration. No public legislation could be attempted which in a greater or less degree was not affected by that absorbing question." Harold Spender, writing immediately after the close of the First World War, thought that it too would spur responsible political action because "the war has not weakened, but has increased her sense of nationality. It has stimulated her pride."[20]

But Bryce knew better years earlier. The state was a subsidiary institution in American culture, and one would wait in vain for it to set the pace of life in the New World. One must recognize, he explained,

> . . . the comparatively limited conception of the State itself which Americans have formed. The State is not to them, as to Germans or Frenchmen, and even to some English thinkers, an ideal moral power, charged with the duty of forming the characters and guiding the lives of its subjects. It is more like a commercial company, or perhaps a huge

[18] Perhaps this is a remnant from the Lockean prescription for limited government. The political apathy of the ordinary American voter and his lack of responsibility and knowledgeability as to the workings of his own government were deplored by the great majority of the Britons. They were sure that ignorance and indifference in a political system in which the people are supposed to rule was a recipe for catastrophe. Sir Philip Burne-Jones was one of a small handful who applauded this apathy. "The absence of political conversation in general society," he decided, "was a great relief after what one has to suffer in that respect in England. . . . Politicians in America are relegated to their proper place in the general economy of things, and do not loom disproportionately out of the picture" (*Dollars and Democracy*, pp. 170–71).

[19] Charles Mackay, *Life and Liberty in America*, pp. 300–1, 308.

[20] Peto, *Resources and Prospects*, pp. 408–9; H. Spender, *A Briton in America*, p. 23.

municipality created for the management of certain business . . . but for the most part leaving the shareholders or burgesses to themselves.[21]

With just a touch of irony, it became fashionable for the British writers to label the American government "conservative." Alexander Francis did not exaggerate when he announced in 1909: "Conservatism has been declared, by all competent observers, to be a characteristic of the American democracy." The eminent historian A. F. Pollard, in a series of published lectures delivered in 1924, thought he had perceived the reason. A fundamental cause for American political conservatism "is to be found in the boundless opportunities for self-expression which the American people found in other fields than politics. Conservatism dominated there because inventive energy, ambition, discontent, and sometimes first class brains, became engrossed in business and in pioneering, and left politics to a vicarious and professional class."[22] A Commonwealth Fund Fellow, writing just before the 1929 Depression, made this same point by comparing the United States of his day with eighteenth-century America. "In both cases an experiment was being carried out, which was watched with the greatest concern by Europe, and especially by England. But whereas in the eighteenth century it was political in the broadest sense, today it is purely economic and politically America is of no more interest to Europe than she appears to be to her own people."[23]

The roots of this strange aversion to a strong and positive government run deep into the American experience and can be grasped from several different angles. Bernard Bailyn, for example, tells of the seizure in 1776 of the College of Philadelphia, the confiscation of its private charter, and its conversion into a new state institution by the Pennsylvania legislature. The legislature also seized the charter of the Bank of

[21] Bryce, *The American Commonwealth,* III, 472. Bryce charged that Tocqueville overemphasized the importance of American political democracy because the Frenchman was really writing a philosophical treatise on democracy "whose conclusions are illustrated from America, but are in large measure founded, not so much on an analysis of American phenomena, as on general views of democracy which the circumstances of France had suggested. Democratic government seems to me, with all deference to his high authority, a cause not so potent in the moral and social sphere as he deemed it" (*ibid.,* I, 5).

[22] Francis, *Americans: An Impression,* p. 232; A. F. Pollard, *Factors in American History,* p. 57. Pollard continued: "Instead of lining the barricades, the dissatisfied American took to clearing forests; a people has little temptation to revolt where it can get land, the common basis for all conservatism, almost for the asking" (*ibid*).

[23] Recorded in Edward Bliss Reed, ed., *The Commonwealth Fund Fellows and Their Impressions of America,* p. 93. Since its inception in 1925 the Commonwealth Fund has asked the British scholars who were awarded two-year grants at American graduate schools to compose reports on their impressions of the New World. Their comments usually run on a higher level than the average book of travel. See also S. Gorley Putt, ed., *Cousins and Strangers: Comments on America by Commonwealth Fund Fellows from Britain, 1946–52.*

North America. "Both seizures had been made in the name of the People and as part of an effort to eliminate enclaves of special, state-protected privilege." Bailyn used this case to raise fundamental questions illustrating the difficulty the state faced of ever acquiring great strength or becoming the dominant institution in American life. The seizures had been made in the name of the people:

> But who were the People? A handful of legislators? Not bankers, not educators whose enterprise would advance the general good? To eliminate all privilege from private groups was, it would seem, tantamount to giving it all to the State. But what was the State in a republican government? Should it have powers against the people themselves? Was not the answer the multiplication rather than the elimination of privilege?

These queries could be relevant only in an egalitarian as opposed to an authoritarian society. The answer to them, Bailyn continued, came thirty years later in the Dartmouth case wherein the Supreme Court in effect restored Dartmouth's old charter and endorsed the right of initiating groups to control their creations. The state must grant these groups equal privileges with all other groups and these privileges can be held even against the state itself.[24]

If the case of state charters in the eighteenth century reveals the dilemma facing the central state in a decentralized society with power so dispersed as to make a weak government practically unavoidable, one can arrive at essentially this same point even by investigating Erik Erikson's apparently unrelated psychoanalysis of American children in the twentieth century. In tracing the career of a mythical typical American adolescent, Erikson asked, "How does his home train this boy for democracy?" This question must be asked even though "the boy has no political sense whatsoever." Erikson concluded that "this boy's family life harbors more democracy than meets the eye," but not "the democracy of the history books." What he described was the democracy of dispersed power and the avoidance of leadership by any responsible or beneficent single force. "The American family . . . tends to guard the right of the individual member—parents included—not to be dominated." The meaning of this political balance of powers in the family is "an automatic prevention of autocracy and inequality. It breeds, on the whole, undogmatic people, people ready to drive a bargain and then to compromise. It makes complete irresponsibility impossible, and it makes open hate and warfare in families rare."[25]

The analogy with the two-party system of America "is clear," and

---

[24] Bailyn, *Education in the Forming of American Society*, p. 47.
[25] Erik Erikson, *Childhood and Society* (2nd ed., New York: Norton, 1963), pp. 315–18 *passim*.

Erikson did not hesitate to make it. But while this family arrangement avoids "uncompromising absolutes" and "uncompromising ideologists," it also cancels out leadership, individualism, and it courts the dominance of "all-around acceptable banalities" both in family life and in national political life. In the final analysis, Erikson must ask of these adolescents when they grow up whether they are "as men, not strangely disinterested in the running of the nation? Are these freeborn sons not apt to be remarkably naive, overly optimistic, and morbidly self-restrained in their dealings with the men who run them?"[26]

David Potter arrived at the junction of child-rearing permissiveness and political weakness via the more familiar road of historical analysis. In his case, he connected these two phenomena with American attitudes toward marriage, all of which were manifestations of the American rejection of authority. "The rejection of authority in American life," in Potter's words, "which has made our child-rearing permissive and has weakened the quality of leadership in our politics, has also meant that the relation of husband and wife is more of a partnership and less of an autocracy in this age and in this country than at any other time or place in Western civilization."[27] Erikson has further suggested that there is not only an analogy between American family life and American politics, but that the absence of a locus of power in the former renders Americans indifferent to the exercise of power in the latter and hence leaves their political system susceptible to "bosses" and limitations on freedom. This potential threat to individual liberty was, as a consequence of the weakness of American government, the second danger which the British visitors, especially America's friends, thought to be of great importance in their critique of American democratic government. They were greatly alarmed at the power held by the "majority" in the absence of responsible leadership, and by the intolerance of the masses for unusual ideas.

THE ALL-POWERFUL PEOPLE

Charles Mackay saw also that this familiar argument concerning "the tyranny of the majority" was directly related to the notion of America's weak government when he concluded his discussion of the latter by claiming that "the great American republic is not a country where there exists as much political freedom for the individual as we enjoy in England." Sixty years later, this sort of contention was still being repeated with great regularity. G. Lowes Dickinson concluded that "there can be

[26] *Ibid.*, pp. 318, 321.
[27] David M. Potter, "American Women and the American Character," *Stetson University Bulletin*, LXII (1962), 21.

little doubt that England is now more democratic than the United States." In 1925, Douglas Woodruff went as far as to call Americans "the least free of all the peoples of the earth." The despot singled out by all these men was not the government, but "Public Opinion, or the Opinion of the Majority; and he is the offspring of Propaganda."[28]

When so many Englishmen, Liberal and Conservative, announced to the world that England was more democratic than the United States, one must recognize that they were having a bit of fun. They were turning the tables on the American Revolutionaries, gaining ironic revenge. Under- lying their wit, however, whispered the differing conceptions that the two nations held concerning what real democracy was—whether it re- volved around the American devotion to the equality of the people and their right to rule or whether the British commitment to dissent was the major requirement. One could almost feel James Hannay's shudder as he commented: "There are several subjects about which it is not wise to talk quite freely in America." One could almost feel Mrs. Humphreys' satisfaction as she declared:

> In coming to America, I had pictured a land of freedom and true citizen- ship: I had never pictured such inequalities and contradictions as con- front one on every side. Has the land which claims freedom as a na- tion's birthright, only erected the Goddess of Liberty as witness of a falsified creed? For there is no more liberty of thought or action in America than in any other country."[29]

EGALITARIAN DEMOCRACY

Sir Philip Gibbs made the best effort among more recent travelers to ex- plain how a land that claims to love freedom could be accused with such vehemence of betraying it. In doing so, he got down to fundamental is- sues. He began by spelling out the nature of the charges being hurled at the United States contemporaneous with his book (1920)—charges which he did not fully accept, but which he thought contained more than a grain of truth:

> The chief charge levelled against the intellectual tendency of the United States may be summed up in one word, "intolerance." Men like George Bernard Shaw, J. A. Hobson, and H. W. Massingham do not find in their study of the American temperament or in the American form of government the sense of liberty with which the people of the United

[28] Charles Mackay, *Life and Liberty in America,* p. 300; Dickinson, *Appear- ances,* p. 149; Woodruff, *Plato's American Republic,* p. 42.
[29] Hannay, *From Dublin to Chicago,* p. 200; Humphreys, *America—Through English Eyes,* p. 138.

States credit themselves, and with which all republican democracies are credited by the proletariat in European countries.

They seem inclined to believe, indeed, that America has less liberty in the way of free opinion and free speech than the English under their hereditary monarchy, and that the spirit of the people is harshly intolerant of minorities and nonconforming individuals, or of any idea contrary to the general popular opinion of the times. Some of these critics see in the "Statue of Liberty" in New York Harbor a figure of mockery behind which is individualism enchained by an autocratic oligarchy and trampled underfoot by the intolerance of the masses.[30]

Gibbs then specified some of the causes that inspired the outbursts of these critics, chief among which were the many arrests of dissenters from the war effort, the formation of citizens' vigilante groups, censorship of various journals in which criticism of the government appeared, and the maltreatment of various radical labor leaders and of Negroes by both the government and the howling mobs that it served. "These people," Gibbs went on with reference to the critics, "believe that American democracy has failed in the essential principle which alone justifies democracy, a toleration of minorities of opinion and of the absolute liberty of the individual within the law. They say that even in England there is greater liberty, in spite of its mediaeval structure. In Hyde Park on Sunday morning one may hear speeches which would cause broken heads and long terms of imprisonment if uttered in New York."

Gibbs did not share the bitterness and scorn of these oversimplifications, but neither did he altogether deny their verity. "To my mind a great deal of this criticism is due to a misconception of the meaning of democracy." And that misconception stemmed, of course, from the failure of these analysts to distingish between egalitarian democracy of the American stripe and libertarian democracy of the British variety. In fact, the closest analogue that this warm ally of the United States could make with America's democracy was not with England, the British Isles, or even Continental Europe, but with the new government of the U.S.S.R. Gibbs stated:

In England it was a tradition of liberal thought that democracy meant not only the right of the people to govern themselves, but the right of the individual or of any body of men to express their disagreement with the policy of the state, or with the majority opinion, or with any idea which annoyed them in any way. But, as we have seen by recent history, democracy is government by the majority of the people, and that majority will be less tolerant of dissent than autocracy itself, which can often afford to give greater liberty of expression to the minority because of its inherent strength. The Russian Soviet government, which professes to be the most democratic form of government in the world, is utterly in-

[30] Gibbs, *People of Destiny*, p. 139.

tolerant of minorities. I suppose there is less individual liberty in Russia than in any other country, because disagreement with the state opinion is looked upon as treachery to the majority rule. So in the United States, which is a real democracy, in spite of the power of capital, there is less toleration of eccentric notions than in England, especially when the majority of Americans are overwhelmed by a general impulse of enthusiasm or passion, such as happened when they went into the war. The people of the minority are then regarded as enemies of the state, traitors to their fellow-citizens, and outlaws. They are crushed accordingly by the weight of mass opinion, which is ruthless and merciless, with more authority and power than the decree of a king or the law of an aristocratic form of government.[31]

Perhaps even more perceptive than Gibbs's Tocquevillean observations were those of Alexander Mackay seventy years before, in 1849. In a few sentences he laid bare the theoretical basis upon which a critic brought up with a British sense of politics could find American democracy tyrannical and, strangely enough, powerless, just as the American could disparage British democracy in those same terms. The Briton considered the American *masses* tyrannical and the *government* powerless; the American believed that too much power resided with the British government and too little with the people. Mackay used the terms "liberty" and "power" in making his inverse comparison between the British and American Constitutions.

> At the basis of the former [the British Constitution] is power, from the spoils of which the superincumbent fabric of popular liberty has been reared; power still retaining all the franchises and prerogatives not conceded by it;—at the foundation of the latter is popular liberty, the necessities of which have called power into existence; power in this case, however, wielding no more authority than has been conceded to it. Liberty in England has been wrung from power—power in America has arisen out of liberty. In the one case, power has been fettered that freedom might expand; in the other, freedom has been restricted that power might exist. Without his charters, the Englishman would have no freedom of action—without his constitutions the American would have no restraint upon his. It is by deeds of concession that the people in England vindicate their liberty—it is by deeds of concession that power in America vindicates its authority.[32]

[31] *Ibid.*, pp. 141–43.
[32] A. Mackay, *The Western World*, I, 176. The tenuous condition of authority in America did not imply instability in the republic: "The safety of the American Republic consists in this, that in establishing it the American people were not suddenly or violently diverted from the political order of things to which they were accustomed. Let parties well consider this before they indulge in sinister predictions as to the instability of the political institutions of America. If the Americans have been successful as republicans, it is because they underwent a long probation to the principle of Republicanism" (*ibid.*, II, 292). Many modern works of American history, e.g., Louis Hartz, *The Liberal Tradition in America* (New York: Harcourt, Brace, 1955), are built on a similar thesis.

Eight years later Phillippo made ostensibly the same distinction, though with a less complete grasp of the implications than Mackay, when he commented that "the constitution of American society" was founded "not on alleged *duty,* as in England,—whence feudalism attained its strength,—but on natural *right;* the principle that now exercises a growingly perceptible influence in the destiny of nations, was the soil in which American institutions were rooted, and out of which they have so vigorously grown."[33]

The pattern of the travelers' critique of American government was clear. Not many Englishmen joined with Charles Mackay in his call for the re-establishment of an "aristocracy of rank," of "preponderating church," or of "overshadowing families . . . to compete with and rival public opinion." Few Britons noted within the American populace, as did Robert Naylor, "a strong undercurrent of feeling which plaintively and silently sighs for a monarchy. Society requires this, honesty pleads for it, and a deep-rooted longing for permanency and rest appeals for it." Nor did many repeat his quaint proclamation: "America, we are to the front of you; for we have, thank Heaven! in reality what your most enlightened people greatly long for."[34]

The majority of the British visitors affirmed the desirability of representative, parliamentary government; they had, after all, been western civilization's spokesmen for the idea for several centuries. But they thought the American approach was backward. The New World invested power in the inexperienced common masses instead of an enlightened body like the House of Commons which could serve as stewards for the people. They recruited for political leaders common, rather than uncommon, men, who pandered to the majority instead of leading it. The Americans were careless about protecting the minority rights that the British valued so highly. The only sense in which American government could be considered "more democratic" than England's was in the principle of universal suffrage. By the Third Reform Bill in 1884 the English had caught up on this point without abandonment of the parliamentary prerogatives they had built up over the centuries. For the bulk of the period covered in this study, then, the British remained singularly unimpressed by American government, in theory and especially in administration and practice; there was little new in it that they wished to imitate. While most British commentators liked the United States, three out of every four of the visitors used in this study were generally negative about the American political system, with the percentage increasing throughout this period except, for obvious reasons, during the First

[33] Phillippo, *The United States and Cuba*, p. 318.
[34] Charles Mackay, *Life and Liberty in America*, p. 300; Naylor, *Across the Atlantic*, pp. 70–71.

World War. That is why so many Englishmen were anxious at the undisputed emergence of the United States at the end of that war as the world's great power. "The United States of America," said one observer, "has a new meaning in the world, and has entered, by no desire of its own, into the great family of nations, as a rich uncle whose authority and temper muct be respected by those who desire his influence in their family quarrels, difficulties, and conditions of life."[35] They were nervous that such a politically inept people should be so powerful diplomatically.

For the first time, thought Annie Smith, the Mother Country was alarmed whenever America showed the slightest signs of coolness to her. Would power go to the heads of the American people? Gibbs thought not: "They are a middle-class empire, untainted by imperial ambitions or ancient traditions of overlordship." C. R. Enock carefully told Americans that they deserved praise for their diplomatic sobriety. But Collinson Owen's logic received substantial support from many other observers. "The heady wine of power," he advised, "may affect republics as well as monarchies, presidents as well as monarchs. It is an attractive pastime for one nation to sway the affairs of the world, especially when it is a novelty." Specifically "it is American nationalism, prosperity, and the desire for still greater conquests in world commerce that we have to deal with, which latterly and not without some reason have been called American Imperialism."[36]

The tendency to undervalue American diplomacy may be attributed to the general British disapprobation of American political democracy. Even as perspicacious and friendly a critic as Denis Brogan, writing in 1932, did not feel that the American government had sufficient elasticity or the people sufficient political sense to deal effectively with the Depression. He even called for a political revolution to overhaul the state.[37] For this mistake Brogan apologized in the preface to a 1943 edition of *Government of the People*.

Effective political leadership, the British generally decided, cannot be expected of the masses. Egalitarianism may have been an effective guiding principle in educating young children, in settling a continent, in enlarging commercial enterprise, in developing the potential of women, and in daily social intercourse. It was inappropriate, though, for the cultivation of intellectual excellence. And it was quite inadequate for the governance of a nation where trained, independent, cool leadership was

[35] Gibbs, *People of Destiny*, p. 98.

[36] A. Smith, *As Others See Her*, p. 177; Gibbs, *People of Destiny*, p. 122; C. R. Enock, *America and England: A Study of the United States; its Relations with Britain; its Part in the Great War; and its Future Influence*, p. 206; Collinson Owen, *The American Illusion*, pp. 269–70.

[37] Denis W. Brogan, *Government of the People: A Study in the American Political System*, p. 386.

necessary and where uncommon ideas must be granted free circulation. The travelers recognized that Americans shunted politics into the background because they were busy clearing forests and erecting new institutions. But the inhabitants of an island whose greatest art was the art of government and whose greatest men went into politics had cause to advise Americans that the world's strongest nation could ill afford much longer to trust its government to second-raters. The different British and American conceptions of and attitudes toward politics persist to our own day.

The British commentators had grave misgivings about the advisability of the American application of egalitarian principles to one other major segment of life—religion. Before attempting, in the final two chapters, to bring these assorted notes together, we must first examine the travelers' impressions of the ways in which Americans worshiped their God.

IX   Churches

Perhaps no other subject stirred such intense feelings among the British observers as the manner in which Americans treated religion. This is directly related to the circumstance that, contemporaneously, no subject stirred Englishmen as much as the state of English religion. Certainly the abdication of power by the national government seemed to matter nowhere more than in the religious sphere. Commenting upon the momentous break from tradition—the formal separation of church and state—Bryce himself called it "of all the differences between the Old World and the New . . . perhaps the most salient." In saying this Bryce touched upon the religious question of the day in England—one that reached deeply into political and educational questions as well. The United States had made a remarkable innovation in history: they had abandoned the idea and practice of an established state church. "They not only divorced the State from the Church, in a strictly political sense, but," stated the Scotsman Alexander Mackay in 1847, "in so doing refused to allow the Church a separate maintenance."[1] That most of the clergy had to rely for financial support upon their respective congregations rendered the situation still more alien, and to some even bizarre.

On a purely abstract level, most Anglican Englishmen simply did not know what to make of this separation. Expressed as a positive innovation, American religion was christened "voluntary religion," whose guiding purpose was to insure "the right of every man to think for himself on all matters connected with religion."[2] Or as Phillippo stated: "Religion is regarded entirely as a matter between man and his God, because man is accountable only to God for his belief." The opponents of the idea of voluntary religion (chiefly Anglicans, of course) referred to the separation negatively as disestablishmentarianism or plain anarchy. Free

[1] Bryce, *The American Commonwealth*, III, 465; A. Mackay, *The Western World*, II, 244.
[2] A. Mackay, *The Western World*, II, 244.

choice, democracy, and individualism could be tolerated in political, economic, and even some social matters; but the line had to be drawn at religion. One dealt here not with institutional arrangements or political theory, but with God, with truth, with eternal values, with matters more universal than even the Declaration of Independence. Englishmen, including some Dissenters, boggled at a theory that elevated the sinner to a position of pre-eminence in selecting that version of God's truth that served him most fitly; American Protestantism, they felt with historical justification, had misread Luther's intentions. Separation of church and state, the critics scoffed, was another name for atheism. Francis Wyse asserted in 1845: "There is no country where infidelity is more generally diffused amidst the bulk of the population through the land." Five years later the Tory Edward Sullivan agreed that "there being no Established Church in America, dissent and unbelief flourish in their rankest growth."[3]

POPULAR AND PRACTICAL RELIGION

Sullivan's jeremiad was an exercise in abstract logic rather than a statement based on observation; he postulated that since no Established Church existed, atheism *must* have flourished. When American religion was scrutinized *in practice* it became immediately apparent that religious worship in the New World was not simply a private matter and "dissent and unbelief" did not flourish. Nearly all Americans went to church every Sunday, and moreover, they seemed to enjoy the new type of devotions that were therein conducted.

Nearly all nineteenth-century commentators affirmed that Americans flocked to their churches in vast numbers. During the Civil War, the first item that struck Edward Dicey was "the immense number of churches. . . . The churches are apparently crowded, and the number of church-goers you see about the streets is larger in proportion to the population than it would be in London. In fact, if you used your eyes only, the first attribute you would ascribe to the Americans would be that of a church-going people." Seventy years later, though by now on the defensive, S. P. B. Mais broadcast over the radio that "instead of finding the churches empty I found them full."[4]

This surprise gave way almost immediately, however, to one of a greater magnitude when they sat down to find out what went on in the

[3] Phillippo, *The United States and Cuba*, p. 226; Wyse, *America: Its Realities and Resources*, p. 270; Sullivan, *Rambles and Scrambles*, p. 32.
[4] Dicey, *Six Months in the Federal States*, II, 204; Mais, *A Modern Columbus*, p. 49.

churches. An anecdote passed on by Morgan Phillips Price in 1934 is worth retelling in full for the way it joined these two points of church attendance and ministerial style. After participating in a few Congregational services in Springfield, Massachusetts, in which standing room only was the rule, the author reported:

> I noticed on other Sundays also that the churches were far fuller than in England. I was particularly struck by the number of young people I saw there. Another thing that impressed me was the fact that the method of conducting the service was in the full sense of the word popular and even unconventional. The preacher began his sermon with an address to the children. He brought an alarm clock into the pulpit, informing the children that he had picked it up on a rubbish-heap, and that the clock had told him that it had been thrown away by its owner because it did not go off when required, was unreliable, and did not speak the truth. He had taken pity on it, and had decided to give it a fresh chance. He had set it to go off at just that moment. Would it mend its ways and be reliable? The whole congregation sat as still as mice. One could have heard a pin drop. As the silence continued, and it became clear that the clock would not speak the truth, a titter was heard, then a guffaw, and then a real peal of laughter, until finally the whole congregation rocked and the church re-echoed with mirth. I saw then why the churches in America are full on Sundays.[5]

The travelers had trouble acclimating themselves to American services, but many of them complained about the readjustment that they had to make when they went back to St. Paul's in London. They had begun to warm to the American minister's simple invocation of common sense, humor, practicality, directness, and informality; upon returning home they commenced to wonder at the mystery, awe, and dustiness of some Anglican services. They especially admired the sermons and the approachability of the American clergymen. The sermons were characterized by the Robertsons as "short practical discourses applicable to the work of everyday life, not dry doctrinal disquisitions manufactured in the study and fit only for the bookshelf." "In American preaching," stated the Reverend Mr. Macrae, "there is little of what is called exposition of Scripture. Almost all sermons are 'topical,' a text being put up as a peg on which the minister hangs his own views of the subject." Not only, chimed in Leng, "are the services alone more interesting: the same may also be said of the sermons. I did not hear one dull or tedious dis-

[5] M. P. Price, *America After Sixty Years*, pp. 107–8. Though it occurred during years in which, as we shall see, the British discerned changing patterns in the quality of American religious worship, this particular episode is quite faithful to the spirit of the nineteenth-century services.

course in America. . . . The difference [from the English variety] is in their being less clerical in their tone and manner and more human."[6]

And the American ecclesiastic himself, appreciatively marveled Joseph Hatton, is "no more strait-laced than an ordinary fellow-traveler, if you met him on the cars, on a steamer, or at a hotel." "American ministers are men," the Robertsons also generously acknowledged, "and don't pretend to be anything but men; they mingle in every-day life, and in the pulpit, or rather on the platform—for pulpits there are none—they speak to the people in the language of the day."[7] At times that language was strong, indicative of an independence of spirit. Mackay stated:

> If their language in the pulpit, and their conduct in the performance of what may be designated as the more private duties of the clergyman, are to be taken as affording any indication of their independence or subserviency, it would not be easy to find a bolder or less scrupulous set of preachers than those who fill the American pulpits. So far from dealing leniently with the shortcomings of their congregations, they deal with them in a manner which many Englishmen would regard as decidedly offensive. Whatever may be the vices of voluntaryism in America, it cannot be properly alleged against it that it muzzles the clergy.[8]

Foster Barham Zincke, Vicar of Wherstead and chaplain to the Queen, agreed that "the clergy are allowed much freedom of expression in America." He cited a conversation with a New Yorker in which the latter "made the following statement of what he supposed was the general practice:—'The way in which we deal with the clergy here is to pay them well, and to encourage them to say exactly what they think. What we pay them for is not other people's ideas and opinions—that we can find in books—but their own.'" The New Yorker also remarked to Zincke that the ministers are expected "'to devote a reasonable portion of their time and all the mental powers they possess to theological study, and then to give us the result.'" Zincke added: "This broad construction of the duty of the clergyman, as a religious teacher, coincides very much with what I was frequently told, that the broad way of thinking was becoming the common way of thinking in almost all the American churches."[9]

[6] Robertson and Robertson, *Our American Tour*, p. 61; Macrae, *The Americans at Home*, p. 589; Leng, *America in 1876*, p. 293. Even the church singing, according to Emily Faithfull, partook of this friendly, earthy quality (*Three Visits to America*, p. 353).
[7] Hatton, *To-day in America*, p. 18; Robertson and Robertson, *Our American Tour*, p. 23.
[8] A. Mackay, *The Western World*, II, 258.
[9] Zincke, *Last Winter in the United States*, p. 18. Zincke referred to Henry Ward Beecher's approach, as most of the travelers did during these years, as the most illustrious example of this type of preaching.

If the minister was to survive, to maintain financial support from his congregation, he could not pander to them. He was expected to scold, but he had to be relevant. "The American clergyman," said Macrae, "whether he be Presbyterian or Baptist, Episcopalian or Independent, has to depend entirely on his ability to supply the spiritual wants of his people. If he proves himself indisposed or unable to do that, no respect is shown him on account of his cloth; he is paid off with as little ceremony as a bungling lawyer or a useless clerk."[10] Zincke defined the American clergyman's role with some acuity as "precisely the same position that the schoolmaster held with respect to the children. What he had to teach was the history and theory of religion; and to show how, as a rule of life, it bore on the ever-varying circumstances of the day. If he could not teach the people these things he was of no use to them." A nice role, a friendly role, even a homey one, thought Zincke; but also one which "ignores altogether that view of the service which makes it an expression of the devotion and of the religious feelings of the congregation itself."[11]

Though the nineteenth-century ministers were treated equally with all other men, and like all Americans had to prove themselves by merit, and though the services they conducted were direct and down-to-earth, the pastors were not politicians. There is a difference between having a "religious teacher" talking the "language of the day" and the propensities of the churches of M. P. Price's day (1934), which "do more social thinking than the local caucuses of the Republican and Democratic parties."[12] The type of religious thinking sketched by the above Britons who visited the New World as late as the second half of the 1870's and the first few years of the 1880's is not a description of the Social Gospel movement. The clerics were transcribing theology into easily understood moral lessons for the parishioners; they were not calling for a political or economic overhaul of American society; they were not exorcizing robber barons, leading civil rights demonstrations, demanding legislation, or in general injecting the churches into the hotter political debates (for or against change) of the day. They preached in general terms and modeled "their sermons more after the style of Christ's own sermons,

---

[10] Macrae, *The Americans at Home,* p. 588.

[11] Zincke, *Last Winter in the United States,* p. 23. In 1912, George Thomas Smart had occasion to regret the absence of ritual and symbolism in American church services: "All this has left something of abruptness in American public worship. The aim is to be sincere, and to be helpful to the weary souls of men in the most direct way; but too often it has been forgotten that joy comes by indirection, and that the light of the fringes of the stars is necessary, as well as their direct transfixing rays" (*The Temper of the American People,* pp. 247–48).

[12] M. P. Price, *America After Sixty Years,* pp. 108–9.

instead of following, as ours commonly do, the epistolary style of St. Paul."[13]

The involvement of the churches in secular, social matters is the subject of three of the best books on American religion during the years 1865–1915 written by native historians.[14] The nature of that involvement has not been consistent and unwavering through time. Its intensity and commitment to social reform gained momentum in the final quarter of the nineteenth century, culminating only then in the Social Gospel unrest. It was nothing new for American churchmen to take a stand on major social problems. At least as early as the Jeffersonian era they had insisted upon the right to speak out on any topic that had moral overtones. And the clergymen had interpreted this right broadly and exercised it with great vigor throughout the nineteenth century. The chief reason for this lay in the tradition of separatism which, added to the absence of any central authority and the general popular acceptance of some form of Christianity, left the churches free to think along these lines. Freedom, however, brought about not a diversity of thought among the churches, but a consensus. From Jefferson's time this consensus tended to support the status quo, and the political influence of the churches was decidedly conservative. But the conservative mold could not remain intact under the impact of "a series of shocking crises" which made themselves felt in the last quarter of the nineteenth century: "From 1877 through the middle nineties, it became more and more difficult to believe that strikes, depressions, unemployment and bankruptcies were part of a Divinely-regulated and unchangeable social order."[15] Social Christianity or the Social Gospel was the response, one which eventually widened into the Progressive movement.

Toward the end of this chapter, the views of a present-day social scientist will be presented defending the proposition that American religion has remained basically consistent throughout our history, and that one sign of this continuity has been the secularity and social involvement of American churches noted by foreign travelers at all times in the past. At this point, however, it should be remarked that while the travelers and the historians tend to bear him out on this general continuity, there is much evidence to indicate that the nature of that involvement changed rather fundamentally toward the end of the nineteenth century.

[13] Leng, *America in 1876*, pp. 293–94.
[14] Aaron I. Abell, *The Urban Impact on American Protestantism, 1865–1900* (Cambridge, Mass.: Harvard University Press, 1943); Charles H. Hopkins, *The Rise of the Social Gospel in American Protestantism 1865–1915* (New Haven, Conn.: Yale University Press, 1940); Henry F. May, *Protestant Churches and Industrial America* (New York: Harper, 1949).
[15] May, *Protestant Churches and Industrial America*, pp. 263–64.

THE UNION OF CHURCH AND NATION-STATE

The meaning behind the popular sermons delivered by decent ministerial chaps before overflow crowds was expressed paradoxically by the British travelers. "One hardly knows," Anthony Trollope confessed, "where the affairs of this world end, or where those of the next begin. . . . There is, I think, an unexpressed determination on the part of the people to abandon all reverence, and to regard religion from an altogether worldly view." There is, said Lord Bryce, "less of a formal separation between the church and the world." Denis Brogan, writing as late as 1940, decided that "the difference between the church and the 'world' has largely disappeared." The British commentators ended up talking not of the separation of church and state, but of the integration of the two, an integration not of institutions, but of values. As Bryce neatly put it: "The whole matter may, I think, be summed up by saying that Christianity is in fact understood to be, though not the legally established religion, yet the national religion."[16] Two notions are implicit in this statement. First, a congruence is suggested between the values of the nation and of the American style of Christianity. Second, a congruence of belief and practice is assumed among the manifold branches of American Christendom, which permits Bryce to speak of *"the* national religion."

There are many indications that the God whom Americans worshiped was an American God, with whom they could identify their own egalitarian and future-oriented aspirations. The formal separation of church and school and of church and state did not prevent the teachers from having the students say prayers every morning or the Presidents of the United States from attending some sort of Protestant service every Sunday. Politicians not only ended every speech by asking for God's blessing on the republic, but all Americans deemed "the general acceptance of Christianity to be one of the main sources of their national prosperity, and their nation a special object of the Divine favour."[17] The churches of the nineteenth century, in their "basic satisfaction with the status quo," were defending a rapidly changing status quo that seemed to bear witness to the marvelous progress of the republic. There was a close identification between the national faith in progress and the national faith in God. The years during and after the Civil War brought

---

[16] A. Trollope, *North America,* II, 96–97; Bryce, *The American Commonwealth,* III, 494, 483; Denis W. Brogan, *U.S.A.: An Outline of the Country: Its People and Institutions,* p. 55.

[17] Bryce, *The American Commonwealth,* III, 474.

the churches no general discontent with the tendencies of American life. As May wrote:

> In the patriotic exaltation of the post-war years, the standard economic doctrines of American Protestantism seemed to be vindicated for all time. In this period when great industrialists were performing gigantic tasks and pouring out their bounty for religious and charitable work, the doctrines of clerical laissez faire were stated with new rigidity and unanimity in classroom, pulpit and press.[18]

The churches applied pervasive egalitarian assumptions to their own situation. They derived their strength from not agitating for any preferential treatment from the state; they understood that in a society which eschewed arbitrary distinctions and inherited privileges, they could only lose by seeking special favors. "So far from suffering from the want of State support," observed Bryce, "religion seems in the United States to stand all the firmer because, standing alone, she is seen to stand by her own strength. No political party, no class in the community, has any hostility either to Christianity or to any particular Christian body."[19] It is partly for this reason that ministers aroused no great antipathy; they regarded themselves as men, and just like the average citizen, the pastors had to compete, without special protection, in order to succeed.

The churches affirmed the egalitarian faith in their relations with one another. They tolerated the existence of the other sects. T. L. Nichols was sure this was true simply because, there being so many different branches of Protestantism, no other course was possible.[20] But his explanation does not account for the interdenominational cooperation that everywhere struck the visitors. More important, Nichols' theory obscures the point that the British visitors thought that the various American sects worshiped in much the same way. The writers did not make any significant distinction between the various Protestant sects, nor even between Protestantism and Catholicism to as great an extent as might be anticipated; all denominations partook in the simple, practical, worldly, common faith that has been called recently "the American religion."[21] Only the miscellaneous exotic groups such as the Mormons, the Shakers, the many fundamentalist and evangelical groups—all of which received more than their share of critical literary attention from the commentators—were not encompassed by this generalization.

[18] May, *Protestant Churches and Industrial America,* p. 263.
[19] Bryce, *The American Commonwealth,* III, 483.
[20] T. L. Nichols, *Forty Years of American Life,* p. 49.
[21] Will Herberg, *Protestant, Catholic, Jew* (Garden City, N.Y.: Doubleday, 1955), used this phrase to characterize faith in the twentieth-century United States. British travel notes would place this brand of religious belief in the nineteenth century as well.

Interdenominational cooperation was a product not only of necessity but of "a growing indifference to minor points of doctrine and church government." Only the most learned authority could convincingly explain to an American the differences between the Methodists, Presbyterians, and Congregationalists. Other tokens of the churches' acceptance of egalitarian premises abounded. "There exist no such social distinctions between different denominations as those of England. No clergyman, no laymen, either looks down upon or looks up to any other clergyman or layman in respect of his worshipping God in another way."[22] It was understood by Americans in their daily intercourse that no man challenges the religious belief of another. As long as he believed in God, one man's faith was as good as anyone else's. Thus, in America, as Edward Dicey noted,

> . . . you never hear anything about religious opinions or discussions. . . . It would be almost impossible for an American to mix much in English society without becoming aware whether his acquaintances were Episcopalian or Unitarians, High Church or Low Church. . . . Now, of the hundreds of people I knew, to a certain extent, intimately in the States, I am not aware to what denomination more than a couple of them belonged. . . .[23]

Toleration among equals more than fearless individualism marked the American religious situation according to James Burn. Equality extended even to church architecture. Indeed Freeman thought the "outward equality of places of worship of all religious bodies is one of the things which decidedly strike as signs of the New World."[24] And corresponding to the general condition of the people, the visitors found few churches to be either awe-inspiring or tawdry, and few that were not clean, well kept, simple, warm, and decent.[25] The integration of religion and the secular society that really mattered was the harmony between the churches and the nation as a whole in respect to values. Americans

---

[22] Bryce, *The American Commonwealth,* III, 477–79. Bryce did not leave this statement of perfect equality unqualified. He did mention that "the pastors of the Presbyterian, Congregationalist, Episcopalian, and Unitarian bodies come generally from a higher social stratum than those of the Methodists, Baptists, and Roman Catholics." This "corresponds pretty closely to the character of the denomination itself" (*ibid.,* p. 479).

[23] Dicey, *Six Months in the Federal States,* II, 205–6. Denominationalism was a major fact of life in Victorian England; toleration was not. Against the Nonconformists and the Tractarians, the Church of England could not afford to be generous.

[24] [Burn,] *The Working Classes in the United States,* p. 61; Freeman, *Some Impressions of the United States,* p. 162.

[25] See, for example, Henry A. Murray, *Lands of the Slave and the Free,* p. 423; and Leng, *America in 1876,* p. 287.

considered a good Christian to be a good American; and a good American was bound to be a good Christian. In Phillippo's words:

> Our American brethren consider that it [true religion] is advantageous to the State,—that it protects liberty,—diminishes the necessity of public restraints,—and, to a considerable degree, supersedes the use of force in the administration of the law, from the consideration that religious men are a law to themselves. They regard religion as the soul of freedom,—the safeguard of the national prosperity and honour,— they believe it unites and concentrates public opinion against injustice and oppression, and spreads a spirit of equity and goodwill throughout the community. They consider, indeed, that pure and unadulterated Christianity is not merely friendly to the civil and sacred liberties of mankind, but that it is the only system on earth by which the sweets of rational liberty, and the full enjoyment of natural rights, can be secured.[26]

When the travelers denied that church and state were functionally separated in the United States, when they insisted that most of the churches were actually integrated into the entire social, political, architectural, and even economic fabric of American life, they were touching upon a more profound harmony—the commingling of all nineteenth-century American beliefs and institutions in the ideal of equality.

BUT IS IT RELIGION?

The Britons could recognize intellectually that the churches had been absorbed into the pattern of equality, but a good many of them could not help but be repelled by the fact. Social institutions may be susceptible to manipulation by man, the travelers could grant, but religion they contended should transcend human and manipulative concerns. Must not true religion leap beyond the conveniences of a national ethos toward the infinite? beyond the practical toward the spiritual? beyond man toward God? Can one truth be as good as another when ultimate meaning is involved? Can the cleric simply be another man? If truth exists, must not it be the same truth under one banner for all men for all time? Has not the theory of equality gone too far when it has invaded the spiritual world? Does what passes in the United States under the name of "religion" constitute "true" religion?

"A semblance of religion," warned Samuel Phillips Day, "must not be taken for religion itself." The proliferation of sects led not to a healthy freedom but, according to Greville Chester, to "utter anarchy in matters of faith." Freeman was sure that the financial dependence of the ministers upon their flocks chained them to positions too "closely

[26] Phillippo, *The United States and Cuba,* pp. 221–22.

confined by public opinion." Matthew Arnold did not think much of a religion that derived its inspiration from "a mind of the third order" like John Wesley's. Everywhere he was disgusted by America's religion of the middle class, "the insufficiency [of which] is now everyday becoming more manifest." True religion, he claimed, must inspire "the discipline of awe and respect," and obviously in the United States "this religion is dying out."[27]

These negative claims, however, were definitely minority opinions in the nineteenth century. Two out of every three visitors who took up the subject championed American religion and denied that any incompatibility obtained between plain, simple religious discourse and reverence. There was, first of all, definite agreement on Bryce's quantitative judgment of the influence of religion in nineteenth-century America as "greater and more widespread in the United States than in any part of western Continental Europe, and I think greater than in England." Few demurred from his statement that "the churches are as thoroughly popular, in the best sense of the word, as any of the other institutions of the country."[28]

But of greater consequence, there was general agreement among the nineteenth-century commentators that American popular religion was religion of quality, of true devotion and spirituality.[29] The visitors during this period felt that Americans not only went to church, but that they went there to pray in a devoted and humble manner. In the nineteenth century the British verdict on the effects of voluntary, popular religion was better represented by such panegyrics as Phillippo's in 1857, which follows here, than by criticism. Phillippo stated:

> America shows the noble and gratifying spectacle of the whole christian church within her borders sustained solely by the voluntary energies of the people, and yet thriving throughout an immense empire, receiving the homage of men of every rank, and sending forth its missionaries to distant realms. Fluctuations there may be; but the tide is ever flowing,— the advancement is actual and permanent.[30]

This kind of writing all but disappeared from descriptions of the condition of religion in twentieth-century America.

[27] Day, *Life and Society in America*, I, 72; Chester, *Transatlantic Sketches*, p. 357; Freeman, *Some Impressions of the United States*, p. 175; M. Arnold, *Civilization in the United States*, pp. 87, 104, 176.

[28] Bryce, *The American Commonwealth*, III, 483.

[29] There were other points of consensus: British condemnation of evangelism; fear of Catholicism, especially of the Irish variety; abhorrence of most of the odder sects of American Christendom. These topics, though of interest, are not, I think, particularly germane to the mainstream of American religion which I am trying to map.

[30] Phillippo, *The United States and Cuba*, p. 229.

CHANGE OR CONTINUITY IN AMERICAN RELIGION

A strong case against the proposition that American religion has changed in the twentieth century was made by the sociologist Seymour Lipset in 1963. The argument for change he summed up as follows:

> It is widely assumed that structural changes inherent in industrialization and urbanization, with consequent bureaucratization and an increase in "other directedness," have resulted in two major changes in American religious practice and belief. First it is argued that many more people outwardly adhere to formal religion and attend church than ever before; and second, that this increase in formal practice does not reflect greater religiosity—on the contrary, it is suggested that American religion itself is now secularized, that it has increasingly adjusted to the sentiments of the general society.

Lipset, however, discovered that

> . . . much of the historical record indicates that these aspects have always distinguished American religion from religion in other nations. American religion, like all other institutions, has made major adjustments in response to changes in the size and scope of the nation, but as the institution most intimately linked with values it has shown the tenacity exhibited by the value system itself.[31]

The author then turned to the historical record, which in this instance consisted largely (as indeed it had to) of foreign travelers' reports, in order to sustain his conclusion. In doing this he produced sufficient evidence to indicate that the presumably modern trends toward large church attendance and the secularity of religion were also common in the United States in the nineteenth century. The weight of the data just sketched in this chapter clearly supports Lipset's contention on this point.

Lipset, too, felt that "both the secular and the all-pervasive character of American religion is a result of its being viewed as part of the 'American Way of Life.' " "In seeking to explain the special character of American religion," he went on, "many of the foreign visitors singled out the effect of the separation of church and state, which resulted in American churches being voluntary organizations"—a statement which, once again, he has a right to make on the basis of the evidence. Lipset concludes:

[31] Seymour Martin Lipset, *The First New Nation: The United States in Historical and Comparative Perspective* (New York: Basic Books, 1963), pp. 140, 141. Lipset's major thesis, that the American value system has remained relatively constant throughout our history, will be taken up in the final chapter.

The emphasis upon equality, between religions as among men, which intensified after the American Revolution, gave the subsequent development of religious institutions in America its special character. Democratic [substitute, for precision's sake, egalitarian] and religious values have grown together . . . [contributing to] the consistency with which both secularization and widespread adherence have distinguished American religion throughout its history. . . .[32]

In stressing this continuity Lipset has not violated the letter of the travel reports. But the spirit of twentieth-century British travel writing departs markedly, as will be seen, from that of one hundred years before. The degree of secularization and political involvement on the part of American churches has intensified and, far more telling, the visitors insist that the reverence of the Americans has degenerated into hypocrisy.

The problem of continuity and change is subtle and complicated. It is easy, without being intellectually dishonest, to find in travel literature any sort of precedent one seeks. It is also undeniably true that one can quite justifiably contend that *compared to Europe,* American religion in the nineteenth *and* the twentieth centuries was more all-pervasive and more secular than that of any European nation.

Yet this kind of data selection can distort and destroy all meaningful discussions of cultural change. The historian must make the effort to free himself from semantic finesse by asking larger questions such as: does twentieth-century man feel God's presence with the same or even a similar quality of intensity as did his predecessors a century earlier? Extraordinary changes have befallen Western man's cosmic thinking since Darwin, Marx, Freud, Einstein, two world wars, and the atomic bomb, and it would be a miracle if religion in the United States continued untouched, flowing along peacefully in basically the same stream as it always had.

ACCIDENTAL COLLOCATIONS OF ATOMS

The historian Carl Becker once compared the "climates of opinion" of the thirteenth, eighteenth, and twentieth centuries. He stated that the first two, though decidedly different, were still basically theistic. But the cosmic process had altered radically in the twentieth century. He wrote of our own times:

The ultimate cause of this cosmic process of which man is a part, whether God or electricity or a "stress in the ether," we know not. Whatever it may be, if indeed it be anything more than a necessary postulate of thought, it appears in its effects as neither kind nor unkind,

[32] *Ibid.,* pp. 158–59, 169.

but merely as indifferent to us. What is man that the electron should be mindful of him! Man is but a foundling in the cosmos, abandoned by the forces that created him. Unparented, unassisted and undirected by omniscient or benevolent authority, he must fend for himself, and with the aid of his own limited intelligence find his way about in an indifferent universe.[33]

Whatever application these assumptions may have to modern physicists, it seems fairly clear that the average twentieth-century American citizen has not yet reached this "advanced" stage of thinking; his affinities with the Enlightenment are probably still somewhat stronger than Becker suggests. But changes of momentous proportions have occurred in our epoch which render, in many circles, the beliefs in equality, in progress, and even in God, quaint relics of bygone days.

The British travelers of the twentieth century recorded serious challenges to these faiths, challenges that were reaching larger numbers of the citizenry. Bryce in 1888 recognized these incursions:

> Whether pronounced theological unbelief, which has latterly been preached by lectures and pamphlets with a freedom unknown even thirty years ago, has made substantial progress among the thinking part of the working class is a question on which one hears the most opposite statements. . . .
> In the cultivated circles of the great cities one finds a good many people, as one does in England, who have virtually abandoned Christianity; and in most of the smaller cities there is said to be a knot of men who profess agnosticism, and sometimes have a meeting-place where secularist lectures are delivered. Fifty years ago the former class would have been fewer and more reserved; the latter would scarcely have existed.[34]

Lipset was quite correct in stressing that widespread church attendance and the secularity of the services in the New World are not unique to twentieth-century religious observance. But he passes over too quickly the proposition that modern Americans might believe in God less intimately than did Americans in former days. "I must say," wrote one observer in 1909, "that in the States I was unable to find any marked religious feeling or natural reverence." Another commentator alleged in 1913: "There is one characteristic common to the worship of all religious bodies of America . . . and that, I regret to say, is the apparent want of reverence."[35] Right or wrong, three out of four of the visitors from 1900 to 1935 made a point of lamenting the sham, superficiality, and hypocrisy which they claimed had corrupted American worship.

[33] Carl Becker, *The Heavenly City of the Eighteenth-Century Philosophers* (1st ed., 1932; New Haven, Conn.: Yale University Press, 1962), pp. 14–15.

[34] Bryce, *The American Commonwealth*, III, 492–93.

[35] Vaile, *Y., America's Peril*, p. 195; Brown, *The Real America*, p. 25.

This nearly reverses the tabulation for the period 1845–85. As closely as can be told, the center of the period of change seems to fall during the years 1885–1900.

A transition beginning as early as the vogue of Spencer in America seemed to gather strength toward the end of the century. In 1896 Samuel Smith remarked with sad reluctance upon how "thoughtful Americans of the best type regard with grave anxiety the decline of religion in many parts of the country."[36] While cries about the decline of religion have been uttered since time began, the cries increased in volume and intensity around this time. George Smart, in 1912, traced one special cause of this transition:

> The world that religion inhabits [he said] is now a world of secular force and science; it is breathless in pursuit; and, though an exciting and interesting world, it is wearying. Men and women become so used to the outer play of life that it seems to be the whole story. The wrestlings of the souls that the elders experienced are not experienced now. Men do not live under the Great Taskmaster's eye because they are too conscious of the gaze of man.

Instrumental in forging this new world was the figure of Charles Darwin. As Smart looked back he noted that "there has been a difficult quarter of a century for theology, which suddenly has sprung upon it the new way of thinking brought about by the evolutionary hypothesis, and yet had to do something with it unprepared and absolutely unequipped." The result of all these challenges almost had to be that "devoutness in the finer and older forms grows rarer in pulpit and pew."[37] Darwin was not the only figure responsible for transformations taking place in American thought at the turn of the century. Challenges came from other European intellects; we need to know more about the influence exerted by Marx, Freud, or even Nietzsche in altering the American view of the nature of reality. Other less intellectual causes for this transformation which undermined the old confident order of the nineteenth century would include the growing strife between management and labor, the recurring economic panics, the flood of "new" immigrants into crowded, slum-ridden cities, the corruption of political life, the power of the millionaire, and the symbolic closing of the frontier. All these forces gained momentum in the last two decades of the nineteenth century.

Nineteenth-century American religious worship may have been too secular to suit some, but a new note began to be struck insistently in the twentieth century. Richard De Bary accused American Protestantism of

---

[36] S. Smith, *America Revisited*, p. 22.
[37] Smart, *Temper of the American People*, pp. 239, 241–42.

"fast becoming a social religion." He referred, in part, to the growing involvement of the churches in politics. Bryce noted the benevolence that Christian belief reinforced in the political life of the republic.[38] The rise of the Social Gospel in the last quarter of the nineteenth century has been well documented by American historians.

But an unsettled world in which old faiths are disintegrating can engender a very different, more conservative political response, and this is what the British tourists emphasized. Stephen Graham amplified this thought when he indicated that where ministers might once have addressed themselves to topical matters, they were now becoming apologists and spokesman for some of the more questionable secular qualities in American life. Ties between the churches and the business ethic in particular began to bother large numbers of observers. Graham defined American Christianity as the religion of "making good." Smart remarked that "no longer does religion make its old appeal to the worker."[39]

C. E. M. Joad, in *The Babbitt Warren,* written in 1925, outlined the way in which the Babbitts salved their scarred consciences on Sundays. "What easier way out of the difficulty [of ungodly behavior the other six days] than to persuade ourselves that God shares our tastes and bestows His blessing on our pleasures, so that, by merely doing what we want to do, we are actually spiritualizing our natures and approaching nearer to Him? And this, in America, is exactly what we do do." Joad then proceeded to take up the advertising executive Bruce Barton's strange vision of "Jesus as a businessman."[40]

In this same spirit the philosopher G. Lowes Dickinson contended that the newspapers had replaced the Bible as America's printed source of inspiration, and that "religion is becoming a department of practical business. The churches . . . vie with one another in advertising goods which are all material benefits: 'Follow me, and you will get rich.' " Dickinson concluded: "This conversion of religion into business is interesting enough. But even more striking is what looks like a conversion of business into religion." Annette Meakin varied the theme a grace note by quoting an American cleric's characterization of America's God as Money. Woodruff said Americans worshipped quantity and progress.[41]

[38] De Bary, *Land of Promise,* p. 265; Bryce, *The American Commonwealth,* III, 499–500.

[39] Stephen Graham, *With Poor Immigrants to America,* p. 12; Smart, *Temper of the American People,* p. 147.

[40] C. E. M. Joad, *The Babbitt Warren,* pp. 171–72.

[41] Dickinson, *Appearances,* pp. 174–75; Meakin, *What America Is Doing,* p. 360; Woodruff, *Plato's American Republic,* pp. 15–16. Woodruff construed "Progress" strictly in its material sense.

If one can believe the British, then twentieth-century Americans worshipped anything but God—and that anything was usually vulgar. This verdict was not unanimous, but for the twentieth century it was decisive.[42] Americans lived in only two dimensions, declared Dickinson: "That missing dimension I shall call religion." Abhorred most of all was the reduction of all values to the terms of business, "the concentration of what, at other times, have been moral and religious forces upon the one aim of material progress." Where Bryce could talk rather positively about a national religion, just a score of years later H. G. Wells could speak for most of his compatriots when he stated flatly that "America has no Church." And the military strategist J. F. C. Fuller decided that the average American is "so unbelieving" as to have "no religion."[43]

Perhaps C. R. Enock expressed the appropriately larger view when he off-handedly dropped the thought that "the 'decadence' of religion is lamented everywhere."[44] Still it must be repeated that this lamentation was uttered by British travelers in the United States with greater regularity in the years between 1900 and 1935 than for the forty years before 1885.

Lipset, the American sociologist, is nonetheless quite right in underscoring the British revelation for both nineteenth and twentieth centuries that Americans had made astounding departures in the history of religious worship in Western civilization. Nowhere else had religion ever been so exclusively addressed to this world, so accessible, so common-sensical, so unmysterious, so simple, so sympathetic to ordinary, every-day human needs. Nowhere else, certainly not in England, had belief in Christianity been so voluntary, or had the Christian churches so readily accepted equality as their *modus vivendi*. The British could, with only the greatest difficulty, recover from their astonishment when they were compelled to admit that the United States had achieved a more perfect harmony between her religious beliefs and her national aspirations than had any nation with an established church.

---

[42] For some exceptions, see Hilaire Belloc, *The Contrast,* p. 182; Craib, *America and the Americans,* pp. 297, 302; Mais, *A Modern Columbus,* p. 49; M. P. Price, *America After Sixty Years,* pp. 107–8. Belloc said that skepticism was further advanced in Europe than in the New World—a statement which, though possibly true, does not necessarily belie the assertions made by the other British critics concerning the decline of American religion relative to earlier periods of the *American* past.

[43] Dickinson, *Appearances,* pp. 174, 179; H. G. Wells, *Social Forces,* p. 329; J. F. C. Fuller, *Atlantis: America and the Future,* p. 70.

[44] Enock, *Farthest West,* p. 278.

X   The Land of Young Adulthood, 1885–1935

I N THE LAST SEVERAL CHAPTERS, the British portrayal of educational, religious, political, and familial customs has sounded confirmation of Viscount Bryce's previously quoted maxim that the United States "is made all of a piece: its institutions are the product of its economic and social condition and the expression of its character."[1]

1860–1900

The innovation of the common schools; the innovation of universal suffrage; the phenomenon of a family in which the wife supervised and in which the child dominated and was indulged; the novelty of religious worship that was not only voluntary and free, but secularized and practical; the lesser departures of one-class railway carriages, upstart "help," and presumptuously friendly manners within a framework in which the prospect of great wealth did indeed seem open to all—all these were the innovations of equality, a generous, forward-looking equality.

The travelers everywhere depicted this dynamic egalitarianism as the chief element by which the United States could be recognized and differentiated from all other civilizations, past or present; and they told of how this republic had translated an abstraction into specific and functioning institutional arrangements. The equality of which they wrote, however, was not a final fact, as witness the ambiguous equality of American women, but rather a tendency whose ultimate and perfect fruition would take place in the future. It had a character of its own: animated by a boundless optimism, moved by faith in the possibilities of all white men, informed and blessed by a land of plenty that promised success to those with the requisite energy and integrity.

[1] Bryce, *The American Commonwealth*, III, 354.

Above all, the commentators portrayed a youthful equality: idealistic, rarely satisfied simply with present achievements, nor with accumulated, uninvested wealth, nor with the cultivated sophistication of the leisured, nor even with millennial goals; but the equality of a people who strove and yearned restlessly, unceasingly upward, energetic, cocky, rough, and humane: who rested their deepest dreams in their children and in their education. This sense of awesome vitality is well captured in comparisons of the republic with England and with Russia. Lady Emmeline Stuart-Wortley in 1850 plagiarized from Tocqueville, but still made sense when she exclaimed:

> Russia and the United States are the two, young, growing, giant nations of the world—the Leviathans of the lands! . . . Those two grand young nations are strong to the race, and fresh to the glorious contest. Far off, in the future, centuries and ages beyond this present hour, is their culminating point. What to other nations may be work and labour, to them is but, as it were, healthful relaxation, the exercising of their mammoth limbs, the quickening of the mighty current of their buoyant and bounding life-blood, the conscious enjoyment of their own inexhaustible vitality.[2]

At a later period, an expert on Russia, Stephen Graham, contrasted that nation with the United States and England in terms of their respective attitudes toward life, death, and work:

> The American working man has a true passion for work, for his country, for everything; the British working man does his duty. We have not the belief in life that the American has—we have not yet the Russian's belief in death. The American breathes full into his lungs the air of life. . . . America loves the strong, the healthy, the pure, because she is tired of Europe and the weakness and disease and sorrow of Europeans.[3]

Just before the turn of the century, all these various tendencies received their fullest expression in the writing of James Fullarton Muirhead. First, he issued the manifesto that "the distinguishing feature of American society, as contrasted with the societies of Europe, is the greater approach to equality that it has made. It is in this sphere, and not in those of industry, law, or politics that the British observer must feel that the American breathes a distinctly more liberal and democratic air than he." Muirhead then went on to indicate the elements of which this air was composed:

> It includes a sense of illimitable expansion and possibility; an almost childlike confidence in human ability and fearlessness of both the pres-

[2] Stuart-Wortley, *Travels in the United States,* p. 72. Sisley Huddleston made the same comparison in the same way eighty years later in *What's Right with America,* pp. 18–19.

[3] Graham, *With Poor Immigrants to America,* p. 14.

ent and the future; a wider realisation of human brotherhood than has yet existed; a greater theoretical willingness to judge by the individual rather than by the class; a breezy indifference to authority and a positive predilection for innovation; a marked alertness of mind and a manifold variety of interest; above all, an inextinguishable hopefulness and courage.

In the sense that equality means equality of opportunity, Muirhead tried to capture the American attitude in negative, paradoxical terms when he said: "The true-born American is absolutely incapable of comprehending the sense of difference between a lord and a plebian that is forced on the most philosophical among ourselves by the mere pressure of the social atmosphere. It is for him a fourth dimension of space."[4]

Even as Muirhead was writing, however, a defensive note began to creep into his soaring prose. He prefaced, for example, his statement of equality as the "distinguishing feature of American society," with "in spite of anything in the foregoing that may seem incompatible"; and he had to follow his encomium to "inextinguishable hopefulness and courage" with a long catalog of the defects, evils, and difficulties which plagued the United States with increasing severity.[5] Muirhead had premonitions of peril for the republic. Hints of those premonitions have been dropped in the last several chapters of this study, all adding up to qualifications, reservations, alterations now beginning to mar the harmonious, synchronized egalitarian scene that marked the travel reports about nineteenth-century America. The portrait of the nation "made all of a piece," a youthful land blessed with natural wealth, buoyed by its mythic beliefs in equality and progress to which that plenty led, and propelled by institutions which incorporated those faiths into daily life and which, by their success, further reinforced the power of those beliefs—this dynamic but harmonious vision appeared to be becoming to more and more Britons less and less apt as the United States moved into the twentieth century.

To draw from the previous chapters some specific examples on the institutional level, one might recall the following. As time went by, the quality of the American faith in the Almighty appeared to be growing tainted. The quality of the various governments, most notably in the growing, immigrant-filled cities, was becoming no less corrupted. Women were increasingly setting the tone of American life as the frontier symbolically closed and families moved to the cities. Children retained their importance, but the common schools were no longer regarded as wonderful. The idealism that Americans had invested in them

[4] Muirhead, *America, the Land of Contrasts,* pp. 28, 274, 276.
[5] *Ibid.,* pp. 28, 277.

seemed to be giving way before the sophistication and research-orientation of the universities.

In this chapter we shall deliberately focus on the travelers' delineation of change as the United States entered the twentieth century. A long look will be directed toward the American affirmation of progress and of the egalitarian principle, as well as to the British impression that the New World was a place best symbolized by the conception of "youth." In the final chapter we shall discuss what these changes may signify.

THE GROWTH OF CLASS DISTINCTIONS

Englishmen had never pretended that class distinctions did not exist in the United States. They had mixed the two related but not identical notions that material wealth was fairly equally distributed throughout the society and the more important idea that one had the *opportunity* to change one's status in the world. But as America moved into the 1880's, as the cities grew crowded with immigrants from eastern Europe, as a class of industrial tycoons accumulated extraordinary fortunes, as labor-management clashes grew in virulence, as periodic economic panics ensued, and as the safety valve of the frontier was announced closed, the British tourists wrote with greater frequency of plutocracy, of class wars, of love of caste distinctions, of labor's discontent, of the extinction of opportunity, of the aristocracy of wealth. As opportunity seemed to be on the wane and as the disparity between rich and poor grew, they even wrote of "inequality" in American life. They wrote of it both as an economic fact and as a spiritual permutation. One must read the words of the travelers themselves to appreciate accurately the great importance that they ascribed to this fundamental transformation.

Emily Faithfull (1884): "Americans boast of their freedom from the Britisher's recognition of different ranks and grades in society, but all candid persons will acknowledge to a growing love of caste distinctions in that country."[6]

Alfred Russel Wallace (1888): "The struggle for wealth and power is always exciting, and to many irresistible. But it is essentially a degrading struggle, because the few only can succeed while the many must fail. . . . [There has resulted in the United States] that mad race for wealth in which they have beaten the record, and have produced a greater number of multi-millionaires than all the rest of the world combined, with the disastrous results already briefly indicated."[7]

[6] Faithfull, *Three Visits to America,* p. 34.
[7] Wallace, *My Life,* II, 197–98.

George Steevens (1896): "Americans have complained that this is the first election [the presidential race of 1896] in which class has been arrayed against class; it will assuredly not be the last. Open warfare between capital and labour will be earlier and bitterer in the United States than in Europe."[8]

Sir A. M. Low (1901): "It would be foolish to ignore the fact that in the United States not less than in England there are classes. . . . Every year the lines are more tightly drawn, and it must be admitted that wealth makes classes."[9]

Sir Philip Burne-Jones (1904): "Of late years there has grown up in America a sort of aristocracy of great wealth, the outcome of the immense fortunes that have been made in a comparatively short time. . . . The members of this small coterie of extremely rich people . . . have arrogated to themselves a position somewhat analogous to our own nobility; and in so doing the have out-heroded Herod."[10]

Richard De Bary (1908): "America expanded, but left some millions of poor men in the train of its unfathomed wealth."[11]

Annette Meakin (1910): ". . . there are only two classes of society in America, the rich and the poor."[12]

Mrs. Tweedie (1913): America "is the land of wealth and it is the land of poverty."[13]

H. G. Wells (1913): "A hundred . . . signs confirm that the huge classless sea of American population is not destined to remain classless, is already developing separations and distinctions and structures of its own."[14]

G. Lowes Dickinson (1914): "America is the paradise of plutocracy; for the rich there enjoy not only a real power but a social prestige such as can hardly have been accorded them even in the worst days of the Roman Empire."[15]

Annie Burnett-Smith (1918): ". . . nowhere in the world are there more classes, between which the dividing line is sharply drawn."[16]

The same refrain was repeated over and over. To be sure, some Britons, few in number, but no less vocal than those above, protested

[8] Steevens, *Land of the Dollar*, p. 305.

[9] Low, *America at Home*, p. 41.

[10] Burne-Jones, *Dollars and Democracy*, p. 108. He continues: "The middle classes accept them cheerfully as the best available substitute for the dukes and duchesses whom, in their heart of hearts, the Americans love so well; and the newspapers help to keep up the fiction" (*ibid.*, p. 109).

[11] De Bary, *Land of Promise*, p. 235.

[12] Meakin, *What America Is Doing*, p. 18.

[13] Tweedie, *America As I Saw It*, p. 16.

[14] Wells, *Social Forces*, p. 331.

[15] Dickinson, *Appearances*, p. 147.

[16] A. Smith, *As Others See Her*, p. 55.

vigorously against this line of argument. John Spender, in a good book written in 1928, fired back that equality "struck me as *the* note of America when I spent three months in the country six years ago, and it strikes me even more when I return to it." And Sisley Huddleston a year later gave as his first major reason for *What's Right With America* the traditional one that "in America there is a real equality of classes."[17] But the tide had turned: the English in the twentieth century ceased to regard the United States as pre-eminently the land of equality and they were convinced that Americans had also abandoned the notion. Other changes followed in the wake of this one.

THE INCREASE OF MATERIALISM

In *The Future in America* (1906), H. G. Wells issued the following dour pronouncement: "The American community," he said, "is discovering a secular extinction of opportunity, and the appearance of powers against which individual enterprise and competition are hopeless. Enormous sections of the American public are losing their faith in any personal chance of growing rich and truly free, and are developing the consciousness of an expropriated class."[18]

As long as opportunity for all existed, or even was believed to exist, the scramble for the attainment of wealth could be carried on unhysterically; the odds favoring success seemed to be fairly high. But when the chances to rise either came to be or were thought to be "infinitesimal" (as Frederic Harrison, in company with many others, later claimed),[19] when society came to be conceived of as divided into rich and poor, the anxiety to get into the rich classification became, in British opinion, overwhelming. Wealth became synonymous with success in life, and its accumulation the *sine qua non* for Americans, according to the British. Unlike in the preceding century, the race for money assumed such staggering, all-consuming proportions that all other values were swallowed up in its path. Business, the travelers said, came to be the only honored career because only in business could one get rich. Principle, whether of the Christian or politically progressive variety, was reduced to a sentimentality easily disposed of by the "realists" who developed a new set of ethics in step with the tendency to enthrone business.

This strain in American life had been noticed long before 1885. The

[17] J. A. Spender, *Through English Eyes,* p. 4; Huddleston, *What's Right with America,* p. 242.

[18] Wells, *The Future in America,* pp. 108–9.

[19] Harrison, *Memories and Thoughts,* p. 181; Wells, *The Future in America,* p. 81.

Marryats and Trollopes of the 1820's and 1830's made it their chief target. Opportunities were already growing scarce, said Pairpont in 1854, when he declared: "The fact cannot be too strongly insisted on, that the interior district of the United States, and Canada, is the only legitimate field for emigrants." A decade later Burn warned that "the battle of labour and capital is frequently being fought here between associated bodies of men and their employers with all the acrimony and ill-feeling which selfishness and blind passion dictate." In 1877, William Saunders mentioned how "the working classes merely follow the example set by capitalists: monopoly and restriction are the evil genii of American life."[20]

In the next decade Lord Bryce, too, testified to a dramatic diminution of material equality, to its baleful effects on the lower classes, and to the tendency to make wealth an end in itself. He noted:

> Sixty years ago there were no great fortunes in America, few large fortunes, no poverty. Now there is some poverty (though only in a few places can it be called pauperism), many large fortunes, and a greater number of gigantic fortunes than in any other country of the world. . . . One may surmise that the equality of material conditions, almost universal in the last century, still general sixty years ago, will more and more diminish by the growth of a very rich class at one end of the line, and of a very poor class at the other end.[21]

Kipling laughed in 1891: "Yes; it will be a spectacle for all the world to watch, this big, slashing colt of a nation, that has got off with a flying start on a freshly littered course, being pulled back to the ruck by that very mutton-fisted jockey Necessity," or, more specifically, "the rapidly diminishing bounty of Nature."[22]

But before 1885, before the time Bryce and Kipling spoke, these dire warnings and imprecations of money-madness were not as typical and inexorable as they later became. The famous cry that the United States was the land of materialism did not really resound with great consistency until the period between 1910 and 1930. "Business is the only virile pursuit," Dickinson (1914) sarcastically remarked. Ramsay Muir (1927) put in that "the nation as a whole regards wealth-making as the highest form of human activity." Business had replaced education as the national panacea, according to J. A. Spender (1928). "The majority of Americans," he observed, "seem to be convinced that if only they stick to business, everything will cure itself."[23]

[20] Pairpont, *Uncle Sam and His Country*, p. 331; [Burn,] *The Working Classes in the United States*, p. 23; Saunders, *Through the Light Continent*, p. 30.

[21] Bryce, *The American Commonwealth*, III, 526, 528.

[22] Kipling, *American Notes*, pp. 235–36.

[23] Dickinson, *Appearances*, p. 199; Muir, *America the Golden*, p. 136; J. A. Spender, *A Briton in America*, p. 316.

The result: a civilization, if the word could still be used, which valued gadgets, goods, and things rather than ideals. De Sumichrast commented upon the "wholly erroneous importance given to mere size and costliness." "What would remain if the material civilization of America disappeared?" demanded the pugnacious Brown.[24]

In his play, *The Apple Cart,* George Bernard Shaw created an American diplomat, Vanhattan by name, who graciously offered the Queen of England the opportunity to have her nation annexed to the United States under the aegis of American money.[25] When asked if the French might not object to such a union, Shaw had Vanhattan reply characteristically: "So long as Paris is full of Americans, and Americans are full of money, all's well in the west from the French point of view." "This falsification of the standard of values," pointed out the youthful Aldous Huxley in 1926, "is a product, in our modern world, of democracy, and has gone furthest in America." Also in 1926, Woodruff advised Americans "that unless they reopen the question of the end of living they will grow dissatisfied and exist wretchedly."[26] In the same year Bretherton added gratuitously:

> The American does not want to think and is rapidly forgetting how to think. He is living more and more in two dimensions, length and breadth with no depth. He wants all the potentialities of life to be analysed for him and to be handed a booklet in which every opinion he may be called upon to hold and every course of action he may be required to pursue can be immediately found by referring to page three or chapter six.[27]

The historian George Knoles in summing up British reaction to American civilization in the 1920's spoke of British resentment of New World prosperity "in the face of continued depression at home. These resentments fed the growing fear of Americanism, to the extent that English visitors saw alarming signs in many of the most trivial phenomena of the Jazz Age. Cocktails, movies, jazz, advertising, and salesmanship all were taken as ominous evidence of a crude, materialistic culture."[28]

---

[24] Frederick C. J. M. S. R. de Sumichrast, *America and the Britons,* p. 219; Brown, *The Real America,* p. 4.

[25] The plan by which this would be accomplished began with American renunciation of independence and the declaration proclaiming it, followed by her return into the British Commonwealth!

[26] George Bernard Shaw, *The Applecart: A Political Extravaganza,* p. 64; A. Huxley, *Jesting Pilate,* p. 276; Woodruff, *Plato's American Republic,* p. 121.

[27] Bretherton, *Midas,* p. 54.

[28] Knoles, *The Jazz Age Revisited,* p. 134. He concluded his work by saying that "American civilization in the 1920's, as the British critics described it, failed to inspire confidence" (*ibid.,* p. 134).

Materialism clearly meant more to the Britons than hunger for money; it meant the bastardization by Americans of value, ideal, and "principle." This thought received an interesting discourse at the hands of Douglas Goldring, who said:

> By "principle" I mean all intellectual integrity, such as that of Socrates or Giordano Bruno; all patriotism worthy of the name; all "causes" for which men have justifiably sacrificed their lives. It is a first step on the ladder of spiritual progress. Principle begins at the point where it is able to defeat self-interest. The man of principle is the unbuyable man. However humble, he can make all the Rockefellers, Morgans, Fords and Mellons look foolish.

This fervent Irish revolutionary then noted "the astonishing inability of the great majority of Americans even to understand the meaning of the word."[29] These indictments of ruthless American materialism are familiar enough; less familiar is the fact that they did not assume a place of overwhelming prominence until the first quarter of the present century; that before that time, the British regarded the Americans, with their wide-eyed optimism and strident proclamations of equality, as out-and-out idealists.

THE LIFE OF EASE

Herbert Spencer, in 1882, warned Americans to stop working so hard. "Exclusive devotion to work," he advised, "has the result that amusements cease to please; and when relaxation becomes imperative, life becomes dreary from lack of its sole interest—the interest in business." This tremendous compulsion to work which gave to American life an "electric" quality had always, from the earliest days of the republic, made immediate and lasting impressions upon British and European travelers. Twenty years after Spencer's statements, Frederic Harrison still spoke of America's "inexhaustible energy"; Low still referred to a nervous, working population; Igglesden still remarked upon the ceaseless, restless hustle of the United States; Huddleston urged Europeans to "borrow American energy, American enthusiasm, American optimism;" and Aldous Huxley composed a modern, appropriate national model to replace, interestingly enough, Liberty, Equality, Fraternity. Huxley's slogan read: "Vitality, Prosperity, Modernity."[30]

[29] Douglas Goldring, *Impacts: The Trip to the States and Other Adventures of Travel,* p. 62.

[30] Spencer, *Essays,* III, 483; Harrison, *Memories and Thoughts,* p. 176; Low, *America at Home,* p. 227; Igglesden, *A Mere Englishman in America,* p. 184; Huddleston, *What's Right with America,* p. 20; A. Huxley, *Jesting Pilate,* p. 280.

The speed, energy, hurry, and hustle of American as compared with European life, continued to sound its edgy note in the travel records well into the twentieth century. Its intensity, if anything, increased. But new overtones could be heard, at first faintly, but later more definitely —overtones suggestive of an American longing for serenity, comfort, relaxation, and fun. Phillippo told, in 1857, of the "few exhibitions for amusement, and but little time or taste for them. . . . There are few to be found in America who are driven by *ennui* to adopt expedients for killing time." Theatres and places of public entertainment were little patronized. "Nor are the American people addicted to holiday sports, or festive celebrations. The principal out-door amusements of the sexes have been said, sneeringly, to be the bar-room and the lecture-room." The author was led to conclude that America "has not many charms for the voluptuous portion of mankind. . . . Nor has America many attractions for the romantic, the fastidious, or the sentimental; but much for the rational, the sober-minded, and the discreet." In 1882, as a sign of changing times, Miss Faithfull had to admit that Americans no longer attended lectures but spent much of their spare time attending the performances of traveling theatrical companies.[31]

Whereas the energy portrayed by the nineteenth-century commentators seemed to be self-sustaining and self-perpetuating, some of those writers in the later portion of the century and after seemed to detect a desire among men of the middle classes to work hard and make their fortune so that they could escape the rat-race of the cities, buy a house on a tree-shaded, quiet suburban street, and begin to take life easy. Arnold Bennett told this story as early as 1911. He began with the young struggling couple caught up in the frantic existence of the city. But they worked hard, accumulated enough money so that freedom could be achieved. "You may see that couple later," wrote Bennett after the goal had been attained, "in a suburban house—a real home for the time being, with a tolerable imitation of a garden all about it." And the husband, no longer harried and jumpy, has ironically become "calmer, milder, more benevolent, and more resignedly worried."[32]

The Earl of Birkenhead, in comparing the businessman of 1900 with the businessman of 1924, noted above all else how the latter more frequently went to the club, drank with the Elks, played golf, and generally relaxed. A good portion of this tendency came, of course, as a reaction against the grueling exertions of the First World War. MacQuarrie had predicted, as the war ended, that Americans would now want some fun. In 1920 Harold Spender wrote that "one strong impres-

[31] Phillippo, *The United States and Cuba,* pp. 98–99; Faithfull, *Three Visits to America,* p. 81.
[32] Bennett, *Your United States,* pp. 175, 176.

sion left by America to-day is that there is more innocent merriment and less sour goodness." He also made a generalization about the "one outstanding feature of American life" that writers a half century earlier would have been hard put even to imagine: "That is the atmosphere of serenity, the calmness of outlook, the confidence in survival."[33]

It was not simply the Great War that seemed to inject this new note into American life. In 1913, speaking of the growing effort to curb immigration to the United States, Stephen Graham sarcastically remarked that the old idealism was giving way before the republic's new destination wherein "everybody is to be well dressed, well housed, comfortable."[34] Materialism and passive pleasure went together; they expressed a certain dissatisfaction with American life which was reflected in a conversation reported by L. P. Jacks during the Depression, but which still echoes today:

> I once asked an American friend, "What is it that makes life in this hell of a city [New York] tolerable to the young people?" His answer was "Sex"; and I remembered a saying of M. Bergson, *"Toute notre civilisation est aphrodisiaque."* "And what makes it tolerable to people like you?" I continued. "It isn't tolerable," he answered, "we all want to escape from it as soon as we have made enough money to buy our freedom"—the first intimation I had of "the philosophy of escape" which I was afterwards to hear much spoken of in other American cities.[35]

It would be foolish to deny the existence of these escapist interests before the 1920's. But it would be blind to deny the novelty of their comparative prominence in the British travel accounts written from 1900 to 1935. Still, in contrast to what we hear today, fewer than half of the foreign commentators wrote of a nation of sloth, of a nation desiring only security, escape, sex, ease, and "fun." Movies and radios were only beginning their ascendancy in the realms of vicarious satisfactions, and the euphoric effects of television lay in the unimagined distance.[36]

[33] Frederick E. S. Smith, the first Earl of Birkenhead, *America Revisited*, p. 7; MacQuarrie, *Over Here*, p. 145; H. Spender, *A Briton in America*, pp. 19, 21.

[34] Graham, *With Poor Immigrants to America*, p. 10.

[35] Jacks, *My American Friends*, p. 38.

[36] Philip Gibbs paid attention to an "institution which [in 1920] occupies a prominent place in every American township. That is the picture-palace. It is impossible to overrate the influence upon the minds and characters of the people which is exercised by that house of assembly. It has become part of the life of the American people more essentially than we know it in England" (*People of Destiny*, pp. 75–76). The Norwegian, Halvdan Koht, writes that "in contemporary intellectual life nothing seems so distinctly American as the 'movies.' . . . Their appearance on the world stage may best be compared with the invention of the art of printing in the fifteenth century. . . . In all

Only occasionally did one of the writers see the now platitudinous comparison between the United States and the dying Roman Empire. Englishmen, as a group, continued to be staggered by the pace and power of American life; but superimposed above all this motion, a few thought they detected a growing desire for surcease.

THE RISE OF COLLECTIVE MAN

A tendency to characterize the American as a conformist, as an "other-directed" figure, has always been present in British travel literature. The observers never regarded Americans as individualists in the sense of having individuality or being intellectually free. The great exception was in economic affairs, where, with wealth apparently within everyone's reach, ingenuity, innovation, and courage were often the hallmarks of the American. When, however, that opportunity seemed to be diminishing, when political freedom was said to be becoming more circumscribed, when individual enterprise was giving way to corporate activity and work to play, American conformist tendencies came to the forefront of British analysis.

George Steevens wrote of this disquieting development in the terms of a nation in "bondage to fashion." C. Reginald Enock in 1909 remarked upon "the condition of uniformity among the people, reminding us of a great ant-army." John Spender discovered "the habit which Americans have of doing everything in common" and he thought "their willing conformity to standards set for them and ready acceptance of things produced in bulk, are a perpetual surprise to Europeans brought up to think of privacy, domesticity, and individual development as things of high value." Joad continued the ant-robot metaphor by writing that "every effort is made in America to secure uniformity—uniformity in conduct, uniformity in clothes, uniformity in thought. America is and seeks increasingly to be the perfect Paradise of Robots."[37]

A few authors, such as Clare Sheridan (just back from Russia) could facetiously find something positive about this standardizing process "that suppresses individuality"; the suppression sped up the assimilation proc-

---

matters relating to movies, America decidedly has the lead. Its influence on the world through this art is immense" (*The American Spirit in Europe: A Survey of Transatlantic Influences* [Philadelphia: University of Pennsylvania Press, 1949], p. 242). The related tendency for Americans to prefer being spectators at professional athletic contests rather than participating themselves is recognized by Muirhead, *America, the Land of Contrasts*, p. 107; Low, *America at Home*, p. 145; and Brown, *The Real America*, pp. 255–56.

[37] Steevens, *Land of the Dollar*, p. 311; Enock, *Farthest West*, p. 319; J. A. Spender, *Through English Eyes*, pp. 317–18; Joad, *The Babbitt Warren*, p. 92.

ess of the immigrants in the New World. Morgan Philips Price had a more mature and serious appreciation of the tendencies of modern life —the industrial complexities, the need for an expanded bureaucracy, for legislative planning, for financial and commercial combines to maximize efficiency and order the needs of an expanding and interacting population. He insisted at the end of the book he wrote in 1934 that a new age was dawning and that new responses to it were of vital importance, for "if America is to live, her citizens must learn to cooperate in house-keeping. A beginning has been made, but the way is long and difficult."[38]

Most of the Britons were not, however, particularly comforted by this spreading uniformity, which they felt was dehumanizing. J. B. Priestley said, in 1937, of the emergence of this new type of animal— the collective man:

> . . . there is something fundamentally hostile to the communal and collectivist ideal in the French, whereas in America, notwithstanding her intrenched capitalism, and her boast of being so strongly individualistic, there is not this fundamental hostility, that in America the battle is already half won. American economists and politicians and newspaper editors may go on and on shouting about their individualism, but the great unconscious drift of American life, it seemed to me, was away from it, set towards a very different shore.

The great hidden force which, according to Priestley, had tugged American life toward the new shore was standardization. "What used to be regarded as one of the chief weaknesses of the collectivist state—its probable tendency towards standardization—has been at work remolding American social life these last two generations." The result, Priestley concluded:

> The collective man, the socialist citizen, is not a weird new type that may arrive in the United States any year now. In almost all but his theories, the average modern American *is* the collective man. His impulsive advances seem to be always away from that famous individualism. He has no objection to mass movement. Nearly everything he does is being done about the same time by a million others. He likes doing exactly what all the others are doing. So does his wife."[39]

THE DECLINE OF OPTIMISM

The vast dichotomy between the American theory of liberty and her practice of collectivization as postulated by Priestley hinged, in part, on

[38] Sheridan, *My American Diary,* p. 135; M. P. Price, *America After Sixty Years,* p. 235.

[39] Priestley, *Midnight on the Desert,* pp. 118, 121.

the extent to which the theory of liberty was important in the United States. As we have seen, most of the nineteenth-century British travelers were impressed with the prevalence of the egalitarian ethos in the New World over the libertarian disposition, and many of them felt that conformity and uniformity did not contradict altogether the logic of that ethos. The writers of the nineteenth-century travelogues always noted that the egalitarian ideal was united with the mighty belief of the Americans in progress. The belief in progress was inimical to standardizing tendencies, for it gave to American equality its dynamic; it made it open, experimental, generous, and hopeful. Its demise in the twentieth century and the shadow this demise cast over the American's optimism and confidence in the future was perhaps, in British opinion, the most basic and pervasive change that they witnessed.

Early in this century Low wrote, in words reminiscent of the most exultant patriot of the nineteenth century but no longer typical of the twentieth, that the American looks upon life

> . . . as waiting for him to conquer it, to win in a larger arena [than the schoolroom] greater and more substantial prizes. To the American everything is before him. He is as convinced that his people are the chosen people, his race the world's greatest race, as he is that nature has endowed his vast continent with more lavish generosity than that of any other land. Everything points to the fulfilment of his destiny—and destiny has declared that he shall march on ever triumphant.[40]

The theme of the American as perennial optimist never entirely faded, just as Bryce's reminder that "the United States are deemed all the world over to be pre-eminently the land of equality" has never fully disappeared from the popular imagination despite the many incursions and challenges made in recent times. The literary critic Ford Madox Ford found that "the note of New York as of all the United States of North America is hope." Huddleston repeated that even at the onset of the Depression "confidence is the keynote of America." Mais came upon "enthusiasm everywhere" and Jacks wrote that Americans continued to live for the future.[41]

But this was not the dominant tone of the twentieth-century travel accounts. As one would expect from the notes assembled in this chapter, the majority of the observers intoned with funereal insistence the onset of disillusion, doubt, difficulty, and even despair in the breasts of Americans. In the statements below, one should note that it is not the Britons

---

[40] Low, *America at Home*, p. 220.

[41] Bryce, *The American Commonwealth*, III, 525; Ford, *New York Is Not America*, p. 290; Huddleston, *What's Right with America*, p. 209; Mais, *A Modern Columbus*, p. 51; Jacks, *My American Friends*, p. 96.

who are gloomy; instead, they portray their New World cousins as worriers and self-doubters in stark contrast to what the Americans were once depicted to be. For example:

William Saunders (1879), anticipating the later trend: "Care and caution had replaced that careless confidence which is the real source of danger in public as in private life."[42]

Samuel Smith (1896): "Many of the best men in the United States regard the future with great anxiety."[43]

John Kendall (1896): "There appears to be a growing feeling that the condition of the middle classes in America is becoming harder as the years go by."[44]

H. G. Wells (1906): ". . . I have chanced upon a time of peculiar significance. The note of disillusionment sounds everywhere. America, for the first time in her history, is taking thought about herself, and ridding herself of long-cherished illusions."[45]

Alexander Francis (1909): " 'The American people finds itself today in the position of a man with a dulled knife and broken cudgel in the midst of an ever-growing circle of wolves.' This temper is far removed from the former national gaiety of heart which the nation, still young, ought to possess and must regain."[46]

J. Nelson Fraser (1910): "There is a general feeling abroad that the health of the people is not what it ought to be."[47]

Elijah Brown (1913): "When one looks at the America of to-day . . . with its insane worship of money and vulgar ostentation, its mismanagement and incapacity in high places, its hurry to get rich quickly at all cost, its bribery and corruption, its low standard of ideals and morals, its trusts and corporations which strangle its commercial life like the limbs of an octopus, its tainted justice, its scandal-loving press, its scamped and jerry-built cities, its packed State Legislatures, its many social problems which it seems quite incapable of solving; when one looks at all this, and sees how far she has fallen short of the fair promises of less than a century and a half ago, and when one sees how little hope there is for the future . . ."[48]

Philip Gibbs (1920): "The people of the United States have learned many other things during the last few years, when all the world has changed, and they stand now at the parting of the ways, looking back

---

[42] Saunders, *Through the Light Continent*, p. 4.
[43] S. Smith, *America Revisited*, p. 22.
[44] [John Kendall,] *American Memories*, p. 270.
[45] Wells, *The Future in America*, p. 287.
[46] Francis, *Americans: An Impression*, p. 16.
[47] Fraser, *America, Old and New*, p. 362.
[48] Brown, *The Real America*, p. 263.

on the things they knew which they will never see again, and looking forward to the future, which is still doubtful to them in its destiny."[49]

Mary Agnes Hamilton (1932): ". . . the all-round depression carries with it a real, if irrational doubt about the future. . . . One cannot help feeling that a doubt about certain immaterial elements—call them leadership, if you will—call them purpose: call them values—is undermining the national self-confidence. Once so serene, so soaring, its wings are certainly not moving at the moment."[50]

All sorts of explanations were postulated for this dramatic, dark shift in the national mood. Kipling was not alone in blaming "the rapidly diminishing bounty of Nature," nor Wells in speaking of "the extinction of opportunity."[51] We recall that others referred to the closing of the frontier, to the racial and class wars brought on by immigration and by rapid population increases as well as by various depressions and inflations, to the power of the wealthy, and to the loss of religious conviction. Very few commentators thought that a growing federal bureaucracy or a national government growing in power was primarily responsible for growth of national self-doubt. Most of the travelers applauded more active governmental adventures and the early New Deal was generally accorded a warm welcome by the Britons.

A more tangible reason for the decline of American enthusiasm was the aftermath of the Great War, which did not seem to end anything except many young lives. World War I, more than any other single event, more than the Civil War, more than the Census of 1890, more than the Depression of 1893, more than the assassination of McKinley, tempered the American's enthusiastic view of the future according to patterns traceable among the bulk of the travel books. The fatuous optimism of the 1920's struck the Britons as a cover-up for a deep insecurity about the future. The second tangible event that shattered American complacency was the Depression, which Miss Hamilton considered as much psychological as economic in its effects. Harold Laski, writing after the world-wide war of 1914 and during the world-wide Depression that began fifteen years later, properly placed the mood itself in a world-wide context. He said, "The general temper of the world is one of profound and widespread disillusionment. Our generation seems to have lost its scheme of values. Certainty has been replaced by cynicism; hope has given room to despair." Even in 1911, before both the war and the Depression, Miss Meakin remarked that "the self-complacency so noticeable in the American of the nineteenth century, and which resulted

---

[49] Gibbs, *People of Destiny*, p. 107.
[50] Hamilton, *In America Today*, pp. 142–43.
[51] Kipling, *American Notes*, p. 236; Wells, *The Future in America*, p. 108.

from his living so far apart from the rest of the world, is now giving way to a narrow introspection."[52]

The weariness of the Old World may have been infiltrating at last the isolated innocence of America, or else the New World was just growing up. Whatever the explanation, it seemed clear to the visitors that the eager, hopeful, cocky view of life once credited to Americans had given way to a greater sadness, or, as not a few Britons conceived it, had become tempered finally with wisdom and humility.[53]

THE YOUTH MATURES

Wisdom and humility had never been attributes with which the British travelers endowed Americans. And while the tone of the foregoing discussion has been rather negative—the decline of liberty, hope, equality, opportunity, and idealism—while it has implied disdainful British depreciation of the performance of the United States in the twentieth century, such an implication would be no truer than its complement: that the nineteenth-century visitors were universally fond of the boastful, egalitarian society. The representation of the uncouth, arrogant, irreverent Yankee dated, it should be remembered, from the earlier period.

All the qualities of nineteenth-century America, inspired, insulting, indifferent, were captured in the metaphor of youthfulness: the swagger and the hope, the roughness and the idealism. In the twentieth century this metaphor seemed to the Britons to be less apt, in part because a maturation process was proceeding that seemed to be softening the primitive, overly assertive edges of the American profile. Through hard

---

[52] Laski, *Democracy in Crisis,* p. 16; Meakin, *What America Is Doing,* p. 363.

[53] That American optimism has been no undiluted blessing is made abundantly clear in a highly stimulating book on United States diplomacy by Robert Heilbroner entitled *The Future as History* (New York: Harper, 1959). Heilbroner contends that the American approach to foreign policy has always been shaped by "the philosophy of optimism," which assumes that Americans can shape the future world in any way they please. Americans have believed this to be true simply because, in the past, they always have been able to impose their will successfully. But today, Heilbroner insists, when atomic weapons are not a monopoly of this nation, "the philosophy of optimism" is tragically outmoded, unrealistic, dangerous, and disillusioning. It could lead either to despair or war. Heilbroner no doubt would agree with Wells's comment in 1906 (*The Future in America,* p. 287) that the United States, by shaking off her optimism, would be simultaneously "ridding herself of long-cherished illusions." Heilbroner's words were written before America's long involvement in the Southeast Asian war—a war which has furnished a dramatic demonstration of his thesis.

times and serious failures, the United States was growing up. But by British standards the nation could hardly yet be called mature. Despite advances in culture, in the arts, and in manners (signaled by the growing ascendancy of the American woman), intellect, civilization, and wisdom had not yet been achieved. Furthermore, ample residues of youthful energy, faith, power, cockiness, and idealism (by European standards) could not be argued out of existence. The United States may not be so young as it once was, the visitors seemed to say, but neither certainly was it yet a man. To meet these conditions from a literary standpoint, a large number of Britons seized upon a new metaphor for a new century to replace the image of America, the youth. America, they decided, had reached the stage of development and the outlook of a college student.

Consider, "It is only when one looks at the recent childhood of America that one realises its amazing growth to maturity. And it is still young, still at college, so to say; still capable of learning, and of readjusting itself to new dignities."[54]

Or, the Americans "have a boisterous sense of importance and prestige, but rather as a young college man is aware of his lustiness and vitality without considering the duties and dangers that have come to him with manhood. . . . The flowering-time of America seems due to arrive, after its growing pains."[55]

Or, "It is not exactly that Americans strike one as young in spirit; rather they strike one as undeveloped. It is as though they had never faced life and asked themselves what it is."[56]

Or, once more, the American "is as a youth at school who has won all the prizes, who at college has carried off the honours."[57]

One naturally suspects that there may be some link between the advent of this curious comparison (these quotations all derive from the first three decades of this century) and the heightened fascination shown on both sides of the Atlantic with American college education, though the connection would probably be more poetic than functional.

The abandonment of the metaphor of youth could be used as an excuse for detraction or tribute as it suited, as always, the propensities of the author. Charles Whibley, for example, declared that the loss of youth signified the end of "the golden age":

In vain you will search the United States for the signs of youth. Wherever you cast your eyes you will find the signal proofs of an eager, grasping age. Youth loiters and is glad, listening to the songs of birds, won-

[54] Humphreys, *America—Through English Eyes*, p. 233.
[55] Gibbs, *People of Destiny*, pp. 157–58.
[56] Dickinson, *Appearances*, p. 173.
[57] Low, *America at Home*, p. 220.

dering at the flowers which carpet the meadow, and recking not of the morrow. America is grave and in a hurry. She is not content to fleet the time carelessly as they did in the golden age.[58]

It was the maturity of the land that struck Mrs. Tweedie as its great virtue. "No, no," she cried, "America is not young. She is in the full force of her strength and maturity. She is a great country, and has a great people, so it is a little childish and peevish to be always sheltering herself under the cloak of babyhood."[59]

One nice turn of events for one who has read these books dating over the past one hundred years is that the twentieth-century British friends of the United States were able to shower their praise of the nation in precisely those terms that the nineteenth-century visitors thought least applicable—the terms of tradition, conservatism, and maturity. Low could appeal to the most respectable Tory when he said, "Yesterday a sprawling infant, today the United States is a full-grown man. . . . Under the light layer of emotion is a solid substratum of the Anglo-Saxon conservatism." Jacks, with only half irony, could make the Americans ancient: "The Americans," he observed, "are really a very old people and though they make a show of despising tradition are as tightly in the grip of tradition as the British, and more so at certain points." And Harold Spender wrote: "Let us get a firm grip of this new fact of world life on this planet. It is not Europe, let us fully realise, but America which is now 'the land of ordered liberty.' It is not America, but Europe, which is now the sport of rash and random experiments. It is not Europe, but America, which now holds fast to the faith of its forefathers."[60] By their testimony, the rash land of youth had become at least as conservative as Great Britain herself.

BETTER MANNERS, HIGHER CULTURE, FINER INTELLECT

The commentators had more direct, less literary means for expressing their respect for the modern United States. For when the youth grows

[58] Whibley, *American Sketches*, p. 299.

[59] Tweedie, *America as I Saw It*, p. 2. Americans, proclaimed Gibbs, "are the new People of Destiny in the world of progress, because after their early adventures of youth, their time of preparation, their immense turbulent growth, their forging of tools, and training of soul, they stand now in their full strength and maturity, powerful with the power of a great, free, confident people" (*People of Destiny*, p. 156). Chesterton wrote a witty exposé of the logical fallacy behind using the metaphor of youth in the first place in *What I Saw in America*, pp. 189–91.

[60] Low, *America at Home*, pp. 4–7; Jacks, *My American Friends*, p. 56; H. Spender, *A Briton in America*, p. 19. See also Freeman, *Impressions of the United States*, p. 292; Archer, *America Today*, p. 56.

up a bit, his manners soften, he gains in tact, consideration, and polite-
ness what he loses in spontaneity. This change, certainly agreeable to
most travelers, and exemplified by their ecstacy over the emergence in
recent decades of the graceful American lady, was recognized as occurring even in Bryce's time. Said Bryce:

> The concurrent testimony of European travellers, including both ad-
> mirers and detractors of democracy, proves that manners must have been
> disagreeable forty years ago, and one finds nowadays an equally general
> admission that the Americans are as pleasant to one another and to
> strangers as are the French or the Germans or the English. The least
> agreeable feature to the visitors of former years, an incessant vaunting
> of their own country and disparagement of others, has disappeared, and
> the tinge of self-assertion which the sense of equality used to give is now
> but faintly noticeable.[61]

At the same time, and more important, there were giant strides being taken intellectually and culturally by the men as well as by the
women of the maturing nation. This advance received long-overdue
acknowledgment from the Britons who, on this subject, had had a past
history of depressing snobbishness. The kind words in behalf of American higher education and American women tell only part of the tale.
If equality had hindered the possibilities for true intellectual excellence, then equality's partial demise in recent times promised, according to the more fair-minded British logicians, new opportunities for the
American intellect. Bryce noted this explicitly when he observed that
by education the

> . . . general level tends to rise. But the level of intellectual attainment
> in that small but increasing class who have studied at the best native uni-
> versities or in Europe, and who pursue learning and science either as a
> profession or as a source of pleasure, rises faster than does the general
> level of the multitude, so that in this regard also it appears that equality
> has diminished and will diminish further.[62]

Joseph Hatton made this same point earlier (1881) when he stated
that "all through American cities and in the best society the tendency
is toward making intellect aristocratic, to give knowledge and culture
foremost places." Another of Sisley Huddleston's explanations for
What's Right with America was "because there is a thirst for knowledge
which is revealed in the remarkably large attendance at the colleges and
universities, in the general love of lectures, and in the sales of popular
books on natural science, philosophy, history, and so forth."[63]

[61] Bryce, *The American Commonwealth*, III, 540.
[62] *Ibid.*, p. 528.
[63] Hatton, *To-day in America*, p. 3; Huddleston, *What's Right with America*,
p. 244.

American achievement in science, theoretical to a greater degree than ever before, as well as technological, attracted greater attention. Developments in literature, architecture, and the fine arts in general fared less well at British hands, but that neglect, too, was rapidly altering in the twentieth century. John Galsworthy credited Americans with "the aspiring eye" and he concluded one of his 1919 lectures with a spirited defense of the American mind. "People are inclined to smile at me," he remarked, "when I suggest that you in America are at the commencement of a period of fine and vigorous Art. The signs, they say, are all the other way. Of course you ought to know best; all the same, I stick to my opinion with British obstinacy, and I believe I shall see it justified."[64]

Ten years later, few Britons could any longer dispute Galsworthy's point. It took too long for the visitors to acknowledge the fine work of various American novelists, poets, composers, performers, painters, historians, sculptors, dramatists, architects, pure scientists, scholars, and philosophers. The British had defined "art" rather rigidly, and the process of accepting new standards came to them only with the greatest difficulty. But at least by the late 1920's it took an unflinching and unseeing observer, a critic of great stubbornness, to call the United States mindless, and the number of these critics appeared to be very small.

GREATER WEALTH, GREATER POWER, GROWING RESPONSIBILITY

Nothing astounded the British visitors in the twentieth century more than: (1) the fantastic wealth of the United States, signaled by her material achievements from the tallest skyscrapers to the fastest automobiles to the tiniest radios; and (2) her extraordinary rise in political, economic, and diplomatic power. Every visitor, depending upon his state of mind, was either thrilled, amazed, frightened, disturbed, or overwhelmed by America's technical wizardry and resultant high living standard (unevenly distributed though many thought it to be). No one took these developments in stride.

Among the material advances, a few devices whose effect was to reduce labor and to provide leisure and pleasure caused the strongest reactions. Automobiles, radios, telephones, movies, refrigerators, and household gadgets of all kinds not only brought great transformations in American life, but augured similar ones for Great Britain and the rest of the planet as well.[65] Patterns for the way the new spare time would be

[64] John Galsworthy, *Addresses in America*, pp. 53, 57.
[65] Bennett, *Your United States*, has a charming passage on "the telephone habit," p. 74.

used emanated, thought the commentators, from the United States. Even at a nadir of the Depression, Harry Greenwall reported how "the rest of the world thinks of America in terms of films, radio and dance tunes."[66]

All the other developments outlined in this chapter pale, however, when placed beside the inescapable conclusion, admitted by the British and the rest of the world, that the United States, not Great Britain, was the most powerful nation in the world. Especially after 1920, only rare, feeble protests were mustered against this proposition. Reactions to this development varied from dismay to envy to exaltation.[67] The policies recommended for Britain in light of this shift in power ranged from wary distrustfulness of the United States to passionate embraces of the blood relative who, if not properly propitiated, could be a dangerous enemy. Collinson Owen advised Americans to shun foreign entanglements,[68] but a far larger number of the writers urged the Americans to avoid isolationism and assume international responsibility commensurate with their nation's power. In fact, the majority of the British observers converged around a common position regarding this accession of power—a position of good, typical British common sense. They recognized who had the power;[69] they admired the Americans for an impressive achievement in the space of an unprecedentedly short span of years; they hoped, even if they had grave doubts, that the United States would assume world leadership with the same kind of responsibility and restraint that England had exercised in the preceding century; and they advised their countrymen to regard the Americans as allies, to cooperate with them as closely and amicably as possible. Acceptance, rather than the jealousy which many assume to be the British response, was the dominant attitude in the travel accounts toward the American accession to power. This note of British resignation seems somewhat pathetic in comparison with the assured self-sufficiency of the pre-Civil War visitors, but it is preferable to the churlishness that one might have expected to encounter many more times than was the case.

We leave it to the final chapter, in which we shall attempt to sort out these various observations about the United States from 1885 to 1935, to determine whether any larger generalizations may usefully be made about this period. We shall also look at the general problem of change and continuity in American values from the perspective of almost a century of comment on the New World found in the British books of travel.

[66] Greenwall, *American Scene*, p. 77.
[67] The United States of America, trumpeted William Archer, "is a rehearsal for the United States of Europe, nay, of the world" (*America Today*, p. 154).
[68] Owen, *The American Illusion*, p. 254. He did this out of fear of American imperialism.
[69] "America leads the pack" said Joad, *The Babbitt Warren*, p. xi.

XI

Change and
Continuity in
American Values

T HE POINT HAS BEEN REACHED at which an effort, in the interests
of clarity, should be made to pull together these various observations
concerning the years from 1885 to 1935. It has been previously stated
that the British view of the United States from 1845 to 1900 fixed itself
on the American attempt to simplify and to incorporate the Enlightenment conception of man's perfectibility and a version of Rousseau's romantic egalitarianism into their own peculiar New World ideological
concoction; and that, furthermore, the Americans fashioned institutions
which expressed these ideas in concrete situations so successfully that
they appeared to confirm the beliefs and perpetuate a happy cycle.

1885–1935

One must not conclude from the foregoing analysis that the British travelers of the period 1900 to 1935 decided that the United States had rejected these creeds altogether and become a slothful, greedy, pessimistic
land of inequality. Condorcet and Rousseau still had a home in American ideology in the eyes of these chroniclers; hopes for the future and
hopes to rise beyond one's inherited status have never disappeared from
the American imagination, and the Britons never insisted that they had.
What may safely be concluded, however, is that the integration the
Britishers postulated between the two American articles of faith and
their institutional manifestations had broken down. Compared to that of
an earlier era, the British picture of twentieth-century America was
muddy, complicated, filled with new, odd shapes, many colors, and lacking a frame. The neat simplicity and balance of the nineteenth-century
portrait had vanished.[1]

[1] The emergence of these new complexities may have two very simple explanations. First, the United States may have, in fact, been growing more com-

So far, we have talked about changes reported by the British between the United States of 1845–1900 and the United States of 1885–1935 in a negative way, as the replacement of a well-defined harmony by an ill-defined dissonance. This is the way Jacks summed up his comparison of the United States between his memories of his 1886 visit and those of his visit in 1933. Idealism, which for him lent that original harmony its definition, "struck [me] very forcibly on my first visit in 1886. . . . No doubt it still survives, but very feebly, if at all, among the people whom it has been my lot to encounter in this year of disillusion."[2]

Must we settle for "muddy picture" or "ill-defined dissonance" as the final word for the British picture of modern America? Did the visitors simply talk miscellaneously about money, culture, leisure, and power, about the sundry demises of idealism, optimism, and equality? Can one construct from these books a faithful, comprehensive model for the twentieth-century United States to replace the one powered by the spirited egalitarian motor at whose thrust the earlier commentators had marveled? The honest answer is that no such similar, clear, and simple order can be imposed upon the travel accounts after 1885, no grand generalization emerges that would not greatly distort the meaning of these works. If any positive generalization can be mustered concerning the British view of America from 1885 to 1935, one must weakly but accurately fall back upon calling this period a transitional one. The old ethos lingered, but not unscarred; a new set of ideas and conditions, many of them quite incompatible with the old, entered the lists to do battle. By 1935, it was not possible for the British to say which values were in the ascendancy; one could only say that Americans appeared to be far more torn and confused than once they had been in the eyes of earlier observers. As H. G. Wells wrote in 1935:

> Putting it in the most general terms, what has happened to America is what has happened to the rest of the world. The American mind has not kept its vision of the world and its thought about social structure up to date. While France goes on with late eighteenth-century political and business ideas, while Germany flounders in the tawdry militarist nationalism of the middle nineteenth century, and Russia clings to revolutionary patterns sixty years out of date, America, like Britain, has been caught short of any vital social and economic philosophy at all. . . . America even now is failing to display any real vigor of intellectual synthesis.[3]

---

plex as she entered the twentieth century, just as these books, taken *in toto*, suggest. Or, second, and not to be ignored, perhaps the British travelers themselves were growing in their understanding of what had always been, in reality, an intricate civilization. I suspect that both explanations are in part true.

[2] Jacks, *My American Friends*, p. 59.

[3] Wells, *The New America*, p. 37.

The turning point at which the older egalitarian synthesis seems finally to have crumbled in the British view came with the advent and aftermath of the First World War. It is this event to which European historians frequently refer as bringing whatever was left of the Enlightenment on the Continent to an end. The "disillusionment" after Versailles gave rise in America during the 1920's to such recognizably contemporary phenomena as the race for "fun," the collective man, the desperate search for security, the rise of the mass media, the final triumph of urban civilization, unparalleled prosperity, and new experiments in morality.

Because this study goes only as far as 1935 it is impossible to affirm whether the travelers perceived a new pattern of American life emerging in the 1920's which they could demark with the same clarity and over as substantial a period of time as they had done in the nineteenth century. But one might note the words of Professor Cushing Strout, who, in his rebuttal to Carl Degler's criticism of the historical soundness of *The Lonely Crowd,* stated:

> As an historian, I should think, instead of minimizing any change in the social character of Americans [which he felt Degler and other continuity-minded historians tended to do], we might find it more profitable and appropriate to look into the 1920's as a seed-bed for those emphases in style which *The Lonely Crowd* has identified so vividly that we can no longer look at our own time without reference to its categories.[4]

But before deciding on the period during which a new era of American culture was ushered in, we must present the case for stressing the continuity of values in American history.[5]

TOO MANY WATERSHEDS

The most persuasive recent argument for emphasizing continuity in American values has been shaped, curiously enough, not by an historian but by a historically aware sociologist, Seymour Lipset. It reveals, in passing, the danger of concluding that fundamental change has occurred in the United States on the basis of evidence that reaches only as far as the 1930's.

Professor Lipset noted the sharp differences between social com-

[4] Cushing Strout, "A Note on Degler, Riesman, Tocqueville," *American Quarterly,* XVI (1964), 102.

[5] Two historical studies that illuminate these various problems of periodization and shed light on the pivotal years surrounding the First World War and after are Henry May, *The End of American Innocence: A Study of the First Years of Our Time, 1912–1917* (New York: Knopf, 1959), and William E. Leuchtenburg, *The Perils of Prosperity: 1914–32* (Chicago, Ill.: University of Chicago Press, 1958).

mentators of the 1930's and those of the 1950's, and he observed that in each instance, these analysts felt that the United States was going through a period unlike any that had previously occurred:

> In the 1930's American social scientists were certain that the country was undergoing major structural changes. In the 1930's they were sure that these changes were making status lines more rigid, that there was a movement away from achieved status back to ascribed status, and that the equalitarian ethic was threatened as a consequence. Such typical writers of the 1950's as David Riesman and William H. Whyte contend that it is the achievement motive and the Protestant ethic of hard work that are dying: they think that the new society prefers security, emotional stability, and "getting along with others."[6]

As evidence for this comparison, Lipset referred to such analysts of the 1930's as Robert S. Lynd, Karen Horney, Harold Laski, and W. L. Warner, who, he claimed, "all agreed that the egalitarian emphasis on American democracy was declining sharply under the growth of the large-scale corporation, monopoly capitalism, and economic competition. They asserted categorically that mobility had decreased, and Warner predicted the development of rigid status lines based on family background." These views were echoed by many of the British observers discussed in the previous chapter. "Twenty years later," Lipset continued, "these interpretations are almost unanimously rejected." The difference, according to Lipset, lies in the altered economic circumstances of the two decades. The Depression "inclined intellectuals toward an equalitarian radicalism, which condemned capitalism and achievement orientation as the source of evils," including even conservatives such as Warner. The return of prosperity in our time has "renewed the legitimacy of many conservative institutions and values" and it has caused some, even self-styled socialists and liberals, to criticize not only "the radical excesses of the former period," but to subject to new scrutiny even the "equalitarian values themselves."[7]

Lipset does not believe these claims that American values were in fact changing very rapidly. He refers approvingly to Marcus Cunliffe's article on "American Watersheds"[8] concerning the often-repeated and mistaken "American propensity to feel that the country is going through a major change at any 'present time.' " This belief arises from the fact of rapid social change in America, from the inclination to repudiate altogether Europe—the symbol of worldly corruption and of the past—and from the sense of mission which makes Americans feel they can control

[6] Seymour Martin Lipset, *The First New Nation: The United States in Historical and Comparative Perspective* (New York: Basic Books, 1963), p. 102.
[7] *Ibid.*, p. 125.
[8] *American Quarterly*, XIII (1961), 479–94.

their fate and which hence causes them to bemoan with a special intensity those tendencies that they find inimical to their mission. These beliefs to the contrary, Cunliffe feels that "there has been a surprising continuity in American history as compared with the histories of European nations."

Lipset's purpose in all this is "to present some of the evidence for my thesis that it is the basic value system, as solidified in the early days of the new nation, which can account for the kinds of changes that have taken place in the American character and in American institutions as these faced the need to adjust to the requirements of an urban, industrial, and bureaucratic society."[9] In this contemporary effort to opt for continuity over change in the American character or the American value system, Lipset rallies to his side many of the leading scholars of our time—Henry Nash Smith, Walt Rostow, Henry Steele Commager, Daniel Boorstin, Louis Hartz, Ralph Gabriel—each of whom, he alleges, has "in a different way, argued the effective continuity of the fundamental ideals of the society."[10]

As further evidence for the continuity of American values Lipset mentions a 1941 study of the American character in which the investigator divided American history into four periods: Pre–Civil War (to 1865), 1866–1917, 1918–29, and 1930–40:

> For each period a list of traits alleged by observers was recorded, and "when the lists for each of the four time periods were compared, no important difference between the traits mentioned by modern observers and those writing in the earlier periods of American history was discovered." Among the traits mentioned in all four periods were: "Belief in equality of all as a fact and as a right" and "uniformity and conformity."[11]

[9] Lipset, *First New Nation*, p. 104. Occasionally, as in the Cunliffe citation, Lipset mixes continuity in American history with that in American values. Generally, however, Lipset stays quite consistently with value structures, and with those we too shall stay.

[10] Henry Nash Smith, *Virgin Land: The American West as Symbol and Myth* (Cambridge, Mass.: Harvard University Press, 1950); W. W. Rostow, "The National Style," in Elting E. Morison, ed., *The American Style: Essays in Value and Performance* (New York: Harper, 1958); Henry Steele Commager, *Living Ideas in America* (New York: Harper, 1951); Daniel Boorstin, *The Genius of American Politics* (Chicago, Ill.: University of Chicago Press, 1953), and *The Lost World of Thomas Jefferson* (New York: Henry Holt, 1948); Louis M. Hartz, *The Liberal Tradition in America: An Interpretation of American Political Thought Since the Revolution* (New York: Harcourt, Brace, 1955); and Ralph H. Gabriel, *The Course of American Democratic Thought* (New York: Ronald Press, 1956). Lipset explains: "Boorstin sees these values or basic premises as 'naturalism.' Hartz calls his version 'liberalism,' while Gabriel speaks of a 'democratic faith' with three aspects" (*First New Nation*, p. 106).

[11] Lipset, *First New Nation*, p. 106, referring to Lee Coleman, "What Is America? A Study of Alleged American Traits," *Social Forces*, XIX (1941), 492–99.

This, of course, leads us to Lipset's own version of which values have been central to the American character since at least the American Revolution, an event that Lipset feels, more than do most historians, signally shaped American beliefs. Two values, often complementary, sometimes antagonistic, but usually interacting in some way, have dominated the American stage: equality and achievement.

> When I say that we value equality, I mean that we believe all persons must be given respect simply because they are human beings; we believe that the differences between high- and low-status people reflect accidental, and perhaps temporary, variations in social relationships. This emphasis on equality was reflected in the introduction of universal suffrage in America long before it came in other nations; in the fairly consistent and extensive support for a public school system so that all might have a common educational background; and in the pervasive antagonism to domination by any elite in culture, politics, or economics.

While we are familiar with this, we are somewhat less so with achievement as a value.

> The value we have attributed to achievement [Lipset explains] is a corollary to our belief in equality. For people to be equal, they need a chance to become equal. Success, therefore, should be attainable by all, no matter what the accidents of birth, class, or race. Achievement is a function of equality of opportunity. That this emphasis on achievement must lead to new inequalities of status and to the use of corrupt means to secure and maintain high position is the ever recreated and renewed American dilemma.[12]

Although his definition of achievement as a value is a bit imprecise, we can have a fairly good idea of what Lipset means when he uses as related terms to achievement such words as "opportunity" and "competition." Its institutional embodiment is "capitalism"; its distortion is "materialism."

Here then we encounter an ingenious way of creating a model for continuity. Not only are the two values sometimes corollary and sometimes antithetical, but they are both open-ended and they permit the scholar to account for actual conflict and change within the wide limits of their meaning. That they touch on subjects discussed in this study in a peculiarly direct and relevant way should be clear by now.

CHANGE AND CONTINUITY IN THE TRAVEL ACCOUNTS

Lipset's work is relevant here not only because it is the most recent, as well as one of the most interesting, in a long line of attempts to throw

---

[12] Lipset, *First New Nation*, pp. 1–2.

light on the American character and because of its confrontation of the change versus continuity debate in American history. It is also important because it uses, as its chief base of evidence to prove the constant pervasiveness of his twin themes of equality and achievement, the writings of foreign travelers to the United States. He employs these data in the standard manner. That is, beginning with his thesis he finds quotable substantiation from the vast travel literature, in this case testimonials proclaiming the existence of the ideals of achievement and equality at various times throughout the period from the American Revolution until the present time. He goes beyond some historians in citing also the secondary summations available in Mesick, Berger, Torrielli, and Brooks.

If we bring to bear the new evidence presented in this study of over 225 post–Civil War British visitors, we find no definite repudiation of Lipset's thesis. The themes of both equality and achievement have indeed been sounded frequently by British commentators from 1860 to 1935. The persistence of the values is undeniable, especially in comparison with those dominant in the nations of the Old World. Yet the material assembled here in previous chapters also suggests great changes in the American value structure; it points to a twentieth-century American culture greatly at variance with the comparatively untroubled, idealistic American civilization of the preceding era. The contrast is not merely a matter of a difference in the tone or feeling which the republic evoked in the travelers of the two periods. There is a substantive philosophical and spiritual difference that evolves around the *faith in progress* in the New World. The earlier American did not doubt himself or his nation's destiny; the later American, says the Briton, does. The earlier American was very young; the later citizen has, as it were, graduated from college at the height of his young adulthood and, while he attempts to remain young, virile, and innocent, he must face up to the difficult, unwonted, and unwanted responsibilities of maturity.

Lipset paid only scant attention to the idea of progress in his analysis, but the British travelers wrote of it constantly. It was not only an idea with an identity separate from the egalitarian principle (unlike the achievement value), but the visitors linked the faith in tomorrow directly with the zeal, optimism, vitality, and transcendent youth by which they came to identify the nineteenth-century republic.

These qualities, furthermore, understood as a stance toward life, lent American equality its upward thrust, and invested the desire to succeed with its zestful rather than its anxious side. And travelers in *this* century have noted that the race to succeed has not always been the joyful affair of charging ahead, but has become now more often a harried effort to "keep up." So even if it can be shown that there has been little abatement of the egalitarian-achievement ethos in modern times, it is possible

that the activities conducted in its name may be carried on in an altogether different, more tentative, spirit than ever before in the New
World.

These are all matters of degree; one should be able to talk about both
change *and* continuity in the history of any nation, depending upon the
point of reference. If in this case Europe is that reference point, then
American values no doubt appear to gain some tenacity. In this century,
though, of two world wars, mass murders, deep depressions, unparalleled challenges to theism, the creation of man's most terrible weapons,
the rise of totalitarianism, and the uncontrolled spread of violence, depravity, race hatred, generation gaps, and bloody revolutions, the belief
in progress, even in America, has not been strengthened. It should not
tax our logic to take seriously the British claim that this faith—which had
once been so central to American mythology—has been undermined in
modern America. It would require a much greater stretch of the imagination, on the other hand, to believe that during the past two hundred
years—the most rapidly changing epoch in the history of mankind—the
value system of the United States had not undergone some very significant alterations.

THE DELUGE AND THERMIDOR

The British travelers as a group, over a long period of time, do *implicitly*
furnish the historian with a positive way of talking about the contrast
between the nineteenth-century New World and twentieth-century
America. If the reader will draw back and view these many books from
a very broad perspective, it will become apparent that the picture of the
United States painted by the Britons from 1845 to 1900 bears resemblance at many points to a society in the throes of revolution. This is not
meant literally, for these years saw the national government stably in
power (except for a few years in 1860's), and were years generally characterized by a respect for law and order. Nothing met Crane Brinton's
specific definition of revolution as an event that witnessed the "drastic,
sudden substitution of one group in charge of the running of a territorial
political entity for another group." There was no sign of "the revolutionary substitution of one group for another, [which] if not made by
actual violent uprising, is made by *coup d'état, Putsch,* or some other
kind of skullduggery [*sic*]."[13]

Yet the nineteenth-century society of the United States as seen by the
British travelers bore several unmistakable attributes of a revolutionary

[13] Crane Brinton, *The Anatomy of Revolution* (1st ed., 1938; New York:
Vintage Books, 1957), p. 4.

society.[14] Four of these stand out. First, the Britons bore witness to an intense idealism, even to an ideology centering around the mythic faiths in equality and progress. If this is true, it seriously contradicts the view of certain American historians, such as Daniel Boorstin, who insist that America has been distinguished from other nations by its *lack* of ideology, by its practical pragmatism that prefers to deal with each case one at a time, specifically and flexibly, without the inhabitions of a priori theory.

Second, the British reported a fervency, an energy, even a religious zeal in the execution of that faith; the Americans seized upon their national destiny with unshakable, unquestioning conviction and set out to achieve it without reservation.

Third, the visitors could not repeat often enough that the Americans had created bold institutional innovations to achieve that destiny. Tradition could not hold them back from setting out upon uncharted seas as they searched for new ways to educate the people, to pray, to apportion political power, to raise living standards, and to revise the relationship of children and of women to the rest of society and to the new needs of the new land. This sense of radical departure and pioneering experimentation dominates British discussion of nineteenth-century American institutions.

And fourth, the commentators insisted that Americans believed they had a destiny, a future, though vague, millennium in which brotherhood and justice would reign, brought about primarily through the education of all men, women, and children.

These four qualities characterize revolution even during the sordid, apparently unidealistic, terroristic phases through which so many of them pass. Brinton speaks of the various reigns of terror as manifestations "of an effort to achieve intensely religious ends here on earth," of the terrorists themselves as behaving "as men have been observed to behave before when under the influence of active religious faith," and of their goals as "the brotherhood of man and the achievement of justice on this earth." What is true for the reign of terror holds also for the preceding revolution itself.[15]

Whatever else the British had to say about the America of the early *twentieth* century, the over-all impression they gave was distinctly not one of a revolutionary society. Instead they described something of a conservative Thermidorean reaction, similar to the one some believe the

[14] Perhaps the traditional conservatism of the British caused them to exaggerate the radicalism of the experiments occurring in the United States.

[15] Brinton, *The Anatomy of Revolution,* pp. 269, 273. Brinton asserts that of the four Revolutions he examined in the effort to arrive at certain uniformities —the Puritan English, the American, the French, and the Russian—only the American Revolution did not have to suffer a Reign of Terror.

Soviet Union began during Khrushchev's regime. A certain cynicism was replacing the ideology. Social zeal, the British seemed to say, was giving way before the desire for personal gratification. The created institutions were no longer felt to possess magic powers. Doubts concerning the future, fears of insecurity, the need for escape—all these motifs the travelers began to substitute for the American's once-invincible faith in tomorrow.

This postrevolutionary era was ushered in by general success as much as it was by the failure to attain perfection. Power, culture, and comfort were being achieved, and they did not fan the flames of idealism. As with other revolutions, success required restraint in the political and global sphere, and it encouraged a turning inward on the personal level; the individual after the revolution becomes impotent to deal with enlarged, complicated political issues, but he is far better able to fend for himself now that he is assured the roof over his head and the next meal. Such is, when viewed in a large framework, the fairly familiar kind of historical situation the twentieth-century British travelers appeared to be recording.[16]

THE TRAVELERS IN PERSPECTIVE

A reading of the books of many British visitors writing over this extended period of time yields a different perspective upon the American past than is usually found in the works of native historians. The travelers generalize more broadly. They focus not on politics, economics, or events but on the large elements of culture, belief, and temperament. They see more in schooling and child-rearing patterns than we do. They tend to see the major change in American values not in the period 1860–65, which native historians favor, but in the years surrounding 1900 and the First World War. They are struck by an extraordinary harmony in nineteenth-century America between the nations's valuation of equality and progress, the political, educational, economic, familial, and religious institutions that the New World created, and the personal qualities of the citizenry. They do not write of such a harmony in the twentieth century. They portray a transition from a culturally revolutionary society to a far more established, even conservative civilization.

The extent to which these insights may be of value to the American

[16] It is interesting to note that the new rhetoric of revolution used by many young people (perhaps inspired in part by the effects of the "Thermidorean reaction"), beginning in the last half of the 1960's, is not filled with hope for the future. While loaded with disgust for contemporary American conditions, it offers fewer millennial hopes than such rhetoric usually does.

historian depends upon a clear awareness of the assets and liabilities of the approach to American society which the foreign observer character-istically takes. He can, quite evidently, *see* freshly, but he does not ex-plain the causes for the phenomena he observes with sufficient back-ground or knowledge. His interpretations and opinions are likely to be of less value than his observations. Where objectivity and knowledge are required the traveler's generalizations are suspect; where a fresh vision and a willingness to say the obvious are in order, the foreign commen-tator can have some very important things to tell us.

Unfortunately, the distinction among these categories is not always clear. While an effort has here been made to strain out British prejudice and eliminate the involved topics upon which the visitor can only display his ignorance, that attempt can only be, at best, partially successful. When a tourist said, for example, that American parents are permissive with their children, this statement often was made in regard to situations he saw. But the very use of words is an interpretation of his impressions, and his opinion of this phenomenon will undoubtedly affect most of the generalizations he will construct from that initial insight. The comments of British travelers, who tended to write "with little fear and little knowl-edge," must always be weighed against other kinds of data.

But caution should not make the American historian too timid to realize the inestimable advantage which any foreign observer possesses over the native, and which James Bryce so well outlined in the introduc-tion to his great volumes on the American commonwealth:

> It may be thought that a subject of this great compass ought, if un-dertaken at all, to be undertaken by a native American. No native Amer-ican has, however, undertaken it. Such a writer would doubtless have great advantages over the stranger. Yet there are two advantages which a stranger . . . may hope to secure. He is struck by some things which a native does not think of explaining, because they are too obvious, and whose influence on politics or society he forgets to estimate, since they seem to him part of the order of nature. And the stranger finds it easier to maintain a position of detachment, detachment not only from party prejudice, but from those prepossessions in favour of persons, groups, constitutional dogmas, national pretensions, which a citizen can scarcely escape except by falling into that attitude of impartial cynicism which sours and perverts the historical mind as much as prejudice itself. He who regards a wide landscape from a distant height sees its details im-perfectly, and must unfold his map in order to make out where each village lies, and how roads run from point to point. But he catches the true perspective of things better than if he were standing among them. The great features of the landscape, the valleys, slopes and mountains, appear in their relative proportion: he can estimate the height of the peaks and the breadth of the plains. So one who writes of a country not his own may turn his want of familiarity with details to good account if he fixes his mind strenuously on the main characteristics of the people

and their institutions, while not forgetting to fill up gaps in his knowledge by frequent reference to native authorities.[17]

Perhaps only Bryce and a few exceptional others took proper advantage of the "distant height." Yet the irony persists that when one wants
to gain the fullest possible understanding of the civilization of the United
States, one is as likely to turn to the works of Tocqueville and of Bryce
as he is to those of any American author.

[17] Bryce, *The American Commonwealth*, I, 10–11.

APPENDIX   The British Travelers

as Amateur

Anthropologists

About a decade ago, Robert G. Athearn began a book about British travelers to the American West by noting that "when the historian learns that his colleague is interested in the comments of these people, he smiles, waves his hand, and deprecatingly says, 'oh, yes, the good old British traveler!' That closes the conversation."[1] This response, a mixture of familiarity and amusement, illustrates the peculiar status of the travelers among American historians. When the historian needs a grand generalization about American life, the British traveler is always on the spot with some tart remark. The historian, too, has shared in the fascination of Americans with what outsiders think of their country. No nation, it is often remarked, has displayed such sensitivity to the opinions of visitors.

One Englishman reported that no more than thirty minutes would elapse upon his meeting a new American before the inevitable question popped up:

> The form of the question varies. Sometimes it is put diffidently, and in the nicest words. Sometimes just the other way. "Does not your mind expand when you consider the institutions of this great country, when you see how like a clock the machinery works, &c.?" This last is a very favourite form. It was asked me many times in exactly the above words.[2]

Most Englishmen did not react sympathetically to such outrageous examples of national boastfulness; but others, like the perspicacious Alexander Mackay, understood that in Britain

> . . . it is difficult to understand this sensitiveness on the part of the American people. England has her fixed position in the great family of nations. . . . We care not, therefore, what the foreigner says or thinks of us. . . . The desire of America is to be at least abreast of England

[1] Robert G. Athearn, *Westward the Briton*, p. xi.
[2] Money, *The Truth about America*, pp. 5–6.

in the career of nations; and every expression which falls from the Englishman showing that in his opinion she is yet far behind his own country, grates harshly upon what is after all but a pardonable vanity, spring-
ing from a laudable ambition.[3]

SOME HISTORICAL USES OF THE TRAVEL REPORTS

The historian, however, seeks more from the traveler than approval or
quotable prose; he seeks information, instruction, and insight. Several
kinds of information are obtainable. In the first place, the traveler in-
advertently reveals a great deal about his own person and his own nation when he comments upon another nation. As any tourist can testify,
he frequently returns home with a keener perception of his native land
than when he began his voyage. He quickly discovers that modes of behavior that he may have assumed to be natural and universal are not;
and this discovery frees him to make judgments and to view his home-
land in a larger perspective. Many students of travel literature have
therefore found this source fruitful for acquiring information on the
native land of the visitors. Andrew J. Torrielli, for example, the author
of *Italian Opinion on America, 1850–1900,* surveyed the subject primarily in order that "generalization may be cautiously drawn on the
state of the Italian mind at this period. . . . Using them [the Italian
visitors], I have planned to present not merely another work on American social history, but rather an examination of average Italian sentiment on problems of continuous moment."[4]

A second use of the travel accounts is the one that Torrielli decided
to dismiss in his own case: their potential contribution to the social history of the country being visited. Since travelers' accounts make explicit
and vivid what local residents take for granted, they provide a kind of
color, detail, and human interest available in no other historical source.
Anything that strikes the tourist as unusual, no matter how trifling, has
generally found its way into print. The result: an odd catalogue of miscellaneous manners and customs of which the native is rarely conscious,
ranging from the American's way of eating to his way of speaking, from
the way he looks to the way he lives. This storehouse of descriptive
paraphernalia has often aided the historian in imaginatively recreating a
feeling for the life of an earlier era.

A third use has occasionally been found for travel reports: suggestive
and far-reaching insights for the historian. One need only mention the
names of Crevecoeur and Tocqueville, of Bryce and Brogan to establish

[3] A. Mackay, *The Western World,* II, 285.
[4] Andrew J. Torrielli, *Italian Opinion on America, 1850–1900,* p. vi.

this point. Sadly, only a few of the visitors have been blessed with the observation and understanding of these men, important because they were gifted with wisdom, not because they were travelers.

Other scattered uses have been found for these accounts, chiefly by specialists who can uncover a good British report on any number of specific topics. Sir Charles Lyell's description of American geology and Richard Burton's study of the Mormons, for example, are practically definitive. Experts are grateful for the diary composed by William Howard Russell at the front during the Civil War, for the book by Robert Somers on Reconstruction, for Henry Stanley's on Indian fighting, for Isabella Bird's on her days in Colorado, and for Sir George Campbell's analysis of racial problems.[5]

Much can be learned about hunting in the Far West from William Baillie-Grohman, about the American feminist movement from Emily Faithfull, or about the American theater from William Archer. One can surround himself with the flora and fauna of the United States through Paul Fountain's works or experience the fear and anticipation of the new immigrant with Stephen Graham. The state of America immediately after World War I has been well captured by Philip Gibbs, spiritualism in this country best detected by Sir Arthur Conan Doyle. George Peel measured the American economic impact on European businessmen more intimately than could any American, and Ford Madox Ford gauged the inner meaning of life in New York City with as much irony and love as has any New Yorker.[6]

This list could be extended indefinitely, but one can gather from this the enormous variety and expertise that British travelers have brought to bear on nearly all aspects of American life. Indeed, one can name practically any subject and assume that some British visitor has composed a book on it.[7]

[5] Lyell, *A Second Visit;* Sir Richard F. Burton, *The City of Saints and Across the Rocky Mountains to California;* Sir William Howard Russell, *My Diary North and South;* Robert Somers, *The Southern States Since the War, 1870–71;* Sir Henry Morton Stanley, *My Early Travels and Adventures in America and Asia Minor;* (Bird) Bishop, *A Lady's Life in the Rocky Mountains;* George Campbell, *White and Black.*

[6] William Adolph Baillie-Grohman, *Camps in the Rockies;* Faithfull, *Three Visits to America;* Archer, *America Today;* Paul Fountain, *The Eleven Eaglets of the West;* Graham, *With Poor Immigrants to America;* Gibbs, *People of Destiny;* Doyle, *Our American Adventure* and *Our Second American Adventure;* George Peel, *The Economic Impact of America;* Ford, *New York Is Not America.*

[7] One subject at least which did escape the attention of the travelers is of importance for the chapter dealing with children. They rarely discussed the preverbal childhood disciplines—weaning, fondling, toilet training, attitudes toward masturbation—matters deemed crucial by neo-Freudians. Only seldom did they refer, and then implicitly, to the Oedipal crisis of four or five, a subject that Freud himself thought most important.

SOME LIMITATIONS

Yet after due acknowledgment to the travelers, historians rightly feel that travel literature can be used as a source only with skepticism and a clear awareness of the visitors' defective vision. Two qualities have been attributed to the British observers which wholly justify the unwillingness of the historians to accept at face value the large body of British claims. They are prejudice and ignorance.

The Problem of Prejudice

These English gentlemen have notorious reputations, in part because they were presumed to be so upper-class. It required (and still requires), so the argument goes, a relatively substantial fortune and freedom to cross the Atlantic. Those who came consequently had to be drawn from the upper class with both the time and the money, the class least likely to appreciate the social experiment taking place in the New World, the class most likely, it was thought, to be prejudiced. Edward Money wrote that "by far the larger number who go to the States are of two classes. 1. The rich, who go for travel, pleasure, and change. 2. The emigrant, who is poor, and who stays there."[8] An examination into the backgrounds of the British travelers after the Civil War reveals, however, that they were actually neither condescending noblemen nor representatives of all classes of British life who could be presumed to be voicing typical British opinions (as Torrielli claimed that his travelers expressed "average Italian sentiment").

It was possible to trace the careers and occupations of over 200 of the 225 authors employed in this study. This discovery is not uninteresting and it certainly could not be duplicated with a typical cross section of the British population. Thirty-three, or one out of every six visitors, occupied himself at home writing novels, poems, and short stories. Twenty-two of them, the second largest group, were journalists, and nineteen served in the government. Fourteen spent their lives as professional travelers and twelve were clergymen. There were ten historians, ten scientists, ten businessmen, and ten scholars in other fields, especially philosophy and economics. The rest of the observers were divided among barristers and judges (eight), publishers and editors (eight), sportsmen and adventurers (seven), soldiers (seven), professional educators (six),

---

[8] Money, *The Truth about America*, p. 3. The subjects of this study belong in the first category.

literary and drama critics (five), professional reformers (five), laborers and farmers (four), artists (three), idle rich (three) and six miscellaneous professions.[9]

At least three points can be made to demonstrate that these people did not represent an average sampling of the British population. First, the occupations that would in fact dominate any survey of the British populace during this period are either altogether absent from this list or have a minimal representation. For example, only 2 per cent of the tourists were farmers or laborers, while almost twice that figure were "sportsmen."[10]

Second, the sample of travelers hardly can be called representative or typical of even the select occupations on this list. Instead one is confronted with a veritable "Who's Who" of barristers, scientists, novelists, and the like. Much of the cast of travelers reads, in fact, like a "Who's Who" of Great Britain from the middle of the nineteenth to the middle

[9] The breakdown by percentages is as follows: novelists—16.5 per cent; journalists—11 per cent; government officials—9.5 per cent; travelers—7 per cent; clergymen—6 per cent; historians, scientists, businessmen, and scholars— 5 per cent each; lawyers and editors—4 per cent each; sportsmen and soldiers— 3.5 per cent each; educators—3 per cent; literary critics and professional reformers—2.5 per cent apiece; laborers—2 per cent; artists and idle rich—1.5 per cent each; and 3 per cent for miscellaneous. In this last class, I have included two wives of small merchants, a wife of a detective inspector, two engineers, and one man of many occupations.

There are many cases in which one man's career spilled over into one or more additional occupational categories. Bryce, for example, was a distinguished M.P. as well as an historian. And just how does one classify H. G. Wells? I have placed each individual in the pigeonhole in which he seems to have made his greatest mark; the results are sometimes arbitrary, but they do not change the total configuration significantly.

I have defined a "British traveler" as any citizen of the British Isles who wrote a book about the United States on the basis of a personal visit to these shores. This is a rather broad definition, especially for more recent times; but since I am more interested here in studying the United States than in the travelers themselves, it seems to me to be a functional one. For the particulars on the career of each traveler, see the annotated bibliography.

[10] It would seem that the more common occupation groups might figure more prominently when the two dozen persons of whose careers I could find no trace were added to the sample. Further, a larger selection of observers than the 225 used in this study might penetrate more deeply into the lower and middle classes. On this latter point, I have investigated the backgrounds of more than fifty of the Britons who were not included in this essay. And although they lacked the renown of those in the original sample, three quarters of them could be located—with three groups accounting for nearly the entire total: magazine and newspaper writers out to make a monetary kill on the lucrative travel book market; public officials and their wives on vacation; and bored barons and baronesses killing deer and parading their titles. This does not yield a typical cross section, even in recent times when the costs of travel have become less prohibitive to larger numbers of Britons.

of the twentieth centuries. Many of these people were renowned not only at home, but throughout the civilized world.[11]

Third, one can combine many of these occupational categories into one large group: those whose careers centered on the act of writing. Those who were engaged as journalists, novelists, editors, historians and various other scholars, drama and literary critics, and professional travel writers could all be called authors. More than half of the travelers fall into this group.[12] Out of over two hundred travelers traced in this sociological excursion, more than one hundred and twenty of them had written books previously and had published at least two other books in addition to their American travelogues, and another forty were afterward to become authors of at least three books.

The British travelers of our study, then, were professional writers, the author-class of Great Britain. This is not quite the same as the upper class socially.[13] But these 160 authors were unrepresentative not only of the general population, but of English writers in general. A disproportionate number of them were superior writers, and taken together they form a kind of intellectual elite of the British Isles from 1850 on. It is self-evident that these people could not be said to speak for "average British sentiment." And although the common stereotype of languid, aristocratic Tory snobs does not apply, the feeling that the observers moved on the highest levels of British life certainly does.

There can be no question that the class background of the visitors inclined them toward a skepticism regarding the various social experiments about which they wrote. Sometimes the prejudice was flagrant, as when P. A. Vaile saw the United States above all as a nation "full of the loathsome seeds of corruption, easy divorce, thirst for dollars, licensed

[11] A brief run-down on a few of the best-known observers in just two fields demonstrates this point. *Novelists and story-tellers:* Rudyard Kipling, Charles Dickens (he paid a second visit in 1867–68), Aldous Huxley, John Galsworthy, Robert Louis Stevenson, Oscar Wilde, H. G. Wells, Arthur Conan Doyle, Arnold Bennett, Hilaire Belloc, G. K. Chesterton, Anthony Trollope. *Historians and philosophers:* Herbert Spencer, James Bryce, A. F. Pollard, Harold Laski, Frederic Harrison, Thomas Huxley, Denis Brogan, Edward Freeman, Lord Acton.

Among the other illustrious tourists, we might mention Matthew Arnold, J. B. Priestley, Henry M. Stanley, Ford Madox Ford, Lord Coleridge and Lord Russell of Killowen (both were Lord Chief Justices of England), Charles Lyell, *et al.* This is a very fragmentary list, but it should give some idea of the level of society from which the British travel authors were in significant measure drawn. At the same time, it should be noted that some of these figures were at the starting point of their careers and that many of the British authors were hacks.

[12] One hundred two out of 202.

[13] Twenty-six of the total of 225 visitors were noblemen. Of these, only seven inherited their titles.

murder and assassination, neurotic and dyspeptic disease."[14] Such a man would see only what he wanted to see. Tory prejudice usually exhibited itself more subtly as the prophecy of Southern victory in the Civil War[15] or as the myopia which saw in permissive divorce laws only an invitation to total corruption[16] or interpreted voluntary religion as an endorsement of atheism.[17] Liberal prejudice was on occasion at work also, such as when the ardent Americophile, Sisley Huddleston, who in 1929 (before the Crash) could find no wrong, would not even doubt the wisdom of prohibition, which "has made of the overwhelming majority of Americans a sober people . . . happy to be rid of alcoholism."[18] Such bias was not typical, but it would be unwise to pretend that the main value of the travel accounts lies in their objectivity.

The Problem of Ignorance

The visitors were not, in most cases, well informed about the United States when they came over. Many of them knew only what they had read in Mrs. Trollope or in the newspapers. Nor did the tourist gain sufficient knowledge on the trip itself. He usually toured the land in one breath. He trekked through only the most obvious showplaces, and even there he emerged with a one-sided picture. If he visited New York, for example, most of his observations derived from scenes in his hotel lobby or his taxi. Then, before it was too late to pay, he rushed to get his incomplete and distorted impressions into print, preferring ostentatious generalization to careful thought lest anyone suspect that he might not speak out of vast experience with the United States.

The men glibly analyzed the American woman, usually on the basis of encounters with those who had invited the British to their homes for lavish parties. They wrote easily of child rearing even though they were seldom in American homes when the children were awake. Only 21 of the 225 visitors were women, from whom one might expect greater acuity in description of the private circumstances of American home life. Small wonder that Max Berger complained of "the limited knowledge of many travellers. This frequently causes them to draw generalizations from a few isolated incidents, generalizations which may not be typical."[19] Anyone who has sampled this literature must soon become painfully aware of how inaccurate so many of these books are, and is likely

[14] Vaile, Y., America's Peril, p. ix.
[15] Samuel Phillips Day, Down South, passim.
[16] Sir Lepel Henry Griffin, The Great Republic, pp. 62–65.
[17] Sullivan, Rambles and Scrambles, p. 32.
[18] Huddleston, What's Right with America, p. 245.
[19] Berger, The British Traveller in America, 1836–1860, p. 6.

to wonder why the authors bothered to write some of them. But the average author published "My Two Days in America," of course, for money. He could hardly be blamed for going on about Mormon bigamy, easy divorce, political scandal, and an interview with "a typical business-man." There existed a booming market for these goods. Naturally many of the authors tended to "emphasize the unusual and to ignore the com-monplace. Most travel books are written for sale. Hence, sensational matter is welcomed rather than deprecated."[20]

Writing a book for sale, however, does not preclude other motives, nor does sensationalism inevitably follow. A large proportion of the au-thors were already well known and respected, and hence could not af-ford to degrade themselves. Many hoped to get invited back to the United States to tour the lucrative lyceum circuit and could not permit themselves the indulgence of gratuitously vilifying their potential hosts. Some writers, like H. G. Wells, wanted to persuade; some, like Dickens, hoped to add to their literary reputation; still others, like Bryce, genu-inely hoped to understand and explain America. Motives were many and mixed, and not all of them were cynical. An increasing percentage of the authors during this period had the experience to avoid this kind of sensa-tionalism. As pointed out earlier, many were professional travelers who had visited other lands stranger even than the United States. A good many more were able to afford more than one trip to the United States before writing their first book on the New World. Emily Faithfull toured the United States in 1872, 1882, and 1884 before she wrote her work on America in the latter year. James F. Muirhead roamed widely in the country in 1888, 1890–93, and 1898 before composing *The Land of Contrasts*. These cases are exceptional, but I used forty-three books which were written after at least a second stay in America. This trend has accelerated in the twentieth century.

Still, the historian should not be blamed for being a bit suspicious about the reliability of these books. He smiles when reminded of the British travelers because, by experience, he has become fully aware of the gullibility of travelers in strange foreign lands, of their instinct to praise or censure automatically, and of their distressing habit of so often being wrong. From all this, one might conclude that the body of travel literature cannot be trusted, that at best one might be able to employ a few selected and well-known books, and use the rest only for the most specialized purposes. Yet this study, for reasons that will now be dis-cussed, employed all 225 authors and their 260 books to ascertain the extent to which "suggestive and far-reaching insights" might be drawn from that literature.

[20] *Ibid.*

PREJUDICE AND IGNORANCE QUALIFIED

A balance should be struck between the admission that British travel works are not paradigms of accurate observation and reporting and the feeling that prejudice and ignorance disqualify these works from serious usage by the historian. Much of the latter view stems from a stereotype of the British travelers which has practically made its way into the popular imagination as well as into the minds of too many scholars. The Briton, as the stereotype goes, came to the United States possessing a title he never earned, a contemptuous heart, and a total blindness to the realities of American life. He came to sneer and abuse; he had never forgiven the colonial for rejecting his guidance. He toured the land with the heightened sensitivity, attachment, fear, and anxiety of the rejected father to his prodigal sons unreturned. Out of his own bitterness, he loathed; out of his own fear, he reviled the odious Americans.

John Graham Brooks helped to perpetuate this exaggerated image when he began his chapter of "The Mother Country as Critic" thus:

> If it is true that no quarrel may take on more virulence than that within one's own family, the fact accounts for the extreme rancor of feeling against England that continued a generation after the War of 1812. I do not see in the evidence a sign that England "hated the United States," as was so often said. Until after the Civil War we were not thought important enough to inspire that feeling. She had merely an unintelligent contempt for us. This led her to ignore or to trample on every sensitive nerve in the national body.[21]

Joined to these misconceptions are two corollary notions: (1) the French and other European critics were somehow fairer and more judicious than their English counterparts; and (2) it took the Civil War to convince the British that the United States deserved more respect as a nation.

All these notions can be placed in more proper perspective once it is realized that no more than a handful of the Britons ever fit the caustic cast of a Mrs. Trollope. The sources of British vituperation of American society were certain magazines such as *Blackwood's,* the *British Review,* and the *Edinburgh Quarterly,* both in their stories about the United States and in their reviews of the travel accounts. They made the Griffins and the Marryats famous by praise and publicity; they hid the more typical works from common knowledge by derision and ommission. As Allan Nevins, Max Berger, and other astute students of the visitors have

[21] Brooks, *As Others See Us,* p. 116.

remarked, the majority of the travelers, at all times, treated the United States fairly and sympathetically. One must not confuse a few touchy critics (especially during the 1830's) and some sour journals with the bulk of British commentators. Nevins tried, over forty years ago, to ease the stereotype:

> The common view among Americans that the republic was an object of condescension on the part of all British critics until it confounded them by its successful emergence from the Civil War, though quite absurd, rests upon several foundations. It is little realized how numerous were our English visitors, and how varied were their objects in crossing the ocean and publishing their books. Most Americans think first of the three travelers who bear names distinguished in the history of English literature, Dickens, Captain Marryat, and Mrs. Trollope; and they happen to have been a rather severe trio. Moreover, it is human nature to remember critics whose judgments were harsh and whose attacks aroused bitter controversy, and to forget the sympathetic writers who said little except in praise.

Nevins then argued that many American historians, John Bach McMaster especially, "have fallen into the error of confounding the early British travel-writers with what the Troy quarterlies and monthlies said about their books." American historians who also "like high colors" have blown up the importance of this magazine censure.[22]

Scholars have been fond of contrasting the jeering Britons with the Frenchmen "full of geniality and even flattery,"[23] especially in the decades after 1776. Frank Monaghan, in the introduction to his bibliography of *French Travellers in the United States* proceeded on this assumption. Compared to the English, he said, "it was enthusiasm rather than bitterness that prejudiced the minds of French travellers to America during the eighteenth century; and during the early years of the nineteenth century . . . America was the object of the admiration, even veneration."[24] Even this claim had died by the mid-1840's; and certainly no one speaks of "Tory condescension" by 1850. This renders somewhat misleading the idea that the Civil War changed Britain's mind about the United States. And for the period studied in this paper, out of 225 authors, only 13 could fit into the Tory stereotype as previously outlined, most of the examples for which derived from the 1830's.[25] More

[22] Nevins, *America Through British Eyes*, pp. 79–80.

[23] Brooks, *As Others See Us*, p. 173.

[24] Frank Monaghan, *French Travellers in the United States: 1765–1932: A Bibliography*, p. viii.

[25] They are, in order of appearance: (1) Edward R. Sullivan, 1852 (publishing dates of their books are used here); (2) Hepworth Dixon, 1867 and 1876; (3) Greville Chester, 1869; (4) Theresa Longworth, 1875; (5) Sir Lepel Griffin, 1884; (6) Roger Pocock, 1896; (7) P. A. Vaile, 1909; (8) William Woodley, 1910; (9) Elijah Brown, 1913; (10) Mrs. Desmond Humphreys,

surprising, of the more than 260 works examined, this writer could find only 67 books which were, on balance, more critical than sympathetic toward the United States. There was, in fact, more extravagant praise than denunciation expressed by British enthusiasts in this period, a fact that supports the reputation of the last two decades of the nineteenth century and much of the twentieth as years of warm Anglo-American feelings. The large majority of British commentators throughout the entire span of American history have attempted to arrive at balanced critical estimates of the American scene; and throughout that period more have returned to Liverpool or Southampton with happy recollections of the United States than have not.

Before one altogether discards the idea that the British travelers were more conservative about American social experimentation than the average Briton, let us examine an unusual sociological inquiry conducted by William Buchanan and Hadley Cantril in 1953—one that might aid us in putting this problem into perspective. Operating in nine countries, including Great Britain and the United States, the investigators asked questions of a sample in each nation designed to reveal differences between the ways in which the "common men" of different nations viewed their own lands and other nations. Among the results they found that most nations were friendly toward the other countries in the study.[26] Furthermore, the United States was the most popular of all lands. In response to the question: "Which country in the world gives you the best chance of leading the kind of life you would like to lead?" next to the respondent's own land, the United States was second in each case.[27] This result held for Britain, too. In another measure of friendliness between nations, both the American attitude toward England and the English feeling toward the United States were decidedly on the positive side.

1913; (11) J. M. Kennedy, 1914; (12) Colonel J. F. C. Fuller, 1926; and (13) C. E. M. Joad, 1927. It should be observed that five of these authors wrote in the years between 1909 and 1914, before the United States had committed her sympathies and dollars to the British cause in the desperate diplomatic maneuvering before the outbreak of World War I. The late 1820's and early 1830's were also somewhat special years in Anglo-American history. The social experimentation of the Jacksonian period coincided with the fundamental British political debate which was to culminate in the Reform Bill of 1832. Feelings naturally ran high on both sides of the Atlantic.

[26] William Buchanan and Hadley Cantril, *How Nations See Each Other: A Study in Public Opinion* (Urbana: University of Illinois Press, 1953), p. 57. The countries were Australia, Britain, France, Germany, Italy, Mexico, Netherlands, Norway, and the U.S. Some of the questions were: "Do you believe that human nature can be changed?" "Which people do you feel most (least) friendly toward?"

[27] *Ibid.*, p. 32. More Americans (96 per cent) named their own country in answer to this question than citizens of any other nation. Australia had the second highest "satisfaction index" with 83 per cent picking their own native land.

When given a list of twelve adjectives with which to characterize other peoples (six positive, six negative), the four that Americans most frequently applied to themselves—"peace-loving," "generous," "intelligent," "progressive"—were, uncritical though they might appear, among the five leading terms that the British applied to the Americans. The British appropriately added to the American pantheon the judgment, "conceited."[28]

This positive response cannot, of course, be applied without qualification to Anglo-American relations a century ago. But perhaps it is not unreasonable to hypothesize that general British feeling among the great numbers of people in the period from 1860 to 1935 was probably a good deal more positive than negative. This hypothesis may explain the paradox that a significant majority of British travelers, drawn from the upper echelons of British society, belonging to the more conservative anti-American elements, nonetheless returned with favorable reports about the United States. They may indeed have been more critical about the United States than the masses of their compatriots, but such a relative statement need not turn the travelers into "Tory Snobs." Statements about the aristocratic bearing of British travelers, true though they may be, might better be interpreted in light of the improving relations between the people of the two nations. Not only were the British less biased than was commonly supposed, but, when compared with their European counterparts, they were positively knowledgeable. Even Brooks and Monaghan lost patience with later French critics; the Frenchmen generalized and philosophized, but they never observed. They wrote their books on the steamers out of Le Havre, dashed mechanically around the States, and had their books on the boulevards almost before they reached home again. America, complained these two scholars, was besieged by scores of French journalists peddling their witty and vacuous epigrams.[29]

The Germans had more regard for facts, but all the Continental Europeans had a basic language problem. When one Harvard professor of French was asked why the French travelers were so "destitute of the slightest critical values," he replied that "they either had no real knowledge of English, or knew it just enough to deceive them into thinking they knew it—which was worse." Brooks grew so tired of the inaccuracy of so many of the Continental visitors, that he paraded before his readers a number of the spelling mistakes of one French commentator, "a highly educated man who has been at least eight years in this country. He was given every chance to correct his proofs." Among the more painful er-

[28] *Ibid.*, pp. 51–52, 54.
[29] Brooks, *As Others See Us*, pp. 176, 178; Monaghan, *French Travellers in the United States*, p. x.

rors were New Hawen, Coan., Broakline (New York's largest borough), New Jersia, Conettocutt! Those who abstained from alchoholic beverages were teatotlars; Chicago ended up as Chicorgua; that famous political reform party was gallicized into the La cofocos. And in complete seriousness, the White House was aptly the "Execution Mansion."[30]

The English historian Edward Freeman argued persuasively that the similarity between England and the United States furnished the Briton with an inestimable advantage over all other foreign travelers in understanding the United States. By his logic one can compare two items much more precisely when they are similar to one another. "It is in such cases, not in those where the things compared are altogether unlike one another, that we note the minutest differences." Freeman used the example of Oxford and Cambridge to show that they are so alike, and so different from all other universities, "that there is a certain curious pleasure in tracing out the endless minute points in which they differ. So it is between England and America. It is the essential likeness which makes us note every point of unlikeness." The English traveler, he contended, bore a peculiar and felicitous relation to the United States. His nation's ways were just close enough to America's to be familiar and comprehensible, and just different enough to make significant contrasts possible. "To me," Freeman stated, "most certainly the United States did not seem a foreign country; it was simply England with a difference. The difference struck me as certainly greater than the greatest difference which had ever struck me between one part of England and another, but as certainly less than the difference which strikes me when I enter Scotland."[31]

The prejudice of the British visitors derived from the limitations of politics, class, and sex which helped to shape their views; ignorance came from inadequate preparation and insufficient opportunities for them to observe the American scene. Some of the political prejudice, however, could be canceled out in part because large numbers of both conservatives and liberals came to visit this country. Class prejudice could be overcome as in the case of Tocqueville, son of an emigré nobleman, or Bryce, the arch-Victorian, just to name the two most brilliant of foreign visitors, both of whom treated us sympathetically. Prejudice could also be used to furnish valuable historical perspectives. The imbalance of sexes remain, but ignorance was somewhat mitigated in the case of the Englishmen by their familiarity with American language and culture.

[30] Brooks, *As Others See Us*, pp. 176–77. Brooks, mercifully, neglected to name the French author, and I, unluckily, could not trace his identity. Simone de Beauvoir has continued this Gallic tradition down to our own day.
[31] Freeman, *Some Impressions of the United States*, pp. 9–10.

AMATEUR ANTHROPOLOGISTS

Even after one has qualified the accusations hurled against the British on the grounds of bias and ignorance, even after one has shown that worse offenders existed, one still has not proven the reliability of the travelers. One may draw "far-reaching insights" from this mass of material only if it can be shown that the polemic, prejudices and lack of wide first-hand knowledge of the American scene did not really matter much for certain purposes. This can be accomplished only as one transfers his attention from that which divided the travelers to that which united them. The Britons raged at each other over whether the United States was good or bad, social equality good or bad, hotels good or bad, and the like. Curiously, however, though their evaluations diverged, more often than not the observations and even the generalizations upon which they were based coincided.

To take social equality, for example, James Muirhead, editor of the American *Baedeker Guides* and a warm ally of the United States, centered much of his attention on this general condition of life when he decided that

> . . . the fact remains that the distinguishing feature of American society, as contrasted with the societies of Europe, is the greater approach to equality it has made. It is in this sphere, and not in those of industry, law, or politics that the British observer must feel that the American breathes a distinctly more liberal and democratic air than he.[32]

Muirhead found in equality a cause for celebration. But Sir Lepel Griffin, agreeing with Muirhead's diagnosis of its extraordinary significance in American life, called it "the monomania of an entire nation." Equality "influences the life of the people in every particular." But, to Griffin, "every particular" carried very different overtones than it did for Muirhead. "The struggle for equality has determined most of the social institutions of the States: domestic service, houses, hotels, cuisine, travelling and education. It has dominated their politics and has perhaps determined their religion." And with what consequences? "It has withdrawn much of the sweetness and light from their social life, and has left literature and art as monotonous a wilderness as their own prairies."[33] To make clear where he stood on this issue Sir Lepel, a rather good replica of the aristocratic Tory snob, decided with pleasure that "with the experience of every country in the civilized world, I can

[32] Muirhead, *America, the Land of Contrasts*, p. 28.
[33] Griffin, *The Great Republic*, p. 73.

think of none except Russia in which I would not prefer to reside, in which life would not be more worth living, less sordid and mean and unlovely."[34]

Standing somewhere between the views of Muirhead and Griffin, Mrs. Trollope's illustrious son Anthony admitted that he personally preferred to live in England where the upper one tenth of society was a privileged class; and since he belonged to it, he could not complain. But he could also extol the glories of an egalitarian society wherein "if you and I can count up in a day all those on whom our eyes may rest, and learn the circumstances of their lives, we shall be driven to conclude that nine-tenths of that number would have had a better life as Americans than they can have in their spheres as Englishmen."[35] The point at issue is not whether Trollope was the fairest judge of the three; it is that they all insisted on the centrality of equality, that their generalizations if not their own feelings about them coincided. When he ceases to focus on the Britons' opinions, the reader will more readily perceive that the British observers converged around a remarkable consensus on a wide variety of subjects.

This uniformity not only of specific observation but of cultural generalization has been noted by two leading American historians, both of whom prepared anthologies of the travelers. Henry Steele Commager asked how sense might be made from so many conflicting conclusions. "At best the view they seem to present to us is kaleidoscopic, at worst chaotic. Can we," he wondered, "draw any conclusions from such diverse points of view?" The reply: "Surprisingly enough a real unity emerges from these heterogeneous selections, and it is not one imposed by any antecedent editorial discrimination but implicit in the material itself."[36] Amplifying upon this somewhat unexpected consensus Allan Nevins noted the following:

> A considerable degree of unity is discernible in the whole mass of British writing on America, and from these hundreds of volumes it is possible to obtain a composite portrait with certain strongly marked lineaments. It is upon the external features of American life, of course, that the general agreement is most emphatic. . . . Much more significant is the general British agreement upon our external social and cultural traits.[37]

This may get us past the problem of prejudice for a moment, but one may not take too secure a sanctuary in the fact that the commentators often agreed. One encounters the disagreeable possibility that their com-

[34] *Ibid.*, p. 4.
[35] A. Trollope, *North America*, II, 74.
[36] Henry Steele Commager, *America in Perspective: The United States Through Foreign Eyes*, p. xv.
[37] Nevins, *America Through British Eyes*, pp. 3–5.

mon misinformation and inexperience with the United States may have
made them all wrong together. There is no satisfactory way of assessing
the reliability of the common findings of the British short of far-flung
research beyond the limits of this study. But one can diminish the
severity of this shortcoming by guessing upon which *kinds* of topics the
travel comments are likely to be useful, and by concentrating on them
while taking less seriously those upon which their observations are
likely to be faulty.

Should the historian, for example, rely on the average British traveler for information concerning the causes of the Civil War, the economic policies of Lincoln, or the effects of Reconstruction on southern
whites? Will the touring Britons accurately comprehend the issues in
the 1896 presidential election, understand the Muckrakers, or correctly
grasp the roots of the Progressive movement? Can he be expected to
appreciate the pressures felt by Wilson from 1915 to 1919, the foundations of American foreign policy in the 1920's, the causes for the Crash
of 1929, or the nature of Franklin Roosevelt's electoral appeal in 1932?
The average observer in his two months of touring could not possibly
answer these questions intelligently. Although this did not deter him
from trying, only rarely did he possess the facts, the familiarity, the
first-hand knowledge, and the experience which answers to these questions demand. Even less often did he bother to do any research on these
subjects. The local analyst does possess these qualities and has done
the research; Americans have written frequently and informatively in
these fields.

The travel reports may be more eye-opening in those areas where
Americans have kept their eyes shut; where they act out of habit or
custom; where they take things for granted and feel no need to speak
about them; where they assume certain ideas automatically, ideas which
have become unquestioned articles of faith (or what we now call the
society's "myths"). The place to look for these items is not in the
printed documents, but in those things which stand right before the
eyes of the native, so close to him that he cannot see them. "Things too
commonplace," observed Berger, "for a native to mention often appear
sufficiently bizarre to the stranger to merit notation and investigation."
Not just things, but ideas too, claimed Commager. "What they [the
travelers] can, and do, tell us," he said, "are mostly the obvious things,
for it is in what a people take for granted that their character can be
read—in the unformulated assumptions, the spontaneous reactions, the
inevitable responses, the articles of faith."[38]

[38] Berger, *The British Traveller in America, 1836–1860,* p. 6; Commager,
America in Perspective, pp. xiv-xv.

The outside observer, hence, can act as a kind of amateur anthropologist perceiving the fundamental ways of behavior and thought of a culture, precisely because they may not be *his* culture's way of behaving and thinking. Because they are different, he notices them; what seems self-evident to the native may be remarkable to the visitor. For this role, too much knowledge can be a liability at times. But what, more specifically, are the kinds of things noticed by the anthropologist? What are some of the assumptions that are second nature to the American? According to Commager:

> We take for granted our pervasive social equality and do not appreciate the nature of class distinctions until we go abroad—until we go even to democratic England and discover the importance of the public-school accent. We take for granted the exalted status of women and the almost universal pampering of children, until we discover how these things alarm or horrify our visitors. We take for granted universal public education—until we familiarize ourselves with the statistics of secondary-school and university education abroad. . . . It is because foreign observers can see America without the assumptions and presuppositions that becloud the American vision, because they can, in fact, see America in perspective, that they are helpful.[39]

The role of women in the society, child-rearing practices, the class structure, the significance of education—these the travelers saw freshly, these the natives took for granted—occupy the center of the stage in this book. To this group we can add assumptions about God and religious practices, the unspoken political attitudes and the fixation on certain political institutions, and the American's conception of himself, his nation, and the future of both.[40] Though this may seem to cover everything, a great deal is actually excluded from this list. The visitors' clumsy efforts at filling in the historical background and the statistical realities of the above subjects are of less value than their larger generalizations. Monographic analyses of particular presidents, elections, and economic panics are better left to the more knowledgeable researches of American scholars. British narratives of American political, economic, and diplomatic history have generally been very inadequate. Narrative, monographic analysis, historical and statistical background make up the form and level of analysis within which most historians

[39] Commager, *America in Perspective,* p. xv.

[40] Other subjects which anthropologists always treat and which many travelers have noticed, such as sports, use of leisure time, humor, and language are remarked upon in Chapter Three. Further topics—diet, rhetoric, heroes, crimes, other deviant behavior, law enforcement, therapeutic practices—are omitted. Omissions of the visitors have been noted at various points in this work since these can be as revealing as that which they explicitly included.

work, and it is just on this level that travel comments are most unreliable. It is at the higher level of abstraction that the visitors have something unique and potentially valuable to offer the native scholar.

If some historians laugh condescendingly at the British travelers, they do so, in part, because they themselves have misused the travelers. By indiscriminately extracting from the Briton whatever may be helpful for the historian's momentary needs, they have thrown discredit upon the entire body of travel literature. Travel accounts, like any other source of data, must be plumbed selectively and carefully. The chief reason for not simply surveying British opinion on all aspects of American life (an easy thing to do with a serviceable cross-filing system) has been to provide credible concentration on the single larger question: can we learn anything significant from the British traveler about the United States between 1860 and 1935?

BIBLIOGRAPHY

BOOKS BY THE TRAVELERS

A LTHOUGH the following list of travel accounts contains over 250 titles, it is a highly selective one, including not more than one half of the total number of such books composed by Britons between 1860 and 1935. The grounds for selection were twofold. First, every travel work mentioned in secondary accounts as being of any possible consequence was obtained from the collections of several libraries across the country. The Library of Congress surpasses all others in this field. I do not think that many travelogues of significance escaped this search.

Second, the list was completed, and a more representative sampling obtained, by a scrutiny of every title in the ample collections of the libraries of the University of California at Berkeley and Stanford University. Not all the books examined in these two categories were included in the Bibliography; those omitted were deemed altogether valueless, even in comparison with the many works of negligible value which appear below.

I have defined a travel account as any book descriptive of the United States by a citizen or resident of the British Isles, based upon a personal visit to the States. There are a few exceptions to this definition noted below, there are a few periodical articles of special value included below, and there are some works which do not lie within the chronological boundaries of this study. Approximately fifteen of the finest studies written between 1845 and 1860 appear below, books which bear directly on the question of whether the years 1860–65 were decisive turning points in American thinking as well as in American political and diplomatic history. A couple of excellent post-1935 books, one by Brogan, another by Laski, are included because of their great general value. Some basic information about each of the authors is included where obtainable. Where one author is represented by two or more books, I have listed his books in chronological order for the sake of logic in following these annotations. These various deviations from strict bibliographical protocol emphasize the personal purposes of this Bibliography. Rather than pretending to be "definitive," it is meant simply to record my own particular experiences with and responses to a large, suggestive, and useful body of material.

Ackrill, Robert. *A Scamper from Yorkshire to the United States, with a Glance at Canada.* Harrogate, 1878.

213

Ackrill published newspapers and was the editor of the *Harrogate Herald*. He liked the United States and did his best to understand items that struck him as odd. This is not a work of systematic analysis, but a collection of informative letters informally written on the spot and sent to friends who put them in Ackrill's newspapers and then successfully encouraged him to publish them.

Acton, Lord John Enerich Edward. "Lord Acton's American Diaries," *Fortnightly Review*, CX (1921), 727–42, 917–34; CXI (1922), 63–83.

The diary of a two-month trip in the United States in 1853 made by the famous English historian (1832–1902) in his youth was discovered and printed sixty-eight years after the fact. Like all diaries, this one moved trippingly from one observation to the next, and no clear, over-all pattern emerged. Most of Acton's entries dealt with conversations he conducted with leading American intellectuals, most of whom lived in the area around Boston and Harvard. Acton's observations were meticulous and accurate; his evaluations neutral and infrequent.

Adams, William Edwin. *Our American Cousins: Being Personal Impressions of the People and Institutions of the United States*. London, 1883.

As the title suggests, Adams felt some anxiety about relations between England and the United States and hoped fervently that the natural ties of family would bring the two nations into closer concord. He was not afraid to confront directly the problems of corruption, immigration, and labor upsets which were raising their heads during his visit in 1882, but he always did so constructively and sympathetically: A further account of his visit to the United States appears in *Memoirs of a Social Atom* (London, 1903).

Aflalo, F. G. *Sunshine and Sport in Florida and the West Indies*. Philadelphia, Pa.: G. W. Jacobs and Co., 1907.

Aflalo (1870–1918), the editor of the *Encyclopedia of Sport*, arrived in San Francisco the day after the San Francisco earthquake. On his way to Florida, he paused to meet with Theodore Roosevelt, and then continued south to take up the main business of his trip: tarpon fishing. Most of this book takes up some "practical and descriptive aspects" of tarpon fishing and other sports.

Archer, William. *America Today: Observations and Reflections*. New York, 1899.

Archer (1856–1924) achieved great fame as a drama critic and he had a love affair with the United States. This book, in its overenthusiasm epitomizes the Anglo-American amity which was reaching a peak at the turn of the century. Archer's 1899 visit, which took him as far west as Chicago, followed by twenty-two years an earlier one. He saw the development in the interim not only of the Anglophilia, but also, as a result of the Spanish-American War, the growing rapprochement between North and South within the United States. He had good words for American literature and the American nourishment of the English language, both on stage and off. He had no bad words.

———. *Through Afro-America: An English Reading of the Race Problem*. London: Chapman and Hall, 1910.

Dedicated to H. G. Wells, "with whom I so rarely disagree that, when I do, I must needs write a book about it," Archer took Wells up on his view of the Negro problem. Wells argued, along with scores of others of course, that there was no "Negro problem"; the problem was with the southern whites. Archer visited the South in 1909 and concluded that the southern white position was comprehensible as soon as one realized that Negroes constituted such a large proportion of the southern population. He also believed that Negroes were somewhat inferior people, and that the happiest solution to the whole racial dilemma would be found in the establishment of a separate, segregated Negro state within the United States.

Argyll, John George Edward Henry Douglas Sutherland Campbell. *A Trip to the Tropics and Home Through America By the Marquis of Lorne.* London, 1867.

The last half of these notes, extracted from letters written during the Marquis' 1866 journey, cover the United States. He made no generalizations about American society, but he did describe with a great deal of verve the political doings in Washington and the border states after the War. The Marquis (1845–1914) also interviewed leading personalities. In later years he made speeches and wrote articles about the United States, and he composed a fictionalized account of his visit to California.

Arnold, Sir Edwin. *Seas and Lands.* London, 1891. The New York, 1891, edition was used.

These letters, reprinted from the London *Daily Telegraph* of which the author was editor, recount an ample sojourn in Japan. Arnold (1832–1904) took just one month (six out of forty chapters) to pass through the United States in 1889 on his way to the Orient. He had little of consequence to say about this nation except to express abundant gratitude for "that unbounded friendliness and faultless grace and goodness" he received everywhere.

Arnold, Matthew. *Civilization in the United States: First and Last Impressions.* London, 1888. The sixth edition (Boston, 1900), was used.

A major treatise composed of startling insights and gross misunderstandings. Arnold (1822–88), a visitor in 1883–84 and again in 1886, never shrunk from grand generalization—an idiosyncracy that explains the combination of perspicacity and distortion which marks this work. Its five essays include two in praise of Ulysses Grant; "A Word about America," written before he ever saw it, describing the United States as a land of "Philistines" (a word not as fully derogatory in his hands as in Mencken's); a modification of this view after he crossed the Atlantic called "A Word More about America"; and the title essay, in which he brought to bear his aesthetic perspective and decided that while America might have solved "the political and social problem" (which England, he felt, had not), it had not solved "the human problem": America was not "interesting." This book lent respectability to the claims of American conservatives.

Asquith, Margot. *My Impressions of America.* New York: George H. Doran Co., 1922.

The wife of the former Prime Minister spent nine weeks on tour in early 1922. A wit and personality in her own right, and author of a lively autobiography, Lady Asquith (1864–1945) wrote a superficial travel account. Pleasant though it was, it was never more than half-hearted in praise or criticism and rarely very informative in description. In all justice to Lady Asquith, it should be pointed out that she could not fully cope with the physical hardships of the incessant lectures and interviews that confronted her, and toward the end of her trek she became weary and peevish.

Aubertin, J. A. *A Fight with Distances: The States, The Hawaiian Islands, Canada, British Columbia, Cuba, The Bahamas.* London, 1888.

A translator and traveler by profession, Aubertin (1818–1900) spent ten months in the New World in 1886–87. He wrote of sights seen and little else. Most of his travels, despite the pithy title, were in the United States. There is a chapter on San Francisco in his *Wanderings and Wonderings* (London, 1892).

Aveling, Edward Bibbins. *An American Journey.* New York, [1887?].

A bitter and often ignorant account of a tour in late 1886. Aveling (1851–98), son-in-law of Karl Marx, duly reported as fact wild stories told him about the seamy side of American life. With his wife, Eleanor Marx Aveling, he later wrote *The Working-Class Movement in America* (London, 1888) and *The Chicago Anarchists* (London, 1888).

Ayscough, John. See Bickerstaffe-Drew.

Baillie-Grohman, William A. *Camps in the Rockies: Being a Narrative of Life on the Frontier, and Sport in the Rocky Mountains, With an Account of the Cattle Ranches of the West.* New York, 1882.

One of the better tales of hunting in the Far West, this book describes the first two of many hunting expeditions (in 1879 and in 1880–81) undertaken by Baillie-Grohman (1851–1921) in the United States. This one took him to the Wyoming Rockies.

Ballantine, William. *The Old World and the New.* London, 1884.

This work belongs more in the category of autobiography or legal reform than of travel literature. Ballantine (1812–87), a serjeant-at-law, did cross the Atlantic in 1882–83, and he did tour the continent (accompanied by Phil Robinson) from New York to Salt Lake City. He did describe many lawyers and judges he encountered along the way and he referred to some of the scenery he saw. But his main thrust was to reform the legal procedure connected with capital punishment, and he came to the United States to seek precedents that might bolster his case. He also came to make some money lecturing.

Barker, J. Ellis. *America's Secret: The Causes of Her Economic Success.* London: J. Murray, 1927.

Barker (1870–1948), an English historian and writer of books about health, came to a prosperous United States determined to discover the key that opened the door to such marvels. Claiming himself to be an expert on American economic matters, he warned England that she had better copy American techniques lest she find herself a totally second-rate power. Barker, in common with most Americans of the late 1920's, could discern no flaws in the economic system.

Barneby, William Henry. *Life and Labour in the Far, Far West: Being Notes of a Tour in the Western States, British Columbia, Manitoba, and the North-west Territory.* London, 1884.

A description of the western states of America and a good portion of Canada, taken from a journal made by the author in 1883. No analysis was intended in this "simple account of our trails, and of the various facts which came under our notice." One of Barneby's traveling companions died of typhoid fever toward the end of the expedition, and his death cast a pall over the entire journey, which made its way sadly and evocatively into the book itself.

————. *Notes from a journal in North America in 1883*. Hereford, [1884?].
Articles taken from the same journal and reprinted from the *Hereford Times*.

Bates, Emily Katherine. *A Year in the Great Republic*. 2 vols. London, 1887.
Words came easily to this lady novelist (1859–1929), who had no trouble filling out two volumes based upon a long coast-to-coast trip. Unfortunately, she rarely delved deeply into things, perhaps because she was enjoying her stay too much to bother. A nicely written and rather pleasant work, especially on domestic matters. She wrote more of the same in *Seen and Unseen* (New York: Dodge Publishing Company, 1908).

Beadle, Charles. *A Trip to the United States in 1887*. London, [1888?].
This English businessman printed the book only for private circulation so that his mother might enjoy reading his letters home in book form. They merely tell of what the author saw, in chronological order, during a happy whirlwind coast-to-coast and back tour in 1887.

Bell, William A. *New Tracks in North America; a journal of travel and adventure whilst engaged in the survey for a southern railroad to the Pacific Ocean during 1867–8*. 2 vols. London, 1869.
The title refers to the Kansas Pacific Railway's survey, for which Bell served as physician and photographer in 1867–68. He tells of his adventures and travels from St. Louis to the Pacific in great detail, including sections on physical geography, botany, and railways. Its many illustrations make this an enjoyable book for frontier buffs.

Belloc, Hilaire. *The Contrast*. London: J. W. Arrowsmith, 1923.
Belloc had a thesis and he rode it to the bitter end. The prolific Catholic novelist-poet-historian (1870–1953) said: "My thesis is that the New World is wholly alien to the Old." He thence delineated a number of stark contrasts: physical, social, political, military, religious, literary, linguistic, and diplomatic. He wanted to tear down the Atlantic bridge over which American ideas were crawling into Europe; he wanted thus to purge Europe of democrats, Protestants, Jews, and other intruders upon the thirteenth-century scene. *The Contrast* recalls Chesterton's picture of the United States with its similar point-of-view, facile prose, flickers of true brilliance, with its never-ending fascination and its wide gap between fact and generalization. Belloc lacked, unfortunately, Chesterton's inestimable grace and humor.

Bennett, Arnold. *Your United States: Impressions of a First Visit*. New York: Harper and Brothers, 1912.
"In seven weeks (less one day) I could not expect to penetrate very far below the engaging surface of things. Nor did I unnaturally attempt to do so." And yet the illustrious novelist (1867–1931), albeit he hazarded few generalizations, managed through acute observation of details and his deft pen to get further below the surface than he claimed. Better than any other writer did he recreate the dynamic surge of American life which surrounded him in New York, Chicago, and Boston. His best and most original chapters were those in which he depicted the

day-by-day routine of all kinds of American citizens, from top to bottom, with special emphasis on the middle. In the end, as Allan Nevins put it, "if the dominant impression of America conveyed by Stead is power, and by H. G. Wells is gigantic disorder, that given by Bennett is vitality."

Berry, C. B. *The Other Side: How It Struck Us.* London, 1880.

A flimsy description of an 1879–80 trek which took the author, a Scottish businessman, as far south as Richmond and as far west as Chicago where he spent much of his time. He pontificated in a slightly sneering manner on such matters as hotels, railways, and other usual tourist trappings.

Bickerstaffe-Drew, The Right Reverend Monsignor Court Francis Browning Drew [John Ayscough]. *First Impressions in America.* London: J. Long, 1921.

A look at various Roman Catholic institutions and practices in America against the background of European Catholicism by a Roman Catholic priest who later became private chamberlain to Pope Leo XIII and Pius X. Bickerstaffe-Drew (1858–1928) began the first of his twenty novels after he arrived at the age of fifty.

Bird, Isabella Lucy. See Bishop.

Birkenhead, Earl of. See Smith, Frederick Edwin.

Birmingham, George A. See Hannay.

Bishop, Isabella Lucy (Bird). *The Englishwoman in America.* London, 1856.

Isabella Bird (1831–1904) was only twenty-three when she visited in 1854. She had not yet developed the warmth and understanding that were to characterize her later travel works. Yet intimations of these qualities could be found in her descriptions of social life and of New York City.

———. *A Lady's Life in the Rocky Mountains,* London, 1879.

This celebrated collection of letters, after going through several editions, has received a handsome new one (Norman: University of Oklahoma Press, 1960), nicely introduced by Daniel Boorstin. Written by perhaps the most empathetic female traveler of the nineteenth century, these letters were based upon her adventures in Colorado in 1873.

Black, William. *Green Pastures and Piccadilly.* London, 1878.

The characters in this happily forgotten novel, one of forty-three by this Scotsman (1841–98), spend the last half of the yarn on American soil, mostly Coloradan. Literary license offers a somewhat more sensitive, if less systematic, perspective than does the ordinary travelogue; and since the protagonists do see a good portion of the United States, some direct information may be gained also. The factual account of his 1876 visit can be found in Sir Thomas Wemyss Reid, *William Black* (New York and London: Harper and Brothers, 1902), which describes some of Black's other novels dealing with America.

Blaikie, William Gardner. *Summer Suns in the Far West: a holiday trip to the Pacific slope.* London, 1890.

Blaikie (1820–99), a Scottish divine of the Free Church of Scotland and theology professor at Edinburgh's New College, and his wife vacationed in the United States in 1889 and visited their son who had settled near Los Angeles. In his own words, "the book is neither more nor less than notes of a holiday trip . . . [which] might be regarded as written in a railway carriage." Although much of it seemed to be so written, the book does contain one of the better descriptions of the yet-unsettled coastal area of southern California. Much the same ground is covered in *Recollections of a Busy Life* (London: Hodder and Storighton, 1901).

Boddam-Whetham, John Whetham. *Western Wanderings: A Record of Travel in the Evening Land*. London, 1874.

An author of travelogues on Central America and various Pacific islands, Boddam-Whetham found the American West rather un-English in taste and manners. He missed the culture but liked the scenery. His distaste, however, reached full flower only when he wrote of the Mormons.

Bretherton, Cyril Herbert. *Midas, or, The United States and the Future*. New York: E. P. Dutton and Company, 1926.

One of the few British books that took dead aim on the Harding-Coolidge era in the manner of American critics. He chastised American civilization as fat and materially overstuffed, intellectually and spiritually undernourished. Bretherton (1878–1939), a barrister, concluded in this little eighty-eight–page essay that a mechanical life had replaced the human, and that intellectual depth had been replaced by "a line." The book, too short to develop ideas, managed nonetheless to make many pungent points.

Bridge, James Howard [Harold Brydges]. *Uncle Sam at Home*. New York, 1888.

The author (1858–1939) attempted to generalize more than most travelers, and though he was not shrewd enough to carry it off, the book is of more than average interest. His discussions of the consequences for Great Britain of American business development seem better informed than the discussions of the other subjects with which he deals.

Brogan, Denis William. *Government of the People: A Study in the American Political System*. New York: Harper and Brothers, 1933.

Nevins said of this work: "Not a book of travel, but a treatise so penetrating and well informed that no survey of British studies of America can fail to give it an important place." Brogan (b. 1900), professor of politics at Cambridge University, wrote this analysis of "the working of the American political system as it is today" in 1932. Eleven years later in a new edition after the turmoil of depression and world war, this latter-day Bryce praised the durable American political system as one "that has passed through these years so little changed in its forms and personnel. . . . Survival is not the only test of a government, but it is a test all the same, and the American system of government has passed that test." Harold Laski wrote the Foreword.

———. *U.S.A.: An Outline of the Country, Its People and Institutions*. London: Oxford University Press, 1941.

One of "The World Today" series in which nations were "summed-up" in one hundred pages with a minimum of eccentricity. As might be expected, Brogan performed his task admirably.

Bromley, Mrs. Clara. *A Woman's Wanderings in the Western World*. London, 1861.

Only the first quarter of the book concerns Mrs. Bromley's experiences in the United States. She visited North and South America in 1853–54, accompanied by a young female friend. Her chatty observations of the eastern seaboard were related as letters to her father, Sir Fitzroy Kelly, M.P.

Brown, Elijah [Alan Raleigh]. *The Real America.* London: F. Palmer, 1913.

"Wipe out American civilization as it is, and as it has been for a hundred years, and tell me to what extent the world would be a loser." The captious Raleigh found nothing admirable in the land where "the higher life of mankind is almost forgotten in a mad debauch of commercial riotousness." Urging England to recognize the contamination that was America (alien blood, of course) and the contempt in which England was held by Americans, Raleigh temperately advised Americans to "return to the swaddling clothes and the nursery." The author was well advised to use a pseudonym.

Bryce, James. *The American Commonwealth.* 3 vols. London, 1888.

Easily the most searching, most complete, most understanding analysis of American society by a Briton. Matched only among all travelers to the United States by Tocqueville for originality and brilliance, Viscount Bryce (1838–1922) probably surpassed the Frenchman in observation of detail, familiarity with the subject (he visited the country in 1870, 1881, 1883–84, and 1887), and a sense of American history. While Bryce concentrated for two volumes on political institutions, his account of social and intellectual forces has not been improved upon. America's warmest friend, Bryce was also her most challenging critic. He was professor of civil law at Oxford (1870–93), began the revival of the study of Roman law, became a Liberal M. P. (1880–1906), was chief secretary for Ireland (he helped prepare the Irish home rule bill) in 1905–6, and Ambassador at Washington (1907–13), and was made a viscount and member of the Hague Tribunal in 1914.

———. *Modern Democracies.* New York: Macmillan Company, 1927. Volume II.

Originally published in 1921, written between 1918 and 1921, the second volume of this work condenses and brings to date much of *The American Commonwealth,* thus anticipating Bryce's later, more conscious two-volume condensation of the classic (which came out in 1922–23).

———. "America Revisited: The Changes of a Quarter Century," *The Outlook,* LXXIX (1905), 733–40, 846–55. New York: Outlook Publishing Company, 1905.

In this two-part article, Bryce compared his impressions of the United States in 1905 with earlier memories of 1870 and 1883. The second article concentrates on politics, while the first deals largely with economic and social considerations. His comparisons, though too miscellaneous to be profound, are nonetheless instructive and reliable. That change "which most strikes the visitor to America to-day is its prodigious material development." Many of Bryce's letters, which frequently reveal more of his personal reactions to America than do his more public utterances, are contained in H. A. L. Fisher's altogether excellent biography, *James Bryce (Viscount of Dechmont, O.M.),* published in two volumes (New York: Macmillan Company, 1927).

Buckley, Michael Bernard. *Diary of a Tour in America . . . by Rev. M.B.*

Buckley, of Cork, Ireland, a special missionary in North America and Canada in 1870 and 1871. Dublin, 1886.

A colorful account of Roman Catholic churchmen and their parishes. Father Buckley (1831–72) added spice to his travels by going around the country raising money for the Fenians and in general making appeals for their cause. His book was edited by his sister, Kate Buckley.

[Burn, James Dawson.] *Three Years among the Working Classes in the United States during the War.* London, 1865.

A peevish exposé of the evils, mostly moral, to which a working-class Scotsman would have been subjected should he have emigrated to the United States. Burn (1801?–89?) compiled a number of unflattering incidents and generalized therefrom. On his return to Scotland, the author discovered that home was even worse than America. The book appeared anonymously as "by the author of *The Autobiography of a Beggar-Boy.*" He was indeed a beggar, who was imprisoned in nearly every jail in the south of Scotland.

Burne-Jones, Sir Philip. *Dollars and Democracy.* New York: D. Appleton and Company, 1904.

On the cover, Sir Philip (1861–1926) painted a lovely impression of the New York skyline with its spires reaching heavenward to a sky filled with dollar signs. Money-madness and the supposedly vast importance of the Four Hundred (he called it "Society") were his themes. Since Burne-Jones spent a year in the United States (1902–3), since as a famous English painter (and son of an even more illustrious one) he had access to the highest places, and since he could write, this book should have shed more light than it did upon the artistic milieu to which he belonged.

Burton, Sir Richard Francis. *The City of the Saints and Across the Rocky Mountains to California.* London, 1861. The New York, 1862, edition was used.

This is the famous explorer and traveler's (1821–90) 500-page description of the Mormons in 1860. One of the finest and fairest accounts of the most controversial community of the time, this work stands as a classic of travel literature. Fawn M. Brodie edited a new version of this work in 1963.

Butler, William Francis. *The Great Lone Land: A Narrative of Travel and Adventure in the North-West of America.* London, 1872.

By the author of many other adventure-travel books, the land referred to in the title of this one was mostly in Canda, but some of the adventures took place in Minnesota and the Dakotas. Butler (1838–1910) was a captain in the British Army investigating British troop needs in Canada in 1869–71. He later became Major General Sir William Francis Butler.

Campbell, Sir George. *White and Black: The Outcome of a Visit to the United States.* London, 1879. The New York, 1879, edition was used.

Nevins describes this as "the best treatise upon the race question." Based upon a trip in the winter of 1878, the judgments on Reconstruction by this canny Liberal Scottish M.P. (1824–92) who had been active and distinguished in administration in India were indeed judicious and temperate. Campbell's observations of the South are more useful than his admittedly sketchy "Bird's-eye view of the United States" with which he began the book, and which he delivered as a lecture in Scotland in 1879.

Campbell, John Francis. *A Short American Tramp in the Fall of 1864.* Edinburgh, 1865.

A series of physical descriptions, largely of the Middle West and the Mississippi region.

———. *My Circular Notes.* 2 vols. London, 1876.

The first fourth of this book covers the American portion of Campbell's world tour in 1874–75. He compiled it from journals, letters, and geological notes written on the run, and like his earlier book, fixes on the terrain—this time farther west. He described himself occupationally as a "brief-less barrister," but this Scotsman (1822–85) achieved recognition as folklorist, meteorologist, and especially as a geologist.

Chambers, William. *Things as They Are in America.* London, 1854.

Chambers (1800–83) was an influential and important publisher in Edinburgh. He visited the Northeast in 1853 and left singing its praises, urging British emigration, and admiring everything American except daily manners and the treatment accorded Negroes. The self-reliance of the average citizen greatly impressed him. Also valuable is his *American Slavery and Colour* (London, 1857).

Chester, Greville John. *Transatlantic Sketches in the West Indies, South America, Canada, and the United States.* London, 1869.

Filled with inaccuracies, innuendo, and ill humor, this book need not long detain the historian. Chester (1830–92), a member of the Royal Archeological Institute of Great Britain and Ireland, reached the United States in 1868 on the last leg of a long trip. Although he devoted half of his stuffy tome to America, he was apparently very tired.

Chesterton, G. K. *What I Saw in America.* New York: Dodd, Mead and Company, 1922.

"I have never managed to lose my old conviction that travel narrows the mind." Thus, in his first sentence Chesterton gave a typical foretaste of what would follow: irony heaped upon paradox. He could have called his travels "Father Brown in Wonderland." As usual with this poet-critic-novelist (1874–1936), many of his generalizations were arresting, but the abstractions drifted so far from observable fact (based upon a meagre six-week tour) that one cannot help forgetting all about America while lost in admiration for Chesterton's prose and wit. His arguments cannot be easily simplified or evaluated, nor can they be ignored, for as a Catholic medievalist, Chesterton brought to bear upon the United States a fresh, critical, outrageous, and significant perspective—especially upon matters of philosophy and values.

[Coleridge, John Duke, Lord.]. History of Lord Coleridge's Tour. In *New York State Bar Association Reports,* VII (1884), 53–166.

England's Lord Chief Justice (1820–94) wrote no book about his lecture tour of 1883, but some of his speeches are in the above journal. See also "Lord Coleridge in America" and "Lord Coleridge Interviewed" in *Saturday Review,* September 1, 1883. A future Lord Chief Justice, Lord Russell of Killowen, accompanied Coleridge and did write a book about the trip.

Colyer, W. T. *Americanism: A World Menace.* London: Labour Publishing Company, 1922.

A typical Communist interpretation of American institutions and American life. Colyer gave the world a choice between America, the world menace, and Communism. George Knoles remarked of this work: "It is surprising, and a little frightening to see that the present-day Communist line [1955] respecting the United States has altered so very little in a third of a century."

[Cook, Joel.] *A Visit to the States: A Reprint of Letters from the Special Correspondent of The Times.* 2 series. London, 1887–88.

The most detailed catalog of the cities, countryside, and scenery of the eastern half of the United States—over eight hundred pages of sights! The anonymous author, long assumed to be an Englishman, was an American named Joel Cook. No analysis.

Cottenham, Mark Everard Pepys, 6th earl of. *Mine Host America.* London: Collins, 1937.

The earl (1903–43) commenced his preface by announcing that "this is little more than a descriptive account of a drive from New York to California and of a flight back." Although a bit modest, he accurately set the limits. Part I of this 462-page "descriptive account" logged his automobile trip from east to west, beginning in late 1935; he filled this section out with much practical information about cars, hotels, food, gasoline in a manner similar to his previous "Motoring Through . . ." books. He continued his off-beat Baedeker in Part II, this time being concerned with practical aspects of flying. On the way, he made some incidental social observations, most interesting of which, considering his aristocratic background, was his strong condemnation of the attitude taken by America's men of wealth toward President Franklin Roosevelt.

Craib, Alexander. *America and the Americans: A Narrative of a Tour in the United States and Canada with Chapters on American Home Life.* Paisley and London, 1892.

A little-known, but rather comprehensive view of the United States arising from a journey in 1891. The author was too kind to America, finding his generous heart kindled with warmth wherever he went and whatever he saw. Most pleasing of all to him was the liberal Christian spirit which he credited the United States with owning in large quantities. His promised chapter on American home life never panned out: he merely described some physical comforts of the home.

Crowe, Eyre. *With Thackeray in America.* New York, 1893.

Crowe (1824–1910) accompanied the illustrious Thackeray (1881–63) during the novelist's six-month lecture tour in 1853. The book uncovers no worthy insights, but it is filled with 117 pen-and-ink drawings of some of the sights and many of the personalities encountered by the two friends during the course of their American wanderings.

Dale, Robert William. *Impressions of America.* New York, 1878.

Dale (1829–95), a well-known Congregational minister and a theologian of great eminence, toured in the fall of 1877. He discussed politics, religion, and general social matters, but devoted half the book to an interesting and informed discussion of public education.

Day, Samuel Phillips. *Down South: or, An Englishman's experience at the seat of the American war.* 2 vols. London, 1862.

Phillips Day (1845–87) covered the events in the South in 1861 for the London *Morning Herald*. His reports rank among the least valuable of those produced by British journalists at this time—most of whom also published their daily stories. His sympathies were fully with the South; he felt that the Northern efforts to "subjugate" the South were futile and criminal. Yet he counseled against direct English involvement in the fighting. His bias was not atypical; but it hampered his powers of observation more than it did Russell's or Dicey's.

————. *Life and Society in America*. 2 vols. London, 1880.

Just a little more than twenty-five years after his first American misadventure, Day returned to get in his last licks. Aiming at the Northeast, the author quoted Hepworth Dixon on the title page, and went on to ridicule and exaggerate in similar fashion.

De Bary, Richard. *The Land of Promise: An Account of the Material and Spiritual Unity of America*. London: Longmans, Green, and Company, 1908.

A perceptive study by an English scholar who spent several years in the United States recuperating, mostly in Colorado, from a breakdown. Eschewing description of "the more obvious appearances of life," De Bary "aimed chiefly at showing what inner and spiritual forces unite all Americans in a certain community of thought, feeling, and action." He built his thesis around a unifying "civic religion" of optimism, geniality, and perfectibility, with which Protestantism, fast becoming "a social religion," strongly allied itself. This faith, he felt, would overcome the obstacles that had forced Americans to think about their shortcomings. Although James Eckman found De Bary's propositions "queer" and "of no great importance," this book, like that by George Smart, deserves, in this writer's opinion, a far wider reading.

Delafield, E. M. [E. E. M. De La Pasture]. *The Provincial Lady in America*. New York: Harper and Brothers, 1934.

Speaking through her fictional creation—the Provincial Lady—Miss Delafield (1890–1943) brightly chattered her way through three months in the United States in the cold winter of 1933. Employing diary form, and offering no relief from her incessant chipperness, the author managed to conceal from her readers any idea that the United States might have been experiencing any economic difficulties at the time.

De Sumichrast, Frederick Caesar John Martin Samuel Rousay. *America and the Britons*. New York: D. Appleton and Company, 1914.

Alarmed over the rapidly declining Anglo-Saxon side of the United States and by the ubiquitous political corruption he could not avoid seeing, the author (1845–1933) still managed to construct a temperate and reasonable overview of American society. He ended his career at Harvard as a professor of modern languages.

Dicey, Edward. *Six Months in the Federal States*. 2 vols. London, 1863.

Dicey (1832–1911) reported from the field on developments of the Civil War for the *Spectator* and *Macmillan's Magazine* and, next to William Howard Russell, historians have found his works, of those of the various journalists on the scene, to be the most useful for their understanding of the conduct of the war. Unlike Russell, however, Dicey prophesied Northern victory, and unlike Russell, he thought this would be a beneficial outcome. He wrote a lean, direct prose and showed not a trace of naïveté.

Dickens, Charles. *American Notes for General Circulation*. London, 1842. The Boston, 1867, edition was used.

The occasion for this new edition of the most noted of all British travel works was the novelist's second visit to the United States in 1867–68, by which time some of the scars he caused in 1842 had healed, and after which time Dickens (1812–70) had softened somewhat his original views. Except for a new, short preface by Dickens, the publishers left the 1842 version intact.

————. *The Letters of Charles Dickens*. "Edited by his Sister-in-Law and his Eldest Daughter." 2 vols. London, 1880.

Dickens' account of his 1867–68 visit appears in the second volume of this particular edition. In what was largely a report of his lecture triumphs, his friendly reception, and his severe cold, Dickens noted that "the changes that I find in the country generally exceed my utmost expectations." He referred to the improved social conditions and alluded to the growth of certain cities. "Strange to say, the railways and railway arrangements (both exceedingly defective) seem to have stood still while all other things have been moving." Also valuable for this visit is George Dolby's *Charles Dickens as I Knew Him: The Story of His Reading Tours in Great Britain and America, 1866–1870* (London, 1884).

Dickinson, G. Lowes. *Appearances: Notes of Travel, East and West*. Garden City, N.Y.: Doubleday, Page and Company, 1914.

A work of profound thought based upon superficial observation. Dickinson (1862–1932), a philosopher and historian best known for *The Greek View of Life*, wrote a number of letters from the United States in 1909 in which he attempted to uncover the basic assumptions of Western and American life. Since the first three sections of *Appearances* dealt respectively with India, China, and Japan, his contrasting American section was characterized by monumental comparisons and a grand philosophical detachment. He did not like American civilization for basically the same reasons as Matthew Arnold: it was a business civilization *sans* culture, and therefore spiritually decadent. He overstated his case (which here has been grossly oversimplified), but in his hands the case was not as platitudinous as might appear; it was searching, illuminating, and, at times, irresistible. This book, too, should be more familiar to American readers.

Dilke, Sir Charles Wentworth. *Greater Britain: A Record of Travel in English-Speaking Countries during 1866 and 1867*. 2 vols. London, 1868. The one-volume New York, 1869, edition was used.

"Through America England is speaking to the world." Thus concludes this strange book by a traveling companion of Hepworth Dixon and the son of Dixon's employer on the *Athenaeum*. Dilke (1843–1911) journeyed around the globe in 1866–67, the year before he began his long, auspicious, brilliant, and ill-fated career as a radical M.P., and he included Polynesia, Australia, and India along with the United States as the parts of Greater Britain: "If two small islands are by courtesy styled 'Great,' America, Australia, India must form a Greater Britain." Any American achievement, Dilke decided, must really be an achievement of the Saxon race. His specific observations were concentrated on California and the West and were rather thin; but he must be commended for not imbibing too much nonsense from his traveling companion. He expressed some interesting later views in *Problems of Greater Britain* (London, 1890).

Dilnot, Frank. *The New America.* New York: Macmillan Company, 1919.

A celebrated journalist and author of a biography of Lloyd George, Dilnot (1875–1946) lived in the United States during the eventful years of 1917 and 1918. He described different responses of various cities to the war and he wrote of "manners and temperament," sticking to a fairly superficial level. Of most interest are his shrewd capsule impressions of some of the leading men of the time with whom he came into contact: Woodrow Wilson, Colonel House, Teddy Roosevelt, Elihu Root, Orville Wright, and Billy Sunday.

Dixon, William Hepworth. *New America.* 2 vols. London, 1867.

Two lurid and sensational volumes that went through eight editions —probably for that reason. Dixon (1821–79), a professional traveler, editor of the *Athenaeum,* and an amateur historian—and no friend of America—examined such typically American groups as the Mormons, Shakers, and Oneida communists. He also exposed the female revolution in which the miserable ladies had resort to their secret weapon: refusal to make babies. Dixon concluded that the native-born population was being depleted and ruin was therefore imminent.

———. *White Conquest.* 2 vols. London, 1876.

In this book, which was even more flamboyant than his earlier best seller, Dixon continued his racist view of life by depicting a death struggle on the North American continent between the Caucasians on the one hand, and the Chinese, Negroes, and Indians on the other. By his 1875 trek, the United States had turned into a "seething jungle," to quote from Nevins. *White Conquest* also sold widely in Great Britain along with other good chillers. Dixon outdid even himself in *Spiritual Wives* (London, 1868).

Doyle, Sir Arthur Conan. *Our American Adventure.* London: Hodder and Stoughton, 1923.

The creator of Sherlock Holmes had another side to his personality, no less alluring, which dominated this adventure: Doyle as spiritualist. Sir Arthur (1859–1930) toured the eastern half of the United States in 1922 lecturing on his beliefs that the souls of the dead live on and that communication with them is elementary. He drew large crowds who were invariably impressed with his warmth and seriousness. His comments on America were incidental, but always well written and most cordial.

———. *Our Second American Adventure.* Boston, Mass.: Little, Brown, and Company, 1923.

A year later, Doyle carried his message to the American West and to Canada. This lecture crusade was the third and last of his spiritual trilogy, which began with *The Wanderings of a Spiritualist* in Australia. Again the scene of combat was neglected; the combat itself dominated the scene.

Dundee *Courier* and Dundee *Weekly News. Artisan Expedition to the World's Fair, Chicago, Organised by the Dundee Courier and the Dundee Weekly News.* Dundee, 1893.

Organized by the above newspapers, two groups of Scottish laborers representing a wide cross section of the population sailed in 1893 to the United States and to Canada: one for a report on American working conditions, the other for a look at Canadian agriculture. The artisan expedition spent a good deal of time shirking their mission at the Chicago World's Fair. Their conclusions on working conditions were palatable for home consumption, and not altogether incredible: the American receives higher pay and has a higher standard of living than his counterpart in Scotland. But he works far harder and longer, has less time for recreation, and generally speaking, "the good is soon taken out of his life. . . . The lot of the home worker will compare favourably with the conditions that are found to prevail in America."

Dunraven, Earl of. See Wyndham-Quin.

Enock, C. Reginald. *Farthest West: Life and Travel in the United States.* London: J. Long, 1910.

A leading English geographer, Enock (b. 1868) began this account with a topographical view of the United States, but moved quickly to a wide variety of topics, none of which he handled in depth. He made much of crime, business and political greed, and was not particularly optimistic about the possibilities for true Anglo-American friendship.

————. *America and England: A Study of the United States; its Relations with Britain; its Part in the Great War; and its Future Influence.* London: D. O'Connor, 1921.

Despite its title, this book treads more completely over the topography of the United States than did *Farthest West;* in fact, Enock provides a rundown of geological and soil conditions in every state of the Union. This consumes half the book, another quarter being wasted by a rather poor attempt at American history. The final quarter treats subjects promised in the title and is worth waiting for. Intelligent and modest, it also illustrates the difference made in Anglo-American relations by joint participation in the First World War. The possibilities for a deep and lasting accord between England and the United States were, he thought, immeasurably greater and more realizable than they were just eleven years before.

Faithfull, Emily. *Three Visits to America.* Edinburgh, 1884.

A leading feminist, Miss Faithfull (1835–95) devoted most of her time to the question of women's rights during her visits in 1872, 1882, and 1884. She talked to nearly every important woman in America in addition to seeking interviews with "the President, senators, journalists, college professors, and artists." She was even one of that small number with the good sense to go out of her way to meet Walt Whitman. Her observations on the feminist movement are unequalled in their knowledgeableness. On other questions, she had nothing new to say, but her comments are unusually well informed, her instincts unusually sympathetic.

Ferguson, Robert. *America during and after the War.* London, 1866.

Ferguson (1817–98), a writer of light travelogues, came to the United States twice: to the North in 1864 and to the South the next year. Most of the book consists of sight-seeing notes, interspersed by interviews with people such as Longfellow, Neal Dow, and Lincoln, and by some discussion of current happenings. He concluded by chastising England's diplomacy during the war.

Ferguson, William. *America by River and Rail*. London, 1856.

The author (?–1887) was a botanist untrained in social analysis. The account of his 1855 railroad and boat travels was pictorial and reached fullest expression in its description of mining in the West. He tended toward Toryism, but harbored generally favorable feelings toward his hosts.

Finlayson, Archibald W. *A Trip to America: A Lecture, delivered by Archibald W. Finlayson, Johnstone, near Glasgow, in the Public Hall of the Johnstone Working Man's Institute, 18th March, 1879*. Glasgow, 1879.

Moderately sympathetic and moderately interesting, but unfortunately failing to touch on the conditions of American labor as his place of lecture would seem to promise. The author made his trip in 1878.

Fitz-Gerald, William George [Ignatius Phayre]. *America's Day: Studies in Light and Shade*. London: Dodd, Mead and Company, 1918.

A lively picture of the United States on the eve of her entry into World War I by a professional traveler. Fitz-Gerald felt that America was growing a new soul, a seriousness of purpose under the "ablest Executive who ever led her to the vindication of her ideals." Yet he bitterly reproached the State Department for its policy toward England and he evoked the image of an utterly chaotic land ruled by money, advertising, newspaper publishers, a land viciously rent by class hatreds. The author delighted in felicity of phrase as an end in itself; this often led him to exaggeration and fantasy.

———. *Can America Last? A Survey of the Emigrant Empire from the Wilderness to World Power together with its Claim to "Sovereignty" in the Western Hemisphere from Pole to Pole*. London: J. Murray, 1933.

By the early days of the New Deal, Fitz-Gerald had come to despise Woodrow Wilson, as well as the United States in general. He ran through American diplomatic history to prove the arrogance, selfishness, spinelessness, and stupidity of American foreign policy and to warn the world against trusting America. As to his title question, Fitz-Gerald's answer was no, unless some powerful conservative leader of the Teddy Roosevelt or Nicholas Murray Butler type could come along and rescue America from her platitudinous hypocrisy. He did not think FDR was that man.

Ford, Ford Madox. *New York Is Not America*. New York: A. and C. Boni, 1927.

Illuminating perceptions and incoherent cryptograms were mixed together in ample proportions by this distinguished critic, novelist, and talented go-between of the *literati* of the 1920's. Posing as one in total ignorance of the United States while knowing only New York, Ford (1873–1939) impressionistically and affectionately sketched Gotham before revealing that the Midwest and not New York represented the real America. He made the contrast vivid, and invidious for the Midwest. New York shared only one quality with the rest of the nation: hope.

———. *Great Trade Route*. London: G. Allen and Unwin, 1937.

Practically an autobiographical stream-of-consciousness tour around much of the world, including ample slices of the United States.

No organization, only flashes, some illuminating, some blinding, none easily paraphrased.

Fountain, Paul. *The Eleven Eaglets of the West*. London: J. Murray, 1906.
This is the fourth of Fountain's portrayals of American nature and game, and probably the most informative. The title refers to the eleven states of the Far West, each of which the author described separately. There is still controversy concerning Fountain's identity; he has been accused of being a monumental liar.

————. *The Great Deserts and Forests of North America*. London: Longmans, Green and Company, 1901.
Also prairies, Indians, and swamps.

Francis, Alexander. *Americans: An Impression*. London: A. Melrose, 1909.
Education in its many aspects—universities, public schools, college fraternities—dominates this detached and analytic book. Francis also dealt intelligently with the bad climate for socialism in America.

Fraser, J. Nelson. *America, Old and New: Impressions of Six Months in the States*. London: J. Ouseley, 1910.
Fraser (1869–1918) tried to cover everything. Here for six months in 1908–9, he assayed subjects ranging from American history to wild life, from scenery to social speculation. He simply did not know enough to avoid superficiality and error. Worried especially by socialism on one side and the trusts on the other, Fraser believed that progress through education could result in the triumph of common sense and moderation. He was a member of the Indian Education Service.

Freeman, Edward A. *Some Impressions of the United States*. London, 1883.
The New York, 1883, edition was used.
The distinguished Oxford historian of the Norman Conquest and secondarily of Greek civilization inaugurated a decade of travel literature that greatly surpassed in quality any other, with the possible but dubious exception of the 1830's. Freeman (1823–92) came in 1881–82, ventured only as far southwest as St. Louis and as far southeast as northern Virginia; but he covered a wide range of topics most expertly. With his unparalleled sense of history, one might have expected a marvelous book, but he did not seem to try very hard. He stuck to details, and his criticisms were specific but obvious. He seemed most concerned with variations in language usage between England and the United States, and his great generalization seemed to be that Americans remain "as English people." Granting these disappointments, this book still ranks among the major achievements in travel literature. His *Lectures to American Audiences* (London, 1882) can also be read with profit.

[Fremantle, Sir Arthur James Lyon.] *Three Months in the Southern States*. London, 1863.
I also used the new edition entitled *The Fremantle Diary* edited by Walter Lord (Boston, 1954). Lieutenant Colonel Fremantle (1835–1901) of the Coldstream Guards traveled behind Confederate lines from April through June, 1863. His diary records with much sympathy each tidbit of frontier adventure and Southern military life he encountered. He refused to believe the South could ever be subdued. Enjoyable reading, but no general analysis of American life.

Frewen, Moreton. *Melton Mowbray and Other Memories*. London: H. Jenkins, 1924.

This is an autobiographical survey of the years 1853–87 in the life of an economist (1853–1924) who seemed to know nearly everyone of importance. He came to the United States in 1878, married an American girl, and spent the larger portion of his life commuting between Liverpool and New York. His most interesting American experience was buffalo-hunting in Wyoming. He wrote several other articles and pamphlets dealing with the United States, mostly on economic matters.

Fuller, Colonel John Frederick Charles. *Atlantis: America and the Future.* London: K. Paul, Trench, Trubner and Company, 1926.

Speakeasies, crime, materialism, and godlessness were portrayed as the fundamental American institutions and attitudes in this foolish book. The colonel (b. 1878), who later became one of the world's leading authorities on military strategy, reconnoitered in the American field for all of six weeks in the late summer of 1924 and first published the core of *Atlantis* in *The National Review*. Happily, this tome —published as part of the same series that gave us Bretherton's caustic but more knowledgable *Midas*—was very short.

Furness, Sir Christopher. *The American Invasion.* London: Simpkin, Marshall, Hamilton, Kent and Company, 1902.

After this Liberal M.P., industrialist, and shipowner (1852–1912) saw the United States in 1901, he returned home to reassure his countrymen in a series of speeches and articles that they need not despair over the American invasion of economic markets that England had dominated for a century. Instead, he constructively advised a strengthening of Commonwealth ties, a step-up in educational development, and a liberal trade policy. The book consists of a reprint of an article from the *Pall Mall Magazine* and the text of a 1902 lecture, the latter telling the story of his actual experiences in the United States.

Galsworthy, John. *Addresses in America, 1919.* New York: C. Scribner's Sons, 1919.

Reprints of seven lectures given by the novelist-playwright (1867–1933) upon the occasion of his second excursion to the United States. Galsworthy maintained great caution in generalizing about his hosts and chose instead to speak harmlessly and warmly in behalf of Anglo-American harmony. He stressed the need for cultural and spiritual yearnings and gladdened his audiences by suggesting that the United States stood at the verge of such a cultural surge, and that she would assume the mantle of world leadership with grace and responsibility. He seemed to hope that his suggestions would bring into being the reality.

George, Walter Lionel. *Hail Columbia! Random Impressions of a Conservative English Radical.* New York: Harper and Brothers, 1921.

Skillfully drawn impressions of New England, Chicago, New York, of women, prohibition, and the American scene in general by a successful novelist (1882–1926). George thrilled to the modernity of the new world in much the same way as H. G. Wells. He preferred Irish Boston to Brahmin Boston, Chicago to London, vitality to intellectuality. Thus, like Wells, George was one of a few who reprimanded America for its overconservatism, for its sentimental affinity for aristocracy, even for its mistreatment of women in a land where "gyneola try" supposedly was the rule. Oddly, the influx of alien peoples upset him.

Gibbs, Philip. *People of Destiny: Americans as I Saw Them at Home and Abroad*. New York: Harper and Brothers, 1920.

The novelist-newspaperman-author (b. 1877) of *Now It Can Be Told* reached the United States in late 1919. "The war was over, and the warriors were coming home with the triumph of victory . . . and there had not yet crept over the spirits of the people the staleness and disillusion that always follow the ending of war." No book surpassed this for its cheerful impression of those halcyon days or for its keen demarcation of America's new role of mature world power. Gibbs felt that this "middle-class empire, untainted by imperial ambition or ancient traditions of overlordship" would be a great force for peace.

Gladstone, Thomas H. *Kansas; or, Squatter Life and Border Warfare in the Far West*. London, 1857.

A description of events in Kansas in 1856 by a correspondent of the London *Times*. Excellent for its evocation of the violent atmosphere pervading "Bleeding Kansas." In America the book was published under the title *The Englishman in Kansas* (New York, 1857).

Goldring, Douglas. *Impacts: The Trip to the States and Other Adventures of Travel*. London: Eyre and Spottiswoode, 1931.

Goldring (1887–1960) wrote many novels, including the compassionate *Odd Man Out*. Only the first sixty-five pages of *Impacts* deal with his American travels. He arrived before the Depression and found an arrogant population intoxicated with power. Goldring, who did not usually experience indignation, experienced it very strongly when he noted the extraordinary new vogue of things American conquering England. Only half-facetiously toward the end did he cry out, "Keep England English."

Gordon, Harry Panmure. *The Land of the Almighty Dollar*. London, [1892?].

A stockbroker by trade, Gordon (1837–1902) wrote of his travels in New York City and Chicago. The book is perfectly commonplace, perfectly friendly, and filled with many quotations in French and Latin.

Graham, Stephen. *With Poor Immigrants to America*. London: Macmillan Company, 1914.

Graham (b. 1884) wrote many fine travel books about Russia, and he never quite left his haunts on this unusual 1913 excursion. He accompanied emigrants (mostly Russian and Slavic) on their momentous voyage to Eden, and he tried to view America through their eyes. With him always was the extreme contrast between Russia and the United States, between backwardness and progress, between the mystical and the material, between tears and hope, between "the religion of suffering and the religion of philanthropy." England, Graham felt, represented the mean. The author's sympathies with all three ways of life helped make this an interesting and humane study.

———. *The Soul of John Brown*. New York: Macmillan Company, 1920.

Graham returned in 1920 to trek through the much-neglected South. He visited many scenes of the Civil War and enjoyed that part of the excursion. But the current plight of the Negroes appalled him

and this feeling was expressed on every page. Yet he managed to con-
of new life."

Newspaperman. London: Grant Richards, 1917.

An English journalist's disjointed journalistic patter. Perhaps in
honor of the joint 1917 war effort, Grant took as his subject Englishmen in the United States and Americans in England. Not surprisingly,
his most useful chapters dealt with the American press. Grant had no
intention of getting serious about anything and said nothing very important.

Greenwall, Harry J. *American Scene.* London: I. Nicholson and Watson,
1937.

A pseudohistory with 1936 as point of reference by a freelance
journalist (b. 1896). The author attempted to paint a large canvas so
that he could explain the background causes of the Depression and
place the New Deal in historical perspective. Instead he underscored
the bizarre, the sensational, exhibiting only the most superficial understanding of American life. Easily the most informative section of the
book is Greenwall's extensive quotation of a stripper and her views on
life and nudism.

Grey, Frederick William. *Seeking Fortune in America.* London: Smith,
Elder and Company, 1912.

The author tried from his youth to make money in North America, most often by farming on homesteading land. Grey never succeeded. The narration of his frustrating experiences makes mildly
interesting reading. His conclusion belied the reputation of the New
World and cast an interesting light on changing times in the United
States. "I am still seeking fortune in America; I have sought it in
Canada, the United States, and Mexico, but it appears as far off in
1912 as ever it did. America is a land of great opportunities, but
rarely for the Briton or the man without capital."

Griffin, Sir Lepel Henry. *The Great Republic.* London, 1884. The New
York, 1884, edition was used.

Griffin (1840–1908) disliked everything about the Great Republic. Visiting coincident with Matthew Arnold in 1883, whom he also
abused, this ill-humored British official in India declared that "America is the country of disillusion and disappointment in politics, literature, art, in its scenery, its cities, and its people." This left little else,
but Griffin made sure to warn his countrymen of the folly committed by America of giving power to "the uneducated masses."
Nevins characterized the author as "an amusing reversion to Mrs.
Trollope. . . . Sir Lepel came just fifty years after his due time, and
we are not likely to look upon his kind again." Unhappily, a few
more Griffins, such as Elijah Brown [Alan Raleigh], did follow.

Guedalla, Philip. *Conquistador: American Fantasia.* New York: Harper
and Brothers, 1928.

The British historian (1889–1944) left off analysis, institutions,
causation, and laws when he embarked on a "willy-nilly" three month
lecturing expedition in 1926–27. He took with him an eye, an imagination, enthusiasm, and a multicolored palette from which he
fashioned a fascinating assortment of revealing sketches of surface

America. No conclusions presented, *Conquistador* bears a resemblance to Kipling's *American Notes* in its virtuoso writing.

Guest, Lady Theodora (Grosvenor). *A Round Trip in America.* London, 1895.

With the hunting season over early in 1894, Lady Theodora, sister of the Duke of Westminster, decided to take a quick trip to the American West to keep herself busy. She set forth the natural wonders which she beheld.

Hamilton, Mary Agnes. *In America Today.* London: H. Hamilton, 1932.

"Today" was early in 1932, when this influential former Liberal M.P., delegate to the League of Nations, biographer, and journalist made her fourth visit in five years to the United States. She used her travel background to contrast previous pre-Depression moods with the new atmosphere in 1932. Concentrating on this mood, Miss Hamilton (b. 1883) argued with great persuasiveness that the psychological depression was far more severe than the economic, that Americans had lost all their hope, that they had nothing inward upon which to fall back. America's historic vitality had, she said, depended too totally on economic success, and without that the nation had no place to turn. A sober, thoughtful, and incorrect little study.

Hannay, James Owen [George A. Birmingham]. *From Dublin to Chicago: Some Notes on a Tour in America.* New York: George H. Doran Company, 1914.

An Irish clergyman by profession, Hannay (1865–1950) made his chief mark as a humorist. These warm and gentle impressions of America were as much concerned with England and Ireland as with the United States, Hannay using comparison to good effect. Rather than generalizing straight-out, he showed things American in a new light via laughter, whimsy, and irony. He ended the book plaintively by noting about his Irish countrymen "that it has always been in other lands, not in their own, that our people succeeded."

Harbord, Maurice Assheton. *Froth and Bubble.* London: E. Arnold, 1915.

A modest autobiography by one who spent most of his life in South Africa and fought in the Boer War. Harbord (1874–1954) spent his early years in the Midwest until 1896, and his adventures make pleasant and unimportant reading in this accurately titled little work.

Hardman, Sir Joseph William. *A Trip to America.* London, 1884.

A minor record of an 1883 sightseeing excursion by a cleric and close associate of George Meredith. Hardman (1833–91) penetrated as far as Yellowstone Park, where he met President Arthur by the campfire.

Hardy, Iza Duffus. *Between Two Oceans, or Sketches of American Travel.* London, 1884.

Not to be outdone by her mother, Lady Duffus Hardy (see next item), Iza (?–1922) followed her to the States in 1881–83, traversing the same territory, and wrote a travel book in the same vein as her mother's. Like Lady Duffus she was a novelist. Iza spent most of her trip in Florida and the Southeast. Perhaps of some interest is her *Oranges and Alligators: Sketches of South Florida Life* (London, 1886).

Hardy, Mary (McDowell) Duffus, Lady. *Through Cities and Prairie Lands: Sketches of an American Tour*. London, 1881. The New York, 1881 edition was used.

A condescending but cheerful spin around the northern half of the country from the East Coast to San Francisco in 1880–81. Lady Mary (1824–91) was a novelist and as such was granted interviews with Longfellow and Oliver Wendell Holmes. Most of her chapters describe her crossing (part of it in an emigrant train in Nebraska) and her pleasing sightseeing trip to California. She also wrote *Down South* (London, 1883).

[Harris, W. A., and Alexander Rivington.] *Reminiscences of America in 1869*. London, 1870.

A little-known, anonymously published, but reliable account of another journey timed to take advantage of the completion of the transcontinental railway. Harris wrote more than two thirds of the book, including two fine chapters on American education. The two Englishmen encouraged the working man to emigrate to the United States, mostly because "a good and gratuitous education is offered to his children."

Harrison, Frederic. *Memories and Thoughts: Men-Books-Cities-Art*. London: Macmillan and Company, 1906.

In this series of recollective essays, the famous positivist and literary critic included a thirty-page remembrance of his two-month tour in 1901. Harrison (1831–1923) rambled and naturally developed no ideas, but he touched lightly and deftly on a number of significant matters from equality to immigration to cultural excellence. He felt that the two most difficult problems confronting the United States were the heightening labor-capital discords and the Negro question. Generally, however, he seemed quite optimistic about America's future.

Hatton, Joseph. *To-day in America: Studies for the Old World and New*. 2 vols. London, 1881. The one-volume New York, 1881, edition was used.

An unexpectedly perspicacious study by a novelist and journalist (1841–1907). He came in 1880 (he also visited in 1876 and 1878) as a reporter for the London *Standard*. But unlike other journalists, he attempted to get beyond simple documentary description. He seemed most concerned with American economic development and American theater—an incongruous combination explained in part by the fact that he accompanied Henry Irving. He also composed interesting chapters on the "free-thinker," Robert Ingersoll, and on American-Canadian relations. Hatton wrote two interesting novels about the United States: *The Queen of Bohemia* (London, 1878) and *Cruel London* (New York, [1883]).

————. *Henry Irving's Impressions of America*. 2 vols. London, 1884. The one-volume Boston, 1884, edition was used.

In 1895, Henry Irving (1836–1905) became the first actor ever to be knighted. This book tells the story of the first (1883–84) of eight American tours made by the famous Lyceum Company in the space of twenty years, bringing drama on a major scale to all parts of the United States. Irving, the company's manager and leading actor, was accompanied by his leading lady Ellen Terry and by the author who duly noted all their interviews and conversations. Irving, not America, was the leading protagonist of this particular scenario. Also pertinent to Irving's first visit are L. F. Austin, *Henry Irving in England and America* (London, 1884) and William Winter, *Henry Irving* (New York, 1885).

Hole, Samuel Reynolds. *A Little Tour in America by the Very Rev. S. Reynolds, dean of Rochester.* London, 1895.

The witty Anglican Dean of Rochester (1819–1904) (and part-time rosegrower) made a rapid trip in 1894–95 as far west as the Rockies, visiting schools, churches, and bishops, looking at horses and flowers. The account is descriptive for the most part, but Dean Hole wrestled momentarily with the fact that education was, in his opinion, too secular and yet the churches, in his opinion, were thriving. He lectured as he went, trying, successfully, to raise contributions to renovate his Rochester cathedral.

Holyoake, George Jacob. *Among the Americans and a Stranger in America.* Chicago, 1881.

A leading spirit in the Co-operative movement and a committed free-thinker, Holyoake (1817–1906) was not alarmed as were many of his contemporaries by the most progressive tendencies in American life. His discussion of emigration, co-ops, emigrant education, and state socialism for the United States make uncommonly interesting reading. His descriptive chapters, on the other hand, are quite commonplace. The bulk of the book, "Among the Americans," was written for the Manchester *Co-operative News.* The shorter article, "A Stranger in America," which is not in the second edition of *Among the Americans* (London, 1881), appeared in the journal, *Nineteenth Century.* Holyoake preferred the American spirit to that of England, which he called "a country where nothing leads to anything, and anything leads to nothing." No surprise then that when T. S. Hudson purchased a copy of this work in 1882 on a train near Chicago he decided that Holyoake *must* be an "atheist." Of comparable interest is his *Travels in Search of a Settler's Guidebook to America and Canada* (London, 1884).

Howard of Glossop, Winifred Mary (De Lisle) Howard, Baroness. *Journal of a Tour in the United States, Canada, and Mexico.* London, 1897.

The baroness (1861–1909) arrived in 1894 for sightseeing purposes. She left four months later in February, 1895, after having hopped from Toronto to San Francisco to Mexico City to San Antonio to Tampa to Washington to Boston, with many stops in between. She had no time for ideas.

Huddleston, Sisley. *What's Right with America.* Philadelphia: J. B. Lippincott Company, 1930.

Huddleston (1883–1952) adored America. He praised without qualification her prosperity, culture, optimism, economic system, intellectual growth, architecture, political system, and even prohibition! He celebrated the United States with all the fervor of a stock speculator of the late 1920's. This is the most ironic of all British travel books, for it was composed in 1928–29 just as the house crumbled. This veteran journalist was so starry-eyed that he had no idea that the first crash might be anything more than a passing phenomenon.

When *What's Right with America* was published, its author might well have blushed.

Hudson, T. S. *A Scamper through America, or, Fifteen Thousand Miles of Ocean and Continent in Sixty Days.* London, 1882.

A day-by-day log of an 1882 chase by an Englishman unwilling to concede a thing to the United States.

Hughes, Thomas. *Vacation Rambles.* London, 1895.

The author of *Tom Brown's Schooldays* collected in this volume all of his "Vacuus Viator" travel letters which had appeared in *The Spectator* from 1862 to 1895. His American travels, which came in 1870, five years after his election as a Liberal reformer to the House of Commons, and then again at scattered intervals between 1880 and 1887, and which took him to Tennessee, Iowa, and the Cumberland Mountains along with the usual cities, constitute about one third of the book. The letters of this Christian socialist (1822–96) were mostly descriptive, but included was the text of a lecture delivered in Boston in 1870, being an apologia for English diplomacy during the Civil War. His comments on education in this book were disappointing though he made up for this lack in several articles. Of interest also is his *Rugby Tennessee* (London, 1881), an account of the cooperative he set up there.

Humphreys, Mrs. Eliza Margaret J. (Gollan). *America—Through English Eyes by "Rita"* [pseud.]. London: S. Paul and Company [1910].

"Rita" (?–1938) wrote short stories and came to the United States for a short two months in 1910. Unfortunately she could not resist blessing the world with her vast knowledge of Boston, New York, Washington, and the true meaning of American civilization. So she penned sarcastic statements about American religion, marriage, men, women, institutions, and cities. Although not always wrong, she was always unnecessarily irritating.

Huxley, Aldous. *Jesting Pilate: The Diary of a Journey.* London: George H. Doran Company, 1927.

A stinging attack on American values by one who was to spend most of his life and was to die in this country. Huxley (1894–1963) was just being recognized as a brilliant essayist when he embarked on a global tour that took him to India, Japan, Burma, and home via San Francisco. His American observations of San Francisco, Los Angeles, Chicago, and New York lasted only twenty-eight pages, but in them he found America's brand of equality leading unequivocally to a state of affairs in which (to paraphrase a French traveler of another century) the majority tyrannized the excellent few.

Huxley, Thomas Henry. *American Addresses: with a Lecture on the Study of Biology.* London, 1877.

Only one of the lectures by this illustrious Darwinist scientist (1825–95), given at the ceremony honoring the opening of Johns Hopkins University in 1876, addresses itself, rather too generally, to the United States. Three speeches given in New York dealt with evolution, and the rest, emanating from England, discussed the study of biology. More of Huxley's impressions of America can be found in "Professor Huxley in America," *New York Tribune,* September 23, 1876 and his *Life and Letters* (New York, 1900).

Hyde, John. *Homeward through America.* Chicago, 1892.

Hyde (1848–1929) rode by train from San Francisco to New York on his way home from the Orient. He described, in a handsome thirty-six page pamphlet, what he saw through the window. He was a Fellow of the Royal Society of literature. He may, however, have been an American paid to write this piece of railway propaganda. This problem remains unresolved at the present.

Igglesden, Sir Charles. *A Mere Englishman in America*. Ashford, Kent: Printed at the Kentish Express Office, 1929.

Igglesden (1861–1949) toured in 1927–28 as one of fourteen journalists invited to travel coast-to-coast by the Carnegie Trust for Universal Peace. He wrote nothing pretentious, but retraced his itinerary with plainness and good sense.

Jacks, Lawrence Pearsall. *My American Friends*. New York: Macmillan Company, 1933.

A sensible, fair-minded, well-informed study by the principal of a Unitarian training college fully acquainted with the United States. Jacks (1860–1955) ranged knowledgeably over such diverse themes as American children and the intelligentsia, the schools and Rhodes Scholars, recreation and self-criticism. Seeing complexities, chuckling ironically at his own generalizations, Jacks wrote one of the finest of all travel books.

[Jebb, Mrs. John Beveridge Gladwyn.] *A Strange Career: Life and Adventures of John Gladwyn Jebb*. Edinburgh and London, 1894.

Jack Jebb (1841–95) managed to live a life of romantic adventure, and he failed to manage well any of his business enterprises. This biography, written by his widow, relates his wandering in the West in the 1870's as well as his later escapades in Mexico. H. Rider Haggard wrote an introductory eulogy.

Joad, Cyril Edwin Mitchinson. *The Babbitt Warren*. New York and London: Harper and Brothers, 1927.

The well-known journalist masquerading as a professor of philosophy at London University had not visited the United States when he wrote this harangue. It is not a travel book, but I have included it as a sample of one of the most extreme and overdrawn indictments of American civilization by a Briton I have ever seen, a widely-read montage of the most bizarre press clippings from the yellowest journals. The author's intention was to damn modern, material civilization, of which the United States stood as symbol, vanguard, and perpetrator, for its utter decadence and its absolute alienation from the Platonic categories by which Joad (1891–1953) chose to measure life: Truth, Beauty, and the Good. I also included the book because of its clever title.

Kelly, William. *An Excursion to California over the Prairie; Rocky Mountains; and Great Sierra Nevada: With A Stroll through the Diggings and Ranches of That Country*. 2 vols. London, 1851.

Kelly happened to reach California in 1849, a circumstance which, in its depiction of the Gold Rush, gives this book a special niche in travel literature. The rest of this work, like the Irish author's later descriptions of life in the Far West, is of minor importance.

[Kendall, John.] *American Memories: Recollections of a Hurried Run through the United States during the Late Spring of 1896 . . .* Nottingham, 1896.

This is an account of a rapid trip through five thousand miles in one month in the spring of 1896, just as the Bryan-McKinley campaign began to gather force. Kendall merely described places, and better yet, included over one hundred clear photographs. Published anonymously.

Kennedy, John McFarland. *Imperial America*. London: S. Paul and Company, 1914.

An answer to the English "peacemongers" who, in 1913, believed that war was evil and that the United States was a friend upon whom England could rely. By emphasizing American history "from an economic point of view" (at a time when this was a fashionable thing to do), Kennedy, a writer of popular political polemics, attempted to prove that the United States had always been imperialist, would continue to be (especially in South America), that her ambitions were antithetical to those of England and Europe, and that the Anglo-American "cant of arbitration and brotherly love" should be replaced by a recognition of Anglo-American conflict—"certainly more manly and more in accordance with reality."

Kipling, Rudyard. *American Notes*. New York, 1891. The Boston, 1899, edition was used.

"I love this People, and if any contemptuous criticism has to be done, I will do it myself." The twenty-five-year old Kipling (1865–1936) did both: he burlesqued mercilessly while identifying closely "with this vulgar, conceited, and magnificent" nation. His descriptions of San Francisco, Chicago, a church meeting, American women, and Mark Twain compare favorably in style with Dickens'. These letters grew out of a trek in 1889 from India to England via the United States and were first printed in the *Pioneer* of India. Pirated in 1891, *American Notes* was generally suppressed because of its apparent vilification of Americans. Kipling's true feelings toward them, however, may be more accurately gauged by his subsequent marriage to an American girl, and his domicile in Vermont from 1892 to 1896. *American Notes* may be overly flamboyant, but its reputation as a bitterly withering indictment of American civilization is certainly unwarranted.

———. *From Sea to Sea: Letters of Travel*. 2 vols. New York, 1899.

The earliest edition contains letters only from 1887 to 1889. Later editions include travel letters up to 1913, including several new American ones. *American Notes* is repeated in full in all editions of *From Sea to Sea*.

Kroupa, B. *An Artist's Tour; Gleanings and Impressions of Travels in North and Central America and the Sandwich Islands*. London, 1890.

Kroupa spent nine years "zig-zagging" across the United States, Canada, Cuba, Central America, and the Hawaiian Islands. He wrote mostly of California and did his own illustrating. The art work surpassed the literary: "I am back from the far west, back from the land of marvels—but my heart lingers there still . . . ," etc.

Laski, Harold J. *Democracy in Crisis*. Chapel Hill: University of North Carolina Press, 1933.

While teaching at Yale Law School in 1931, Professor Laski (1893–1950) delivered the Weil Lectures in April of that year at the University of North Carolina, from which this significant work grew. Neither a travel book nor Laski's greatest study of America (*The American Democracy* appeared in 1948), its analysis of the dilemma of capitalist democracies during the Depression bears inclusion on this list simply for its acuity.

————. *The American Democracy: A Commentary and an Interpretation.* New York: Viking Press, 1948.

A monumental study, sweeping in scope and deep in understanding, in which the themes of progress and equality are played prominently from the first page on. "No state, until our own day, has done so much to make the idea of progress a part of the mental make-up of man. No state, either, has done more to make freedom a dream which overcame the claims both of birth and of wealth" (p. 3). In addition to the usual chapters on politics, religion, education, culture, etc., Laski also wrote about "the professions," the press, cinema and radio, labor, and "the Spirit of America." His tendency was to treat American civilization statically, as following out a consistent, relatively unchanging pattern since her early beginnings. Some of the book seems a bit dated already, but it must be read by all serious students of American society.

Latham, Henry. *Black and White. A Journal of a Three Months' Tour in the United States.* London, 1867.

A running journal of a very fast journey (December, 1866–March, 1867), mostly in the Southeast, and about racial relations, a book which the author, a barrister, correctly described as superficial. He appended four topical chapters of fair quality: on the Negro, the Indian, the Fenians, and the Alabama Claims.

Lawrence, George Alfred. *Silverland.* London, 1873.

Lawrence (1827–76) always identified himself on his title pages as "the author of Guy Livingstone," a novel written in 1857 by which he assumed he would be carried to eternal fame. His 1872–73 venture was his third in the United States, the first coming during the Civil War when he unsuccessfully tried to join the Confederate Army. The second trip was in 1866, and out of these two experiences he constructed three books. He wrote, airily, of sights in California, of the Mormons, of Chicago after the fire, of Nevada silver mines, and of some interviews.

Leng, Sir John. *America in 1876: Pencillings during a Tour in the Centennial Year: With a Chapter on the Aspects of American Life.* Dundee, 1877.

After a pleasant journey across the land, including a visit to the Centennial Exhibition in Philadelphia, this distinguished Scottish businessman (1828–1906), who was especially concerned with emigration prospects for his countrymen, settled down to his three most important concluding chapters. One dealt with education, the second with the churches, and the third with "general aspects," including the ins and outs of acquiring free land. He was impressed. At the time of writing, Leng was editor of the Dundee *Advertiser;* later he entered Parliament as a Liberal for Dundee and was knighted in 1893. A useful book.

Leslie, Shane. *American Wonderland: Memories of Four Tours in the United States of America (1911–1935).* London: M. Joseph, 1936.

Spicy, opinionated, enjoyable comments on everything American by the Irish humorist and Jonathan Swift scholar—a writer with whom Leslie (b. 1885) seemed to have much in common.

Linklater, Eric. *Juan in America.* New York: J. Cape and H. Smith, 1931.

A terribly funny spoof on American civilization written by a charming essayist after his tenure as a Commonwealth Fellow (1928–30). Linklater (b. 1899) inaugurated his "Juan in . . ." series with this volume and he has carried on with it many times since then. The tone of the satire can be gathered from the title of his most amusing chapter: "The Land of Infinite Possibility." Although he stretched things perhaps more than he had to do, the humor was more often friendly than sarcastic. The book has been translated into German.

Longworth, Maria Theresa, Viscountess Avonmore [Therese Yelverton]. *Teresina in America.* 2 vols. London, 1875.

Teresina (1832?–81) traveled twenty thousand miles around America in 1872–73 upon a very high horse from which she never descended. Bad manners and no Society bothered this busy authoress. She wrote three other books dealing with the United States.

Lorne, Marquis of. See Argyll.

Lovett, Richard. *United States Pictures Drawn with Pen and Pencil.* [London,] 1891.

The author (1851–1904) spent ten years as a boy in the United States and lived through the Civil War before returning to England as a missionary Tractarian and author of *The Printed English Bible.* The book is critical and reasonably accurate, but does not derive its chief value from the prose.

Low, Sir Alfred Maurice. *America at Home.* London: G. Newnes, 1908.

Like Archer, Stead, and Muirhead before him, the journalist Low (1860–1929) could not conceal the almost mystic awe in which he held the United States, with its wealth, power, and future prospects. Like Muirhead's, this high admiration was not a thing of the moment, but had grown steadily after a long residence in the nation. Also like Muirhead, Low's observations are frequently original and unusually penetrating. His analyses of politics, American women, differences between eastern and western United States, and his portrayal of America's growing manhood justify the ranking of this book among the major travel works. But he did not sustain this excellence; many of his chapters missed the mark badly, and his exaggeration of American money-madness limited his over-all understanding of the nation.

———. *The American People: A Study in National Psychology.* 2 vols. Boston and New York: Houghton Mifflin Company, 1909 and 1911.

Low left the United States in 1900 after twenty years residence to begin work on this, his magnum opus. It took him eleven years to complete this study of "the origin, growth, and development of the American people and to trace the causes that have produced a new race." He disclaimed the title of historian, preferring "historical psychologist" instead, since national character and not narration interested him. His thousand-page effort to supplement or even supplant Bryce is heroic and of great significance, but never really rises to either great history or great psychology.

Lucas, Edward Verrall. *Roving East and Roving West.* New York: George H. Doran Company, 1921.

After sections on India and Japan, the distinguished essayist (1868–1938) and associate editor of *Punch* devoted the last half of the book to the United States, based upon a scant eight weeks in 1919. The prose naturally had great charm, but nothing very important was written.

Lucy, Sir Henry William. *East by West: A Journey in the Recess.* 2 vols. London, 1885.

The first half of the first volume dealt with the author's passage through America on his way to China, Japan, and India. Lucy (1845–1924) earned little money as a parliamentary reporter, well known as he was as "Toby, M.P.," and spent most of this section expressing his dismay at the high cost of living and traveling in the United States. Undoubtedly this increased his general petulance and made him especially irritable over poor road paving and over that great American deficiency—the scarcity of dogs in New York and Chicago. Lucy was knighted in 1909 during his long tenure (1881–1916) as the writer of the "Essence of Parliament" for *Punch*.

Lyell, Sir Charles. *A Second Visit to the United States of North America.* 2 vols. London, 1849.

The renowned geologist wrote less about his own field after this second trip (in 1845–46) than the first in 1841–42. His sociological comments were perspicacious, but undeveloped—especially those hypothesizing the origins for American religious and economic equality. He regarded the common school system as the United States' most valuable and exemplary institution. Lyell (1797–1875) also surveyed conditions in the South more expansively in this useful work than in the equally valuable *Travels in North America* (2 vols.; London, 1845).

MacDonell, A. G. *A Visit to America.* New York: Macmillan Company, 1935.

A cheerful anecdotal tale of a cross-country tour in 1934, in which the author (1895–1941), a journalist, dwelled excessively on the delights of San Francisco. His most serious criticism concerned America's lack of historic monuments.

Macgregor, John. *Our Brothers and Cousins: A Summer Tour in Canada and the States.* London, 1859.

An economist (1825–92) who feared democracy and Catholicism too nervously to report reliably.

Mackay, Alexander. *The Western World, or, Travels in the United States in 1846–47: Exhibiting Them in Their Latest Development, Social, Political and Industrial.* 3 vols. London, 1849. The Philadelphia, 1849, two-volume edition was used.

Although recognized by those who have read it as the finest antebellum British travel work on America, *The Western World* remains relatively unread. This is unfortunate since the analyses of this Scots newspaper correspondent, geographer, Free Church minister, educational writer, and barrister are comprehensive, insightful, and based upon long acquaintance with the United States. Mackay (1808–52) deftly alternated description and analysis, displaying special skill upon American political institutions. He hoped to convince his countrymen that the United States would have to be reckoned with in the future as a great power, and that she did many things that England would do well to emulate or at least appreciate. A thoroughly intelligent and good-natured study.

Mackay, Charles. *Life and Liberty in America: or, Sketches of a Tour in the United States and Canada in 1857–8.* 2 vols. London, 1859. The New York, 1859, edition was used.

It is hard not to be disconcerted by Mackay's constant assurances that the fuss over slavery was just a passing phase, even though the bulk of this prolific Scottish poet-composer-journalist's description of cities and politics in 1857–58 has much merit. Charles Mackay (1814–89) has been praised, however, more than he deserves, perhaps out of confusion with his unrelated namesake, Alexander, perhaps because of his connection with a well-known book on *The Mormons: or Latter-day Saints* (London, [1851]) with which he has mistakenly been identified as author. The real author (anonymous) was Henry Mayhew. Mackay edited the work. Mackay's later personal retrospects, *Forty Years' Recollections* (London, 1877) and *Through the Long Day* (London, 1887) touch upon his American experiences.

MacQuarrie, Hector. *Over Here: Impressions of America by a British Officer.* Philadelphia: J. B. Lippincott Company, 1918.

Lieutenant MacQuarrie of the Royal Field Artillery was injured during the First World War at Ypres. After convalescence he was ordered to the United States to inspect production of guns and carriages. He spent over a year, most of it in Bethlehem, Pennsylvania, from late 1916 to early 1918 making friends, writing, having a good time, and even doing his duties. His sunny book portrays only incidents, but has interest for its display of a special kind of Anglo-American affection growing out of the joint sacrifice. The author also anticipated the mood that would conquer America in the 1920's, for he thought, perhaps wishfully, that all people would soon want to gather rosebuds and relax.

Macrae, David. *The Americans at Home.* 2 vols. Edinburgh, 1870. The one-volume 1952 edition (Dutton, New York) was used.

The most important travel work composed after Alexander Mackay's and before the spate of first-rate books produced in the 1880's. Macrae (1837–1907), a Scottish minister-scholar, arrived in 1867–68 and wrote with intelligence, wit, and vigor. Best known for his sketch of the early Reconstruction South, the author managed to touch upon nearly every aspect of American life (including much trivia) with assurance and knowledge. His observations on American religion deserve special notice. Revised editions of this book came out in 1874, 1908, and 1952; in 1871 it had appeared under the title *Home and Abroad, Sketchings and Gleanings* (Glasgow, 1871).

———. *America Revisited and Men I Have Met.* Glasgow: J. Smith and Son, 1908.

Macrae paid another visit just over thirty years later and with bewilderment and nostalgia compared the new surface of things with the old. Again he spent much time in the South, but his reminiscences lacked the precision and force that characterized *The Americans at Home.* "America Revisited" occupied only the first third of this posthumously published volume, the rest telling of "Men I Have Met," from Charles Dickens to George Gilfallan.

Mais, S. P. B. *A Modern Columbus*. Philadelphia: J. B. Lippincott Company, 1934.

A written version of a series of radio addresses given en route through the United States by a prolific author and popular announcer for the B.B.C. Mais (b. 1885) flattered each city from which he spoke to his American and English audiences and admitted to no higher purpose than "to make you want to visit the places I visited."

Marshall, Walter Gore. *Through America; or, Nine Months in the United States*. London, 1881. The London, 1882, edition was used.

An unimportant book based upon trips in 1878 and 1879. The author spent most of his time with the Mormons and in California, extolling the scenery of the latter and condemning the "monstrous social scandal" of the former. *Through America* is graced by more than seventy-five engravings, including some good glimpses of New York and San Francisco.

Massie, James William. *America: The Origin of the Present Conflict; Her Prospect for the Slave, and Her Claim for Anti-Slavery Sympathy; Illustrated by Incidents of Travel During a Tour in the Summer of 1863 Throughout the United States, from . . . Maine to the Mississippi*. London, 1864.

As a result of the Ministerial Anti-Slavery Conference held in June, 1863, Massie (1799–1869) headed a delegation to the United States in that summer. Its purpose was to demonstrate to American antislavery leaders that they could expect at least some moral support from sympathizers in England. Massie offered insight into a passionate English position occasionally overlooked by scholars. This longstanding foe of slavery in America wrote several antislavery books before this account, most famous of which was *Slavery the Crime and Curse of America: An Expostulation with the Christians of that Land* (London, 1852).

Maycock, Sir Willoughby [Robert Dottin]. *With Mr. Chamberlain in the United States and Canada, 1887–88*. London: Chatto and Windus, 1914.

Maycock (1849–1922) accompanied the impressive Liberal statesman, Joseph Chamberlain, as Assistant Secretary on a mission to settle the Canadian Fishery question. The negotiations culminated in the Chamberlain-Bayard Treaty, which the U.S. Senate failed to ratify. The book, though about Chamberlain's activities and not about America, and though filled with reprints of newspaper articles about Chamberlain, provides an unusual perspective into the diplomacy of the time, into American journalistic practices, and into Chamberlain's personality.

Meakin, Annette M. B. *What America Is Doing: Letters from the New World*. Edinburgh: W. Blackwood and Sons, 1911.

From May to November, 1910, Miss Meakin (?–1959) sent thirty-five letters back to London, which a year later turned into this book. Although a professional travel writer who had travelogues of Russia and Spain to her credit, she here showed a curious weakness of observation. Her letters climbed the heights of trivia and when ideas intruded, they were invariably in the form of extended quotation from other authors. She could have written this book without ever leaving her study in London.

Merewether, Henry Alworth. *By Sea and Land; Being a Trip through Egypt, India, Ceylon, Australia, New Zealand, and America, All Round the World*. London, 1874.

Merewether was for thirty years a clerk at the Parliamentary Bar. In 1871 he retired and in 1872 set out on a trip around the world. His American descriptions are short (five chapters) and minor, but warm. He claimed that he came to America "a British Tory" and left declaring: "Of all the places in the world where a man may be most comfortable, most independent, and may do best, America is the place for me."

Money, Edward. *The Truth about America*. London, 1886.

The exposé implied by the aggressive title would have been justified by the remarkably temperate author. Money purchased 160 acres in the Antelope Valley of California from an American agent in London. Instead of Eden he found a desert. After this appalling discovery, and coming up with no other possibilities in California, he bought a ranch near Colorado Springs. This too did not work out and so after five months in 1885, Money had had enough and sailed for home prepared "to put a certain class of emigrants on their guard against the machinations of a few agents in London, who victimize them not a little." He had a right to complain more than he did.

Muir, Ramsay. *America the Golden*. London: Williams and Norgate, 1927.

Muir (1872–1941) lectured in the United States in 1926 "as a member of the committee which is carrying out the Liberal Industrial Enquiry." A Liberal M.P. in 1923–24, professor of history at Manchester, and editor of a liberal magazine, Muir examined industrial conditions in the United States to ascertain what innovations might properly be applied to British industrial policy. The wide distribution of ownership struck him most forcibly, and he devoted much of this specialized but sensible little book in urging this course upon Great Britain.

Muirhead, James Fullarton. *The Land of Contrasts: A Briton's View of His American Kin*. Boston, 1898. The third edition (London: J. Lane, 1902), entitled *America, the Land of Contrasts . . .* , was used.

This is the best single-volume travel study of the United States. Muirhead (1853–1934) edited the Baedeker handbook to the United States, *The United States, with an Exursion Into Mexico* (Leipzig, 1893), and in preparation for *Land of Contrasts* and the handbook he traveled everywhere in the land in 1888, 1890–93, and 1898. Few knew the country more thoroughly than he. His working model emphasized the polarities that mark American life, transcended only by the unifying force of the egalitarian principle. Although one could not always be sure where Muirhead spoke for himself and where he paraphrased others, his chapters on American women, children, sports, humor, newspapers, literature, and practical travel conditions (he called this "Baedekeriana") rank very high for shrewdness and reliability.

Murphy, John Mortimer. *Rambles in North-Western America from the Pacific Ocean to the Rocky Mountains*. London, 1879.

As indicated in an incredible subtitle, this is a rather detailed survey "of the physical geography, climate, soil production, industrial and commercial resources, scenery, population, educational institutions, arboreal botany, and game animals" of the Far West. Perhaps it may be of interest to naturalists, as the author knew the land well from many years' experience. He was an amateur botanist, paleontologist, and geologist and is said to have mastered nineteen Indian languages. Murphy may have spent more time in America than in England.

Murray, Amelia M. *Letters from the United States, Cuba, and Canada.* 2 vols. London, 1856. The one-volume New York, 1856, edition was used.

Miss Murray (1795–1884) is best known for her ardent antislavery position which, when published, forced her resignation as a maid of honor to Queen Victoria (since court officials were not permitted to publish anything with political implications). These thirty letters tell mostly of her abolitionism and of certain botanical interests. She visited, largely in the South, in 1854–55.

Murray, Henry A. *Lands of the Slave and the Free, or, Cuba, the United States and Canada.* 2 vols. London, 1855. The one-volume second edition (London, 1857) was used.

The author (1810–65), a captain in the Royal Navy, insisted that his observations were "free from political bias." He protested too much, for his views, formulated in 1855, were very Tory. He reserved his sharpest barbs, often rather intelligently, for the center of his target: the idea of equality.

Naylor, Robert Anderton. *Across the Atlantic.* Westminster, 1893.

"The Society of Arts of Great Britain" made one of those group pilgrimages in 1893—this to the Chicago World's Fair. Naylor, one of the members on the group plan, and a writer of picturesque tales, somehow composed over three hundred pages based upon a two-week sojourn. He filled much of the space with his own verse, which must rank among the worst ever published.

Nevinson, Henry W. *Farewell to America.* New York: B. W. Huebsch, 1926.

This much anthologized thirteen-page essay by the noted journalist, writer, and Labor Party member first appeared in *The Nation and the Athenaeum* of London. Nevinson (1856–1941) delightfully extracted, one by one, all those oddly and brightly colored little stones that make up the American mosaic as he waved to each one in turn, "Good-bye, America. I am going home."

Newman, Francis William. *Character of the Southern States of America.* Manchester, 1864.

By a Latin professor at University College in London, prolific writer, and leading scholar on religious and political matters (1805–97), supporter of Mazzini, Kossuth, and women's suffrage, and Protestant brother of John Henry Newman. This brief eighteen-page "letter to a friend who had joined the Southern Independence Association" presents a strong denunciation of the Confederacy and of England's foreign policy during the Civil War. It is not based upon a visit to this country, but it is nonetheless of interest.

Nichols, Beverley. *The Star-Spangled Manner.* New York: Doubleday, Doran and Company, 1928.

Proclaiming himself Britain's answer to Richard Halliburton, young Nichols (b. 1899) dashed to the United States eager to establish his glamor. In no time at all he had interviewed and portrayed Calvin Coolidge, Big Bill Thompson, Gloria Swanson, Charles Lindbergh, Andrew Mellon, Anita Loos, and Henry Ford. He captured the glitter of the stars, but had no ideas of his own to speak of. The highlight of the book is Nichols' funny account of American funerals and cemeteries, anticipating Evelyn Waugh and Jessica Mitford.

Nichols, Thomas Low. *Forty Years of American Life, 1821–1861.* 2 vols. London, 1864. The one-volume 1937 edition (Stackpole Sons, New York) was used.

Neither a book of travel nor by an Englishman, this book still commands attention because of its point of view. Nichols (1815–1901), an American reformer and M.D., emigrated to England in 1861 in protest against the Civil War. His memories of four decades of his youth fill in complexities that the ordinary visitor could not hope to take in.

Ollivant, Joseph Earle. *A Breeze from the Great Salt Lake.* London, 1871.

In the first thirty pages, this English educator outlined his trip along the new mail route from New Zealand to New York via Honolulu and San Francisco. He slowed down enough to view the Mormons (fairly dispassionately), and he reproduced in its entirety a sermon by Brigham Young.

Orpen, Mrs. Adela. *Memories of the Old Emigrant Days in Kansas, 1862–1865.* London: W. Blackwood and Sons, 1926.

A charming recollection of Mrs. Orpen's life on the prairie sixty years before when she was a little girl between seven and nine years of age.

Owen, Collinson. *The American Illusion.* London: E. Benn, 1929.

Owen (1882–1956) loved to write; he turned out novels, travel books, and countless newspaper and magazine articles. In *The American Illusion,* his facility with words, his verbal portraits, and his prose rhythms leave the strongest impression. Basically anecdotal in organization, Owen still criticized plentifully; yet all his criticisms, such as those which unfavorably contrasted America's "spiritual interests" with Europe's—criticisms which he seemed to feel originated with him—were old hat as far as the Americans were concerned.

Ozanne, T. D. *The South As It Is, or, Twenty-One Years' Experience in the Southern States of America.* London, 1863.

Not strictly a traveler, this English clergyman lived in the South from 1841 to 1862, and in Philadelphia five years before that. The burden of this somewhat sanguine effort was to justify the Southern way of life and point out the dangers of hasty emancipation.

P., J. *A Chat about America: October and November, 1884.* Manchester, 1885.

A privately printed book of letters comparing the United States in 1884 with conditions seen on a trip thirteen years before, all on a rather superficial level.

Pairpont, Alfred J. *Uncle Sam and His Country; or, Sketches of America in 1854–55–56.* London, 1857.

Humble, genial, superficial, and miscellaneous sketches by one who came to Boston for employment in a business firm. He actually spent most of his time from 1854–56 in Dorchester, Massachusetts; this allowed for some intimate glimpses into small-town American life.

————. *Rambles in America, Past and Present*. Boston, 1891.

Pairpont returned to his New England haunts for nine years beginning in 1882, adding many new items to his curiosity shop of American customs. He recalled very warmly his earlier days in Dorchester as one returning home after a long absence.

Peel, Arthur George. *The Economic Impact of America*. London: Macmillan and Company, 1928.

Peel was one of the leading English businessmen among many who came to the United States in the 1920's to seek the secret of success. Unlike others, Peel (1868–1956) did not conclude dismally that England's commercial pre-eminence had been forever usurped, but in an informed pep talk begged his countrymen to realize that "the place of Great Britain in world economics is not less, but more important, than formerly, and that her future will be even greater than her past."

Percy, Lord Eustace. "State and Municipal Government." Pp. 31–58 in Gaillard Lapsley, ed., *The America of Today*. Cambridge: Cambridge University Press, 1919.

Lord Percy (1887–1958), a former Secretary at the British Embassy in Washington, delivered one of eleven lectures given, mostly by Americans—including George Santayana and Henry Seidel Canby—during the summer of 1918 at Cambridge University dealing with American subjects. His talk constitutes one of the few British discussions of this topic and is informative. He also lectured on "Social Legislation and Administration" (pp. 59–88).

Peto, Sir S. Morton. *The Resources and Prospects of America*. London, 1866.

A leading Liberal M.P. from Norwich (1847–54), Finsburg (1859–65), and Bristol (1865–68) and an outstanding railroad builder, Peto (1809–89) landed in 1865 with one question on his mind: would the United States be solvent in the future? He compiled figures and tables on agriculture, manufacture, commerce, railways, etc., and concluded unequivocally that the American future (the South included) was a bright one indeed. He saw clear economic gains rising from the ashes of the Civil War, and advised England to befriend the United States. His good advice resulted from sound scholarship and vast experience.

Phillippo, James M. *The United States and Cuba*. London, 1857.

Perhaps the finest emigrant guide of the period. The author (1798–1879), a missionary to Jamaica, compiled this handbook more from secondary than first-hand sources. Yet it is accurate, complete, and interesting. Of greater interest than its accuracy, however, was Phillippo's enthusiasm and his utter lack of hesitation in advising Europeans to pull up their roots and try the soil of the New World.

Pidgeon, Daniel. *Old-World Questions and New-World Answers*. London, 1884.

Instead of a scenic adventure across the forests and canyons of a continent, this civil engineer invited his readers to accompany him "on a short flight through the roaring valleys of Massachusetts and Connecticut." Pidgeon wanted to investigate industry, technology, and economic conditions, and for this Lowell, Lawrence, and Holyoke provided his havens. Many fresh observations within what was, for the Briton, an uncommon range of experience.

Player-Frowd, J. G. *Six Months in California*. London, 1872.

A study of California with the emphasis on natural resources: flora, agriculture, zoology, wine, geology, and four chapters on minerals. Not much about people.

Pocock, Roger. *Rottenness: A Study of America and England*. London, 1896.

This writer of tepid stories raised himself high to deliver a furious jeremiad against the sickness of Anglo-American life and institutions. Calling for a return to Christ, Pocock (1865–1941) directed his wrath into three channels: political, social, and economic corruption. Nothing in contemporary life pleased him.

Pollard, A. F. *Factors in American History*. New York: Macmillan Company, 1925.

In 1924, this worthy historian of Tudor England and professor of constitutional history at University College, London, delivered the Sir George Watson Lectures in American history—lectures which formed the heart of this volume. Writing more a book of history than travel, stressing the common foundations in the British Middle Ages for both modern America and England, Pollard (1869–1948) nonetheless knew the United States from more than the documents. He had held, for example, several previous American lectureships, including one at Cornell in 1913.

Porteous, Archibald. *A Scamper through Some Cities of America: Being a Record of a Three Month's Tour in the United States and Canada*. Glasgow, 1890.

Perfectly typical.

Porter, Thomas Cunningham. *Impressions of America*. London, 1899.

A member of the Chemical Society, Physical Society, and Astronomical Society of London, Porter (1860–1933) rushed to the Far West to take stereoscopic photographs of the scenery. As the author candidly admitted, the more than fifty photographs published were worth far more than the prose.

Price, Morgan Philips. *America After Sixty Years: The Travel Diaries of Two Generations of Englishmen*. London: G. Allen and Unwin, 1936.

In the third section of this book, the author (b. 1885), a Labor M.P., detailed his impressions of the United States in 1934–35 and the attempts of the nation to evolve a new economic approach to the Depression. Price sympathized with Franklin Roosevelt. As an agriculturist, the author spent most of his time not in the well-traveled East, but in the farming country of the Midwest, the South, and California studying these difficult economic problems and offering humane and sympathetic comments. But the book has two other portions, and they furnish a stimulating contrast: first, the diary of his father Capt. (later Major) William Edwin Price (he too was a member of Parliament) of an 1869 visit immediately after the completion of the Union Pacific; and second, his parents' description of their honeymoon in 1878 in the West and South of the United States. These earlier diaries are fairly commonplace; the value lies in their juxtaposition to the son's account, bringing home dramatically in one work the extraordinary metamorphosis undergone by the United States in just sixty years.

Price, Sir Rose Lambart. *The Two Americas: An Account of Sport and Travel with Notes on Men and Manners in North and South America.* London, 1877. The Philadelphia, 1877, edition was used.

Slightly more than the first half of the book centers in the second America: South America. Still, this spare-time soldier traveled widely for a year (1875–76) in the United States, preferring to write of his hunting experiences in the West (which he loved) rather than of his sociological eastern experiences. Sir Rose (1837–99) distrusted republican institutions, but he enjoyed hunting enough to be fond, as a whole, of the United States.

———. *A Summer in the Rockies.* London, 1898.

More hunting and sightseeing twenty years later, in 1897.

Priestley, John Boynton. *Midnight on the Desert: Being an Excursion into Autobiography during a Winter in America, 1935–36.* New York and London: Harper and Brothers, 1937.

From a little hut in Arizona, erected in a couple of days by ranchhands upon the casual request of the author, the noted novelist and critic (a frequent visitor to American shores) assembled this fascinating, rambling potpourri. Writing part autobiography, part reflections on man, part analysis of the United States, Priestley (b. 1894) brought to bear his peculiar brand of unorthodox perceptions on all three levels. Among his observations concerning the United States: (1) psychologically, Americans were more naturally collectivist than individualist; (2) outdoor Americans were a better breed than the indoor variety (he loved the Southwest, despised Hollywood and New York); (3) American life had dreamlike, ghostlike, unreal qualities; (4) the world would soon be a replica of the United States. An arresting book.

Rae, William Fraser. *Westward by Rail: The New Route to the East.* London, 1870. The London, 1871, edition was used.

Rae (1835–1905) railroaded from New York to San Francisco in 1869—another early bird on the Union Pacific. A light, commonplace work with the only critical comments reserved for the poor Mormons. Rae was correspondent for the London *Daily News* and translated Hippolyte Taine's *Notes Sur L'Angleterre, 1860–1870* into English in 1873.

———. *Columbia and Canada: Notes on the Great Republic and the New Dominion.* London, 1877.

Rae used his second venture to the United States during the Centennial year to compose a pseudohistory or retrospect of the nation and the eastern cities instead of another travel book. Though not gifted with an original mind, he had a genial disposition and a deep desire for Anglo-American accord. Rae also wrote a novel about a tour through America, *An American Duchess* (London, 1890–91).

Reed, Edward Bliss, ed. *The Commonwealth Fund Fellows and Their Impressions of America.* New York: The Commonwealth Fund, 1932.

The Commonwealth Fund Fellows are England's equivalent of the Rhodes Scholars. Reed herein assembled a potpourri of impressions from some of the Fellows' reports for 1925–1931 (the first years of the program) which they all had to compose. All studied for a minimum of two years at American graduate schools. No coherent point of view can be extracted from this miscellany, but the scattered comments show perception far beyond that of the ordinary traveler. The editor divided the anthology into three portions, dealing respectively with the physical features of the land, "The American People," and the universities. A reservoir of valuable unpublished observation must be resting quietly in the Fund's London files.

Rivington, Alexander. See [Harris and Rivington].

Robertson, William, and W. F. Robertson. *Our American Tour: Being a Run of Ten Thousand Miles from the Atlantic to the Golden Gate, in the Autumn of 1869*. Edinburgh, 1871.

Yet another Union Pacific ride and another typical version of "Through the Window-Pane." The authors had a kind of Manichaean view of the United States: total wickedness in ceaseless struggle with Christianity. They tremulously hoped and believed the latter would prevail.

Robinson, Philip Stewart. *Sinners and Saints: A Tour across the States, and Round Them; with Three Months among the Mormons*. London, 1883. The Boston, 1883, edition was used.

Tabbed by his publishers as "the new English humorist," "Phil" Robinson (1847–1902), part-time poet, naturalist, traveler, and expert on India, did write with considerable, if self-conscious charm. More than half of this tale of an 1883 trip is, however, not at all funny: it is one of the fairest, most sympathetic and knowledgeable outlines of Mormon culture produced by a Briton, and it valuably answers much of the vilification which his colleagues turned out. The remainder of the book tends to be overly precious.

Russell, Charles Russell, Baron. *Diary of a Visit to the United States of America in the Year 1883*. New York: United States Catholic Historical Society, 1910.

This is a day-by-day log by one who in 1894 became Lord Chief Justice of England. Russell (1832–1900), a Liberal M.P. at the time of this trip, accompanied his predecessor Lord Coleridge and "the great orator of the day, W. M. Evarts, Barrister." Russell went from coast-to-coast (Coleridge only reached Chicago), observed accurately, and recorded a refined and discerning, if not original, commentary. He returned again in 1896 as Lord Chief Justice to lecture to American lawyers on the subject of arbitration, but kept no diary the second time.

Russell, Sir William Howard. *My Diary North and South*. 2 vols. London, 1863.

Over 850 pages of extracts from the notebooks and diaries of this most powerful correspondent of the London *Times* in 1861–62. Convinced that the Union could never be restored (even though he was not unsympathetic to the North), his "truthfulness" in reporting impelled Stanton to deny "Bull Run." Russell (1820–1907) passes to visit battle areas, thus ending his journalistic usefulness in 1862. A third volume, dealing chiefly with Canada, but including three chapters on the United States appeared in 1865. Indispensable reading, of course, for anyone interested in the Civil War. Fletcher Pratt's edition of *My Diary North and South* (New York: Harper, [1954]) is handy.

———. *Hesperothen: Notes from the West: A Record of a Ramble in the United States and Canada in the Spring and Summer of 1881*. 2 vols. London, 1882.

Russell returned to America in 1881 with the Duke of Sutherland's party. He hardly ventured below the Mason-Dixon line, spending most of his time in the Far West. Though perhaps valuable because of the author's eminence, I found that Russell's observations lacked the keenness they once had, that his comparisons between 1861 and 1881 were of the most banal sort, and that he had grown testy with time. His working generalization concerned the immorality, corruption, violence, and crime that typified American life—proofs all of the failure of free education. He concluded with an interesting chapter on the American Indian.

————. *Letters of William Howard Russell to the London 'Times' on the Civil War in America*. Washington, D.C., 1914.

A paste-up reproduction, done by the Library of Congress, of actual clippings of Russell's letters to the *Times* from March 29, 1861, to April 5, 1862. An invaluable, but hard to read historical document. For all of Russell's work, the best biography is John Black Atkins, *The Life of Sir William Howard Russell, C.V.D., LL.D.* (2 vols.; London: J. Murray, 1911).

Sala, George Augustus. *My Diary in America in the Midst of War*. 2 vols. London, 1865.

Sala (1828–95) was the war correspondent for the *Daily Telegraph* in 1863–64, and like most of his colleagues was pro-South. Young, headstrong, and no Russell, short on wisdom and understanding, he still wrote vigorously and enthusiastically and can be read with profit.

———— *America Revisited: From the Bay of New York to the Gulf of Mexico, and from Lake Michigan to the Pacific*. 2 vols. New York, 1880. The two-volume enlarged second edition (London, 1882) was used.

When Russell returned to America twenty years after the Civil War, he had grown more petulant and opinionated than he ever had been. When Day returned, he refused to admit that he had even been indiscreet, and he remained unchanged. Sala had matured and confessed that he had been "very prejudiced, very conceited" in 1863–64. He traversed twenty thousand miles, predominantly in the South and Far West. His comments were genial, sparkling, chatty, and superficial. (One reviewer characterized it as "bubbly champagne turning flat with the years.") They were first published as letters to the London *Daily Telegraph*. Of more than passing interest are the four hundred illustrations which very nicely accomplish their purpose. For a more intimate insight into the feelings of this major Victorian, see *The Life and Adventures of George Augustus Sala. Written By Himself* (2 vols.; New York, 1895).

Saunders, William. *Through the Light Continent, or, the United States in 1877–8*. London, 1879.

A disjointed but stimulating and critical topical analysis by a journalist who later became a Liberal peer. He was one of England's earliest champions of the land policies of Henry George. He eventually became a socialist. The title seems to be a spoof of Stanley's *Through the Dark Continent*, published in 1878. Actually, the United States emerged as rather dark in this book: its optimism was vanishing because of increasing economic difficulties, the ugly rise of class conflict, and growing political corruption. Saunders (1823–95) especially concerned himself with agricultural and financial developments and their impact upon potential emigration. Weak on religious and social aspects of American life, the author never resorted to innuendo and wrote a thoughtful and sober work of some significance.

Shaw, George Bernard. *The Applecart: A Political Extravaganza.* London: Constable and Company, 1930.

In all his writings, Shaw (1856–1950) rarely spared the United States and its vulgarity, plutocracy, and insufferable cockiness. The Fabian in him prophesied that America would erode, through the power of capital, that which was best in Western civilization. All of these themes cropped up in *The Applecart* when the English King wisely, in order to preserve English independence and superiority (especially over the Irish), refused America's Machiavellian offer to cancel the Declaration of Independence and thus rejoin (and therefore take over) the Empire. No travel book, this play has been included as a symbol of Shaw's trumpeted protest against democracies everywhere which have failed to live up to their ideals.

Shelley, Henry Charles. *America of the Americans.* New York: C. Scribner's Sons, 1915.

One of the Scribner series outlining some factual tidbits about various nations from Japan to Turkey to Holland. Only the most obvious data about American government, education, literature, inventions, etc., penetrated into this volume. It resembles another work of Shelley's: namely, *Inns and Taverns of Old London.*

Sheridan, Clare. *My American Diary.* New York: Boni and Liveright, 1922.

Mrs. Sheridan (b. 1885) was the daughter of another traveler, Moreton Frewen. In the year preceding her 1921 American visit, she had been in Russia just after the turbulence of Revolution, doing busts of leading Soviets, Lenin and Trotzky included. When she came to the United States to complete her not unsympathetic story of the Bolsheviks, *Mayfair to Moscow,* to lecture on the subject, and to exhibit her sculpture, she commanded quite an audience. Her diary tells little of the United States itself except for some of the get-togethers with many American personalities and artists which she chattily chronicled. Yet it has use as an unusual source for revealing early American reaction to the Russian Revolution.

Shipley, Arthur Everett. *The Voyage of a Vice-Chancellor: With a Chapter on University Education in the United States.* Cambridge: Cambridge University Press, 1919.

The eminent biologist (1861–1927) and vice-chancellor of Cambridge University breezed through many American universities for two months at the end of 1918. The book, a day-by-day record of his doings, is pleasantly uninformative.

Smart, George Thomas. *The Temper of the American People.* Boston: Pilgrim Press, 1912.

An unread, unknown, and unusually perceptive study by an English citizen who took up residence in the United States and was eventually naturalized. Commencing with a chapter entitled "Fact, Idea, and Freedom in America," and following with imaginative chapters on the American "sense of history," "metropolitan and suburban emotions," "industrial attitudes," etc., Smart attempted to illuminate various aspects of the American's consciousness of himself. Much of this work was boring and pompous, but not enough so to negate the thoughtfulness, literacy, and originality everywhere evident in this obscure little book.

Smith, Annie S. [Annie Burnett-Smith]. *As Others See Her: An Englishwoman's Impressions of the American Woman in War Time*. Boston: Houghton Mifflin Company, 1919.

A homey volume of human interest in praise of the war effort made by American women. Miss Burnett-Smith (1859–1943), a Scottish novelist, worked for seven months in 1918 on food conservation and war relief under Hoover and talked to lots of American women, many of whose conversations she simply transcribed. Provides some insight into American marriages and family life.

Smith, Frederick Edwin, the first Earl of Birkenhead. *My American Visit*. London: Hutchinson and Company, 1918.

A bore of a book. The Attorney-General of England visited from Christmas, 1917, to January 30, 1918, because "it was thought desirable that some British Minister should at the moment visit the United States and Canada." Birkenhead (1872–1930) put down everything that leaped into his mind and never bothered to sort things out. He was a Conservative M.P. from 1906 to 1918, and later served as Lord-Chancellor (1919–22) and Secretary of State for India (1924–28).

———. *America Revisited*. London, 1924.

The earl returned in 1923 for more of the same, this time including the South and the West in his itinerary. Most of this volume is composed of lectures he delivered in the United States and Canada. Their tone may be realized by noting how often Birkenhead called for a restoration of "realistic idealism" in foreign policy, along with other such juicy items.

Smith, Samuel. *America Revisited*. Liverpool, 1896.

A little pamphlet packed with generalization. Smith (1836–1906), a Liberal peer (1882–85 for Liverpool and 1886–1905 for Flintshire), came just two months after the 1896 presidential election, and of course commented upon it and upon the dangers posed by "the foreign element" and by Trusts. But his real achievement lay in his intelligent remarks about American education, women, natural beauties, the sections, race relations, and the future of the nation—all in twenty-three pages! This was the third of his four American visits, all of which are chronicled in *My Life-Work* (London: Hodder and Stoughton, 1902).

Somers, Robert. *The Southern States Since the War, 1870–71*. London, 1871.

A thorough, careful, insightful study of the South during Reconstruction by a successful Scottish newspaper editor (1822–91). Carrying with him an equability and an awareness of complexity which only exhaustive knowledge can provide, Somers' analysis, which focused on economic and agricultural factors, is easily the most useful single work written by a Briton on the postwar South.

Somerville, Edith Anna Œneone. *The States Through Irish Eyes*. Boston: Houghton Mifflin Company, 1931.

An anecdotal and quite inconsequential recreation of a 1929 excursion to various odd spots up and down the eastern seaboard by a friendly, gossipy Irish lady (1858–1949). She drew eight sketches for the book. She wrote thirteen other books and was an active feminist.

Soulsby, Lucy Helen Muriel. *The America I Saw in 1916–1918*. London: Longmans, Green, and Company, 1920.

An amiable book by a former headmistress of a prominent boarding school in England, the Manor House School. Miss Soulsby stretched an intended two-month visit to two years for one reason: to travel around the country and into the schools making friends in the interest of Anglo-American wartime solidarity. She was a one-woman ambassadress, trying to assure Americans that they may believe the English "like us." She visited homes, discussed education, and decided that the one word which best described America was "lovable." The historian can benefit from her comments about American families.

Spencer, Herbert. *Essays: Scientific, Political, and Speculative*. 3 vols. New York, 1892.

The philosopher (1820–1903) did not write a book describing his visit in 1882. He arrived at the apex of his popularity and the nadir of his frail health; he thus attempted to avoid the limelight and traveled around under an assumed name. His views on the country were made known in two ways: (1) a contrived interview conducted by his host, Professor Edward Livingstone Youmans; (2) a speech he delivered at a banquet in his honor just preceding his departure. The interview and speech can be found in the last essay of these three volumes or in Youmans' full account of *Herbert Spencer on the Americans and the Americans on Herbert Spencer* (New York, 1883). Spencer's own comments on the trip, including some from his diary, can be found in Herbert Spencer, *An Autobiography* (2 vols.; New York: D. Appleton and Company, 1904), II, 457–81.

Spender, Harold. *A Briton in America*. London: W. Heinemann, 1921.

Spender (1864–1926) lectured in 1920 as a delegate to the Mayflower Council. He reworked some letters he wrote en route into a moderate, fair-minded evaluation of the "conservative" America emerging from the Great War. The author included an interesting appendix called "Dickens and America" in which he argued authoritatively that Dickens' view of the United States after his 1868 visit had become far more positive than after the famous 1842 journey. Moreover, he said that the same improvements noted by Dickens had continued apace from 1868 to 1920.

Spender, John Alfred. *The America of Today*. London: E. Benn, 1928. Published in New York (Frederick A. Stokes Company, 1928), under the title *Through English Eyes*.

One of the soundest and most comprehensive, if overly flattering, analyses of American society in this century. Spender (1862–1942), who turned out many books of history and the contemporary scene, participated in government, and served as a Liberal editorialist, came to the United States in 1921 and returned in 1927–28 as the first Senior Walter Hines Page Fellow. He handled separate subjects more effectively than the unifying threads of equality and "collective vitality" which he tried to weave through the whole pattern, although he never insisted on these larger generalities. His best chapters deal with the racial problem, commerce, American journalism, and foreign policy.

Stanley, Sir Henry M. *My Early Travels and Adventures in America and Asia Minor*. 2 vols. London, 1895. The New York, two-volume, 1895 edition was used.

Four years before he found Livingstone, the twenty-five-year-old Stanley (1841–1904) sent off a series of letters to the *Missouri Democrat* of St. Louis concerning his experiences on General Hancock's Indian campaigns. These became the basis for the first volume of the above title after its author had become quite famous. He did not particularly like Indians. Stanley became a Unionist M.P. (1895–1900). Another account of his American experiences will be found in his *Autobiography*, ed. Dorothy Stanley (Boston: Houghton Mifflin, 1909), and an account of his lectures in 1886–1899 is in James B. Pond, *Eccentricities of Genius* (London: Chatto and Windus, 1901).

Stead, William Thomas. *The Americanization of the World, or The Trend of the Twentieth Century*. New York: H. Markley, 1902.

Reflective of the Anglo-American *rapprochement* at the turn of the century, Stead's book, the work of a great crusading journalist, not only expressed no dismay at the world-wide spread of American ways of doing things, but celebrated it with full gusto. He found Americanization proceeding not only in economic areas, but in diplomacy, education, literature, politics, science, art, language, religion, and the place of women: that is, in all the concerns of life. Stead (1849–1912) asked Englishmen to embrace this process thankfully and constructively and to forge powerful British-American ties. Stead's enthusiasm may have been unwarranted, but his portrayal of the spreading world-wide influence of the United States in all phases of life has not been belied by time. He was editor of the *Pall Mall Gazette* (1883–90) and started the *Review of Reviews* in 1890. Stead wrote more critical American studies in 1894 and 1897 dealing with Chicago and with New York.

Steevens, George Warrington. *The Land of the Dollar*. Edinburgh and London, 1897.

The London *Daily Mail* assigned Steevens (1869–1900) to cover the Bryan-McKinley election of 1896. His chronological narrative remains one of the liveliest records of that colorful and significant campaign. But the liberal Steevens took in more than the campaign in this book. The title refers not only to the silver debates, but to the general materialism and "demonstrative character" of the Americans (only beginning with money matters and election bouts), understanding of which he called a "master-key which would unlock most of the puzzles in the American." In all respects, an interesting book. Steevens also wrote *With Kitchener to Khartoum* and *The Tragedy of Dreyfus*.

Stevenson, Robert Louis. *Across the Plains, With Other Memories and Essays*. London, 1892. The New York, 1897, edition was used.

Stevenson married a Californian, Mrs. Osbourne, who literally nursed him back to life. The first of twelve essays in this collection (the title essay) tells of that 1879–80 journey by emigrant train to California, at which destination the betrothal would take place. The depressing transit, necessitated by poor finances, was a miserable one for the young author as well as for his fellow-passengers. The other American essay recreates the unspoiled beauties of the Monterey Bay area. These essays, reprinted in several later editions, have value for their little peek into the world of the young Stevenson (1850–94). All of Stevenson's various books on the U.S. have recently been gathered together in James D. Hart, *From Scotland to Silverado: Comprising the Amateur Emigrant: "From the Clyde to Sandy Hook," and "Across the*

Plains" The Silverado Squatters & Four Essays on California (Cambridge, Mass.: Harvard University Press, 1966).

Stirling, James. *Letters from the Slave States*. London, 1857.

Still a widely read version of life in the antebellum South by a Scot jurist (1805–83) who traveled through all the East (except New England) in 1856–57. He did not like Dixie or slavery, but he did not think the world, let alone the United States, was nearly ready for full equality. In fact, he attributed American economic and political success not only to industriousness, but to racial characteristics as well. An interesting work.

Strachey, John St. Loe. *American Soundings: Being Castings of the Lead in the Shore-Waters of America Social, Literary and Philosophical*. London: Hodder and Stoughton, 1926.

A generally uncritical panegyric of the United States and her heroes, by the editor of *The Spectator,* composed just before his death. Strachey (1860–1927) tended to wax poetic about all he encountered, but a man of his wisdom could not help but make some shrewd observations. He devoted a number of chapters to the celebration of a number of "representative" Americans (he borrowed the word from Emerson): Jefferson, Lincoln, Emerson, Whitman, and lesser contemporary figures.

Stuart-Wortley, Lady Emmeline Charlotte Elizabeth (Manners). *Travels in the United States*. 3 vols. London, 1851. The one-volume Paris, 1851, edition was used.

Lady Emmeline (1806–55) had a kindly maternal disposition toward the wild American child-nation. This straightforward gossipy tale of a tour in 1849–50 is thin in insight but rich in feminine observation. Perhaps of greatest interest are this prolific poetess-novelist's reported meetings with such men as Daniel Webster, Abbot Lawrence, Louis Agassiz, Benjamin Silliman, W. H. Prescott, and President Zachary Taylor. Only a bit more than one third of the book does, in fact, concern the United States: Mexico and Panama fill out the volume. Lady Emmeline's daughter Victoria accompanied her on this trip and composed *A Young Traveller's Journal of a Tour in North and South America during the Year 1850* (London, 1852). See the account of both in Mrs. Henry Cust, *Wanderers: Episodes from the Travels of Lady Emmeline Stuart-Wortley and Her Daughter Victoria, 1849–1855* (London: J. Cape, 1928).

Sullivan, Sir Edward R. *Rambles and Scrambles in North and South America*. London, 1852.

One of the more popular denunciations of the United States by one who was obviously awed and cowed by the mighty strides being taken by the young giant. Sullivan (1826–99), son of a Tory yachtsman, spent most of his time in 1850 getting into trouble on the American prairie. He substituted epigrams for analysis, but many of them were good ones.

Swansea, Henry Hussey Vivian, 1st Baron. *Notes of a Tour in America: From August 7th to November 17th 1877*. London, 1878. The London, 1879 edition was used.

This industrialist and Liberal Welsh peer wrote accurately as long as he stuck to what he knew: business. But things went a bit awry, as even

Matthew Arnold made clear, when Swansea (1821–94) switched to politics and advised Americans to make their Congress hereditary, and to elect a King! This was surprising in light of his experience of over four decades in the House of Commons and of his steady support of Gladstone.

Tallack, William. *Friendly Sketches in America*. London, 1861.

This is a prison-reforming Quaker's report of feuds within Quaker groups in the United States. Tallack (1831–1908) traveled widely in 1860, and also published an essay about California from the same trip —a thrifty and resourceful thing to do.

Teeling, Luke William. *American Stew*. London: H. Jenkins, 1933.

Teeling (b. 1903), an author and traveler with political interests, did not want to be a tourist. So by hook or thumb he let people take him around haphazardly: he wanted to see a "real" family and stay in a "typical" off-the-beaten-track little town. Instead he reported on the bizarre and the silly things he encountered. Teeling gave us glimpses of such typically American places, for example, as a Doukhobor village, a Rosicrucian cottage, and Aimee Semple MacPherson's home!

Thompson, Cecil Vincent Raymond. *I Lost My English Accent*. New York: G. P. Putnam's Sons, 1939.

A very amusing adventure in Americanization. Thompson (1906–51) came to America in 1933, a journalist who reported about a strange, alien land filled with funny and ugly curiosities—this, the theme of the earlier portion of the book. Within a few years, he married an American girl—another reporter, no less—and everything changed. He found himself no longer an Englishman, "no longer painfully shy, no longer ridiculously reserved. . . . I liked New York, and I did not want to return to London." He did the shopping and, like other American males, deferred to his wife. But alas, he never really understood very much about his new country.

Tod, John [John Strathesk]. *Bits about America*. Edinburgh, 1887.

A slight, happy, unpretentious, little-known record of a three-month excursion in 1887. The Scottish author wrote books for young people and their families with a religious, moralizing bent. In this book, he never stopped being cheerful and recollected at random within a topical rather than chronological framework.

Townshend, Samuel Nugent. *Our Indian Summer in the Far West: An Autumn Tour of Fifteen Thousand Miles in Kansas, Texas, New Mexico, Colorado, and the Indian Territory*. London, 1880.

Lots of large, wonderful photographs assembled by an expert on agriculture in the American West (1844–1910).

Tremenheere, Hugh Seymour. *Notes on Public Subjects, Made During a Tour in the United States and in Canada*. London, 1852.

The author, a Whig barrister and mines inspector who spent four months in the United States and Canada, was most interested in whether American educational practices were suited to Great Britain. He concluded negatively for the reason that the separation of religion and education threatened to remove moral values from learning, and Tremenheere could not help noting that those who received a free secular education were reluctant to attend Sunday school. His chapters on other subjects are of less value. Tremenheere (1804–93) spent 31 years in the public service and was instrumental in securing the passage (through his work on royal commissions) of more than a dozen parliamentary acts ameliorating the conditions of the working classes.

Trollope, Anthony. *North America*. 3 vols. London, 1862. The Leipzig, 1862, three-volume edition was used.

The author of *Barchester Towers* returned to the scene of his mother's battleground in 1859 and then again in 1861 to delve more deeply into American political institutions (a study "fitter for a man"), and probably a bit to assuage the wounds inflicted by the acid *Domestic Manners of the Americans*. Trollope (1815–82) treated Americans with some charity, he drew many superb word portraits, and he covered many, many topics fully. The main fault was that he wrote too much, over one thousand pages; the book meanders, is ill organized, and the author never gets things right about political organizations. Withal, this stands as a significant, comprehensive, exhaustive, albeit exhausting, achievement. More manageable is the fine modern edition of *North America,* ed. Donald Smalley and Bradford Allen Booth (New York: Knopf, 1951).

————. *The Tireless Traveler*. Edited by Bradford Allen Booth. Berkeley and Los Angeles: University of California Press, 1941.

This is a collection of twenty letters written by the novelist to the Liverpool *Mercury* in 1875. Trollope had then gone to Australia, with stops along the way. The last letter relates his complete boredom with San Francisco through which he passed on his way to New York and London along the Union Pacific. "There is almost nothing to see in San Francisco that is worth seeing." This letter has been published as *A Letter from Anthony Trollope Describing a Visit to California in 1875* (San Francisco: Colt Press, 1946). Many of the characters in Trollope's novels of course are Americans.

Tweedie, Ethel Brilliana (Harley) [Mrs. Alec-Tweedie]. *America As I Saw It, or, America Revisited*. New York: Macmillan Company, 1913.

Mrs. Alex-Tweedie (1862–1940), a prolific writer of travel books and a lady with illusions of grandeur (she so wanted to be a member of Royalty), saw the United States three times: in 1900–1, 1904, and 1912–13. The last visit occasioned this thick book, emerging from a series of articles commissioned by the New York *Times*. She tripped gaily from subject to subject, resembling an embryonic Hedda Hopper at times, repeating maliciously how sensitive Americans were to criticism. Yet she keenly observed manners and oddities, and though she repeated others incessantly, her details of the day-to-day habits of women and men in the home and at parties are instructive.

Vachell, Horace Annesley. *Life and Sport on the Pacific Slope*. London, 1900. The 1901 edition (Dodd, Mead and Company, New York) was used.

This work contains material of more general interest than promised by the title. Vachell (1861–1955), an English writer, married a California girl and lived in her state for the last seventeen years of the nineteenth century. He wrote of what he knew best: ranching, fishing, hunting. But he also included three valuable chapters on the western male, female, and child. He liked them, but did not hesitate to spell out the crassness and charlatanerie (his word) which he felt marred their characters and that of the West in general. Many of his novels depict life in California.

Vaile, P. A. *Y., America's Peril*. London: F. Griffiths, 1909.

An exercise in fulmination. Originally just entitled *Y,* as a facetious commentary on the haste of Americans, the longer title refers to the fact that the *Y*ankee, or the American in general, is his own worst enemy. The joke reflects accurately on the taste and quality of this entire production. What kind of country does "Y" inhabit in 1908? One marked by "corruption, easy divorce, thirst for dollars, licensed murder and assassination, neurotic and dyspeptic disease." And so on for almost three hundred pages in the venerable tradition of Mrs. Trollope and Hepworth Dixon. Vaile also wrote other classics of analysis, including *Modern Golf.*

Vincent, Mrs. Howard [Ethel Gwendoline (Moffatt) Vincent]. *Forty Thousand Miles Over Land and Water*. 2 vols. London, 1885.

The wife of London's Director of Criminal Investigations charged herself with keeping a record of their travels through North America, New Zealand, Australia, India, and Egypt in 1884–85. They devoted seven weeks and one fourth of the book to the United States. Mrs. Vincent (1861–1952) said nothing in particular.

Vivian, Sir Arthur Pendarves. *Wanderings in the Western Land. With Illustrations from Original Sketches By Mr. Albert Bierstadt and the Author*. London, 1879.

A rugged and entertaining tale of big-game hunting in the Rocky Mountains in 1877–78 by an M.P. and illustrious colonel in the Welsh infantry. Vivian (1834–1926) also recreated the countryside of Yosemite, northern California, Colorado, Wyoming, Utah, etc., with the help of ample illustrations from his own and Albert Bierstadt's pen. Vivian had a grand time and successfully transmitted to his readers a feeling for the vast, untouched, and glorious wilderness.

Vivian, Henry Hussey. See Swansea.

Wakefield, Alderman Sir Charles Cheer. *America To-day and To-morrow: A Tribute of Friendship*. London: Hodder and Stroughton, 1924.

A former Lord Mayor of London (in 1915–16) chose to view the United States from the vantage point of his other career—businessman. He greatly appreciated the business civilization of the 1920's to the point that his reviewer in *The Spectator* called the review, "By Ford to Utopia." Wakefield (1859–1941) headed a speech-making mission appointed to present various English-American memorials in 1922.

Wallace, Alfred Russel. *My Life: A Record of Events and Opinions*. 2 vols. London, 1905. The New York two-volume edition (Dodd, Mead and Company, 1905) was used.

Discoverer simultaneously of the theory of natural selection with Darwin (to whom he sent his views), Wallace (1823–1913) made the lecture circuit of the United States in 1886–87. His recollections of the journey take up approximately ninety pages of the second volume of this interesting autobiography, and they tell mostly of his meetings with the geologists, biologists, botanists, and Darwinists of America into whose milieu Wallace amiably takes his readers. He was much concerned also over the spoliation of American natural resources and of the growing inequality of wealth.

Watkin, Sir E. W. *Canada and the States. Recollections 1851 to 1886*. London, 1887.

Watkin (1819–1901), an eminent railway entrepreneur, had no qualms about labeling himself: "Anyone who reads what follows will learn that I am an Imperialist—that I hate little-Englandism." As a Liberal and Liberal Unionist M.P., he devoted many of the years 1851–86 struggling "for the union of the Canadian Provinces, in order that they might be retained under the sway of the best form of government—a limited monarchy" (Victoria's, of course). He brilliantly endeavored to bring about this union through the net of railways. Fortunately for American independence, Watkin's forays into the United States were infrequent, and they usually were for the purpose of swelling his own pockets. Portions of his earlier book, *A Trip to the United States and Canada: In a Series of Letters* (London, 1852), are included in *Canada and the States*.

Weld, Charles Richard. *A Vacation Tour in the United States and Canada*. London, 1855.

Weld (1813–67) dedicated this work to his half-brother, Isaac, who fifty years earlier made a similar excursion and wrote a widely read account of his experiences. Charles was a barrister, publisher, and, most importantly, historian of the Royal Society who regarded himself as continuing the earlier chronicle. He went, in 1850, only as far south as Norfolk and as far west as Chicago. His book is quite ordinary.

Wells, H. G. *The Future in America: A Search after Realities*. New York: Harper and Brothers, 1906.

H. G. Wells (1866–1946) had a lifelong fascination for the future which drew him almost inevitably to the United States. His first trip, a short seven-week jaunt in 1906, culminated in one of the most stimulating of all travel books. Wells wanted to know not simply that America was "on the go"; he demanded to know where. This demand, when combined with his Socialist orientation, led him to explore problems such as those posed by immigration, the increasing inequality of wealth, child labor, etc., in ways dissimilar from all other travelers. Although Wells was sometimes excruciatingly vague, this deficiency was overcome by the unusual number of novel perspectives supplied by the author, such as, for instance, his analysis of the American view of progress.

———. *Social Forces in England and America*. New York: Harper and Brothers, 1914.

One sixty-page essay, "The American Population," out of twenty-six shorter pieces deals directly with the United States. Wells continued his call for a form of socialism, or at least something other than chaos, in American economic development. He raised other pertinent problems, too; for example the awful dilemma posed for the Emancipated Woman by the choice between home and independence.

———. *The New America, the New World*. New York: Macmillan Company, 1935.

Wells paid two more visits, in 1934 and 1935, to determine whether the New Deal could provide the economic direction and leadership to the United States and the West in general that the West so sorely needed, and which Wells, for years, had been urging. Impressed in this eighty-page essay with Franklin Roosevelt as a human being, Wells sadly found the president being backed into a corner by what he called "raucous voices and the inexplicit men." Wells had become more pessimistic in 1935 after his short-lived hope of the previous year; in fact, he had, by this time, become a thoroughly disillusioned and bitter man about society in general. He felt that the United States had no plan and that, in the broadest sense, there was insufficient education to make the necessary kind of plan possible.

Whibley, Charles. *American Sketches*. Edinburgh: W. Blackwood and Sons, 1908.

The scholar here wrote several critical essays on a number of widely assorted topics: the criminal underworld, literature and language, patriotism, the press, and impressionistic sketches of various cities. They are gracefully written, and offer occasionally some fresh slants. Whibley (1859–1930) argued, for example, that patriotism impersonates liberty in the United States; he also rejected the metaphor of a youthful America and substituted for it the image of a gaunt, humorless old man seeking a single-minded and joyless success.

Wilde, Oscar. *Impressions of America*. Edited, with an Introduction by Stuart Mason. Sunderland: Keystone Press, 1906.

Only five hundred copies were printed of this lecture delivered in England by the illustrious dramatist (1854–1900) in 1883, immediately following his two American trips (in 1882 and 1883). The editor composed an instructive thirteen-page introduction recounting some of the facts of Wilde's journey. The lecture itself runs only sixteen pages, and although it naturally makes enjoyable reading, it offers nothing that need detain the historian. The lecture also appears in *The Writings of Oscar Wilde* (15 vols.; New York: A. R. Keller, 1907), III, 231–52. A detailed narrative of the tour may be found in the fat, juicy volume written by Lloyd Lewis and Henry Justin Smith, *Oscar Wilde Discovers America* (New York: Harcourt, Brace [1936]).

Winget, William. *A Tour in America and a Visit to the St. Louis Exposition*. Torquay, Scotland, 1904.

Winget recorded his impression of the fair which commemorated the hundredth anniversary of the Louisiana Purchase; he then proceeded westward to see his daughters. Slight and thoroughly inconsequential.

Woodley, William. *The Impressions of an Englishman in America*. New York: W. J. Woodley, 1910.

A spiteful, ill-tempered, anti-Semitic account by a self-styled "imperial yeoman" of his travails in New York, Philadelphia, Boston, Salt Lake City, and San Francisco. Woodley also recoiled from Chinamen, Negroes, Mormons, from equality, and thus from America. Mercifully he left for Canada halfway through this self-printed masterpiece.

Woodruff, Douglas. *Plato's American Republic*. London: K. Paul, Trench, Trubner and Company, 1926.

This book was published as part of the pamphleteering "Today and Tomorrow" series (which also included Bretherton's *Midas* and Fuller's *Atlantis*). Woodruff (b. 1897), a member of the editorial staff of the London *Times*, like the other two authors, found much in America to fault. He dressed his criticism, however, in the garb of the great Socratic dialogue. This permitted him not only to be facetious, but also to impart the illusion of the author's philosophic detachment. The result: a book often terribly unfair, but also humorous and occasionally enlightening.

Wyndham-Quin, Windham Thomas, 4th Earl of Dunraven. *The Great Divide: Travels in the Upper Yellowstone in the Summer of 1874.* London, 1876.

Superb scenery in Montana and Wyoming is recreated here by this active Irish politician (1841–1926). Also included are much-outdated statistical data that were omitted from the 1925 edition, entitled *Hunting in the Yellowstone* (New York: Outing Publishing Company, 1914), edited by Horace Kephart. Accounts of other visits will be found in *Past Times and Pastimes* (2 vols.; London: Hodder and Stoughton, 1922).

Zincke, Foster Barham. *Last Winter in the United States; Being Table Talk Collected during a Tour Through the Late Southern Confederation, the Far West, the Rocky Mountains, and etc.* London, 1868.

A very useful collection of miscellaneous "table talk" by the Vicar of Wherstead. Zincke (1817–1893) traveled widely in the United States in 1867 and his many varied comments display good-will and much common sense. He reserved his most instructive observations for the common-school system, which he greatly admired. He wrote another work on the United States, *The Plough and the Dollar; Or, The Englishry of a Century Hence* (London, 1883) in which he uncannily predicted that by 1980 there would be 200 million British and 800 million Americans.

SECONDARY SOURCES

In the last one hundred years, there has been a steady but slow trickle of historical writing about the visitors to American shores. The first one appeared a century ago: Henry T. Tuckerman, *America and Her Commentators: With a Critical Sketch of Travel in the United States* (New York, 1864). Although he naturally could not get very far into the period under consideration in this study, his work is thorough and not at all out-of-date. His analysis of Anthony Trollope was of especial value.

Forty-four years elapsed before the next book, John Graham Brooks, *As Others See Us: A Study of Progress in the United States* (New York: Macmillan Company, 1908), was published. Like Tuckerman, Brooks surveyed all foreign travelers, not just the British, but for an additional four decades and in one hundred fewer pages. The result was a terribly superficial survey, useful only here and there, as in his chapters on Bryce and H. G. Wells.

Three short articles were composed between 1908 and the time of the first major systematic analysis of the British travelers by Jane Mesick in 1922. E. D. Adams, "The Point of View of the British Traveller in America," *Political Science Quarterly*, XXIX (1914), 244–64, divided the visitors into five neat decades between 1810 to 1860, Britons coming to the United States for different reasons in each decade. Lane Cooper, "Travellers and Observers, 1763–1846," *The Cambridge History of American Literature* (New York: Macmillan Company; and Cambridge: Cambridge University Press, 1917), I, 185–214, included many foreigners in his survey, while F. S.

Dellenbaugh, "Travellers and Explorers, 1846–1900," *The Cambridge History of American Literature* (New York: Macmillan Company; and Cambridge: Cambridge University Press, 1921), III, 131–70, dealt only with Americans.

In 1922 and 1923 two important works, both still widely used, came out. Jane Louise Mesick, *The English Traveler in America, 1785–1835* (New York: Columbia University Press, 1922), is a careful and complete groundbreaking analysis of this early period. Miss Mesick may be faulted for failing to make two critical distinctions: (1) she never determined in what areas travel comment might be more or less useful than in others; and (2) she treated the fifty-year period as a static whole, unchanged and unchanging. Thus, she compiled a comprehensive compendium of comments on all subjects, but she did so uncritically and without consideration of change.

Allan Nevins, *American Social History As Recorded By British Travellers* (New York: Holt and Company, 1923), reissued and brought up-to-date under the title of *America Through British Eyes* (New York: Oxford University Press, 1948), is easily the most far-ranging of all books about travelers. Nevins covered the years in this anthology from 1789 to (in the latest edition) 1946. He divided this long period into five portions, each corresponding to the purposes and qualities of the travel reports: from 1789–1825 they came for "utilitarian inquiry"; 1825–45 was the period of "Tory condescension"; unbiased portraiture" characterized 1840–70; 1870–1922 (the period most closely corresponding with this study) he called simply "analysis"; his final period, added on for his last edition, departs from these categories and describes the conditions witnessed by the Britons as "boom, depression, war." Nevins began each section with a critical essay and then excerpted from some of the best travelers. Among those anthologized who figure prominently in this paper are: Charles Dickens, Charles Lyell, Alexander Mackay, William Howard Russell, Anthony Trollope, David Macrae, Herbert Spencer, Matthew Arnold, James F. Muirhead, James Bryce, Henry Nevinson, J. A. Spender, Collinson Owen, Mary Agnes Hamilton, Morgan Philips Price, and C. V. R. Thompson.

An eager dissertation writer, James Eckman (see below) treated Nevins badly in his study. Eckman accused Nevins of inaccuracy on many fronts: Nevins "altered the original texts"; his references are incorrect; his bibliography is inexcusably sloppy. Eckman, in fact, devoted three full pages to exposing Nevins' bibliographical errors, and some of them are not at all trivial. Nevins' latest edition, which came out two years after Eckman's attack, did not correct the blunders. Nevins was also attacked for serious errors of judgment, but after all the criticism has been acknowledged, one must still admit that a careless Nevins still has a great deal to offer. His introductory essays, though a bit diffuse, are informed by a knowledge of history which makes it possible for him to understand which travelers know what they are talking about and which do not, which observations are true and which are not. This gives his work an inestimable value.

No book about the British travelers was published for another twenty years. Max Berger's published dissertation, *The British Traveller in America, 1836–1860* (New York: P. S. King and Staples, 1943) remains the best single monograph on the general subject. It followed three earlier unpublished doctoral dissertations covering the same period of time which I have not read: S. H. Reed, "British Travelers in the United States, 1835–1870" (American University, 1931); J. D. T. Hamilton, "The South as seen by

British Travellers, 1800–1860" (University of Mississippi, 1938); and W. E. Chace, "The Descent on Democracy" (University of North Carolina, 1941). Berger's work is well organized, well researched, and well written: in some ways it is a model monograph. Berger might be criticized for being too miscellaneous, for not weighing in a sufficiently critical manner the value of different travel observations, for jumbling together in each chapter, as though they were comparable, comments which functioned on several different intellectual levels, and for, in general, not exercising his own critical faculty. Despite the foregoing, it may safely be said that no book on the travelers is more useful than Berger's. Special praise should also be extended for his complete and informative annotated bibliography.

Only four studies, besides that of Nevins, have been made which touch directly on general matters of the post-Civil War period. The two most comprehensive of these are unpublished theses of limited value. The other two are books which deal only fragmentally with the later period. Paul Ashby, "America Through the Eyes of English Travelers, 1880–1929" (American University, 1932), is a Master's thesis based upon only fifty-six volumes. It achieves little because it attempts little. Ashby's main conclusion, that most of the British observations were critical, seems to contradict Nevins' assertion that the likes of Sir Lepel Griffin belonged to an earlier era. In many ways, however, his work is intellectually more imaginative than the fuller one turned out by Eckman. James Eckman combined these two points of view in the final conclusion of his unpublished doctoral dissertation, "The British Traveler in America, 1875–1920" (Georgetown University, 1946).

> It seems to the writer that there are two main conclusions to be drawn from analysis of British travel literature between 1875 and 1920. First, as Ashby pointed out, evidence of disapprobation and sometimes hostility does persist in the writings of the visitors from England, and such evidence occurs more often than Professor Nevins has chosen to delineate it. Second, there is a very decided increase in the respect manifested by Englishmen toward America—a respect based essentially upon recognition of the power and world position of the nation. [Pp. 306–7]

This is the chief generalization of Eckman's study. Each chapter is complete in itself for carefully and thoroughly summarizing, without conclusion, the full spectrum of travel opinion of various unrelated topics. Eckman, for example, chose to conduct his research on the following subjects: American manners, women, the cities, the press, the language, "the peoples of the land," politics, the West, ingenuity, and Anglo-American relations. He did not make clear why he chose these instead of, say, the topics deemed most important in this, in Ashby's, and in other studies: religion, education, equality, or children. I did find Eckman's study useful for its fine bibliography which listed 134 volumes, and for its model of clean prose and painstaking research. Robert G. Athearn, *Westward the Briton* (New York: Scribner, 1953) deals with the British view of the American West from 1860 to 1900. The author covered a fairly wide range of topics within his narrow geographical context which consisted mostly of Colorado, and which did not include California. But what he intended for the most part was to recreate the colorful side of a romantic era, much celebrated in movies and television, through the eyes of the Britons. He laid stress on the stagecoaches, the saloons, six-guns, cowboys and Indians. He achieved his purpose signally: the book is thoroughly enjoyable and informative, and it corrects many of the myths that have grown up about the American West of this period, without sacrificing its larger mythic quality. George Harmon Knoles, *The Jazz Age Revisited: British Criticism of American Civilization During the 1920's* (Stanford, Calif.: Stanford University Press, 1955) concerns itself with the 1920's not only from the point of view of the travelers but of all Britons who wrote about the United States during this transitional era. Professor Knoles added an interesting innovation in his annotated bibliography: he listed the verdicts of all the British book reviews he could reasonably trace for each book, as part of his effort to ascertain the general spirit of British criticism of America in this period.

Two distinguished historians compiled travel anthologies in the 1940's. Henry Steele Commager, ed., *America in Perspective: The United States through Foreign Eyes* (New York: New American Library, 1947), began with a general, but characteristically lively fourteen-page introduction. His selections are drawn from travelers of all nations, including the following who figured in this study: Dickens, Alexander Mackay, Edward Dicey, James Burn, Matthew Arnold, Bryce, George W. Steevens, George Birmingham, Walter Lionel George, and Denis Brogan. Only Continental Europeans are included in Oscar Handlin, ed., *This Was America: True Accounts of People and Places: Manners and Customs: As Recorded by European Travelers to the Western Shore in the Eighteenth, Nineteenth, and Twentieth Centuries* (Cambridge, Mass.: Harvard University Press, 1941).

The best introduction to the study of French visitors is contained in Frank Monaghan's bibliography, *French Travellers in the United States, 1765–1932* (New York: New York Public Library, 1933). Andrew J. Torrielli, *Italian Opinion on America, 1850–1900* (Cambridge, Mass.: Harvard University Press, 1941) has looked at the Italians. Thomas D. Clark has completed the editing of his monumental *Travels in the Old South* (3 vols.; University of Oklahoma Press, Norman: 1956–59) and *Travels in the New South* (2 vols.; University of Oklahoma Press, Norman: 1962). Most of these travelers are American. Professor Ada Nisbet of the English Department at U.C.L.A. is near completion of her list of all *British Comment on the United States: A Chronological Bibliography, 1832–1900*. This should prove a boon to all researchers in Anglo-American history. I should like to thank her for her kindness in checking over this bibliography and in offering me many helpful suggestions for improving it.

Index

Achievement ethos, 68, 69, 186, 188
Ackrill, Robert, 39
Adams, W. E., 32, 34, 39
Affluence. *See* Wealth
Albany, N.Y., 39
Alec-Tweedie, Mrs. Ethel, 86, 119, 165, 179
Anglophilism, 5, 6
Anthony, Susan B., 115
Anti-intellectualism, 67–68, 73, 80, 84, 86; movement away from, 180
Archer, William, 85, 88, 117, 197
Argyll, John G. E. H. D. S. C., Marquis of Lorne, 28, 30
Aristocracy. *See* Social classes in America
Aristotle, 130
Arnold, Sir Edwin, 98
Arnold, Matthew: and business community, 6; U.S. lecture tour, 12–13; American reaction to, 12–13; on social classes, 12–13, 58; on newspapers, 45; on wealth, 66; on coherence in society, 74; on women, 118; mentioned, 23, 73, 127
Athearn, Robert G., 195
Atheism, 144, 157, 200–1
Atlantic City, N.J., 32
Aubertin, J. J., 47
Aveling, E. B., 31

Baillie-Grohman, William, 197
Bailyn, Bernard, 101, 104, 135
Balfour's Education Act, 20, 86
Ballantine, William, 37
Baltimore, Md., 32
Barneby, William Henry, 37*n*
Becker, Carl, 156–57
Beecher, Henry Ward, 147*n*
Beggars, 59, 61
Bell, William, 36*n*
Bellamy, Edward, 70
Bennett, Arnold, 8, 83, 86, 103, 170
Bentham, Jeremy, 16
Berger, Max: *The British Traveller in America*, v; on U.S. response to travelers, 4–5; on Anglophilism, 6; quoted on British views on U.S., 56, 76, 126, 210; on travelers' lack of knowledge, 201; mentioned, 189, 203

Bergson, Henri, 110, 171
Bird, Isabella. *See* Bishop, Isabella (Bird)
Birkenhead, Earl of. *See* Smith, Frederick Edwin
Birmingham, George A. *See* Hannay, James Owen
Bishop, Isabella (Bird), 80, 94, 109, 196
Boddam-Whetham, J. W., 27
Boorstin, Daniel, 94, 187, 191
Boston, Mass., 28–32 *passim,* 35, 38
Bretherton, C. H., 67, 128, 168
Bright, John, 17
Brighton, 34
Brinton, Crane, 190, 191
Brogan, Denis, 113, 142, 150, 196
Bromley, Clara, 26
Brooks, John Graham, 189, 203, 206
Bruno, Giordano, 169
Bryce, James: on American West, 34; on cities, 39; on American democracy, 63–64; on material equality, 64, 167; on belief in future, 71; on republican institutions, 74–75; on education, 88, 90; on women, 108, 113, 114, 116*n*, 120, 121; on the state, 128–30 *passim,* 134–35; on church and religion, 144, 154, 157, 158, 160; on separation of church and state, 150, 151; on manners, 180; on foreigner's perspective, 193–94; mentioned, 12*n*, 28, 126, 161, 174, 196, 199*n*, 202, 207
Buchanan, William, 205
Bureaucracy, 173, 176, 180
Burn, James, 42, 107, 109, 119, 152, 167
Burn, W. L., 17
Burne-Jones, Sir Philip, 42, 65, 96, 114, 134*n*, 165
Burnett-Smith, Annie. *See* Smith, Annie S.
Burton, Sir Richard, 197
Bury, J. B., 55
Business: ethics of, 51, 159, 166–67; status of, 67, 166–67; contrasted to politics, 127–28, 134–35; and religion, 159

267

268 INDEX

Businessman, American, 42–43, 170; and British intellectuals, 5–6
Butler, W. F., 37*n*

California, 29, 36–38 *passim*
Cambridge University, 91, 207
Campbell, Sir George, 31, 111, 197
Campbell, J. F., 43
Canada, 167
Cantril, Hadley, 205
Carnegie, Andrew, 6, 9, 12
Catholicism, American, 151
Central Park, 29
Chamberlain, Joseph, 17
Charleston, S.C., 34
Chester, Greville, 25*n*
Chesterton, G. K., 8, 179*n*
Chicago, Ill.: Kipling on, 14, 36; rapid growth of, 34–35; Great Fire of, 35; government of, 133, 207; mentioned, 9, 37, 40
Children, American: lack of corporal punishment of, 79; sentimentality toward, 79; hopes centered on, 83; contrasted to English children, 94, 104, 105; financial competitiveness of, 94–95; companionship with parents, 101–2; companionship between sexes, 115; permissiveness toward, 95–100 *passim*, 103, 136–37; as symbol of progress, 124; mentioned, 51, 161, 163
Chivalry in America, 106–7, 111
Christianity, 150, 153, 159, 160. *See also* Religion
Churches, 145, 152. *See also* Religion
Cincinnati, Ohio, 34, 39
Cities, 34, 39, 40, 163, 164, 175. *See also names of specific cities*
Civil rights, 148
Civil War: increased English respect for U.S. as a result of, 6–7, 203, 204; influence on European politics, 7; decline of tourism in the South following, 32–33; travelers' views of, 33*n*, 134, 201; effect on American values, 53; political institutions during, 133; mentioned, 23, 56, 63, 72, 90, 145, 150, 197
Clark, G. Kitson, 15
Class structure. *See* Social classes in America
Clergymen, 146–49 *passim*
Cleveland, Ohio, 39
Clothing, 43–44
Cobden, Richard, 17
Co-education, 115

Colleges and universities, 87–90 *passim*, 108, 164, 177, 180
Colorado, 197
Colorado Springs, Colo., 39
Commager, Henry Steele, 187, 209, 210
Common school, 163, 188
Condorcet, Antoine Nicolas, Marquis de, 81, 357
Conformity. *See* Uniformity in American life
Congress, U.S., 63, 126
Conservatism, 135, 149, 159, 179, 186, 192
Constitution, U.S., 9, 64, 65, 140
Copyright, problems of, 5, 7
Corruption. *See* Political corruption
Cremin, Lawrence A., 77, 81
Crowe, Eyre, 95
Crèvecoeur, J. Hector St. John, 41, 196
Crime, 46, 84, 200–1
Cunliffe, Marcus, 186–87

Dartmouth College, 136
Darwin, Charles, 156, 158
Darwinian theory, 19–20
Day, Samuel Phillips, 153
DeBary, Richard, 80, 103, 165
Declaration of Independence, 99–100, 145
Degler, Carl, 185
Delmonico's (restaurant), 9, 11
Democracy, American: contrasted to British, 63, 64, 65, 130, 133, 137–41 *passim;* Tocqueville's concept of, 63, 64; ideal vs. actual, 63, 64, 129; and equality, 63, 64, 65, 186; and uniformity, 64; and universal suffrage, 64, 130–32 *passim*, 141; and child-rearing, 103, 136, 137; faults of, 128–29; and tyranny of the majority, 130, 137–38; and political exclusion of Negro, 131; disillusionment with, 133; conservatism of, 135; and individual liberty, 137–41 *passim*
Denver, Colo., 37
Depew, Chauncey M., 12
Depression, 133, 142, 171, 176–77, 186, 221
Detroit, Mich., 34
Dewey, John, 79
Dibelius, Wilhelm, 5
Dicey, Edward: on wealth, 65, 66; on American society, 69; on family relations, 101; on churches, 145, 152
Dickens, Charles: visit to U.S., 3–4, 8; anger at literary piracy, 6; describes